Meridians feminism, race, transnationalism

VOLUME 22 · NUMBER 2 · OCTOBER 2023

SPECIAL ISSUE
Mosaic

Ginetta E. B. Candelario

Editor's Introduction

Solidarity needs to be renewed between the others, between and among
the marginalized and exploited.
— Sreerekha Sathi, "When My Brown Got Colored"

Moreover, such critique has the potential to reveal the political intimacies
that can develop among differentially racialized groups, expose colonial
pseudofeminisms, and help forge more robust intersectional and transnational feminist solidarities.
— Zeynep K. Korkman, "(Mis)Translations of the Critiques of Anti-Muslim
Racism"

I believed that my path to healing had to incorporate all of life's experiences so as to create the mosaic that makes up the picture of my life. My
challenge was to add enough beautiful pieces so that this mosaic eventually
sparkled.
—Doris H. Gray, *Leaving the Shadow of Pain*

According to the *Oxford English Dictionary*, a mosaic is "a variegated whole
formed from many disparate parts,"[1] which perfectly captures this issue's
geographically, historically, intellectually, and artistically wide-ranging,
and diverse yet interrelated contents. Each piece—whether poetry, *testimonio*, essay, creative nonfiction, or interview—touches on key themes
iterated in unique ways depending on the context. Featuring work focused
on Afghanistan, Canada, Haiti, India, Mexico, Tunisia, Turkey, Sri Lanka,
Puerto Rico, and the United States mainland, this *Mosaic* issue reveals a

MERIDIANS · feminism, race, transnationalism   22:2 October 2023
DOI: 10.1215/15366936-10640374 © 2023 Smith College

broader picture of the complex, contradictory, and challenging nature of enacting transnational or intersectional feminist solidarities within and across borders, whether physical, political, ethno-racial, or ideological. Coincidentally, I write this introduction as each of the countries, diasporas, and issues examined here are prominent in the current news cycle: the politically exacerbated impacts of natural disasters (Turkey, Puerto Rico); religious fundamentalism's impact on women and girls (Afghanistan, India); civil unrest and the repression of civil society (Haiti, Mexico); ethno-nationalist violence against ethnic minority populations (India, Sri Lanka, Tunisia); nativism, xenophobia, and anti-Blackness (Canada, United States); and authoritarianism's resurgence in states claiming to be democratic (Afghanistan, India, Turkey, Sri Lanka, Tunisia). As always, women and feminists of every stripe are at the forefront of organizing nationally and transnationally in response to these upheavals, adding their "beautiful pieces" to the mosaic of their locale's story.

We open this issue with Devaleena Das's "What Transnational Feminism Has Not Disrupted Yet." This *Counterpoint* succinctly summarizes key moments in and debates within and about transnational feminist scholarship in the United States, offering an alternative paradigm and praxis inspired by African American women's quilt-making methods and aesthetics, which Das calls a "quilted epistemology" and argues is exemplified by Indian-Kenyan poet Shailja Patel's performance *Migritude*.[2] Das argues that *Migritude*'s "quilted epistemology acknowledges . . . that migrants are challenged not only to communicate via translations that distort information and meanings, but that they are forced to translate themselves—their sense of self—into unfamiliar societies and cultures" as they confront, challenge, or contend with historical and contemporary power relations, whether those that they carry with them or those that they encounter on their journeys.

Continuing with the theme of challenges inherent in translation, Zeynep K. Korkman's *Essay*, "(Mis)Translations of the Critique of Anti-Muslim Racism and the Repercussions for Transnational Feminist Solidarities," analyzes "the travails of transnational feminist solidarity with 'Black aka Muslim Turks' who appropriated globally resonant progressive critiques of anti-Black and anti-Muslim racism while featuring a racist, neo-imperialist, and misogynist political agenda." This brilliant piece deftly explains the history and contemporary deployment of race, religion, gender, and sexuality by competing political factions in the long aftermath of the Ottoman empire's end, and it elucidates how Turkey's current regime accordingly "complicates our transnational feminist reflexes" toward solidarity with projects that ostensibly enact "Black" power. Simply stated, Turkey's AKP government and the Erdogans have been able to recruit the support of progressive transnational feminists such as the Somali-American representative Ilhan Omar and the University of California, Berkeley, Pakistani-American anthropologist Saba Mahmood for their repressive regime under the guise of transnational feminist solidarity against anti-Muslim/anti-Black racism, even as the Erdogan regime stepped up its violent repression of Kurdish ethnic minorities, the poor, secular women and feminists, LGBTQ+, dissident scholars, and other progressive civil society actors. Korkman writes, "Such intricacies are revealed as central and constitutive when we approach the terrain of transnational feminist analysis and struggle with a double consciousness, such as that which comes from being a subject of and being subjected to, on the one hand, the academic and political hegemony of the U.S. empire and, on the other, the neoimperial and authoritarian ambitions of the . . . state."

Picking up on this theme, Dia Da Costa's *Essay*, "Writing Castelessly: Brahminical Supremacy in Education, Feminist Knowledge, and Research," intends to make clear the particularities of white supremacy and racism in an Indian postcolonial context where official castelessness operates alongside the social fact of casteism. Da Costa narrates how the "caste terror, humiliation, segregation, [and the] sexual violence needed to secure [the] caste endogamy" central to sustaining and naturalizing Brahminical supremacy is systematically elided in Indian higher education but has become clear and visible thanks to Dalit-Bahujan and Adivasi critiques at home and globally. At the same time, Da Costa argues that, similar to white feminist impulses to solidarity with their others, Brahminical feminist impulses to solidarity with Dalit-Bahujan peoples can quickly become politically, professionally, and morally self-serving. Thus "we [must] ask[,] . . . Do we know what it means to be prepared, or worthy of teaching Dalit-Bahujan scholarship?" As Meena Kotwal, feminist Dalit journalist and founder of *The Mooknayak*, pointed out in a recent *New York Times* interview, thanks to increasing Hindutva violence spurred by Prime Minister Narendra Modi's Bharatiya Janata Party, these questions are as urgent today as they were a century ago when the Dalit scholar Dr. Bhimrao Ambedkar contested Mahatma Gandhi's implicit support for Brahmin caste-dominance (Singh 2023). At the same time, the evolving nature of this issue is also why Da Costa asked that we include the original dates of submission and final acceptance published at the end of her piece.

Not surprisingly, these questions travel with Indian (im)migrants as well, as feminist Brahmin scholar Sreerekha Sathi narrates in her *Testimonio*, "When My Brown Got Colored: Living Through/In the Times of white and Brahminical Supremacy." Sathi explores the connections between her experience of racialization as nonwhite in the United States and her caste privilege, writing, "ironically, while the Indian/South Asian diaspora in the United States experiences racism and may even resist it, few have tried to recognize and unlearn their own caste practices and privileges which they transport from India." Yet the experience of arriving in Trump-era United States and living in Charlottesville, Virginia, during the white supremacist invasion of the city and university inspired by the president moved Sathi to reflect on the connections between her Brahminical caste privileges at home and abroad, and her simultaneous racialization as nonwhite in the United States. Sathi eschews simplistic claims of solidarity based on a shared experience of subordination, as well as the impulse to recruit Dalit appreciation for her efforts. Given that she had "found it suffocating to be forced to listen to progressive white members of the Charlottesville community talking of the dangers and the threats they had to face in fighting white supremacy," Sathi acknowledges that she is "uncomfortably placed in the process."

Similarly, Grace L. Sanders Johnson's *Media Matters* piece, "Picturing Herself in Africa: Haiti, Diaspora, and the Visual Folkloric," offers an empathetic yet critical analysis of Haitian feminist anthropologist Madeleine Comhaire-Sylvain's complex positionality as an elite, Afro-descendant feminist critic of the U.S. occupation in Haiti who spends years working and living among the white Belgian colonizers of the Congo because of her marriage to white Belgian anthropologist Jean Comhaire. Sanders Johnson's sophisticated "close reading" of Comhaire-Sylvain's photographic archive of her time in the Belgian Congo is an innovative contribution to our understanding of "alternative imaginings and framings of national and global Black belonging" that avoids simplistic presumptions of race or gender solidarities in the context of intersecting and competing imperialisms, settler-colonialisms, and nationalisms. Serendipitously, in analyzing Comhaire-Sylvain's photography, Sanders Jonson draws on the work of our cover artist, Haitian-American anthropologist Gina Athena-Ulysse, whose piece "Indigo" offers a "meditation on aesthetic identity" as part of the "Tools of the Trade or Women's Work" Kwi series (Athena-Ulysse 2024).

Cherise Fung's "In the Name of Sovereignty: Rethinking the 'Tiger Bitch' and the Terrorist Bomber in Nayomi Munaweera's *Island of a Thousand Mirrors*," turns our attention to the challenges of teasing out the meaning of agency for protagonists whose subject positions are multiply paradoxical. To that end, she draws on Jasbir Puar's theory of "queer assemblage," which makes intersectionality's internal and external contradictions and conflicts visible. Through a close reading of the novel's central protagonist, Sarawshti—a Tamil woman navigating competing Sri Lankan nationalist patriarchal terrains, politics, cultures, and ideologies in the aftermath of her rape—Fung homes in on two moments in *Island of a Thousand Mirrors* in which to offer the possibility of a way out of the dual dead ends presented to Sarawshti by competing patriarchies. Fung argues that life after social death becomes fleetingly possible in two moments of solidarity between Sarawshti and other women, each instance of which alludes to a path that might allow for the subaltern protagonist's transformation from victim to survivor. Although that possibility is not ultimately realized, "an alternative understanding of cross-ethnic and transnational feminist solidarities that move beyond normative sovereign subjectivity . . . to focus more on how various social forces 'merge and dissipate time, space, and body' against the fiction of a stable, coherent identity across linear space and time" is signaled.

In "A Conversation with Doris H. Gray on the Power and Limitations of Restorative Justice across History, Culture, and Gender," education scholar Rosetta Marantz Cohen and Gray offer a less ambivalently hopeful take on the possibility of solidarity between women engendering liberation for all. The interview was inspired by Gray's recent book, *Leaving the Shadow of Pain: A Cross-cultural Exploration of Truth, Forgiveness, Reconciliation and Healing*, which she worked on during a residency at Smith College in the spring of 2018 where she met Cohen. In the interview, Gray discusses how two different historical traumas—the German Holocaust and the Tunisian Zine El Abidine Ben Ali dictatorship—and two personal traumas she experienced in Morocco, the death of her daughter and the rape and torture she was subjected to just a few months later, "complicate the idea that truth telling and revelation is a universal key to healing" from the trauma caused by state violence against targeted populations. Gray's personal experience of loss, violation, and trauma afforded her a sense of connection with the hundreds of Tunisian women she interviewed over the course of seven years, women who "came forward with the truth about their torturous pasts."[3] Gray argues that solidarity between such differently situated traumatized subjects is possible. If we recognize that "all—to various degrees—have been on the receiving and giving end of injustice. . . , [then we can develop] a sense of connection to others." At the same time, we must also recognize the consequences of *not* having traumatizing violations acknowledged and redressed.

The effect of not having trauma acknowledged in the aftermath of violence is heart-wrenchingly evoked in Korean-Canadian Nancy Kang's poem, "Bruise Blue." This poem obliquely yet searingly narrates a teenage girl being attacked by boys who "had swarmed, expectant, / in the back bleachers, ripping skirt and shirt." Subsequently refused the solace and comfort of her "Daddy's retreating shoulders" and subject to the "cold-hard trigger / of [her] [m]other's tongue" in lieu of the comfort she sought, the girl "vows next time to be vengeful, private, agile, / and kinetic, so as never to be caught, / surrounded again / without weapons." This is a classic trauma response, one that is central to survival, but it limits our ability to connect with those who come in our lives long after the blue bruises have faded.

The challenges of coping with both Canadian and heritage-country gender and sexual ideologies, norms, and violence are taken up by Saher Ahmed and Amrita Hari in "Young Afghan-Canadian Women's Negotiations of Gendered Cultural Scripts and Hybrid Cultural Identities." This *Essay* focuses on "Afghan-Canadian second-generation women's gendered expectations related to marriage . . . to understand how they interpret and negotiate these gendered cultural expectations within their diasporic community, while simultaneously adapting to more mainstream cultural gender expectations of the society they reside in." Based on ten qualitative in-depth interviews, and drawing on her status as an insider in the community, Hari found evidence of "agency, autonomy, and independence" alongside "instances of conformity" to both Afghan and Canadian gender norms, insights that she argues were facilitated by her culturally competent rapport with her informants.

The need to develop deep, habitus-based knowledge of (im)migrant communities to understand and advocate effectively for them is also evoked in Michaela Django Walsh's moving creative nonfiction piece, "Between Skin and Stone: A Letter to My Son, Lienzo." In it Walsh issues "an invitation into conversations about place and belonging, levity and resistance" by explaining the meaning of the name she has given her son, whose namesake is a type of stone wall that comprises "heart- and fist-sized stones" woven together (*hilado*) by the builder and that winds its way throughout the Mexican landscape. For Walsh, rather than being a barrier, a *lienzo* is "a" "passage" that offers "a way of embodying space that is connective, intimate, ancient . . . [and imbued with] strength and yield," and a reminder of her son's grounded connection to his mother's people in Mexico and their vulnerable diaspora in the United States. For the author-mother engaged in migrant advocacy—given ongoing policy attempts, to cross the U.S.-Mexico border is as difficult, dangerous, and deadly as possible (see Alvarez 2023)—it is ever-urgent to ensure that her son recognizes his relationship to this land and its people.

Latina advocacy and community organizing is also the subject of "'We Are Orlando': Silences, Resistance, and the Intersections of Mass Violence" by Julie Torres. This *In the Trenches* piece documents the formation of "Proyecto Somos Orlando" by a group of mostly Puerto Rican women in the immediate aftermath of the Pulse nightclub mass murder in June of 2016 who realized that the predominantly Latin@ survivors and victims' families required truly culturally competent support and resources. From translation services to mental health care to the navigation of medical, legal, and financial support systems, the need to invest in deep rather than shallow cultural competence quickly became clear to these women when city and local organizations either failed to provide needed services or did so perfunctorily and temporarily. Torres writes, "Like the discourse of 'multiculturalism' . . . and diversity . . . , the liberal move to become 'culturally competent,' without any real investment in equity and inclusivity, does little more than reinforce capitalist and racial projects." By contrast, in demanding advocacy that evidenced "the ability to analyze and respond to the 'cultural scenes' . . . and 'social dramas' . . . of everyday life in ways that are culturally and psychologically meaningful for all the people involved," the Somos Orlando women honored both the dead and those they left behind.

Uniquely Puerto Rican responses to the dying are poetically addressed in Erika Abad's poem "Farm of Forgetting," which recounts the narrator's complicated responses to her Puerto Rican grandmother's dying in the aftermath of Hurricane María. She both honors the matriarch's power to gather her "beloveds" to her deathbed where they accompany her to the end and decries the implicit expectation that the narrator leave behind "all the

secrets, all the unnamed wounds . . . [and] scars," which that same powerful woman was responsible for. Sadly, however, our narrator reminds us
that death does not necessarily bury the wounds that are left behind on the
living. Perhaps the attempt to fortify "the roots that bind" even those she
"never wanted to love" was the most powerful legacy of the matriarch's
paradoxical life and death.

Picking up on the theme of women's central roles in the work of properly
memorializing the dead, Kami Fletcher's "Black Women Undertakers of
the Early Twentieth Century Were Hidden in Plain Sight" historicizes the
central role Black women played in the development, maintenance, and
expansion of Black undertaking skills and industry. In the context of
white racial terror from enslavement to Jim Crow, and contemporary
white supremacy, caring for the Black dead "became an act of resistance, a
step toward publicly claiming humanity . . . a form of remembering life"
and refusing white power over and after Black death. As Fletcher carefully
documents, Black women played a crucial—if often overlooked—role, one
that supported Black life by offering the culturally competent spaces and
rituals for mourning and memorializing that they were uniquely equipped
to undertake.

In a similar vein, Lashon Daley's "When Diane Tells Me a Story" is a
Testimonio about how her "othermother"—award-winning storyteller
Diane Ferlatte—helped her mourn her mother's passing. Daley writes:
"That is the power of the Black oral tradition: not only does it change
lives, creates and solidifies bonds that may not have formed otherwise,
it also strengthens the connective tissues that unite Black women. When
Diane tells me a story, she's passing down generations of wisdom,
morals, and histories—histories of Black women that have been pushed
aside . . . [and] stories of the oppressed, . . . rebellion, . . . and change."
In turn, when Daley tells this story, she honors Diane, her mother, and all
the Black women whose solidarity in carrying "Bundles of Worries" yielded
awareness of blessings such as a "mother's unrelenting love" and "ever-
growing bond[s]" with othermothers like Diane.

Finally, we close with this year's winner of the 2023 Elizabeth Alexander
Creative Writing Award for Poetry, "American Beech" by Yalie Saweda
Kamara. The *Meridians* Creative Writing Advisory Board described this
winning submission as "an extraordinary poem, tapping into the latent
wordplay of its title, gorgeous imagery like the leaf as raft, and a clean,
strong sense of form. It is a perfect example of what a poem can do in a

relatively small space, if one exploits the power of metaphor, sound, and phrasing." For my part, given what precedes it, I find the poem's final lines particularly apt final words for this issue, which was curated with the faith that putting widely disparate pieces in touch with one another would yield something beautiful. "How mighty. The God portal of human touch," Kamara muses, expanding on her earlier evocation of "haptic grace." I agree—when we are touched by the other's inherent grace, when we bring our broken fragments into contact, we create the possibility of experiencing the divine mosaic that is humanity in its most authentic form. May we all be so blessed.

Notes

1   *Oxford English Dictionary*, s.v. "mosaic," December 2022.

2   A video of Patel discussing *Migritude* is posted under the *Meridians* website's "On the Line" feature.

3   Sadly, little more than a decade after the Arab Spring, Tunisia is ruled by autocrat Kais Saied, who has adopted the United States's "great replacement theory" together with local anti-Blackness in order to scapegoat sub-Saharan (im)migrants for his regime's failed economic policies. This has had deadly consequences for vulnerable populations that have been targeted by vigilantes with impunity (NPR 2023).

Works Cited

Alvarez, Priscilla. 2023. "Biden Administration Rolls Out New Asylum Restrictions Mirroring Trump-Era Policy." *CNN Politics*, February 21. https://www.cnn.com /2023/02/21/politics/asylum-policy-biden-administration/index.html#:~:text=The %20Biden%20administration%20released%20a,a%20departure%20from% 20decadeslong%20protocol.

Athena-Ulysse, Gina. 2024. "Tools of the Trade or Women's Work," forthcoming, *Meridians: feminism, race, transnationalism*, vol. 23, no. 1, spring 2024.

Gray, Doris. 2020. *Leaving the Shadow of Pain: A Cross-cultural Exploration of Truth, Forgiveness, Reconciliation, and Healing*. Berlin: Logos.

NPR (National Public Radio). 2023. "International Institutions Are Protesting Tunisia's Racist Crackdown on Migrants." *Morning Edition*, March 8. https://www.npr.org /2023/03/08/1161859583/international-institutions-are-protesting-tunisias-racist -crackdown-on-migrants.

Singh, Karan Deep. 2023. "With Stories of Her Oppressed Community, a Journalist Takes Aim at the Walls of Caste." *New York Times*, March 6. https://www.nytimes .com/2023/03/06/world/asia/india-caste-discrimination-dalit-journalist -mooknayak.html?smid=nytcore-ios-share&referringSource=articleShare.

Devaleena Das

....

What Transnational Feminism Has Not Disrupted Yet
Toward a Quilted Epistemology

Abstract: Examining the critical genealogy of transnational feminism, this essay proposes a feminist theoretical model called quilted epistemology derived from the Black feminist art of quilting. Aiming to strengthen transnational feminism, quilted epistemology intends to resolve some of the existing limitations of transnational feminism and embrace multiple and incompatible feminist knowledge positions from the Global South to the Global North.

In 1994 Inderpal Grewal and Caren Kaplan's publication *Scattered Hegemonies: Postmodernity and Transnational Feminist Practices* marked a pivotal moment in feminist scholarship by elucidating that transnational feminist intervention must be concerned with not only women-centric social injustices but also immigration and citizenship, globalization, and neoliberalism to address how one oppression intersects multiple other oppressions. In addition, the awareness of multiplicity of feminist evolutions in diverse cultural contexts provided a new impetus to seek a paradigmatic feminist framework that would encompass all those multiple forms of feminism and engage in an intersectional analysis of issues related to social injustices at the local, national, and global levels. From the time of the publication of *Scattered Hegemonies*, attempts were made to solidify diverse feminist epistemological models. This includes Chilla Bulbeck's (1998: 210) theory of "Braiding at the Borderlands," by which she refers to white feminists' obligation to consider the connection of power between them and women of color.

MERIDIANS · feminism, race, transnationalism   22:2 October 2023
DOI: 10.1215/15366936-10637591 © 2023 Smith College

However, Mikki Kendall's aphorism #SolidarityIsForWhiteWomen (2013) raised the question how of solidarity is possible when colonial and capitalist mentalities dominate mainstream feminism. Chandra T. Mohanty (2003) called for a "feminism without borders" by carefully focusing on politics of representation, essentialisms, and universalism that could lead to exclusionary politics. In the context of post-9/11 U.S. policies, transnational feminists (Bacchetta et al. 2002) in the United States vehemently critiqued Western military interventions in Muslim countries that supposedly "saved" oppressed Muslim women (Abu-Lughod 2013) but in reality pursued Islamophobia, neocolonialism, and imperialism. The debate about Islamophobia was further scrutinized by Jasbir Puar's (2007) groundbreaking theory of homonationalism. Homonationalism explains how wealthy white queer communities gain acceptance in Canada and the United States through consumerism and economic mobility. In the process, their homosexuality is co-opted by nationalist sentiment in U.S. foreign policies to claim that Muslim nations are homophobic while the Western world is egalitarian.

Indeed, transnational feminism unsettled mainstream feminist and Eurocentric queer scholarship by excavating how race, gender, sexuality, and other social categories are appropriated to justify imperialism and other forms of state violence. However, as Richa Nagar and Amanda Lock Swarr (2012: 4) argue, the descriptor transnational does not hold the same salience in the Middle East, South Asia, or Africa. I argue this is due to geopolitical locationality, linguistic barriers to intellectual resources, and the myopic division that exists between scholarship and activism that creates resistance to the flow of knowledge between the Global North and the Global South. Most importantly, I claim that feminist epistemology is often seen as metalinguistic, but in reality, it serves only an academic audience in the West. Therefore, transnational feminists need to explore other epistemological possibilities to dialogue among diverse feminist groups in the Global South and the Global North.

By critically tracing the journey of transnational feminism as a theoretical framework and a movement with aspiring intentions, applications, and outcomes, in this essay, I identify and examine issues that are inadequately addressed in transnational feminism. Remembering Laura Briggs and Robyn C. Spencer's (2019: 254) cautionary call that transnational feminism is a "quickly growing but contested field" fraught with "potentialities and continued erasures," I will address the strengths and limitations of transnational feminism in order to propose a feminist epistemological

model germinating from the Black feminist practice of quilting. My purpose in proposing this model is to strengthen transnational feminism by
challenging the belief that the Global North is the touchstone that vali-
dates feminism. To elucidate the application and feasibility of my model, I
analyze the Kenyan poet Shailja Patel's text *Migritude* (2010). Taking a cue
from feminists of color, my proposed epistemological model advocates
loosening the geopolitical knots of Euro-Americanness embedded in
transnational feminism for a nonsegregationist "comradeship" and collaborative feminist knowledge formation. My theoretical model embraces
the philosophy crafted by the Australian Aboriginal activism led by Lila
Watson: "If you have come here to help me you are wasting your time, but if
you have come because your liberation is bound up with mine, then let us
work together."[1]

Critiquing Mainstream Feminism
Since one of the goals of transnational feminism is to decolonize mainstream feminism, before I present the full scope and argue the viability of
my proposed epistemological model, I would like to clarify what I mean by
mainstream feminism. Mainstream feminism, alternately called bourgeois
or white feminism, is an ideological movement that has its roots in the
most publicly visible first- and second-wave feminisms of nineteenth- and
twentieth-century Euro-America.[2] White feminism here does not mean
that all white feminists are practicing mainstream feminism; rather, it
refers to how mainstream feminism, as a class- and race-privileged movement, politically legitimizes whiteness as a racial habitus. In the process, it
engages in an exclusionary, one-dimensional feminism that deals with
upper-middle-class white women's liberation and denies the intersectionality of structural racism, classism, capitalism, ableism, and ethno/
homonationalism that are interlinked to sexism.

In *Me, Not You: The Trouble with Mainstream Feminism*, Alison Phipps (2020:
5) defines mainstream feminism as Anglo-American public feminism that
includes media or popular feminism, institutional feminism, corporate
feminism, and policy feminism, "the feminism that tends to dominate in
universities, government bodies, private companies and international
NGOs [nongovernmental organizations]. . . . This is because it wants
power within the existing system, rather than an end to the status quo."
Borrowing the title of her book from the #MeToo campaign, Phipps ascer-
tains that the phrase *me too* was coined by the Black feminist and civil rights
activist Tarana Burke, but it was appropriated by Hollywood star Alyssa

Milano, who proclaimed that it is about "me," the white suffering self, "and not you," the Black woman. Phipps identifies the cardinal layout of mainstream feminism as "political whiteness" (6) drawn from narcissism, racial capitalism, heteronormative family structures, appropriation, monopolization of Indigenous lands and wealth, and exploitation of people of color. Kendall's essay collection *Hood Feminism* (2020) is another powerful indictment of how mainstream feminism has failed to address hunger and food insecurity, gentrification, eviction and homelessness, gun violence, Black maternal mortality, discriminatory access to health care and education, and extreme poverty leading to survival instincts such as sex work or selling drugs.

Moreover, mainstream feminism motivates corporate feminism whose ultra-inclusive consumerist mantra is that the more consumer products women buy, the more liberated they are. Roxane Gay (2014) identified this among celebrities like Beyoncé Knowles-Carter, Emma Watson, and Jennifer Lawrence, whose claiming feminism "for themselves has become the spoonful of sugar to make that medicine go down." Supporting corporate feminism means supporting consumerism, which leads to production of harmful chemicals, carbon emissions, water wastes, and landfills. For example, as transnational feminists have explained, the consumerist ideology of mainstream feminism encouraged the foundation of the Kabul Beauty School in Afghanistan. Opened with the aid of the North American and European fashion industries in post-9/11 Afghanistan, this school buttressed cultural imperialism and hid "the structuring violence of geopolitics and transnational capital in favor of a liberal ideal of women's freedom" (Nguyen 2011: 360). This same imperialist practice is reflected in Laura Bush's (2016) introduction to the anthology entitled *We Are Afghan Women: Voices of Hope*,[3] in which she glorifies U.S. military intervention to "protect" Afghan women from the atrocities of the Taliban. In rebutting Bush's feminist imperialism, Afghan activist and parliamentarian Malalai Joya (2009) denounced the idea of a savior nation protecting another nation and explained that mainstream feminism uses the "protector and protected myth" to justify U.S. attempts to exploit Afghanistan's potential for becoming a major site for production, circulation, and consumption that enriches the West.

Transnational feminist thinking emerged precisely to challenge the imperialism of mainstream feminism and its scattered hegemonies, and yet it has not been widely adopted outside the West and is largely ignored elsewhere. Ironically, then, transnational feminism, which aims to dismantle mainstream feminism, is operationalized primarily as a way for

Western feminists to execute internal critiques of dominant Western cultural and political phenomena. Transnational feminism has not realized its potential to become a venue for feminist dialogues across borders. I will suggest reasons and remedies for this later in the essay.

But even as I do so, I am keenly aware that I am writing this academic discourse in a colonial androcentric language from a privileged U.S. academic position that addresses mostly, although not exclusively, more privileged academic readers and that, because of geopolitical and economic limitations on publishing and circulation practices, excludes many others. These factors obviously limit my argument. However, as an immigrant who has taught and practiced feminist scholarship in India, Australia, and the United States, I bring my unique experiential knowledge to the project of developing an ever-evolving feminist epistemology in hopes of facilitating its travel beyond national and geographical boundaries. I also aspire to use my scholarship and the social location in which it is rooted to alter educational spaces like universities that do not necessarily foster the growth toward social justice because they are not spaces free from hegemonic and elitist practices. Therefore, to undo Euro-American axes of knowledge and to constantly engage into critical renovation and productive destabilization of transnational feminism that is on the verge of becoming just another fixed, inorganic product of Western imperialism, I propose a feminist epistemological theory. This theory elucidates methods for synergizing feminist knowledge through alliances among political movements, scholars, and artists from multiple sites outside the United States. But, before laying out my theory, I reflect on the existing strengths and inadequacies in transnational feminism as it currently operationalizes.

Slicing and Splicing Feminism

In the early 1990s, some U.S.-based interdisciplinary feminist scholars began to realize that feminism must respond to globalization, and so they developed the framework of transnational feminism to facilitate feminist analysis of globalization and its economic, political, cultural, and geographical processes (fig. 1).[4] These scholars also intended transnational feminism to serve as a corrective to the ethnocentric, if not colonizing, impulses of international feminism and to Robin Morgan's concept of global sisterhood (1984), by centering the struggles, contradictions, and interrelations of Black, Chicana, postcolonial, Indigenous, and Muslim feminisms (fig. 2) in feminist scholarship, teaching, and activism (Nadkarni and Gooptu 2017). This step was taken because global feminism assumes a

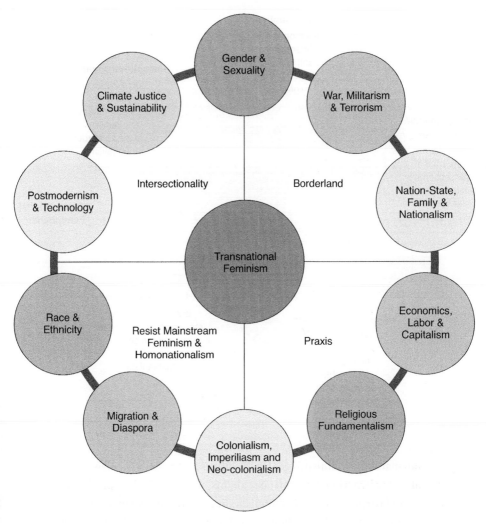

Figure 1.

false paradigm of global sisterhood that asserts women around the world are a homogenous group. This, of course, reduces all women's oppression to a singular, homogenous experience that is inevitably normed around white, middle-class, cisgender, heterosexual, Western women's experiences. The problem with international feminist analysis is that it uses a nationalist framework influenced by U.S. policies. In other words, international feminism ignores its inherent emphasis on nation-state and the asymmetries of power and wealth that organize relationships among the world's regions (Kaplan and Grewal 2002).

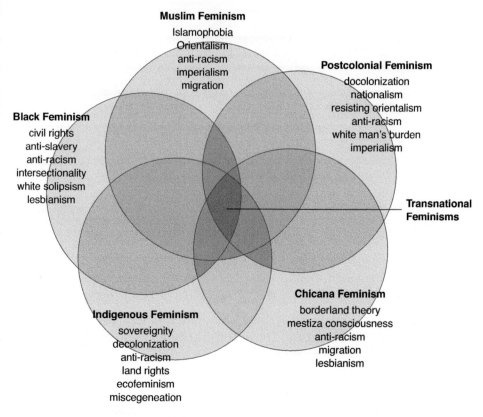

Muslim Feminism
Islamophobia
Orientalism
anti-racism
imperialism
migration

Postcolonial Feminism
docolonization
nationalism
resisting orientalism
anti-racism
white man's burden
imperialism

Black Feminism
civil rights
anti-slavery
anti-racism
intersectionality
white solipsism
lesbianism

**Transnational
Feminisms**

Chicana Feminism
borderland theory
mestiza consciousness
anti-racism
migration
lesbianism

Indigenous Feminism
sovereignity
decolonization
anti-racism
land rights
ecofeminism
miscegeneation

Figure 2.

Transnational feminism's goal is to address and remedy the flaws of global and international feminist paradigms, particularly their participation in and perpetuation of Orientalism, Eurocentrism, and white women's savior complex (Abu-Lughod 2013). For example, the Turkish feminist Meyda Yeğenoğlu (1998: 102) claims that sisterhood predicated on a hierarchical relationship is a tool in a colonial project. Grewal and Kaplan (1994) and M. Jacqui Alexander and Chandra Talpade Mohanty (1997) problematize how the "savior sisters" who practiced the Global North's intersectional feminism essentialized the center-periphery binary—the disparities that, on the other hand, global feminism erased in the name of solidarity. African American feminists offer similar critiques of global and international feminism. For example, some argue that global feminism co-opts the word *sisterhood* from African American women, who have historically used the word to replace the term *auntie*, which whites used to refer to a Black nursemaid for a white family.

Likewise, many African American and Native American activists have rejected white feminist sisterhood and located solidarity not with white women but in their own families, which have suffered eugenic sterilization and genocide at the hands of whites. Thus, Audre Lorde (1984: 111), while critiquing the "pretense to a homogeneity of experience covered by the word sisterhood," identifies her Black lesbian self as the "sister outsider." Similarly, in her seminal article entitled "Trashing: The Dark Side of Sisterhood," Jo Freeman (1976) aka Joreen introduces the concept and practice of "trashing" in feminist groups and warns not to be trapped in the "sweet promise of sisterhood" because it is a "knife" (1976: 51). She argued that women are forcibly conformed to the ideal of sisterhood that leads to the trashing culture.

Postcolonial feminism, like transnational feminism, aimed to remedy the oppressions embedded in global and international feminisms, but some feminists see it as problematic. For example, the term *postcolonial*, apparently suggesting that colonization no longer exists, holds no validity for Indigenous feminists who continue to be colonized today, not only psychologically but also literally in the seventeen non-self-governing territories still under colonial rule, according to the United Nations.[5] On the other hand, postcolonial feminism that has emerged from South Asian and African anticolonial thought argues that the prefix *post* does not imply the end of colonialism. Rather, it is concerned with the lingering forms of colonialism that continue to exist long after the formal end of the European empire, especially in the brutal onslaught of global modernity that imposed neoliberal policies such as privatization and austerity on the world economy despite the cost in human suffering (Loomba 2005; Gandhi 1998). Nevertheless, Indigenous feminists have not adopted these perspectives, owing to their desire for a feminist paradigm that more directly responds to the conditions of twenty-first-century colonization. Irrespective of the differences in ideologies, both postcolonial and Indigenous feminisms provide productive grounds for unpacking colonialism, sovereignty, and embedded racism.

Two theoretical pillars of transnational feminism that respond to the errors of global, international, and postcolonial feminisms and add valence to the prefix *trans* are borderlands theory and theory of intersectionality, respectively. Susan Stryker, Paisley Currah, and Lisa Jean Moore (2008: 11) explain that *trans* is used as a way to "disrupt or unsettle . . . conventional boundaries" and thus "resists premature foreclosure." It also signifies that transnational feminism is not just a movement or a theory; it is a framework, a methodological and analytical tool, and pedagogical strategy. Chicana feminist Gloria Anzaldúa's (1987) concept of borderlands as a third country or a hybridized space among Anglo, Mexican, and Indigenous cultures is an important framework in transnational feminism for theorizing physical, psychological, intellectual, sexual, metaphorical, spiritual, and technological borders and borderlands. What Anzaldúa calls borderlands, the Argentinian-born feminist María Lugones (2003: 59) calls liminal space, "where one becomes most fully aware of one's multiplicity." This liminal space is committed to the theory of "intersectional analysis," which has its roots in the work of Black feminists such as Anna J. Cooper, bell hooks, Patricia Hill Collins, and Angela Davis and was named and developed by legal Black feminist scholar Kimberlé Crenshaw (1989). Significantly, Crenshaw rejected single-axis studies of gender, sexuality, race, class, and nationality. The common methodological strand between intersectionality and borderland theory is their creative and political destabilization of interlocking systems of oppression.

Transnational feminism asserts that the same theory of destabilizing boundaries can be applicable for some instances but not to the others. For instance, in Davis's (1989) self-reflective essay on her 1970s trip to Egypt, she explains that though she belongs to the marginalized Black community in North America, her U.S. citizenship gave her privileges over the Egyptian women she encountered in the borderland between African American and Egyptian cultures. Three decades later, in 2011, Davis was part of a group of eleven feminists who visited Palestine.[6] Some of these women of color grew up in the Jim Crow South or in apartheid South Africa; others were Indigenous women who lived on Indian reservations in the United States. They were shocked to see the violation of Palestinian rights in the West Bank and the Gaza Strip. Indeed, this experience made Davis and her group aware that in a transnational "matrix of oppressions" (Collins 2000: 297), different social classifications and dominations are interconnected while boundaries start to fade. However, in other contexts, transnational feminism as manifested in Anzaldúa's borderlands theory is not liberating. For example, Mizrahi anthropologist Smadar Lavie (2011: 101) argues that Mizrahi Jewish women and Palestinian women who have Israeli citizenship "do not want to be in this 'third country,' dispossessed of their lands, languages, and culture."[7] This latter case demonstrates that transnational feminism should acknowledge that not all borderlands promise coalition. While Davis's and the Egyptian women's alliance was possible, for Lavie, the lived horror of border zone trauma in the West Bank and Gaza was unbearable. So she concluded: "Each theory has its own life. First unthinkability. Then exciting praise for its new set. . . . Then its long process of becoming obsolete" (115).

Lavie's observation is particularly important because it enables us to understand that the material realities of experience can sometimes exceed existing feminist theories, and this premise underlies my critique of transnational feminism. I am not arguing that transnational feminism is essentially colonizing or appropriative. Rather, I am suggesting that it is not effective in all circumstances and, additionally, that it must promise possibilities for revision and expansion. The solution that I am proposing is an epistemological model of my own invention that is grounded in the African American art of quilting. I do not intend to co-opt the metaphor, for I have learned from Black feminists their tremendous power to build Underground Railroad, contribution to the abolitionist movement, publication of anti-colonial chronicles of history, and protest against social injustices. Also, I do not intend to universalize this epistemological framework but to argue that our search for a fixed feminist epistemological model is nonviable.

Disjunctions in Transnational Feminism

While transnational feminism has unsettled the hypernationalist formulation enmeshed within American academia, its adequacy is not evaluated outside the American and Canadian academic spaces: "Locked in opposition to the nation-state, transnational research often mirrors the borders of the sovereign, bounded form of the nation it seeks to move beyond" (Fernandes 2013: 7). Furthermore, the descriptor *transnational*, without its political valences, runs the risk of becoming ornamental (Briggs, McCormick, and Way 2008). Though the proliferation of the transnational feminist framework is the outcome of Black, Chicana, Muslim, Indigenous, and postcolonial feminism, it has not explicitly incorporated East and Central European and Antipodean (Australia and New Zealand) feminisms. It has also failed to offer a useful approach to analyzing cross-border relations between sovereign Native nations. As Mayeli Blackwell (2006) argues, Indigenous feminism is already transnational, owing to its Indigenous nation-to-nation commitments across multiple borders. Therefore, even if transnational feminism has deconstructed academic imperialism that posits the impermeability of knowledge formation, it is sometimes myopic to its own epistemic privileges.

Kaplan and Grewal (2002) and Leela Fernandes (2013) have argued, in fact, that the U.S.-centric concept of transnational feminism is dangerous because it erases meaningful differences and reduces world history and cultures to U.S. institutional practices. For example, U.S.-centered transnational feminism is normed around the dominant United States and its institutions even as it resists many of them. Another example is, while U.S.-centered transnational feminism offers a sharp critique of nationalism as patriarchal in light of U.S. twentieth- and twenty-first century neo-imperialist foreign policy, the Kurdish Female Militancy has feminized nationalism as they fight for Kurdish sovereignty and battle Da'ish (ISIS) in northern Syria and Iraq. In their article "Reconsidering Nationalism and Feminism: The Kurdish Political Movement in Turkey" (2018), Nadje Al-Ali and Latif Tas have explained this more elaborately. Adopting Anthony Smith's (1983: 158–59) distinction between ethnocentric and polycentric nationalism and Ranjoo Seodu Herr's (2003: 139) concept of justifiable and unjustifiable nationalisms,[8] they argue that that the Kurdish women's movement cannot be equated with Western feminists' "opposition to their own government's national and international policies, [and their tendency] to view nationalism as a vehicle to further patriarchy" (Al-Ali and Tas 2018: 453). Al-Ali and Tas traced the history of Kurdish nationalism in alliance with Kurdish leftist politics of the 1960s and 1970s in the face of the Turkish government's repression of Kurds, human rights abuses against them, and attempts at criminalizing (in order to erase) Kurdish ethnicity. Based on their field research and oral interviews of Kurdish and Turkish women activists, they conclude that nationalist sentiment is a key element of Kurdish feminist consciousness and that it is the basis for a "sophisticated and nuanced critique of the patriarchal nature of the nationalist movement as well as the nationalist character of the Turkish feminist movement" (469). This demonstrates that transnational feminists' rejection of nationalism entraps it within the boundaries of the nationalist epistemic that it seeks to subvert.

    Another critique that I want to elucidate here is how major transnational feminist works by Grewal, Kaplan, Alexander, and Mohanty, to name a few, have not sufficiently addressed that the market value of higher education is determined at the intersection of power, capitalist appraisements, education's gatekeeping role in relation to class status, and a geopolitical hegemony dominated by Western universities. This results in a systemic devaluation of non-Western university degrees and the deskilling and de-credentializing of many categories of professionals and academics migrating from the Global South to the Global North. This academic industrial complex, invisible from the vantage point of transnational feminists' epistemic privilege, has contributed to the myth that knowledge generated in a non-Euro-American space is theoretically inadequate.

Ramón Grosfoguel (2012: 81), the Puerto Rican sociologist who resists Eurocentric fundamentalism in Western universities' epistemic structures, identifies this phenomenon as "epistemic racism/sexism." Grosfoguel argues that white male epistemic privilege is rooted in the Cartesian ego-politics of knowledge, and that gender, queer, and ethnic studies, which emerged as part of the civil rights movement in the United States, are crucial to decentering that privilege. According to Grosfoguel, for this reason, non-Eurocentric and alternative epistemologies from non Euro-Amercian places are disqualified, subalternized, and discredited. Borrowing Boaventura de Sousa Santos's concept of "ecology of knowledge" or epistemic diversity, Grosfoguel calls for replacing the monocultural Western "university" with a "pluri-versity" that incorporates "inter-epistemic" knowledge (84). To this end, he argues that a collective and integrative approach to experiential learning stemming from, reflecting on, and influenced by women, the queer community, and people of color within and outside the academic space of the Global North is needed to develop constructivist alternate feminist elucidations of the exercise of power and knowledge productions. My model of quilted epistemology aims to provide the infrastructure necessary for transnational feminists to support such an endeavor.

Quilted Epistemology

My proposed epistemological model is based on the principle of several paths (activism, performance, visual, communal, experiential, dialogical, and musical) to knowledge formation. The impetus to create this model is the need to replace the "pyramidal model" (Connell 2015: 59) of knowledge production with not only a more equitable paradigm but also one that is more organic. According to the Australian social scientist Raewyn Connell, hegemonic knowledge is produced in the Global North, which she likens to the apex of a pyramid, and it trickles down to the Global South. Connell's diagnosis is helpful in understanding how Western economics and cultural imperialism contribute to the neoliberal educational enterprise and inflate, for instance, both the supply and demand of educational degrees from Western universities while devaluing non-Western credentials and deskilling the professionals who hold them. In contrast, my model of quilted, multivalenced knowledge production includes knowledge gained within and beyond institutional engagement, nonprivatized Indigenous knowledge, and knowledge that emerges from marginalized standpoints, such as scholars who do not have the privilege bestowed by research budgets, federal funding, freedom of migration, visa access, and admittance to often geographically distant research sites because institutional policies limit their use to employees or citizens of particular nations.

My notion of "quilted epistemology" originates in Black women's art of quilting, which is so often featured in stories of oppression, human resilience, creativity, and wisdom unleashed in the pioneering texts of Alice Walker, Maya Angelou, Faith Ringgold, Joyce Carol Oates, Marge Piercy, and Toni Morrison.[9] For instance, Ringgold, known for her unique combination of painting, quilted fabric, and storytelling, thematizes intersectionality and structural multiplicity of interlocking systems of oppression in her works. In Morrison's Beloved (1997), the quilt is the metaphor of multiple voices. Walker's womanist quilt is spiritual and ecofeminist, signifying lesbian and sisterly bonding in The Color Purple (1982).

Why quilting? The history of African American quilting is connected to grassroots anti-oppression activism, and community labor, all of which resist globalization and are key elements of transnational feminism. The political journey of Africans who were forced into chattel slavery in America is sewn into this unique art form, and the quilts as well as the collaborative processes employed to create them reflect their cultural heritage and alliances. With the passage of time, enslaved Black ancestors' collaborative artwork crossed cultural boundaries and was mediated by its adoption by indentured servants and Irish and Asians who were abused laborers.[10] These oppressed communities' power to coalesce and promulgate knowledge about their struggles is crucial for the transnational feminist framework. Furthermore, Maude Wahlman and John Scully (1983) claim that the Black women's textile aesthetic reflects multiple, offbeat rhythms of colors and schemes that create unpredictability and fluidity of movement. This polyrhythmic tufting, or the skill of holding all the discarded clothes together, highlights Black women's variety of experiences, frameworks of operation, and understanding of the world. It prevents competitive individualistic enterprise and promotes equity, as found in the oldest crazy-quilt patterns, made of mismatched pieces of clothes, twigs, and cotton. Grounded in an ethics of community bonding across diversity, quilting as a sociopolitical tool can provide an epistemological understanding to transnational feminism, lending it the sense of tufting diverse branches of feminist thoughts.

Feminist knowledge production is consistently marginalized in academia, just as quilting is classified as a craft and is not included in fine arts.

Indeed, in fine arts, the perceived merit as well as price is most often located in the product, whereas the process is as valuable as the artifact when it comes to Black women's quilting. Among African American women, quilting encompasses meditative processes, observations, and contemplation on cultural values and creativity. Quilting demands an intuitive understanding of geometry, texture, and the chemistry between the people who used the cloth and the quilt. Therefore, quilting is praxis, an interweaving of theory and action. A quilted epistemology that propagates care as liberatory, therapeutic, and healing can resist mainstream feminist advocacy of the carceral prison complex and mitigate the trauma caused by gun violence in the United States, suffered disproportionately by BIPOC (Black, Indigenous, people of color), especially African American, communities. Evidence of this curative potential of quilting is offered by the experiences of incarcerated men who have made quilts for homeless people and victims of domestic violence (Friederich 2019). For example, male inmates in Jefferson City Correctional Center in Missouri quilt for charity from 8:30 a.m. to 3:30 p.m. five days a week, as part of a restorative justice program. The quilters' self-esteem and sense of connectedness to the larger community both increase, which is rehabilitative. If the intergenerational patchworks in quilting have survived attempts to erase the history of oppressions, a feminist epistemology grounded in the praxis of quilting also can be restorative.

For these reasons, quilting is more effective than mapping—a term that reeks of colonial oppression but is often used by transnational feminists in their attempts to articulate a heterogeneous feminism in decolonizing the dominant Eurocentric, phallocentric, colonialist, racist, and elitist mode of knowledge formation. In contrast to the restorative, communitarian nature of quilting, mapping is conceptually and practically linked to the colonial practice of cartography, and it involves a process of ordering and anchoring. It is a tool for global economic expansion.

In *Mapping Colonial Conquest* (2007), Norman Etherington argues that cartography is the product of powerful social forces produced by colonizers. Radhika Mohanram (1999: 143), adopting J. B. Harley's analysis of how "maps are never value-free images" based on the selection of their content and dynamics of power in social relations, reminds us that naming the Australian continent terra nullius in early maps was a Eurocentric technique of "a systematic forgetfulness of antecedent spatial configurations." Mapping erased, wrote over, or displaced Indigenous conceptions of space. Furthermore, maps often serve national propaganda; therefore, a mapped

feminist epistemology is at risk for producing authoritarian, propagan-
distic exegesis. Morrison (1989: 8) once warned, "Canon building is empire
building. Canon defense is national defense." Analogously, mapping is
prone to propagating neo-imperialism under the auspices of transnational
feminism by imposing borders around knowledge rather than traversing
and disrupting them to form hybridized knowledge along the lines that
Anzaldúa (1987) discusses in *Borderlands/La Frontera.*

In contrast, quilting is not only therapeutic, but it also resists propagating national and state agendas while facilitating epistemic disobedience
(Mignolo 2010), unfixing possessions, and considers borders permeable,
which should be a priority for transnational feminism. Alexander and
Mohanty (2012: 41), in their attempt to "destabilize the old cartographic
binaries set up by the academy and by the pedagogic and spatial practices,"
interrogate to what extent we are mixing, juxtaposing, and creating leak-
ages between theory and praxis. They further assert that the mobilization
of knowledge in privatized academic spaces involves a set of cartographic
rules that "unjustly organize human hierarchies in place and reify uneven
geographies" (27) and "necessarily produce insiders and outsiders in the
geographies of knowledge production" (28). Mohanram (1996: 50), pointing at the "hegemony of [Western] scholars," further interrogates the
application of theoretical frameworks produced in the Northern Hemi-
sphere, such as mapping and transnationalism, to the Southern Hemi-
sphere: "The scholar in the South is faced with a difficult choice—either
use frameworks which reveal their Northern bias or be read only locally."
For these reasons, I argue that mapping perpetuates boundaries and irre-
versibility, while quilting encourages chaotic and rhythmic complexity of
descriptions and interpretations; multiple and self-reflective learning
experiences; and a blurring of disciplinary, cultural, geographical, institutional, and individual boundaries. The art of quilting, like theory, which,
according to Edward Said (1983: 227), evolves as it encounters acceptance
and resistance in different cultural environments, entails weaving and
stitching across borders. Hence quilting becomes an excellent transnational feminist epistemological model for fostering multiple creative
agencies and coalitional consciousness.

Shailja Patel's *Migritude*

The Kenyan poet, playwright, performer, and activist Shailja Patel's text
Migritude (2010), inspired by the eighteen saris her mother collected for the
daughter in a battered red suitcase for thirty years, is an elucidation of

holistic feminist knowledge produced through quilted epistemology. *Migritude*, a plurality of genres, including poems, monologues, and letters, tells of Patel's lived reality of cross-continental migration as a South Asian diasporic in East Africa, a South Asian African diasporic in the Global North (the United States and the UK), and a fugitive in Australia.[11] As she moves around the three continents, Patel creatively quilts political histories of colonization, empires, war, violence, the flow of global capital, racism, and indignities through autobiographical narratives. In her creativity, quilting means dwelling in multiple temporalities and shifting identities, "melding genres and dissolving boundaries" (138), looking beyond existing data, and reclaiming truths in innovative ways: "I brought Migritude. A tapestry of poetry, history, politics, packed into a suitcase, embedded in my body, rolled out into theatre. An accounting of Empire enacted on the bodies of women" (96). Patel is quilting from the strands of her body; she goes on weaving the intergenerational and cross-continental quilt of untold histories and colonial narratives of the oppressed bodies.

Before the publication of the text, *Migritude* was performed from 2005 until 2008 in the United States, Zanzibar, Austria, Kenya, Italy, Zimbabwe, and South Africa. This example of quilted epistemology involves an inherent unsettling of boundaries. In each performance, *Migritude* adapts to a new audience in a new culture; its form constantly reincarnates, mutates, and discovers multiple creative outlets, just like migrants themselves: "By dawn, we may be on the move, forced to reinvent ourselves in order to survive" (10). Since performance is collaborative, and her writing practice is singular and undertaken in isolation (86), Patel attempts to make the text of *Migritude* highly mobile by synthesizing multiple voices of oppressed women from colonial periods ranging from Roman to British. Different modes of storytelling by different voices in the text, including her mother's, displace Patel's one-dimensional perspective. This collaborative knowledge production is what quilted epistemology aims at: a conclamation rather than a single feminist voice posing as the only source of knowledge.

Migritude, when transposed from performance to text, is juxtaposed with body arts and images of transportation designed by Chez Bryan Ong, Jen Chou, and Pritsana Kootint-Hadiatmodjo to speak of scientific racism during European Enlightenment, while the transport vehicles symbolize migration. Additionally, the interplay of languages (Kiswahili, English, Gujrati, Hindi, Urdu, and Punjabi) within the text and its translation into other languages assert the theme of displacement and multiple enactments of identities. Again, the model of, in this case, quilted language offered by *Migritude* contrasts with transnational feminism's failure to sufficiently address the phenomenon that Anzaldúa (1987: 58) calls "linguistic terrorism," which consists variously of systemic erasure of one's native language, in tandem with forced acquisition of a dominant language or dialect (frequently "standard" English), language discrimination, linguicism, and the politics of gendering of languages (Hall 2010). Unlike transnational feminism, quilted epistemology acknowledges, as Patel (2010: 137) explains, that "translation adds another layer to the migration," meaning that migrants are challenged not only to communicate via translations that distort information and meanings, but they are also forced to translate themselves—their sense of self—into unfamiliar societies and cultures. In *Migritude*, Patel thus turns to Matrubhasha or mother tongue (51) as an important rhetorical tool (136), and one is reminded of Gayatri Chakraborty Spivak's (1992: 189–90) words: "Rather than imagining that women automatically have something identifiable in common, why not say, humbly and practically, my first obligation in understanding solidarity is to learn her mother-tongue." Hence Patel takes the initiative of inserting her first language, Gujrati, in the text of *Migritude* to humbly remind that globalization should not erase one's cultural roots, which is a focus that is not prominent in transnational feminism.

Migritude's use of disembodied voices onstage and in the text destabilizes imperial mapping. One the one hand, *Migritude* refers to untold histories archived in the bodies of migrants. On the other hand, it records oral testimonies of Kenyan women who survived sexual violence and torture by British officers. They speak of how their bodies were burnt with cigarette butts; boots and bottles dipped in petrol were thrust into their vaginas; and they were forced to walk on hot coals, publicly raped, put into sacks, doused in paraffin, and set on fire by British officers during the colonial period. These women strapped their sick babies to their backs and were not allowed to look at them until after the babies died (Patel 2010: 18). Thus "Migritude breaks silence—personal, familial, global, historical" (100). These heart-wrenching, horrifying testimonials are meant to serve as a prophylactic against future violations, for, as Patel states, "history buried becomes history repeated" (128).

As the staged version of *Migritude* performatively demonstrates this hidden violence perpetrated on colonized bodies, this act of creating social awareness regarding the horrors of colonialism becomes activist in nature. Thus, through her journey and evolution as an activist- artist, Patel generates the theory of migritude, a migrant attitude. This migrant attitude complements the twentieth-century (literary and political) negritude movement pioneered by Francophone African and Caribbean writers, including Martinican Aimé Césaire, who coined the term, and Léopold Sédar Senghor, who expanded the theory. The philosophy of action of the negritude movement was restoring pride in African cultural values and pushing back the inferior status imposed on Africans by European colonizers. If negritude resists colonialist structuring of Blackness, then *Migritude* resists anti-immigrant sentiments. *Migritude* not only encourages Black and Asian diasporic voices to speak "unapologetically, fiercely, lyrically for themselves" (143) but also evokes memories of transatlantic slave trade, racial capitalism, the British importation of thirty-two-thousand indentured Indian laborers to Africa to build railways, and systemic violence against immigrants. Consequently, Patel's neologism *migritude* resonates with the possibilities of activist coalitions that have failed to arise out of transnational feminism: "It has the arresting coruscating, academic luster of a freshly minted neologism, but also has harsher/oppressed undertones of 'nigger,' 'meager/maigre,' 'magreb/maigreb'" (143). *Migritude*'s integration of academic feminism by taking the lead from the theory of negritude and activism in the form of stage performance demonstrates the advantage of a quilted epistemology.

This paradoxical coupling enables *Migritude*'s raging activist voice to interrogate why the gutters of Berkeley are not swamped with plastic bottles, as are the ditches of Nairobi (36). It also proclaims that the geopolitical disparity between the Global North and the Global South is a new episode in an imperialist series that started with the murder of twenty-five-thousand Kenyans under British rule. Britain then forced the Kenyan government to borrow 12.5 million pounds from the British in order to raise the funds to pay the UK to end colonial rule. Literally, Kenya was coerced into borrowing money from Britain to cover the cost of buying its own territory. The evil of colonialism has morphed in the name of globalization: "Chai became a beverage invented in California" (7), Palestine is the new social justice summer camp for wealthy American teens (34), and "Pepsi buys water rights in Central Africa" (36). Thus *Migritude* is a quilt of "decolonizing aesthetic" (185), crafted out of experiential, creative, activist, academic, and performative knowledge that is more effective than transnational feminism in resisting the latest phase of colonialism.

Furthermore, a quilt is a reservoir of history, an album of memory, a visible autobiography, and it promises digressions from colonial spatial anxieties in a way that transnational feminism cannot. For instance, Patel's use of saris in her performances invites mainstream audiences into a politically innovated, quilted feminist knowledge formation by appropriating and transvaluing Orientalism. Saris, she says, "are the containers of history, politics, economics, woven into fabric, codified into shape and pattern" (141). The saris, like quilts, are more than a piece of cloth. Resisting her mother's initial intention of using them as wedding gifts to her daughter, Patel deploys those saris as more than cultural objects to break the silence of violence and struggle embedded in their softness. In her performance, the saris are knotted and, like body parts, become organic. As these saris have witnessed how the empire killed children (80), Patel presents an embodied history that women have been carrying through generations: "I know what I carry in my suitcase. I carry my history. I carry my family. Over my saris, I wear my sisters" (41). She embraces the saris to explore her own lesbian identity and challenges Eurocentric and nativist, anti-immigrant stereotypes associated with both saris and lesbianism. If the conservatives in postcolonial nations misrepresent lesbianism as a Western importation, then the homonationalist sentiment in the West propagates the notion that non-Western societies are homophobic, fundamentalist, and backward. Patel resists such political framings by embracing saris, a non-Western attire, which is also a symbolic marker of heteronormative conjugal space in South Asian culture. In the process, she subverts all these dominant stereotypes based on geographical temporalities, ethnicity, and sexualized/racialized identities.

Thus the saris in *Migritude* weave personal history with global politics and shift "from self-protective silence to political expression" (100). As such, the saris expose the vicious caste politics in India, where the weavers who make those precious clothes remain untouchables. The saris are also a reminder of domestic violence, strangulation, and burning of women by throwing paraffin on the silk. The saris that can make women appear vulnerable by enveloping them in yards of colorful, intricately designed cloth are also worn by women warriors when they fight battles, women farmers in the fields, and women laborers on construction sites. The saris also bespeak textile politics, racial capitalism, and the destruction of Indian handlooms and spinning wheels by the British who forcibly took control of Indian cotton production and "hunted down the terrified weavers, chopped off their index fingers and thumbs" (122). At the same time, the saris are reminiscent of the flourishing Indian Ocean trade between Africa, Arabian Peninsula, India, and Southeast Asia.

For Patel the saris awaken her memory of the women tortured in Kenya by the British soldiers, the Maasai women's protest, the rise of the Mau Mau freedom fight in Kenya, and the U.S. military invasion of Iraq and Afghanistan. The saris are evocative of the Ugandan military officer Idi Amin's 1972 coup, which overthrew the democratically elected government of Uganda. Amin, popularly known as the Butcher of Uganda, served as the president from 1971 to 1979. Backed by Britain, Israel, and the United States, during the coup, Asian women were targeted for rape, and Amin expelled the Asian population living in Uganda and Kenya. As Patel unfolds each sari during her performance, she demonstrates her awareness that a "third-generation Asian Kenyan will never be Kenyan enough" (28), that immigrants push themselves "to the breaking point" (41), that they "repair instead of replace" (34), and "what we wear under our saris is unachievable perfectionism" (41). Transnational feminism has not delineated this power of feminist craft as a viable artistic medium to decolonize history, thereby not pointing toward its subversive potential. Quilted epistemology not only radically shatters the gendered hierarchy between art and craft but also integrates the power of craft into feminist knowledge formation.

Just as a quilted epistemology fuels Patel's layered, cross-cultural critique of imperialism globally and locally, it is also capable of strengthening coalitions among feminists that are inclusive, which contrasts with the America-centric tendencies of transnational feminism. Applying Michel Foucault's concept of "subjugated knowledge" to the relationship of higher education as an institution and Black feminisms in the United States, Patricia Hill Collins (1997) argues that the white hegemonic model of knowledge production suppresses Black women's epistemology. Similarly, postcolonial, Chicana feminist Chela Sandoval's *Methodology of the Oppressed* (2000) and Maori feminist Linda Tuhiwai Smith's *Kaupapa Māori Methodology* (1999b) argue that knowledge generated as Indigenous community practice is not recognized in white academic space. Smith's *Decolonizing Methodologies* (1999a) is a strong critique of the Eurocentric research concepts that often exploit Indigenous populations. The Aboriginal feminist critic Aileen Moreton-Robinson (2004: 75) beautifully explains how in Aboriginal philosophy knowledge facilitates humbleness: "The more that I know the less that I know because there are other forms of knowledge that exist beyond us as humans." Patel is aware of this struggle for space that women and queer communities of color experience. Therefore, she has been critical of the Nigerian novelist Chimamanda Adichie, who, in an interview with the French journalist Caroline Broueby, derided postcolonial theory: "Postcolonial theory? I don't know what it means. I think it is something that professors made up because they needed to get jobs" (Musila 2018). In her reply on Twitter, Patel (2018) says:

> The irony is that Chimamanda's parents are both academics. Her mother was the University of Nigeria's first woman registrar. . . . That postcolonial theory Chimamanda derides . . . is what got books by African writers on the national curricula in African countries. . . . Who put *Purple Hibiscus* on college reading lists and syllabi . . . ? Academic feminists, versed in postcolonial theory. Who fought to have women and Black people admitted at Princeton, Yale, Harvard, where Chimamanda enjoyed fellowships? Academic feminists and postcolonial theorists.

While this conflict between the two distinguished Global South feminists of color is a reminder that transnational feminist solidarity is not easily forged, a quilted epistemology could establish that both Patel and Adichie are fighting to promote resistance to monolithic knowledge formation by replacing it with embodied and dialectical engagement of experiences. Adichie's (2009) warning about the "danger of a single story" is similar to Patel's rupturing of the prevalent linearity of time in "The Journey," the last part of *Migritude* that explains how knowledge involves an unending process of learning.

Quilted epistemology offers solutions to the many problems that transnational feminism creates and perpetuates, especially the separationism that is the consequence of its roots in hegemonic Western epistemological traditions, even as it attempts to remedy the flaws inherent in global and international feminism. The Cherokee two-spirit poet Qwo-Li Driskill (2016) argues that separationism militates against transformative education, which is one of feminism's overriding goals. And, though Driskill notes that a union between Native two-spirit studies and the Western paradigm of LGBTQ+ studies is not possible, a "doubleweaving" of the two could provide a good balance. Doubleweaving, one of the oldest and most difficult traditions in basketry, creates two independent designs: one on the outside of the basket and one on the inside. Doubleweaving is also a Cherokee rhetorical strategy, in which two seemingly disparate rhetorical approaches exist concurrently. Likewise, quilted epistemology doubleweaves intellectual agency of both the Global South and the Global North.

This does not discredit all the monumental works that academic feminists and queer studies scholars of the Global North have been doing for decades. It encourages knowledge that originates from activists and social movements like Black Lives Matter, Standing Rock, the Chipko movement, the contemporary Revolutionary Association of the Women of Afghanistan (RAWA), the Palestinian feminist-queer grassroots organization Aswat, and others around the world. Leela Fernandes (2013: 9, 7), crediting transnational feminism for dislodging artificial nation-state boundaries and for making feminist scholarship an interdisciplinary site, warns that transnational feminism should not become "a disciplinary device within interdisciplinary research and theory" or "a territorialized concept." To avoid such an outcome, a quilted epistemology invites pluralist ontological relations between the knower, the known, and the process of knowing, as explained by bell hooks (1995: 158) when she described how her quiltmaker grandmother Sarah Oldham discovered new worlds by quilting new pattern every time:

> Sarah Oldham, my mother's mother, was the style radical. Her aesthetic sensibility was grounded in a more traditional appreciation for the natural world, for color and harmony. As a quilt maker she was constantly creating new worlds, discovering new patterns, different shapes. To her it was the uniqueness of the individual body, look and soul that mattered. From her I learned the appropriateness of being myself.

Devaleena Das is associate professor and program director of women's, gender, and sexuality studies at the University of Minnesota Duluth. She has published on corporeal feminism, transnational feminism, feminist new materialism, and Asian and Australian feminisms. She is coeditor of *Unveiling Desire: Fallen Women in Literature, Culture, and Films of the East* (2018) and *Claiming Space for Australian Women's Writing* (2017). Her forthcoming book entitled *Anatomophilia: The Liberation of the Body* explores alternative theories of human bodies based on narratives in real life, literature, art, religious myths, and performances. She teaches courses on body studies, health humanities, transnational and postcolonial studies of sexuality and race, feminist research and methodologies, politics of knowledge formation, and migration and diaspora studies.

Notes

I am grateful to McMaster University, Canada, where I presented this essay as a talk in the Transnational Feminism Workshop organized in 2018. I am thankful to the invited transnational feminist scholars and the organizers of that workshop for their rigorous and generative comments on this essay. I also thank my feminist friend Prof. Colette Morrow for taking time in reading this essay and for providing helpful feedback. Finally, I would like to express my appreciation to the anonymous readers of *Meridians*.

1   Watson uttered these words at the 1985 United Nations Decade for Women Conference in Nairobi. As an Aboriginal activist, she understood the frustration of her Aboriginal communities in identifying the colonial savior complex among white people who even after the 1967 referendum, the antiapartheid protests of 1971, and the 1972 Aboriginal Tent Embassy on the lawns of Parliament House practiced neocolonialism and unconscious biases in the name of help. Like Audre Lorde who repeatedly reminded us that it is not the responsibility of Black women to educate white people, Watson also argued that Australian white settler communities need to decolonize and self-help themselves to prevent colonization.

2   Several feminist movements that stand outside the middle-class white feminist groups were existing in the United States as well as across the globe. To name a few: Black feminism, Chicana feminism, Moroccan women's struggle to change the Family Law Code, women's resistance to military dictatorship in Chile, South Korean women's protests against oppressive working conditions, Egyptian feminist Huda Sharaawi's formation of the Egyptian Feminist Union, Indian women's activism in the Chipko movement, Charlotte Maxeke's leadership in building the first South African women's organization called the Bantu Women's League in 1918, and the Indonesian feminist Raden Adjeng Kartini's captaincy in starting the first Indonesian primary school for girls in 1879. These feminist movements did not draw media and public attention, given their marginalized positions, unlike the feminist waves in the United States and UK.

3   The book is published by the George W. Bush Institute with its political agenda and ideology. It is interesting to note that Hillary Clinton, Condoleezza Rice, and Sheryl Sandberg have endorsed the book. For example, Clinton comments on the back cover: "For over a decade, Laura Bush has been an ally and advocate for the women of Afghanistan and, in particular, has worked to ensure that the voices of Afghan women are heard. In this book, she shares inspiring stories that not only capture the suffering of Afghan women, but also show their tremendous courage and resilience and the contribution they are making to build a better future for Afghanistan."

4   The feminists include Inderpal Grewal, Caren Kaplan, Chandra Mohanty, Jacqui Alexander, Gloria Anzaldúa, Ella Shohat, Gayatri Spivak, Maria Mies, KumKum Sangari, Mary Layoun, Uma Chakravorty, Norma Alarch, Cynthia Enloe, Nelly Richard, Aihwa Ong, Catherine Hall, Vron Ware, and Hazel Carby, to name just a few.

5   See United Nations' website for details on the non-self-governing territories defined under chapter 11 of the Charter of the United Nations, https://www.un .org/dppa/decolonization/en/nsgt.

6   The feminists include Rabab Abdulhadi, Ayoka Chenzira, Angela Y. Davis, Gina Dent, Melissa Garcia, Anna Romina Guevarra, Beverly Guy-Sheftall, Premilla

Nadasen, Barbara Ransby, Chandra Talpade Mohanty, and Waziyatawin. This group issued a strong statement endorsing the boycott, divestment, and sanctions movement and rejected the argument that to criticize the State of Israel is anti-Semitic.

7 Mizrahi are descendants of the Jewish community based in the Middle East and North Africa.

8 Based on Anthony Smith's classification of nationalism as ethnocentric and polycentric, Herr calls nationalism Janus-faced. She identifies polycentric nationalism as morally justifiable because it is based on the desire to be equal with other nations in the world and in the process creates a sense of community, self-determination, national sovereignty, independence, and pluralism. In contrast, she identifies ethnocentric nationalism as unjustifiable because it is based on concepts such as power and value and gives way to xenophobia, fanaticism, ethnic cleansing, and bloodshed.

9 I reclaim the quilting metaphor to resist all the complicit stereotypical binaries associated with quilting: masculine-feminine, art-craft, needle-pen, white-Black, young-old, and public-domestic. The art of quilting is often gendered as women's activity, but there are plenty of examples of geometric "soldiers' quilts" or "convalescent quilts" made by men involved in Crimean War or during British colonialism. For more details, see Daley 2017. It is important to mention here Joe the Quilter (1750–1826), famously known for his handiwork in England, Ireland, Scotland, and America. In *Historic Quilts* (1939) published by the American Historical Company in New York, Florence Peto profiles several men quilt makers. In 1998 the Anacostia Museum exhibited fifty quilts made by African American men ranging in age from nine to one hundred years across the United States.

10 To know more on this cross-cultural art of quilting, see America's quilting history at http://www.womenfolk.com/historyofquilts/multicultural.htm.

11 Born and raised as a third-generation East African Asian in Kenya, Patel moved to London and San Francesco later in her life while her parents migrated to Australia.

Works Cited

Abu-Lughod, Lila. 2013. *Do Muslim Women Need Saving?* Cambridge, MA: Harvard University Press.

Adichie, Chimamanda Ngozi. 2009. "The Danger of a Single Story." TED, October 7. YouTube video, 19:16. https://www.youtube.com/watch?v=D9Ihs24Izeg.

Al-Ali, Nadje, and Latif Tas. 2018. "Reconsidering Nationalism and Feminism: The Kurdish Political Movement in Turkey." *Nations and Nationalism* 24, no. 2: 453–73.

Alexander, M. Jacqui, and Chandra Talpade Mohanty. 1997. *Feminist Genealogies, Colonial Legacies, Democratic Futures.* New York: Routledge.

Alexander, M. Jacqui, and Chandra Talpade Mohanty. 2012. "Cartographies of Knowledge and Power: Transnational Feminism as Radical Praxis." In *Critical Transnational Feminist Praxis*, edited by Amanda Lock Swarr and Richa Nagar, 23–45. New York: State University of New York Press.

Anzaldúa, Gloria. 1987. *Borderlands/La Frontera: The New Mestiza*. San Francisco, CA: Aunt Lute Books.

Bacchetta, Paola, Tina Campt, Inderpal Grewal, Caren Kaplan, Minoo Moallem, and Jennifer Terry. 2002. "Transnational Feminist Practices against War." *Meridians: Feminism, Race, Transnationalism* 2, no. 2: 302–8.

Blackwell, Mayeli. 2006. "Weaving in the Spaces: Transnational Indigenous Women's Organizing and the Politics of Scale." In *Dissident Women: Gender and Cultural Politics in Chiapas*, edited by Shannon Speed, R. Aída Hernández Castillo, and Lynn M. Stephen, 240–318. Austin: University of Texas Press.

Briggs, Laura, Gladys McCormick, and J. T. Way. 2008. "Transnationalism: A Category of Analysis." *American Quarterly* 60, no. 3: 625–48.

Briggs, Laura, and Robyn C. Spencer. 2019. "Introduction." *Meridians: Feminism, Race, Transnationalism* 18, no. 2: 253–60.

Bulbeck, Chilla. 1998. *Re-orienting Western Feminisms*. Cambridge: Cambridge University Press.

Bush, Laura, and George W. Bush Institute. 2016. *We Are Afghan Women: Voices of Hope*. New York: Scribner.

Collins, Patricia Hill. 1997. "Comment on Hekman's 'Truth and Method: Feminist Standpoint Theory Revisited": Where's the Power?" *Signs: Journal of Women in Culture and Society* 22, no. 2: 375–81.

Collins, Patricia Hill. 2000. *Black Feminist Thought: Knowledge, Consciousness, and the Politics of Empowerment*. New York: Routledge.

Connell, Raewyn. 2015. "Meeting at the Edge of Fear: Theory on a World Scale." *Feminist Theory* 16, no. 1: 49–66.

Crenshaw, Kimberlé. 1989. "Demarginalizing the Intersection of Race and Sex: A Black Feminist Critique of Antidiscrimination Doctrine, Feminist Politics, and Antiracist Politics." *University of Chicago Legal Forum*, no. 8: 139–67.

Daley, Jason. 2017. "The Centuries-Old Tradition of Military Quilting Is Getting Its First Exhibition in the US." *Smithsonian Magazine*, August 10. https://www.smithsonianmag.com/smart-news/quilts-made-soldiers-go-display-first-time-180964215/.

Davis, Angela. 1989. *Women, Culture, and Politics*. New York: Random House.

Driskill, Qwo-Li. 2016. *Asegi Stories: Cherokee Queer and Two-Spirit Memory*. Tucson: University of Arizona Press.

Etherington, Norman. 2007. *Mapping Colonial Conquest: Australia and Southern Africa*. Crawley: University of Western Australia Press.

Fernandes, Leela. 2013. *Transnational Feminism in the United States*. New York: New York University Press.

Freeman, Jo. 1976. "Trashing: The Dark Side of Sisterhood." *Ms. Magazine*, April, 49–51, 92–98.

Friederich, Rachel. 2019. "Itching to Be Stitching: Airway Heights Inmates Donate Quilts." Department of Corrections Washington State, September 25. https://www.facebook.com/WACorrections/posts/the-most-rewarding-part-of-the-quilting-program-is-that-it-enables-staff-and-inc/2483736171747041/.

Gandhi, Leela. 1998. *Postcolonial Theory: An Introduction*. New York: Columbia University Press.

Gay, Roxane. 2014. "Emma Watson? Jennifer Lawrence? These Aren't the Feminists You're Looking For." *Guardian*, October 10.

Grewal, Inderpal, and Caren Kaplan, eds. 1994. *Scattered Hegemonies: Postmodernity and Transnational Feminist Practices*. Minneapolis: University of Minnesota Press.

Grosfoguel, Ramón. 2012. "The Dilemmas of Ethnic Studies in the United States: Between Liberal Multiculturalism, Identity Politics, Disciplinary Colonization, and Decolonial Epistemologies." *Human Architecture: Journal of the Sociology of Self-Knowledge* 10, no. 1: 81–89.

Hall, Donald E. 2010. "Can We Teach a Transnational Queer Studies?" *Pedagogy* 10, no. 1: 69–78.

Herr, Ranjoo Seodu. 2003. "The Possibility of Nationalist Feminism." *Hypatia: A Journal of Feminist Philosophy* 18, no. 3: 135–60.

hooks, bell. 1995. "Beauty Laid Bare: Aesthetics in the Ordinary." In *To Be Real: Telling the Truth and Changing the Face of Feminism*, edited by Rebecca Walker, 157–66. New York: Anchor Books.

Joya, Malalai. 2009. *A Woman among Warlords: The Extraordinary Story of an Afghan Who Dared to Raise Her Voice*. New York: Simon and Schuster.

Kaplan, Caren, and Inderpal Grewal. 2002. "Transnational Practices and Interdisciplinary Feminist Scholarship: Refiguring Women's and Gender Studies." In *Women's Studies on Its Own*, edited by Robyn Wiegman, 66–81. Durham, NC: Duke University Press.

Kendall, Mikki. 2000. *Hood Feminism*. New York: Viking.

Kendall, Mikki. 2013. "#SolidarityIsForWhiteWomen: Women of Color's Issue with Digital Feminism." *Guardian*, August 14. https://www.theguardian.com/commentisfree/2013/aug/14/solidarityisforwhitewomen-hashtag-feminism.

Lavie, Smadar. 2011. "Staying Put: Crossing the Israel–Palestine Border with Gloria Anzaldúa." *Anthropology & Humanism* 36, no. 1: 101–21.

Loomba, Ania. 2005. *Colonialism/Postcolonialism*. London: Routledge.

Lorde, Audre. 1984. *Sister Outsider*. Berkeley, CA: Crossing Press.

Lugones, María. 2003. *Pilgrimages/Peregrinajes: Theorizing Coalition against Multiple Oppressions*. New York: Rowman & Littlefield.

Mignolo, Walter D. 2010. "Epistemic Disobedience, Independent Thought, and Decolonial Freedom." *Theory, Culture and Society* 26, nos. 7–8: 159–81.

Mohanram, Radhika. 1996. "The Construction of Place: Maori Feminism and Nationalism in Aotearoa/New Zealand." *NWSA Journal* 8, no. 1, Global Perspectives: 50–69.

Mohanram, Radhika. 1999. *Black Body: Women, Colonialism, and Space*. Minneapolis: University of Minnesota Press.

Mohanty, Chandra T. 2003. *Feminism without Borders: Decolonizing Theory, Practicing Solidarity*. Durham, NC: Duke University Press.

Moreton-Robinson, Aileen. 2004. *Whitening Race: Essays in Social and Cultural Criticism*. Canberra: Aboriginal Studies.

Morgan, Robin. 1984. *Sisterhood Is Global: The International Women's Movement Anthology.* New York: Anchor Books.

Morrison, Tony. 1989. "Unspeakable Things Unspoken: The Afro-American Presence in American Literature." *Michigan Quarterly Review* 28, no. 1: 1–34.

Musila, Grace A. 2018. "Chimamanda Adichie: The Daughter of Postcolonial Theory." *Al Jazeera*, February 4. https://www.aljazeera.com/opinions/2018/2/4/chimamanda-adichie-the-daughter-of-postcolonial-theory.

Nadkarni, Asha, and Subhalakshmi Gooptu. 2017. "Transnational Feminism." In *Oxford Bibliographies in Literary and Critical Theory*, edited by Eugene O'Brien. New York: Oxford University Press.

Nagar, Richa, and Amanda Lock Swarr. 2012. "Introduction: Theorizing Transnational Feminist Praxis." In *Critical Transnational Feminist Praxis*, edited by Amanda Lock Swarr and Richa Nagar, 1–20. Albany: State University of New York Press.

Nguyen, Mimi Thi. 2011. "The Biopower of Beauty: Humanitarian Imperialisms and Global Feminisms in an Age of Terror." *Signs: Journal of Women in Culture and Society* 36, no. 2: 359–83.

Patel, Shailja. 2010. *Migritude.* New York: Kaya.

Patel, Shailja (@shailjapatel). 2018. "The irony is that Chimamanda's parents are both academics." Twitter, January 27, 2:47 a.m. https://twitter.com/shailjapatel/status/957158183935578112.

Peto, Florence. 1939. *Historic Quilts.* New York: American Historical Company.

Phipps, Allison. 2020. *Me, Not You: The Trouble with Mainstream Feminism.* Manchester: Manchester University Press.

Puar, Jasbir. 2007. *Terrorist Assemblages: Homonationalism in Queer Times.* Durham, NC: Duke University Press.

Said, Edward. 1983. *The World, the Text, and the Critic.* Cambridge, MA: Harvard University Press.

Sandoval, Chela. 2000. *Methodology of the Oppressed.* Minneapolis: University of Minnesota Press.

Smith, Anthony. 1983. *Theories of Nationalism.* New York: Holmes & Meier.

Smith, Linda Tuhiwai. 1999a. *Decolonizing Methodologies: Research and Indigenous People.* London: Zed Books.

Smith, Linda Tuhiwai. 1999b. *Kaupapa Māori Methodology: Our Power to Define Ourselves.* Vancouver: University of British Columbia Press.

Spivak, Gayatri Chakravorty. 1992. "The Politics of Translation." In *Destabilizing Theory: Contemporary Feminist Debates*, edited by Michèle Barrett and Anne Phillips, 177–200. Stanford, CA: Stanford University Press.

Stryker, Susan, Paisley Currah, and Lisa Jean Moore. 2008. "Introduction: Trans-, Trans, or Transgender?" *WSQ* 36, nos. 3–4: 11–22.

Wahlman, Maude, and John Scully. 1983. "Aesthetic Principles in Afro-American Quilts." In *Afro-American Folk Art and Crafts*, edited by William Ferris, 79–97. Boston: G. K. Hall.

Yeğenoğlu, Meyda. 1998. *Colonial Fantasies towards a Feminist Reading of Orientalism.* Cambridge: Cambridge University Press.

Zeynep K. Korkman

(Mis)Translations of the Critiques of Anti-Muslim Racism and the Repercussions for Transnational Feminist Solidarities

Abstract: As critiques of anti-Muslim racism travel transnationally, they get translated in relation to complex histories of imperialism, colonialism, post-colonialism, and nationalism. These (mis)translations produce unexpected uses and abuses of anti-Muslim racism as an academic and political concept, with significant consequences for transnational feminist solidarity. This article explores, as a case in point, the emergence of a "Black Turk" identity in millennial Turkey where pious Muslim identity, once marginalized under a secularist state, has reasserted itself by deploying an analogy of Black to pious Muslim. Obscuring the nuances of local power relations, the pious Muslim/secular fault line was oversimplified and mistranslated into the resonant American idiom of the Black/white binary. This analogy and the progressive critiques of anti-Black and especially anti-Muslim racisms were then instrumentalized by an increasingly authoritarian and gender-conservative Islamist Turkish government to legitimize its repressive agendas, even succeeding to garner unexpected sympathy from some feminist politicians and academics in the United States. Naive confidence that such dichotomous racial/religious categories and familiar political vocabularies can guide feminist analyses and politics risks employing a seemingly transnationalist and anti-imperialist but in truth U.S.-centric understanding of non-U.S. struggles for social justice and thwarting potential transnational feminist solidarities.

MERIDIANS · feminism, race, transnationalism   22:2 October 2023
DOI: 10.1215/15366936-10637672 © 2023 Smith College

How do the critiques of anti-Muslim racism travel transnationally? What kinds of translations and mistranslations accompany their travels? How do local, national, and transnational scales and variant histories of imperialism, colonialism, postcolonialism, modernization, and nationalism inform these processes? What are the uses and misuses of anti-Muslim racism as an academic concept as well as a tool of political strategy? This article explores these questions with an eye toward their consequences for transnational feminist analysis and solidarity.

Black feminist scholars have long acknowledged the central role that racial and other axes of difference and inequality play in shaping the knowledges we produce and our capacities for solidarity (Davis 1981; Lorde [1984] 2012). Similarly, transnational feminists have emphasized the challenges posed to the building of global lines of solidarity by the power differentials between first- and third-world countries, noting how knowledge is always produced under the imperialist gaze (Mohanty 1984, 2003b). They have also addressed the need to understand the specificity of local contexts while insisting on building transnational linkages and coalitions among gender and sexual minorities whose fates are already co-imbricated through processes of imperialist and capitalist domination (Alexandar and Mohanty 2013; Mohanty 2003a). In the particular context of forging transnational solidarities between Middle Eastern Muslim and (white and non-white) U.S.-based feminists, scholars have underlined the importance of avoiding the imperially tinted mission of saving Muslim women from an essentialized and culturalized Islam, situating women instead within their particular and complex social, economic, and political contexts, analyzing the very production of (gendered, religious, racial, and other) lines of difference, and last but not the least, practicing reflexivity and (un)learning when transnational solidarity gets revealed, yet again, to be a troubled and unstable process (Abu-Lughod 2002; Salem 2018; Siddiqi 2014). Feminist scholars of Turkey in particular have attended to the travel and translation of Western political and analytical categories to scrutinize academic knowledge production and its political implications, especially in relation to the politics of Islam, modernity, gender, and sexuality (Gürel 2017; Savci 2021). This article draws on these insights to scrutinize the contents and discontent of transnational feminist solidarity under the growing racialization of Muslims and the mounting social valence of anti-racist discourses. In such a milieu, the article details unpredictable articulations of racial and religious categories and unexpected affinities between feminists and other political actors in a transnational context.

As a Muslim-majority country where ambitious state secularism and authoritarian Islamist governance have both been brokered through gendered civilizational tropes, Turkey provides a rich context in which to explore the volatility of racial categories and anti-racist discourses and the ensuing complexities for transnational feminist analyses and politics. In twenty-first-century Turkey, whiteness and Blackness have acquired new and contested meanings. At the intersections of the transnational flows of anti-Black and anti-Muslim racisms and anti-racist struggles and the civilizational and class-based politics of Turkish secularism and Islamism, two novel social categories have emerged: "White Turks" (*beyaz* or *ak Türkler*) and "Black Turks" (*siyah* or *kara Türkler*). Wholly distinct from, yet implicitly in conversation with the racial dichotomy of white and Black in the United States, the term *White Turks* came to denote the secular, urban, upwardly mobile or upper-class elites and *Black Turks* the religious, provincial, lower-class non-elites. The use of color as the distinguishing marker signaled the essentialization of these categories through their association with physical, embodied characteristics and seemingly unassimilable differences. Once this discourse was in place, Black Turk identity was appropriated by the Islamist Turkish government led by Recep Tayyip Erdoğan and the Justice and Development Party (Adalet ve Kalkınma Partisi, hereafter AKP) in its quest to garner legitimacy locally and internationally by drawing on globally resonant critiques of anti-Black and anti-Muslim racisms. The *Black Turk* label helped AKP identify with the politically resonant, Islamicate category of "oppressed" (*mazlum*), situating the party on the side of the pious Muslims who have been historically marginalized by the Turkish secularist project. More importantly, it helped the party to become legible to progressives worldwide and hide the increasing state authoritarianism and violence executed under the party's reign, from the sacking of academics, judges, and other civil servants critical of the government to the racialized killings of Kurdish civilians. It is in this way that the fault lines of Turkish society were mistranslated into a Black/white dichotomy, which was then understood via the lens of anti-Muslim racism in ways that deeply resonated in the United States. The global post-9/11 and later post–Black Lives Matter political and academic progressive sensibilities reinforced the potential appeal of the Turkish formula specifying the relationship of pious Muslim to secular Muslim as analogous to that of Black to white, thereby eliding the complicated and locally embedded becomings of religion, race, ethnicity, class, gender, and sexuality. These sensibilities have fostered unexpected affinities between some U.S.-based, progressive feminist women of color and the gender-conservative and authoritarian Islamist government of Turkey, leaving feminists in the United States with strange bedfellows. It is in this context that this article calls for a troubling and nuancing of our at times unstated analytical tools and political attunements as transnational feminists exploring the gendered makings of race and religion in relation to the globally circulating forms and critiques of anti-Muslim racism (Korkman and Razack 2021).

In post-9/11 United States, the racialization of and violence against Muslims has solidified Muslimness as a line of difference and oppression and Islam has been essentialized and vilified in gendered and sexualized terms to justify local and global subjugation of Muslim populations. The article warns that, in an eagerness to understand and support Muslim Middle Eastern others in such a time and place, feminist scholars may inadvertently end up (re)essentializing Muslimness as an always and already oppressed position, instead of situating it as a contingent product of particular social, political, economic, and historical conditions. Similarly, in a time and place of accumulated and escalating anti-Black racism and violence and anti-racist mobilization in the United States, anti-racist political and analytical sensibilities may produce an easy confidence that (claims to) Blackness invariably and singularly connotes a position of oppression to be in solidarity with, instead of situating particular assertions of Blackness within specific racial and other formations that produce them. It is in this way that, in the name of attending to racial and religious differences in our efforts to forge feminist solidarity, we might end up homogenizing and exporting familiar categories of difference, and blunting our political and analytical attunements.

This article invites us toward a situated and laborious process of nuanced understanding that is required for solidarity. In this spirit, I analyze below the travails of transnational feminist solidarity with "Black aka Muslim Turks" who appropriated globally resonant progressive critiques of anti-Black and anti-Muslim racism while featuring a racist, neo-imperialist, and misogynist political agenda. I place this troubling encounter within a complex and moving terrain where the floating signifiers of race and racialized religion operate in the globally made yet locally specific Turkish context. I painstakingly track the gendered operations of

categories of Blackness and Muslimness as they are attached through phenotypical and other embodied or essentialized markers to subjects as varied as Ottoman-era slaves, Arab Muslim peoples, cadres of Turkey's current
Islamist government, and Black Muslim peoples of Africa. The complexity
of the account below is neither accidental nor incidental; it attests to the
attention and nuance required to parse out the analytical categories and
the political stakes of a refined feminist analysis and politics. The article
provides a thorough picture of Turkish politics of race, religion, and gender
that potentially, and hopefully, complicates our transnational feminist
reflexes. In doing so, I seek to situate us as transnational feminist scholars
in one of the many complex and moving political terrains we work in, not to
freeze ourselves in relativism or restraint but to (un)learn together with
mutual respect and generosity so that we can tenaciously labor to cultivate
lines of solidarity.

The Many Discontents of the Critiques of Anti-Muslim Racism

As a U.S.-based feminist scholar of gender and religion who originates
from and works on a Muslim-majority Middle Eastern country, I am
inspired to scrutinize the translations and mistranslations of the critiques
of anti-Muslim racism with a view to unraveling its feminist consequences.
To borrow W. E. B. Du Bois's ([1903] 2008) articulation of the feeling of two-
ness characterizing Black subjects in the United States specifically and
processes of racialized subjectification more broadly, I write with a "double
consciousness." On the one hand, I find dissecting the discourse of anti-
Muslim racism a valuable pedagogical and conceptual tool. As an immigrant from Turkey residing in post-9/11 United States, I live under anti-
Muslim racism. And as a professor of gender studies at a North American
university, I am keen to teach to my U.S.-based students the gendered and
sexualized workings of anti-Muslim racism. More precisely, I teach how
U.S. imperial ambitions in the Middle East and violence against Muslim
populations are justified and institutionalized through the profiling of
Muslim men as aggressive/oppressive and of Muslim women as in need of
saving (Abu-Lughod 2002; Razack 2008). I lecture on how in 2001 Laura
Bush gave an influential radio address in which she described the war on
terror as a pseudofeminist civilizing mission to liberate Afghan women
oppressed by Muslim terrorists. I explain to my students how white men
who kill American civilians are usually not given the label of terrorist, but

especially not when, in the name of heteromasculinist white supremacy, they commit mass murders of Muslims or people they mistake for Muslims (Grewal 2013).

As we seek to understand such violent entanglements of religion, race, and gender, anti-Muslim racism serves as a powerful lens for analysis and critique. It highlights the systemic, pervasive, and historically embedded patterns of discrimination and violence that shape the fortunes of racialized groups. It situates the contemporary racialization of Muslims via gendered and sexualized tropes within the larger context of colonial racial formations and the legacy of European imperialism (Naber 2008; Rana 2007). Moreover, such critique has the potential to reveal the political intimacies that can develop among differentially racialized groups, expose colonial pseudofeminisms, and help forge more robust intersectional and transnational feminist solidarities.

On the other hand, anti-Muslim racism can be a slippery concept that may be used to legitimize rather than critique projects of racialized and gendered domination. While the concept of anti-Muslim racism is useful to me academically and politically as a resident of and scholar based in the United States, the picture changes when I think as a scholar and citizen of Turkey, a Muslim-majority country with a long history of state-sponsored political and ethnoracial repression, mass political purges and political imprisonments, military coups, states of emergency, and urban warfare waged against its racialized citizens. In contemporary Turkey, I am subjected to the Islamically accented gender conservativism, authoritarianism, and neoimperialism of the Turkish state, which, to further its repressive agenda against its own racialized others, deploys an instrumentalized critique of anti-Muslim racism and selectively borrows from anti-racist discourses (Adar and Yenigün 2019; Arat-Koç 2018).

Oriented toward both American and Turkish audiences, my scholarship reflects a double consciousness. One side of my academic labor analyzes the gendered and racialized dimensions of anti-Muslim civilizing projects, including a long-standing Turkish one, and places them in conversation with the broader contexts of imperialist and white-supremacist race making. The other reveals the ways that critiques of anti-Muslim racism have been used as a pretext for violent projects of state authoritarianism, ethnoracial repression, and reactionary gender conservatism. This latter effort requires a critique of the universalizing logic that unproblematically extends Euro-American analytical and political categories to our understandings of and engagements with the rest of the world. In the context of transnational feminist research and solidarity, this double consciousness and its analytical and political demands become particularly sticky and germane. To explicate the situated rationale for this two-tiered approach, I offer below an analysis of Turkey's politics of religion and race so as to enumerate their combined repercussions for feminist analysis and politics.

The Making of the Secular Muslim White

Turkey was initially founded in the early twentieth century on the ruins of an empire on the brink of European colonization and against the backdrop of the global dominance of Western Europe. In this context, Turkish nationalists positioned themselves as carriers of a civilizing mission to fashion a new nation on par with its Western counterparts. Part of early Turkish claims to belong to the West included appeals to racial science. To prove via empirical evidence that the Turk was of a superior, aka white, race, and the ethnic and religious minorities were of inferior races, the Turkish government supported eugenics research involving the measurement of skulls as an indicator of intelligence especially in the 1930s. Using the familiar Western techniques of pseudoscientific racism, Turkey was able to translate the ethnic and religious markers of otherness that had earlier held sway into racial ones (Maksudyan 2005). Alongside the ethnic, religious, and civic registers of nationhood through which Turkishness has been variably and complementarily imagined and institutionalized, a biologically conceived, supranational category of the Turkish race continues today to inflect nationalist ideology as well as state policy such as immigration and citizenship criteria (Parla 2019). At the same time, race conceived as biological essentialism has gradually become a rather muted social category in the civilizational project of Turkish secularist nationalism, relatively deemphasized following the early feverish republican drawing of a race line. Nevertheless, in the process, the Turk has become implicitly if not self-assuredly white (Ergin 2008).

The Turk's whiteness depended on his secularity in this early twentieth-century formulation.[1] Under pressure of the designation of Islam, and the figure of the Turk, as the very other of a white, Christian identity (Razack 2022), and in keeping with the Enlightenment idea that (Muslim) religion belonged to the realm of the backward and the irrational (Moallem 2021), Turkish nationalists believed that the undue influence of Islam in society was a major obstacle to realizing the secular, civilized, white version of Turkishness they were crafting. In keeping with the meaning of secularism as a project of modernity buttressed by the implied superiority of European Christian culture, they adopted a French-inspired but functionally and institutionally distinct version of secularism, *laiklik*, in which the state authoritatively restricts and manages the presence of religion in the public sphere. This formula entailed the production of a state-administered and sanitized version of Sunni Islam and the criminalization of all other kinds of religious institutions, affiliations, symbols, and practices (Berkes 1998; Parla and Davison 2008).

Importantly, the Turk was to be secular *and* Muslim. If Turkish secularism was ambiguous or at times even hostile toward various facets of Islamic belief and practice, Turkish nationalism since its conception in the late Ottoman era has drawn heavily on Sunni Islam to delineate Turkishness. For this reason, the crafting of a secular Muslim Turkish nation centrally depended on the violent removal of non-Muslims from the nation-to-be through ethnoracial cleansing policies of the late Ottoman and republican eras, including the Armenian genocide and the Greek-Turkish population exchange (Suny 2017; Iğsız 2018).

To help contain the contradiction between competing nationalist investments in Muslimness and secularity, those parts of religion distanced by secularism were rebranded as traditions and superstitions passed on to Turks via Arabic influences that had corrupted the nation (Gökalp 1968). In this way, secularization was reframed as nationalization (of Islam), which was required for the ethnoracial purification of the society. In the process, the Arab peoples, alongside the Kurds, were constructed as backward and inferior others of the Turkish nation (Akturk 2010; Zeydanlıoğlu 2008). Importantly, *Arap* in Turkish connoted not only the ethnic or national identity of the Arab peoples but also the racial category of Blackness (Boratav and Eberhard 1951). Turkish identity thus depended on its ethnoracial others, whose wrong or excessive kind of Muslimness delineated the contours of the enlightened, secular, "white" Turkishness.

The Turkish politics of nation, religion, and race has been closely entangled with its politics of gender and sexuality (Göle 1996; Kandiyoti 1991). Informed by Enlightenment and Orientalist perspectives, Turkish nationalist secularists held Islam in its traditional garb and public expressions, particularly women's veiling and segregation, responsible for the oppression of women in society. This Orientalist approach would perfuse the policy agendas of a wide range of parties within the Turkish political landscape, including those of various brands of feminism (Kadioğlu 1994). Set in ethnoracial terms, parts of the country such as the Kurdish region were deemed as having too much religion and tradition, and understood as gender conservative and overburdened by "traditional" practices such as honor crimes (Koğacıoğlu 2004). Turkish nationalists focused a good part of their early twentieth-century secularizing reforms on the field of gender relations, such as abolishing sharia family law and introducing mandatory coeducation. At the same time, Turkish nationalists struggled under the postcolonial tension of remaining distinct from the West, all the while striving to become like it. Under the weight of this paradox, women were tasked with walking the tightrope of being modern but modest; shedding the headscarf but wearing below-the-knee-length skirts; being Western secular and Turkish Muslim in just the right measure (Kadıoğlu 1996). Under these pressures, many elite women of the republican generation remained beholden to the reformist state despite its suppression of an early feminist movement (Çakır 2007).

The gendered entanglements of nation, religion, and race in Turkey owed as much to the remaking of the ideal Turkish woman as to the historically accumulated patterns of sexual violence directed against women who have been pushed outside the ethnoracial and religious normativity. To begin with, there is the heritage of Ottoman slavery, which was not legally defined by race, even as phenotype, gender, religion, ethnicity, and geographic origin shaped in complex ways who was enslaved and what kind of slavery they were assigned to. A considerable portion of the Ottoman slave population consisted of women, many of whom were household slaves, including concubines (Zilfi 2010). Circassian (aka "white") slaves were valued over Brown and Black slaves and seen as best suited to serve as household laborers and concubines, with the latter hoping to gain (if rarely achieving) higher status by bearing heirs or becoming legal wives to Ottoman notables (Toledano 1981). Such racialized allocation of phenotypically "white" women, whose light-colored hair or eyes were regularly remarked on (Ben-Naeh 2006), rendered them sexually available through the institution of concubine slavery. Furthermore, in the late Ottoman and early republican era, non–(Sunni) Muslim women, especially Christian women who would be increasingly associated with the West and Christianity/whiteness, would become targets of systematic racist/nationalist sexual violence and appropriation in the making of the Turkish nation as the

Sunni Muslim kind of white. The paradigmatic case in point was the systematic abduction, rape, and transfer to Muslim households as laborers, concubines, or wives, and even transfer to slave trade, of Armenian Christian women and girls during and in the aftermath of the early twentieth-century Armenian genocide (Ekmekcioglu 2013). The gendered and racialized heritage of Ottoman slavery and the historically layered and persistent patterns of violence against non-Muslim women would continue to weigh on the meanings of "white" looks for women in late Ottoman-era and republican Turkey.

Where a quest for authenticity has long troubled nationalist modernization and complicated its desires to Westernize and whiten the nation, "excessively" Western/white embodiment for both men and women has been burdened with the stigma of effeminacy for "dandy" men (Gürbilek 2003) and sexual availability for "fallen" women (Yıldız 2012), pushing such figures outside the moral order of heteronormativity and national community. For example, "evil blond" female actresses of the Turkish cinema have been resigned to play supporting femme-fatale roles (Altinay 2012: 127). More recently, in the context of large-scale labor migration from the post-Soviet region to Turkey, the name Natasha has become a shorthand for "sex worker" and is used as an insult for, or a way of approaching, blond women (Gülçür and İlkkaracan 2002). At the same time, a sense of masculinist entitlement to Armenian women continues to inform popular consciousness, reflected among other things by racist misogynist sayings that insinuate Armenian women's sexual availability, such as, "If you are Armenian, you should put it out without asking" (Yılmaz 2014). Throughout the history of Turkish modernization, a fear of over-Westernization and a desire mixed with resentment for the West have imbued white-looking/Christian bodies with suspicion and outsider/foreigner status, alongside some degree of white privilege. In this context, the proximity to whiteness implies a double bind of, on the one hand, status derived from closeness to a globally valued whiteness and the risk of losing, on the other hand, the status and protections granted to insiders/nationals through gendered and sexualized stigmatization and violence.

Shifting Politics of Gender, Religion, and Ethnoracial Identity

The Islamically accented AKP came to power in 2002 under the leadership of then Prime Minister and now President Erdoğan. The rise of AKP was a particular culmination of Turkish nationalism's inherent tensions with regard to religion and secularity. While from its beginnings the secularist Turkish state had placed the new institutions of Islam in the hands of the government, it was in the 1950s when religion was mobilized with increasing visibility and fervor with the end of the single-party rule of the secularist Republican People's Party (Cumhuriyet Halk Partisi). In this period, the new government's religious populism included gestures aimed at tempering the secularist reforms of the early republican era and providing heightened tolerance for Islamic practices and symbols in the public sphere. Religion was rallied even further in the post-1980 military coup era with the reinstatement of Islam as an antidote to popular leftist mobilization, thereby paving the way for the rise of political Islam in the 1990s (Yavuz 2003). During this period, feminists grew increasingly critical of the state and the constraints of modern modesty imposed by its nationalist project. But they remained nevertheless broadly secular and disinclined to ally themselves with emerging Muslim feminist voices (Sirman 1989).

While in its relative assertiveness concerning religion the party stood in tension with the modern Turkish republic's secularist state tradition, AKP's brand of politics offered no relief from the authoritarian character of Turkish secularism. Indeed, under the AKP, the state further entrenched its monopolistic hold over "legitimate" religious forms by endorsing a particular kind of Sunni Islam over other expressions of Islam and by suppressing variant religiosities such as Alevism, unorthodox Muslim groups, and non-Muslim religious communities. Under the AKP, too, the reach of the official state religious apparatus, the Presidency of Religious Affairs (Diyanet), has expanded, to function in more institutional and discursive realms than ever before, involving itself in new tasks such as the provision of family counseling (Kocamaner 2019).

At the same time, especially in the early years, the AKP's critical relationship with the secularist state tradition rendered it vulnerable to Turkey's secularist power holders, including the relatively powerful military (Akça and Balta-Paker 2013). To stay in power, the party initially depended on a broad hegemonic coalition. Inspired to some extent by the AKP's legitimate critique of the top-down nature of Turkish authoritarian secularism, this coalition included liberal, leftist, and at times ethnic and religious minority voices (Tuğal 2016). The involvement of such heterogenous groups fostered optimism for a more liberal democratic organization and expression of diverse brands of religiosity in the public sphere. The possibility of recovering from the wounds of a fractured republican national identity that had rejected a significant part of itself in the name of modernization seemed possible. It also provided some hope for a possible further visibility and inclusion of ethnic minorities, especially Kurds. The AKP would be the first in Turkish history to openly, albeit not formally, enter into peace negotiations with the country's Kurdish guerrilla organization, the Kurdistan Workers' Party (Partiya Karkerên Kurdistanê, PKK), which has been fighting for the liberation of this racialized minority group for over three decades, and to recognize several basic civic and cultural rights for the Kurdish population.

The AKP would also inherit a growing Islamist movement in Turkey that would come to destabilize the gendered dynamics of Turkish secularism. It was the activism of young pious women, typified in the figure of the veiled university students who especially in the late 1990s vigorously fought for their right to attend classes wearing their banned headscarves, that helped prepare the ground for AKP's rise to power. The public presence of these educated, urban, and pious Turkish women lay bare the shortcomings of Turkish secularism. They were excluded from the nationalist-modernist promise to uplift Turkish women, since secularist policies banning various forms of religious expression in the public sphere deprived these veiled women of their right to education. Their visibility also rendered redundant the secularist equating of piety with a passive, ignorant femininity (Göle 1996). While they were sent home, so to speak, in the first years of the party's rule and had to wait for more than a decade under AKP rule for the right to wear veils in public institutions, some of these pious activist women developed feminist sensibilities and voices, advancing a dual critique of secularist as well as Islamist challenges they face as pious Turkish women (Unal 2015). Their presence gradually incited mainstream Turkish feminism to face its own exclusionary mechanisms, making way for a more inclusive third-wave Turkish feminism that included Muslim and Kurdish feminists. As required by Turkey's European Union harmonization process, the AKP also passed several gender-equality reforms in its early years, allowing for a more amenable context in which feminists could fight for gender equality.

These seemingly corrective aspects notwithstanding, the party was by no means a beacon of democracy. From its beginnings, its coalitions with minoritized sections of society were instrumental, temporary, and limited in scope. Over the last decade, the party's rule and the style of its leader, Erdoğan, now a president with extended powers, have turned increasingly authoritarian. This has meant not only the violent repression of dissent but also the broad imposition of religiously flavored gender conservatism and undisguised anti-feminism. This shift is reflected in the uptick in misogynist discourse and violence, government back-pedaling on a range of gender egalitarian measures and policies, and outright political attacks on the country's vibrant feminist and LGBTQ+ movements, including the banning of International Women's Day and Pride marches and the arrest of protestors (Korkman 2016). That the AKP has sought to justify such repression in religiously accented ways as a defense of "homegrown and national" gender norms and family structure, situated over and against secular and allegedly over-Westernized and unnational masculinities and femininities and feminisms, is of critical import here (Mutluer 2019).

Turkish state's growing authoritarianism and gender conservatism has been accompanied by the escalation of its violent project of ethnoracial domination. In an international context destabilized by the Middle Eastern schemes of the world's neoimperial superpowers, Turkey has been concocting its own neoimperialist dreams, promoting a return to the medieval glory of its predecessor, the Ottoman Empire, and seeking to expand military and political influence in the Muslim Middle East and Africa. This regional neoimperial turn has meant intensifying the internal colonial project of repressing the Kurdish ethnic minority and reigniting warfare against the Kurds, including against Rojava in Syria.

White Turks, Black Turks
In the 2000s the AKP worked strategically to legitimize its dual reactionary gender-conservative and violent neoimperial projects. Part of this legitimizing effort was the appropriating and then repurposing in caricaturized form a throughgoing critique of anti-Muslim discrimination that had been assembled by local Turkish activists and scholars in dialogue with transnational critiques of anti-Muslim racism. Condensed in the figure of the Black aka pious Muslim Turk, this "critical" caricature was then used to justify an intensification of government-led gendered and ethnoracial oppression. Hijacking progressive discourses, AKP members began marking themselves and their Sunni Muslim constituencies, whom they designated as Turkey's sole pious Muslims, with racial metaphors. The party's supporters were now "Black Turks," and the party was there to champion them and other oppressed Muslims around the world. Black Turk identity encompassed the heretofore otherized racial markers of Muslim bodily

comportment, clothing style, and speech, and the physical features associated with nonwhite "Easternness," set against those features associated with the heretofore unmarked White Turks and their secularism, their Westernized lifestyles, and their upward mobility. In the local and global struggles against anti-Muslim (and anti-Black) racists, the AKP thus situated itself on the side of the morally good and politically righteous victims.

The concept of the White Turk was initially coined in the 1990s as a class-based critique of the privileged socioeconomic position of urban, secular, Westernized, ethnically unmarked, upwardly mobile Turks. The *White Turk* label resonated with the historically embedded "whiteness" of the ruling cadres of the late Ottoman and early republican eras, many of whom were from the Balkans and were often more Westernized and secularized in comparison to the Anatolian residents of the country (Bilici 2009). The founder of the republic, Mustafa Kemal Atatürk, himself was born in Ottoman Salonika (Thessaloníki in modern Greece) and had blond hair and blue eyes that were proudly featured in nationalist iconography. In conversation with this history, in the 1990s the term *White Turk* marked both the elite positioning of those associated with older secularist-nationalist and newer neoliberal consumerist patterns of distinction and the physical markers, such as lack of facial or body hair, that were read as proxies for such elite status (Bora 2013). The "whiteness" of these contemporary Turks gained meaning in a context in which looking white(r)—connoted by racially marked physical features such as lighter complexion, hair, and eye color—was conflated seamlessly with other embodied markers of distinction, such as accent, demeanor, grooming, and dress.

In the aughts, this White Turk discourse was taken up positively as an identity by self-proclaimed White Turks who unabashedly articulated a "class-based racism" (Bora 2013: 90) that ridiculed without sympathy its others, namely the poor, the Kurdish, and the pious. Embraced as an identity, the White Turk discourse politically articulated the growing anxieties of the secular middle classes about neoliberal precaritization, congealing them into a culturally essentialist, racist form of class hatred. In this context, Muslim identity stood as a shorthand for urban/rural origin, education, and income- and wealth-related inequalities (Demiralp 2012). Informed by long-standing legacies of Orientalism and the novel context of global neoliberalism, whiteness provided the Turks who claimed it with the prestige of modern, Western status and distinction from their traditional and Eastern others. In the context of neoliberal multiculturalism and capitalist globalization, White Turks aspired to join the transnational bourgeois elite as "new whites," non-European peoples previously excluded from whiteness but now whitening through class privilege vis-à-vis their conationals (Arat-Koç 2010). Turks' identification with whiteness gained further valence in the post-9/11 racialization of Muslims, when the already precarious Turkish claims to whiteness were further weakened with the increasing racialization and hypervisibility of Muslim identity (Yorukoglu 2017).

This Black/white metaphor linking racial hierarchies to other forms of social stratification was increasingly mobilized by the AKP to highlight the hegemony since the founding of the republic of secularists and the concomitant marginalization of Muslimness. Until recently, the secular, Westernized sections of Turkish society held an elite monopoly over the valued forms of cultural capital and comportment, while the pious Islamic habitus written into the body as men's facial hair and women's veil signified otherness and inferiority (Göle 1996). Indeed, especially in the early years of its rule, AKP struggled to convert its increasing political and economic power into cultural prestige. This was in turn linked to the party's then relatively marginalized position in Turkish politics in which the secularist army held significant power and to the marginal status of Muslimness in the post-9/11 world. Appealing to Black (aka Muslim) Turks as wronged citizens who had long been held down by an authoritarian secularist state solely because of their religiousness, the party claimed legitimacy as the voice and savior of disadvantaged masses (Adar and Yenigün 2019; Bora 2013; Arat-Koç 2018; Demiralp 2012). The Black/white metaphor connoted both the AKP's weak sociopolitical position relative to the hegemony of secularism within the Turkish state as well as the larger affiliation of Muslimness with socioeconomic and cultural marginalization. Importantly, this metaphor effectively translated the local Islamist/secularist tension into the globally resonant vocabulary of race.

During the two decades of AKP governments, however, the legitimacy and monopoly of a secular habitus as the signifier of distinction have been challenged. In this period, a publicly pious Muslim middle and upper class with a newly valued religious habitus and attendant consumption habits has emerged, while the (secular and pious Muslim) masses faced increased poverty and precaritization under neoliberalization programs. In this light, using the racialized metaphors of Black and white to reduce Turkey's internal relations of domination to that of a pious Muslim/secular

(Muslim) dichotomy is cynically inaccurate. The Black Turk metaphor instead operates as a tool with which the AKP government can continue to claim victim status, despite its growing hold over state capacities and the increasing wealth of some of its clientele, and to ideologically tame the growing class disparities among various segments of the pious Muslim population (Arat-Koç 2018).

The Black/white metaphor and the resultant claims to anti-racism also function to obscure Turkey's own anti-Blackness. The equating of *Black* with the pious Muslim Turk renders invisible the growing population of Black immigrants who contend with blatant anti-Blackness in Turkey and the Afro-Turks, the Black citizens of Turkey, many of whom are descendants of Ottoman-era Black slaves. Their political struggles are so irrelevant to the AKP that Erdoğan even used the word *zenci* to identify himself as a Black Turk, much to the chagrin of Afro-Turks (Ferguson 2014). The word *zenci* refers not to the color black but exclusively to a Black person or a "negro," to deploy a resonant but crude translation that does not do justice to the specificities of these terms in Ottoman/Turkish- and English-language contexts.

The identification of the pious Muslims of Turkey with Blackness construed in a binary opposition to secular as white further disguises the repression of other racialized groups in a country that is home to numerous religious and ethnic minorities. These minorities include the racialized Kurdish peoples of Turkey, who in recent decades have been increasingly subjected to the familiar strategies of race making: from the marking of certain physical characteristics as definitional of an essentialized Kurdishness, to the igniting of fears of Turkish demographic and cultural decline in the face of growing numbers and visibility of Kurds (Ergin 2014). The AKP's use of Blackness thus helps conceal the fact that the racial and ethnic hierarchies undergirding the Turkish nation have been further cemented under its rule.

This association of Muslimness with Blackness resonates in the current global context of the racialization of Muslims and the progressive and activist mobilization against it, from which the AKP seeks to benefit. As part of its identification with Blackness as the moral/political position of the oppressed, the AKP makes concerted efforts to brand itself as kin to the Black power movement. Its strategies have included Erdoğan's unsuccessful bid to attend Muhammed Ali's funeral, the renaming of the street where the U.S. embassy is located in Turkey's capital city of Ankara as Malcom X

Street, and an interview broadcast by Turkey's state news agency with one of Malcom X's daughters, who commented that by welcoming Syrian refugees inside its borders, Turkey is acting in accordance with her father's legacy. In an effort to boost its support at home and in the diaspora and to expand its international influence by positioning itself as the protector of racialized Muslims, the AKP government has also invited non-Turkish Muslims abroad to contact Turkish embassies with reports of anti-Muslim discrimination and violence (Adar and Yenigün 2019).

On the academic front, the AKP government has been cultivating a network of intellectuals working on issues of imperialism and Islamophobia, for example, when the government granted Turkish citizenship and an academic home in a pro-AKP private university to the persecuted Palestinian American scholar, Sami Al Arian (Adar and Yenigün 2019). Similarly, the government-controlled and state-owned media channel, TRT World, generally busy propagandizing for the Turkish bid for hegemony, has, in a highly calculated way, handed its megaphone over to progressive scholars working on anti-Muslim racism, featuring, for example, an opinion piece by a U.S.-based feminist scholar, Jessica Winegar (2016), on the harassment and self-censorship of critical teaching and research about the Israeli occupation of Palestine in the United States. At the same time, of course, Turkey has been busy with the mass criminalization of over one thousand Academics for Peace, a group of critical academics who petitioned against military violence and human rights abuses in the Kurdish region and for the resumption of peace talks between the Turkish government and the Kurdish guerrilla organization PKK under the auspices of anti-terror laws. Indeed, the AKP government's claims to Black Turk identity and its co-optation of the critiques of anti-Muslim racism come in handy in otherizing its (secular) opponents at home as self-Orientalizing, Islamophobic internal enemies (Adar and Yenigün 2019). By laying claim to an authentic Turkishness, the AKP is able to foster a populist authoritative political agenda at home and a neoimperialist agenda abroad (Adar and Yenigün 2019; Arat-Koç 2018).

These local and international deployments of the critiques of anti-Muslim racism with an analogy of Muslim to Black also complement party-connected civil society and state-level efforts to build an influence on the African continent. These efforts include mobilizing faith-based humanitarian nongovernmental organizations (NGOs), Islamic schools, economic cooperation, and targeting (often but not exclusively) Black Muslim populations in sub-Saharan African countries with developmental, educational, and humanitarian projects. These efforts are enabled because the party no longer distances itself from Turkey's Islamic past and Ottoman heritage, and consequently its Arab (and Black) Muslim neighbors, some of whom lived in areas previously under Ottoman imperial rule. Instead, the Ottoman era is now being reclaimed by the AKP as a benevolent period of ethnoreligious toleration. These activities are also motivated by and fortify the AKP's religiously framed image as a global benefactor of the oppressed (Çelik and İşeri 2016; Guner 2020). In addition to cultivating Turkey's prestige and support for its foreign policy agendas in these countries, these efforts "whiten" the so-called Black, aka pious Muslim, Turks. Paternalistically helping their less fortunate Arab and Muslim brothers, Turkish Muslims become white relative to the Black Muslims they encounter in Africa. The whitening Black Turks donate money to Islamic NGOs to help African children; they visit sub-Saharan African countries as moral entrepreneurs investing and uplifting Black Muslims. Here Turks distinguish themselves as morally good, humanitarian, Muslim kinds of whites as opposed to the bad, imperialist, Christian kinds of whites. As the "Black Turk" is transformed into a new brand of "white Muslim," whiteness, previously associated with state secularism, Western modernity, and elite status, is repurposed as a moral position in AKP's quest for legitimacy at home and abroad (Guner 2020; Langan 2017). Building on the long-standing racialization of Arab Muslims as the racialized others of Turkish nationalism while freshly bringing them into the nation's proximity as Muslim but nonwhite brothers, the AKP's African endeavors thus further complicate the contentious claims to Blackness and whiteness advanced by the various segments of Turkish ruling elites.

Transnational Feminism with Strange Bedfellows

These many local and transnational (mis)translations of critical discourses present us with a paradox, for they represent both opportunities for unscrupulous actors like the AKP to procure political legibility and pitfalls feminists can fall into. The AKP's complex attempts to instrumentally mobilize Black/Muslim/oppressed identity in the service of a Turkish neo-imperialist project have helped cement the party's hegemony locally and abroad by positioning it against anti-Muslim racism. In forging such a position, Erdoğan and his party have succeeded to some extent in pursuing their authoritarian and neoimperialist agendas of oppression and violence with impunity, at times garnering support even from progressive audiences in the United States, including, alarmingly, feminists with a vision of transnational solidarity.

Ilhan Omar, a Muslim woman of color serving since 2019 as a U.S. congressperson for Minnesota, is well known for her progressive politics in and beyond the United States, including her support for the Palestinian struggle and her critique of U.S. foreign policy. She is also recognized as a feminist ally, including in the academic community, as evidenced by her invitation as a keynote speaker at the National Women's Studies Association 2020 Conference. Yet Omar has forged a surprising affinity with the AKP. In 2019 she met personally with Erdoğan and other Turkish officials, accepted a donation from a U.S.-based nonprofit lobby working on behalf of the Turkish government, and was photographed with Halil Mutlu, Erdoğan's cousin and the organization's cochair (Evans 2019). She was the only Democratic representative to vote against the U.S. sanctions that sought to end Turkey's invasion of the Kurdish territories in Syria (Nahmias 2019). She also refrained from supporting a bill that recognized the Armenian genocide and explained her position by reciting Turkish foreign policy talking points, saying that the issue should be decided academically away from political pressure (Arkin 2019). In effect, Omar ended up advocating for the Erdoğan government's foreign policy interests in the United States at the expense of departing from her usual progressive and party politics. It is possible that Omar, who was born in Somalia, sympathizes with Turkey's extensive humanitarian efforts there (Bajalan and Brooks 2019). After sustained criticism for her pro-Erdoğan stance, Omar recently signed a letter petitioning Turkey to include political prisoners in its plans to release inmates as a measure to contain the COVID-19 pandemic, suggesting that she is refining her understanding of Turkish politics (Petti 2020).

The unexpected affinities between the AKP and transnational feminists found another example in academia. In December 2016 WikiLeaks released the hacked email correspondence of one of President Erdoğan's sons-in-law and then a minister of finance, including emails forwarded to him by his wife and Erdoğan's daughter, Esra Erdoğan Albayrak. Among these were emails penned by the late Pakistani American anthropologist Saba Mahmood, who was a doctoral committee member of Albayrak while she was pursuing a graduate degree at the University of California, Berkeley. The messages were dated 2013–14, the precise period in which the Erdoğan government was unleashing a wave of repression in response to the Gezi protests. Dubbed the "Turkish summer" that followed quick on the heels of the "Arab spring," the Gezi protests of 2013 were a mass mobilization in protest of the AKP government in which hundreds of thousands took to the streets, with feminist and LGBTQ+ activists on the front lines. In response, the AKP government, quite fragile at the time and under pressure from a major corruption scandal that included most members of the Erdoğan family, framed the protests as a(nother) secularist plot against the party. During the years of political instability and growing authoritarianism that followed the Gezi protests, Erdoğan personally and repeatedly alleged that a group of male protestors had attacked "our veiled sister," in an attempt to recast the multifaceted discontent with the AKP as a divide between pious Muslims and secularists (Korkman 2017). Yet during these times of rampant government repression in which police violence left dozens of protestors dead and many thousands wounded, in December 2013, Mahmood wrote to Erdoğan's daughter in tones sympathetic not only to her but also to her family: "I can imagine how hard this past year has been for you, your family, and for Turkey in general" (WikiLeaks 2016), citing the "religious-secular divide" as being "more trenchant than it ever was [sic]."

The hacked emails included a draft of Albayrak's dissertation on state-sponsored religious secondary education in Turkey in relation to secularism, piety, and gendered mobility. The dissertation, in which Albayrak identified herself as the daughter of the Turkish prime minister as a methodological aside, included a dedication with a tribute to her father, described as her "all time hero" and "a true visionary" (WikiLeaks 2016). The research focused on the graduates of religious secondary schools, from which Recep Tayyip Erdoğan and Esra Erdoğan Albayrak themselves have graduated, and emphasized the chances of mobility these schools offered to the pious and the disadvantaged. It particularly highlighted the plight of female students, whose families might not have otherwise sent them to secondary school if it were not for these religious schools where, unlike other public schools, girls were physically segregated from boys and wore a headscarf. However, following the so-called postmodern, coup-by-military memorandum of 1997, which pressured the prime minister to resign and his government to dissolve and called for a stricter implementation of various secularist policies such as the headscarf ban in public institutions including universities, these students would find their higher education and civic employment chances obstructed. The research noted how some of these graduates would join the ranks of veiled university students whose political activism helped pave the way for the AKP's electoral successes in the 2000s. Albayrak framed her analysis of the female graduates of Turkey's public religious schools with reference to Mahmood's conceptualization of pious women's agency. She explained that her research subjects did not (necessarily) articulate a resistance to religious or traditional patriarchal gender norms, but they were nonetheless agentic in their struggle against the secular elites, institutions, and norms, including secular feminist ones.

The argument that veiled women have been put at a significant disadvantage by and resisted Turkish secularism, as explored in Albayrak's research, certainly helped advance a feminist critique. However, in the decades since the AKP has come to power, to exclusively and instrumentally emphasize the plight of pious Muslim women at the hands of an oppressively secularist state has been overdeployed as a political legitimation strategy by the party. In this context, when Albayrak introduced her work in 2013 as her "way of resisting injustice" (WikiLeaks 2016), she tightly aligned her study with the then well-used and abused AKP emphasis on the plight of pious Muslims under secularism. Providing feedback on this dissertation draft, Mahmood concluded: "Now more than ever before, it is really really important that you tell the story you are telling in your dissertation. The world needs it, we need it, and the academia will be better for it." Mahmood signed the email, "In solidarity with you and your struggle."

Mahmood's messages that stretched well beyond student encouragement and seemed to include a gesture of support for the Erdoğan family and possibly even the political mission of the party that the family became synonymous with, when leaked three years later in 2016, created quite a scandal in the Turkish academic community. Many felt betrayed by this respected progressive scholar's unlikely allegiance to the Erdoğan family at a time when their political agenda was so patently turning toward authoritarianism. The sense of betrayal was perhaps more acute, given that Mahmood was one of the international signatories of the Academics for Peace petition sent to the AKP government less than a year before the 2016 WikiLeaks files. The petition critiqued the militarized violence and human rights abuses in Turkey's Kurdish region and the intensification of ethnoracial aggression against the Kurds. Signatories were belligerently targeted by President Erdoğan himself, removed from their academic posts en masse, and subjected to criminal trails and arrests on charges of "propagandizing for a terrorist organization."

That Mahmood might have expressed support for the Erdoğan family and the AKP government carries weight because Mahmood is not just any scholar. The late Saba Mahmood is recognized in U.S. academia as perhaps *the* scholar of gender and religion in the Muslim Middle East. Her work on Egyptian Muslim women's political activism is appreciated for having pushed feminist theory beyond its Eurocentric and secularist vision of women's agency as resistant or autonomous (Mahmood 2001, 2011). It encourages a much-needed critique of imperialist secular frames that limit feminist capacities to recognize and come to terms with women's political agency in its myriad forms, including women's active support for gender-conservative religious movements. However, it also poses new challenges for feminist analysis, which, in the name of disengaging from cultural imperialism, finds itself faced by cultural relativism and reductionism, precluding a multifaceted translation and critique of the other (Bangstad 2011; Vasilaki 2016). Muslim actors are blanketly generalized as "agentic," while centralizing the critique of imperialism ironically denies historicity/locality to social subjects beyond the empire (Abbas 2013).

As suggested by her statements of empathy and support for members of the Erdoğan family in the context of her scholarship, Mahmood's understanding of the Turkey of the 2010s may have led her to believe that, by professing a critique of secularism and purporting to foster Muslim women's political agency, the Erdoğan family—and even the AKP government with which it became synonymous—was engaged in a political struggle with which feminist academics ought to show solidarity. In this case, Mahmood's prioritization of secularism's repressive aspects and its limited visions of women's agency ironically ended up privileging the critique of the European imperial project over the feminist critique of other local and transnational forms of power. By assigning greater import to the pious Muslim/secular dichotomy, a dichotomy that both stands in for and elides the historically mutable and multifaceted relations of domination that shape Turkish society, Mahmood rendered irrelevant all other axes of power and local politics. As a result, a scholar whose transnational feminist interventions have helped Western feminism cast off its secular Eurocentric optic wound up recentering the very imperial categories she sought to decenter, eliding in the process other geographically and epistemologically peripheral, yet locally and regionally salient, projects of racial, gendered, and classed domination, such as the AKP projects at home and abroad.

Such reduction of the power dynamics in Turkey to a pious Muslim/secular axis, and in other instances, its subsequent equating with the Black/white racial binary, elide the intersectionality of class, religion, race, ethnicity, nationality, and, last but not the least, gender and sexuality. In doing so, such reductionism aligns with the claims to authenticity and righteousness that the AKP mobilizes via its Black Turk identity, claims that have proven to be dangerous and even fatal for those pushed outside the ethnoracial and religious community and otherized in gendered and sexualized terms, from non-Muslim or white-looking women to LGBTQ+ individuals.

Conclusion

As discourses travel transnationally, as they are appropriated and translated across time, space, and specificity, they come to operate in distinct, sometimes unexpected ways, aligning with struggles for and resistance against disparate and changing modes and nodes of power. Understanding the complexities and contradictions our critical discourses generate as they are translated into dissimilar contexts is particularly important to transnational feminist scholars working on the intersections of gender, race, and religion. Such intricacies are revealed as central and constitutive when we approach the terrain of transnational feminist analysis and struggle with a double consciousness, such as that which comes from being a subject of and being subjected to, on the on one hand, the academic and political hegemony of the U.S. empire and, on the other, the neoimperial and authoritarian ambitions of the Turkish state.

Race, and racialized religion, operate in contemporary Turkey in curious ways. Turkey's republican-era racist claims to a secular whiteness, originally mobilized in the service of a civilizational project in which modernity was defined implicitly as Christian and white, continue to inform both the AKP's ongoing claims to a "Black aka Muslim" Turkishness and its new neoimperialist claims to a "White Muslim" identity. At a time when the global politics of white supremacy and racial justice increasingly infuses the Turkish national landscape, and the post-9/11 racialization of Muslims continues to haunt Turkish assertions of racial identity, the Turk's place in racial hierarchies is negotiated again and again, producing a variety of secularist, Turkist, Islamist, and Ottomanist articulations of whiteness and Blackness. Set in a thoroughly transnational landscape, the Turkish misadventures in race provide a productive inflection point from which to examine the local and specific articulations of race in relation to global whiteness and white supremacy (Guner 2020; Arat-Koç 2010), and against the supposed stability and universality of Euro-American categories of race at odds (Ergin 2016).

These Turkish misadventures in race also provide a productive inflection point from which to think about transnational feminism and its discontents. The White Turk discourse was able to penetrate those popular liberal and secularist brands of Turkish feminism that emulated civilizational and culturalist approaches to women's oppression, leading them to focus on the emancipation of the allegedly hyperoppressed "non-White Turk" women at the expense of developing a coalitional and intersectional understanding of gendered inequality (Arat-Koç 2007). Furthermore, in their relations with women in neighboring Middle Eastern countries, these Turkish feminists were seduced, by their desire to align with a global whiteness, into the imperially tinted role of the exemplary "good Muslim" (Arat-Koç 2007), thereby hindering transnational solidarities in the region and serving imperialist agendas.

Yet the (mis)translations cut both ways. As we have seen with the examples of Ilhan Omar and Saba Mahmood, the Black Turk discourse and its attendant equating of Muslim with the oppressed operate with ease within the terrain of feminist politics in post-9/11 United States. Obscuring the nuances of local power relations, the pious Muslim/secular fault line in Turkey gets oversimplified and mistranslated into the resonant American idiom of the Black/white binary. Easy confidence that Black/white, pious Muslim/secular binaries can guide feminist analyses and politics hides the gendered, classed, and racialized negotiations of power and identity in the here and now. It also disregards how "local" Muslim actors themselves actively engage with thoroughly gendered and transnational anti-Muslim discourses and their critiques in understanding and presenting themselves as situated subjects (Deeb 2009). Most importantly, such naive confidence employs a seemingly transnationalist and anti-imperialist but in truth U.S.-centric understanding of non-U.S. struggles for social justice, thus thwarting potential transnational feminist solidarities.

But what is to be learned from these translations and mistranslations? How do we translate without imposing our already existing frameworks on the rest of the world in all its complexity? What are we left with when our critical frameworks do not translate well? After hearing from the friend of a friend that the op-ed she penned on the persecution of pro-Palestine academics in U.S. academia was featured in what turned out to be a pro-Erdoğan government media outlet, the feminist anthropologist Jessica Winegar channeled her upset into taking responsibility. She offered a public apology on social media and donated the modest honorarium she had received to Scholars at Risk, an organization that helps place abroad those scholars who are persecuted in their home countries, including a large number of scholars from Erdoğan's Turkey. It is in this spirit of fostering critique and change right alongside cultivating generosity and compassion for ourselves and each other that I write this article. In a thoroughly transnational terrain of (anti-Muslim) racisms and rising authoritarianisms that demand understanding and resistance of equal caliber and in equal part, we might simply have to continue to labor toward locally grounded and transnationally resonant analyses with which to foreground our transnational feminist solidarities, even as we wrestle with the many translations and mistranslations our efforts unavoidably get tangled up with.

....

Zeynep K. Korkman is assistant professor of gender studies at University of California, Los Angeles. Her research explores the gendered relationships between affect, labor, religion, and feminist politics, with a focus on Turkey. Her book, *Gendered Fortunes: Divination, Precarity, and Affect in Postsecular Turkey*, was published in 2023 by Duke University Press.

Notes

I am grateful to all the participants of "Feminist Approaches to Understanding Global Anti-Muslim Racism Workshop" that Sherene H. Razack and I co-organized at UCLA in 2019, where I presented an earlier version of this article. Special thanks to Sherene H. Razack for numerous spirited conversations that inspired this article and for her feedback on this work in its different incarnations. I am indebted to Melissa Bilal, Lara Deeb, and Ruken Şengül for providing valuable and nuanced feedback on an earlier version of this article. Can Açıksöz generously contributed his ideas, encouragement, and feedback to this article. I am also thankful to Theresa Truax-Gischler for her substantive editing. Finally, I thank the editor, Ginetta E. B. Candelario, and the anonymous reviewers of *Meridians* for their time and helpful suggestions.

1   This formulation was never fully stabilized or contradiction free, and it would come under particular pressure in the twenty-first century with the gradual entrenchment in state power of the Islamist nationalist AKP, whose claims to Muslimness, Blackness, and whiteness are discussed later in the article.

Works Cited

Abbas, Sadia. 2013. "The Echo Chamber of Freedom: The Muslim Woman and the Pretext of Agency. *boundary 2*, 40, no: 1: 155–89.

Abu-Lughod, Lila. 2002. "Do Muslim Women Really Need Saving? Anthropological Reflections on Cultural Relativism and Its Others." *American Anthropologist* 104, no. 3: 783–90.

Adar, Sinem, and Halil Ibrahim Yenigün. 2019. "A Muslim Counter-Hegemony? Turkey's Soft Power Strategies and Islamophobia." *Jadaliyya*, April 16. https://www.jadaliyya.com/Details/38646.

Akça, İsmet, and Evren Balta-Paker. 2013. "Beyond Military Tutelage? Turkish Military Politics and the AKP Government." In *Debating Security in Turkey: Challenges and Changes in the Twenty-First Century*, edited by Ebru Canan-Sokullu, 77–92. Lanham, MD: Rowman & Littlefield.

Akturk, Ahmet Serdar. 2010. "Arabs in Kemalist Turkish Historiography." *Middle Eastern Studies* 46, no. 5: 633–53.

Alexander, M. Jacqui, and Chandra Talpade Mohanty. 2013. *Feminist Genealogies, Colonial Legacies, Democratic Futures*. New York: Routledge.

Altinay, Rustem Ertug. 2012. "From a Daughter of the Republic to a Femme Fatale: The Life and Times of Turkey's First Professional Fashion Model, Lale Belkis." *WSQ* 41, nos. 1–2: 113–30.

Arat-Koç, Sedef. 2007. "(Some) Turkish Transnationalism(s) in an Age of Capitalist Globalization and Empire: 'White Turk' Discourse, the New Geopolitics, and Implications for Feminist Transnationalism." *Journal of Middle East Women's Studies* 3, no. 1: 35–57.

Arat-Koç, Sedef. 2010. "New Whiteness(es), beyond the Colour Line? Assessing the Contradictions and Complexities of 'Whiteness' in the (Geo)Political Economy of Capitalist Globalism." In *States of Race: Critical Race Feminism for the Twenty-First Century*, edited by Sherene Razack, Malinda Smith, and Sunera Thobani, 147–68. Toronto: Between the Lines.

Arat-Koç, Sedef. 2018. "Culturalizing Politics, Hyper-Politicizing 'Culture': 'White' vs. 'Black Turks' and the Making of Authoritarian Populism in Turkey." *Dialectical Anthropology* 42, no. 4: 391–408.

Arkin, Daniel. 2019. "Ilhan Omar Faces Blowback after Voting 'Present' on Armenian Genocide Resolution." *NBC News*, October 30. https://www.nbcnews.com/news/us-news/ilhan-omar-faces-blowback-after-voting-present-armenian-genocide-resolution-n1073991.

Bajalan, Djene, and Michael Brooks. 2019. "Ilhan Omar and the Turkey Question." *Jacobin*, January 11.

Bangstad, Sindre. 2011. "Saba Mahmood and Anthropological Feminism after Virtue." *Theory, Culture & Society* 28, no. 3: 28–54.

Ben-Naeh, Yaron. 2006. "Blond, Tall, with Honey-Colored Eyes: Jewish Ownership of Slaves in the Ottoman Empire." *Jewish History* 20, no. 3: 315–32.

Berkes, Niyazi. 1998. *The Development of Secularism in Turkey*. London: C. Hurst.

Bilici, Mücahit. 2009. "Black Turks, White Turks: On the Three Requirements of Turkish Citizenship." *Insight Turkey* 11, no. 3: 23–35.

Bora, Tanil. 2013. *Notes on the White Turks Debate: Turkey between Nationalism and Globalization*. London: Routledge.

Boratav, Pertev N., and W. Eberhard. 1951. "The Negro in Turkish Folklore." *Journal of American Folklore* 64, no. 251: 83–88.

Çakır, Serpil. 2007. "Feminism and Feminist History-Writing in Turkey: The Discovery of Ottoman Feminism." *Aspasia* 1, no. 1: 61–83.

Çelik, Nihat, and Emre İşeri. 2016. "Islamically Oriented Humanitarian NGOs in Turkey: AKP Foreign Policy Parallelism." *Turkish Studies* 17, no. 3: 429–48.

Davis, Angela. 1981. *Women, Race, and Class*. New York: Random House.

Deeb, Lara. 2009. "Piety Politics and the Role of a Transnational Feminist Analysis." *Journal of the Royal Anthropological Institute* 15, no. S1: 112–26.

Demiralp, Seda. 2012. "White Turks, Black Turks? Faultlines beyond Islamism versus Secularism." *Third World Quarterly* 33, no. 3: 511–24.

Du Bois, William Edward Burghardt. (1903) 2008. *The Souls of Black Folk*. Oxford: Oxford University Press.

Ekmekcioglu, Lerna. 2013. "A Climate for Abduction, a Climate for Redemption: The Politics of Inclusion during and after the Armenian Genocide." *Comparative Studies in Society and History* 55, no. 3: 522–53.

Ergin, Murat. 2008. "'Is the Turk a White Man?' Towards a Theoretical Framework for Race in the Making of Turkishness." *Middle Eastern Studies* 44, no. 6: 827–50.

Ergin, Murat. 2014. "The Racialization of Kurdish Identity in Turkey." *Ethnic and Racial Studies* 37, no. 2: 322–41.

Ergin, Murat. 2016. *Is the Turk a White Man?: Race and Modernity in the Making of Turkish Identity*. Leiden: Brill.

Evans, Zachary. 2019. "Erdogan Ally Met with Omar, Contributed to Her Campaign." *National Review*, October 31. https://www.nationalreview.com/news/erdogan-ally -met-with-omar-contributed-to-her-campaign/.

Ferguson, Michael. 2014. "White Turks, Black Turks, and Negroes: The Politics of Polarization." In *The Making of a Protest Movement in Turkey: #occupygezi*, edited by Umut Özkırımlı, 77–88. London: Palgrave Macmillan UK.

Gökalp, Ziya. 1968. *The Principles of Turkism*. Translated by Robert Devereaux. Leiden: E. J. Brill.

Göle, Nilüfer. 1996. *The Forbidden Modern: Civilization and Veiling*. Ann Arbor: University of Michigan Press.

Grewal, Inderpal. 2013. "Racial Sovereignty and 'Shooter' Violence: Oak Creek Massacre, Normative Citizenship, and the State." *Sikh Formations* 9, no. 2: 187–97.

Gülçür, Leyla, and Pınar İlkkaracan. 2002. "The 'Natasha' Experience: Migrant Sex Workers from the Former Soviet Union and Eastern Europe in Turkey." *Women's Studies International Forum* 25, no. 4: 411–21.

Guner, Ezgi. 2020. "The Soul of the White Muslim: Race, Empire, and Africa in Turkey." PhD diss., University of Illinois at Urbana-Champaign.

Gürbilek, Nurdan. 2003. "Dandies and Originals: Authenticity, Belatedness, and the Turkish Novel." *South Atlantic Quarterly* 102, nos. 2–3: 599–628.

Gürel, Pelin E. 2017. *The Limits of Westernization: A Cultural History of America in Turkey*. New York: Columbia University Press.

Iğsız, Aslı. 2018. *Humanism in Ruins: Entangled Legacies of the Greek-Turkish Population Exchange*. Stanford, CA: Stanford University Press.

Kadioğlu, Ayşe. 1994. "Women's Subordination in Turkey: Is Islam Really the Villain?" *Middle East Journal* 48, no. 4: 645–60.

294 MERIDIANS 22:2 · October 2023

Kadioğlu, Ayşe. 1996. "The Paradox of Turkish Nationalism and the Construction of Official Identity." *Middle Eastern Studies* 32, no. 2: 177–93.

Kandiyoti, Deniz. 1991. "End of Empire: Islam, Nationalism, and Women in Turkey." In *Women, Islam, and the State*, edited by Deniz Kandiyoti, 22–47. London: Palgrave Macmillan UK.

Kocamaner, Hikmet. 2019. "Regulating the Family through Religion." *American Ethnologist* 46, no. 4: 495–508.

Koğacıoğlu, Dicle. 2004. "The Tradition Effect: Framing Honor Crimes in Turkey." *Differences: A Journal of Feminist Cultural Studies* 15, no. 2: 119–51.

Korkman, Zeynep Kurtuluş. 2016. "Politics of Intimacy in Turkey: A Distraction from 'Real' Politics?" *Journal of Middle East Women's Studies* 12, no. 1: 112–21.

Korkman, Zeynep Kurtuluş. 2017. "Castration, Sexual Violence, and Feminist Politics in Post–coup Attempt Turkey." *Journal of Middle East Women's Studies* 13, no. 1: 181–85.

Korkman, Zeynep K., and Sherene H. Razack. 2021. "Transnational Feminist Approaches to Anti-Muslim Racism." *Meridians* 20, no. 2: 2061–270.

Langan, Mark. 2017. "Virtuous Power Turkey in Sub-Saharan Africa: The 'Neo-Ottoman' Challenge to the European Union." *Third World Quarterly* 38, no. 6: 1399–1414.

Lorde, Audre. (1984) 2012. *Sister Outsider: Essays and Speeches*. Berkeley, CA: Crossing.

Mahmood, Saba. 2001. "Feminist Theory, Embodiment, and the Docile Agent: Some Reflections on the Egyptian Islamic Revival." *Cultural Anthropology* 16, no. 2: 202–36.

Mahmood, Saba. 2011. *Politics of Piety: The Islamic Revival and the Feminist Subject*. Princeton, NJ: Princeton University Press.

Maksudyan, Nazan. 2005. "The Turkish Review of Anthropology and the Racist Face of Turkish Nationalism." *Cultural Dynamics* 17, no. 3: 291–322.

Moallem, Minoo. 2021. "Race, Gender, and Religion: Islamophobia and Beyond." *Meridians* 20, no. 2: 271–90.

Mohanty, Chandra Talpade. 1984. "Under Western Eyes: Feminist Scholarship and Colonial Discourses." *boundary 2* 12/13, no. 1: 333–58.

Mohanty, Chandra Talpade. 2003a. *Feminism without Borders: Decolonizing Theory, Practicing Solidarity*. Durham, NC: Duke University Press.

Mohanty, Chandra Talpade. 2003b. "'Under Western Eyes' Revisited: Feminist Solidarity through Anticapitalist Struggles." *Signs* 28, no. 2: 499–535.

Mutluer, Nil. 2019. "The Intersectionality of Gender, Sexuality, and Religion: Novelties and Continuities in Turkey during the AKP Era." *Southeast European and Black Sea Studies* 19, no. 1: 99–118.

Naber, Nadine. 2008. "'Look, Mohammed the Terrorist Is Coming!': Cultural Racism, Nation-Based Racism, and the Intersectionality of Oppressions after 9/11." In *Race and Arab Americans before and after 9/11: From Invisible Citizens to Visible Subjects*, edited by Amaney Jamal and Nadine Naber, 276–304. Syracuse, NY: Syracuse University Press.

Nahmias, Omri. 2019. "Ilhan Omar Blasted for Voting against Turkey Sanctions Bill." *Jerusalem Post*, October 30. https://www.jpost.com/american-politics/ilhan-omar -votes-against-turkey-sanctions-bill-harms-civilians-606271.

Parla, Ayse. 2019. *Precarious Hope: Migration and the Limits of Belonging in Turkey.* Stanford, CA: Stanford University Press.

Parla, Taha, and Andrew Davison. 2008. "Secularism and Laicism in Turkey." In *Secularisms*, edited by Janet R. Jakobsen and Ann Pellegrini, 58–75. Durham, NC: Duke University Press.

Petti, Matthew. 2020. "Ilhan Omar Pushes Turkey on Kurdish Prisoners." *National Interest*, May 19. https://nationalinterest.org/blog/skeptics/ilhan-omar-pushes -turkey-kurdish-prisoners-155916.

Rana, Junaid. 2007. "The Story of Islamophobia." *Souls* 9, no. 2: 148–61.

Razack, Sherene. 2008. *Casting Out: The Eviction of Muslims from Western Law and Politics.* Toronto: University of Toronto Press.

Razack, Sherene. 2022. *Nothing Has to Make Sense: Upholding White Supremacy through Anti-Muslim Racism.* Minneapolis: University of Minnesota Press.

Salem, Sara. 2018. "On Transnational Feminist Solidarity: The Case of Angela Davis in Egypt." *Signs: Journal of Women in Culture and Society* 43, no. 2: 245–67.

Savci, Evren. 2021. *Queer in Translation: Sexual Politics under Neoliberal Islam.* Durham, NC: Duke University Press.

Siddiqi, Dina M. 2014. "Solidarity, Sexuality, and Saving Muslim Women in Neoliberal Times." *WSQ* 42, nos. 3–4: 292–306.

Sirman, Nükhet. 1989. "Feminism in Turkey: A Short History." *New Perspectives on Turkey* 3: 1–34.

Suny, Ronald Grigor. 2017. *"They Can Live in the Desert but Nowhere Else": A History of the Armenian Genocide.* Princeton, NJ: Princeton University Press.

Toledano, Ehud R. 1981. "Slave Dealers, Women, Pregnancy, and Abortion: The Story of a Circassian Slave-Girl in Mid-nineteenth Century Cairo." *Slavery & Abolition* 2, no. 1: 53–68.

Tuğal, Cihan. 2016. *The Fall of the Turkish Model: How the Arab Uprisings Brought Down Islamic Liberalism.* London: Verso.

Unal, Didem. 2015. "Vulnerable Identities: Pious Women Columnists' Narratives on Islamic Feminism and Feminist Self-Identification in Contemporary Turkey." *Women's Studies International Forum* 53 (November–December): 12–21. https://doi .org/10.1016/j.wsif.2015.08.003.

Vasilaki, Rosa. 2016. "The Politics of Postsecular Feminism." *Theory, Culture & Society* 33, no. 2: 103–23.

WikiLeaks. 2016. "Berat's Box." March 15. https://wikileaks.org/berats-box/emailid /3501.

Winegar, Jessica. 2016. "How Academia in the US Self-Censors on Israel and Palestine." *TRT World*, November 22. https://www.trtworld.com/opinion/how -academia-in-the-us-self-censors-on-israel-and-palestine-3818.

Yavuz, M. Hakan. 2003. *Islamic Political Identity in Turkey.* Oxford: Oxford University Press.

Yıldız, Hülya. 2012. "Limits of the Imaginable in the Early Turkish Novel: Non-Muslim Prostitutes and Their Ottoman Muslim Clients." *Texas Studies in Literature and Language* 54, no. 4: 533–62.

Yılmaz, Mehmet Onur. 2014. "Türkiye'de Çocuğa karşı Ayrımcılık Raporu." Ankara: Gündem Çocuk Derneği.

Yorukoglu, Ilgin. 2017. "Whiteness as an Act of Belonging: White Turks Phenomenon in the Post 9/11 World." *Glocalism* 2: 1–22.

Zeydanlıoğlu, Welat. 2008. "The White Turkish Man's Burden: Orientalism, Kemalism, and the Kurds in Turkey." In *Neo-colonial Mentalities in Contemporary Europe? Language and Discourse in the Construction of Identities*, edited by Guido Rings and Anne Ife, 155–74. Newcastle: Cambridge Scholars.

Zilfi, Madeline. 2010. *Women and Slavery in the Late Ottoman Empire: The Design of Difference*. Cambridge: Cambridge University Press.

Dia Da Costa

....

Writing Castelessly

Brahminical Supremacy in Education, Feminist Knowledge, and Research

Abstract: This article combines historical and life-writing approaches to demonstrate how caste is made invisible in histories and structures of education, canonical knowledge, and research. As a dominant-caste (*savarna*) Bengali academic, the author follows caste-oppressed feminists to offer a methodological intervention that challenges several ways in which castelessness is reproduced in feminist scholarship. The author asks why *savarna* write castelessly. "Writing castelessly," wherein caste reflexivity is absented from analysis, solidarity, and teaching, is one manifestation of *savarna* feminists' historical-material relation to caste. Narrating regional caste histories of *savarna* Bengalis, the author shows that her practice of writing castelessly is founded on material structures of power—historically claimed monopolies over culture and education, land, labor, and political representation. Relatedly, another reason *savarna* write castelessly is that disciplinary training in social sciences in higher education taught the author to think, feel, read, and write castelessly. Finally, the author traces the reproduction of these disciplinary structures in her scholarship. Ultimately, this self-critique grounded in historical and material relations of caste seeks a feminist readership invested in public accountability and denaturalizing Brahminical merit in academia.

....

We [Dalits] are to see academics studying Indian society as casteless people! This, when we are faced with universities and institutes boasting 95% of faculty belonging to a handful of castes. . . . [T]he question, *how can we debate caste without naming the caste location*, should have been a

MERIDIANS · feminism, race, transnationalism   22:2 October 2023
DOI: 10.1215/15366936-10637690 © 2023 Smith College

no-brainer. But it needed engagement because we are touching on an issue
in which academics and feminists have been complicit: invisiblising caste.
—Anu Ramdas, "Casteless Academe, Name-Calling Dalits?"
....

Critiques of Brahminical feminism by the caste-oppressed, at least since
the 1990s, within and beyond the Indian academy, have built the present
moment in which it has become impossible for dominant-caste feminists
to continue to invisibilize caste. Multiple factors in the Indian context led
to the significant growth of published critiques by caste-oppressed scholars to shape the field of Dalit studies (Rawat and Satyanarayana 2016: 4).
This article combines historical and life-writing approaches to revisit specific ways in which caste is made invisible in Brahminical histories and
structures of knowledge, education, and research. I write as a dominant-
caste Bengali Brahmin whose now-secure professional life within disciplines of South Asian critical development studies, sociology of education,
and feminism in the North American "imperial university" (Chatterjee and
Maira 2014) continues to be built on Brahminical supremacy, in India and
its diaspora. Like white supremacy, Brahminical supremacy gains its
power by constructing a specific, dominant view of the world as neutral
and natural. Making Brahminical supremacy in education legible is thus a
task with stakes akin to denaturalizing whiteness and refusing its claims
to normalization.

I focus on one manifestation of dominant-caste (*savarna*) feminists' historical and material relation to caste, which I characterize as writing
castelessly. Writing castelessly involves practices of sweeping the question
of caste power under a heavy rug even though caste pervasively determines
our lives, learning, research, and resistance. The Pakistani, Shi'a Muslim,
caste-oppressed, feminist scholar Shaista Patel's incisive words capture the
practice powerfully: "Brahmin scholars who write about caste without
making their positionality and intentions clear, without carefully and eth-
ically centering Dalit-Bahujan theorizing in non-fetishizing ways" (Patel
2019). I would not have come to this intention of making caste violence
apparent in education and Brahminical feminist writing if caste-oppressed
peoples had not pointedly and patiently called for dominant-caste people
to address caste in our families, social networks, and personal and professional lives (Ramdas 2012a, 2012b; Soundararajan and Varatharajah 2015).

Twice now my writing on making Brahminical supremacy legible has
generated comments about playing into imperial hands by enabling

age-old divide and rule among differentially colonized people, echoing concerns in broader debates (see, for example, John 1996: 23–25). Raised with an acute awareness of U.S. imperialism, I take this critique seriously. Reading this through caste however, I want to remember that Brahmins have been the stereotypical non-Western informants whose contribution to knowledge structurally enabled British colonialism. What does it mean, then, for me to plead distance from imperial collusion today when Dalit-Bahujan call Brahminical supremacy to account? Moreover, can we quiet savarna anxieties about following Dalit leadership and perhaps become informants of a different kind—the kind who betray Brahminical supremacy in service of an anti-caste, anti-imperial feminist politics? Raising rather than answering such questions, I try to articulate methodologies that refuse to distance savarna feminist writing from the historical and ongoing collaboration between white and Brahminical supremacy.

Analogous to the race ignorance of white feminism, the historian Anupama Rao (1999: 208) defines Brahminical feminism as "the possibility of occupying a feminist position outside caste: *the possibility of denying caste as a problem for gender.*" Brahminical feminism is grounded in the millennia-old caste system scripted by Brahmins who placed themselves at the top of the hierarchy and monopolized control over religious and secular knowledge. Writing in the 1930s, the Dalit theorist, visionary leader, and primary author of the Indian constitution, B. R. Ambedkar, said that the caste system was not "merely division of labour, but also a division of labourers" because people are born into it and their humanity is defined by it (Ambedkar and Rodrigues 2002: 263). Four hierarchically organized groups—Brahmins (priests, learned), Kshatriyas (kings, warriors), Vaishyas (merchants, traders), and Shudras (working classes)—are part of the system (savarnas). Others known as *avarnas*, such as Dalits (literally meaning crushed) and *adivasis* (Indigenous peoples) are considered polluted and placed outside its fold. Taking cues from anti-caste writers, I use the term *savarna* to mean the first three dominant castes (to which most academics belong); *Brahmins* to refer to those who gain the most from systemic caste violence; and *Dalit-Bahujan* to refer to all caste-oppressed peoples, including Dalits, *adivasis*, Shudras, Muslims, and others (Teltumbde 2010; Karunakaran 2016). Brahminical supremacy and feminism are not practiced by Brahmins alone, and the complex regional practices of caste often differ significantly. However, the fundamental principles of caste violence were scripted by Brahmins, upheld by rulers, and challenged by Dalit-Bahujan.

In thinking through "writing castelessly," I stay with Dalit-Bahujan and anti-caste critiques of Brahminical supremacy and castelessness in feminism (Pawar and Moon 2008; Ramdas 2012a, 2012b; Patel 2016, 2019; Rege 2000), history (Jangam 2015), and sociology (Guru 2002; Deshpande 2003; Rawat and Satyanarayana 2016), not least because they have insisted on studying caste as a problem and not just as a social system (Mandal 2020). Alongside Dalit-Bahujan scholarship, the savarna sociologist Satish Deshpande's historical identification of castelessness provides a grounding anchor. Deshpande (2013: 33) argues that castelessness "holds the key to caste" because projecting savarna castelessness was the "extra-electoral coup" through which savarna transformed their "caste capital into modern capital" over the course of the twentieth century. For him, castelessness was actively built through debates between savarna nationalist leader Mohandas Gandhi and the liberatory, anti-caste politics of Ambedkar over separate electorates. Separate electorates would afford the caste-oppressed the opportunity to elect representatives from their own communities rather than joint electorates dominated by savarna politics. Ultimately, in the 1930s, savarna politics won. Instead of separate electorates, reservations in education and employment granted by seemingly casteless dominant-caste benefactors made the caste of the caste-oppressed hypervisible (32, 35).

Some Brahmin scholars have eagerly responded to the anti-caste call. In the last ten years, or so, while savarna like myself publicize our solidarity and feverishly publish our anti-caste credentials, we nonetheless fundamentally fail to reckon with our familial, everyday, institutional histories of caste supremacy, even as we stake Brahminical claim over anti-caste scholarship. Some savarna strive to "say it first," hiding the Dalit-Bahujan backs and knowledge our "merit" stands on, and North American publishers steeped in white and Brahminical knowledge amplify savarna hunger for anti-caste relevance, while setting caste as the next trend. Old structures die hard. Those of us who would like to think of ourselves as anti-caste Brahmin feminists are beginning to realize, often for the first time, what caste-oppressed people knew all along: the limits of Brahminical power and knowledge. Notwithstanding Brahminical monopolizing of knowledge to construct what Dalit theorists have called "caste apartheid" (Soundararajan 2022), anti-caste Brahmins cannot simply think and imagine our way into a casteless existence. Our claimed space in anti-caste writing seems utterly useless in bringing about a caste-annihilated reality—tied as our lives stubbornly remain to material structures of protected caste inheritance, from hoarding wealth, land, and labor, to having recognizable names, endowed positions in imperial universities, beautiful houses, well-fed and well-schooled kin, and valuable savarna professionals who protect us.

Rather than reproducing caste apartheid by claiming castelessness or by being cagey about our lives while Dalit-Bahujan lives are constantly on display, savarna academic feminists can make the specific caste-based architecture of our lives manifest. My purpose is thus to articulate a specific methodology that begins accounting for the characteristic histories of my education, disciplinary training, and solidarity scholarship. I do this to challenge "Brahminical ignorance," which, after Charles Mills (2008) is a structurally generated "need to not know" extant Dalit anti-caste knowledges (Da Costa 2022). That I would not have noticed this in feminist writing, including my own, without the labor of caste-oppressed scholars speaks to my own pervasive Brahminical ignorance.

After contextualizing the problem of casteless feminist writing in the first section, I seek to address the basic question: why do savarna write castelessly? Because I am Bengali Brahmin, in the second section, I focus on Bengali Brahmin regional history to show that writing castelessly is founded on material structures of caste. I connect histories of caste power—Brahminical control over knowledge, land, labor, and political representation—to education. In Bengal, in periods of intense flux and anti-colonial nationalist formations, the appearance of Brahminical attachment to liberal postcolonial modernity serviced active Brahminical investment in consolidating caste distinction. These material relations of social power ground the normative, modern savarna Bengali Brahminical epistemological standpoint. In short, savarna write castelessly because Brahminical supremacy structurally affords us this luxury, including that of remaining decidedly unaware of how powerful our caste makes us, and how pervasively it scripts our life stories.

In the third section, I provide another answer by arguing that savarna write castelessly because we are taught to do so. For those of us trained in Indian sociology in the 1990s, the sociological canon on caste deepened castelessness by primarily teaching caste as a structuring force in the lives of others, while practicing an unethical separation of scholar from knowledge production (Deshpande 2003; Ramdas 2012a, 2012b; Rawat and Satyanarayana 2016). Finally, I trace the mark of this disciplinary training in my own scholarship, which returns me to my central concern with challenging the castelessness of postcolonial transnational feminism.

Focusing on discussions of reflexivity, I demonstrate that when it comes to caste in academia, the line between savior and solidarity research is not definitive because both rely on accessing the lives of others. Accounting for Brahminical supremacy requires giving public access to savarna lives, interests, thought, and feeling in order to denaturalize Brahminical merit and challenge the reproduction of writing castelessly. Certainly transnational feminist scholars have long seen "critical transnational feminism as [an] inherently unstable praxis whose survival and evolution hinge on a continuous commitment to produce self-reflexive and dialogic critiques of its own practices rather than a search for resolutions or closures" (Nagar and Swarr 2010: 9). In this spirit, I conclude by noting the broader implications of the argument and imagining fellow Brahminical feminists invested in refusing castelessness in our academic homes.

The Problem of Writing Castelessly
Brahminical supremacy as a foundational feature of South Asian academic trajectories, thought, and life is typically elided in savarna scholarly writing, despite crucial contributions by these very scholars to postcolonial, transnational, and anti-racist feminisms and sociology. For example, in her celebrated and still-urgent article, Chandra Talpade Mohanty (1984) advanced critiques that refused Western feminism's reification and relativizing of third world women's "difference" in unidimensional, victimized terms for Western eyes. Revisiting this essay in 2003, Mohanty reiterated her commitment to an "analytically inclusive methodology" (234) and noted: "Beginning from the lives and interests of marginalized communities of women, I am able to access and make the workings of power visible—to read up the ladder of privilege" (231). Crucially, Mohanty located her analytical and political bearings by noting she is as much insider as outsider, "under" Western eyes as "inside" Western eyes because of her imperial and class position in the U.S. academy (228). In the 1984 essay itself, her critique of Western feminism was already leveled not just against white feminists but also "third world women in the West, or third world women in the third world writing for the West" (336). However, read alongside the Dalit anti-caste feminist Anu Ramdas's (2012a, 2012b) critique of Indian academics circulating as casteless, Mohanty's writing—with its critique of Western feminism, reliance on lives of marginalized women for an inclusive methodology, and self-reflexive discussion of her class and imperial location—is notably casteless, practicing an invisibilizing of caste.

It would be incorrect to say that Mohanty ignores caste altogether. In "Under Western Eyes," caste briefly features through Maria Mies's work on lace makers, which Mohanty (1984: 344–46) holds as exemplary for recognizing how caste-based patriarchy shapes capitalist relations. Elsewhere Mohanty (1997: 12–14) notes that Mies shows how "indigenous hierarchies" of caste and gender shape women's participation in the international division of labor. Noticing that caste structures worker identity, Mohanty argues that "the definition of social identity of women as workers is not only class-based, but in fact, in this case, must be grounded in understandings of race, gender and caste histories and experiences of work" (27). But a nod to revealing caste in the lives of others is not the same as making caste power legible within the structures of savarna feminism itself—a task that Mohanty evades.

In another prominent example, Bengali Brahmin feminist Gayatri Spivak's critique of postcolonial, imperial, and liberal reason fails to confront its casteism. Spivak has repeatedly argued that postcolonial feminist intellectuals in the imperial university have to notice our complicity in becoming commodified "native informants" for the West. By clearly locating themselves, postcolonial feminists must refuse to perpetuate, Spivak insists (1999: 167; 1990: 125), an education steeped in a "sanctioned ignorance" that trades in an "interested denial" in service of imperial class projects and the international division of labor. But why does Spivak's (1990: 125–26) insightful critique of the postcolonial intellectual's vigorous and "interested denial of something that is present crucially and in excess" largely evade the excessive presence and crucial mediation of her caste-inherited role as inter/national intellectual worker and the knowledge produced therein? Spivak is hardly unaware of caste power, as is apparent from her writing on sati (widow immolation) or Mahasweta Devi. Nonetheless, Spivak's (1999: 170) call to "raise the persistent voice of auto-critique" does not stand the test of her evident structural need to write castelessly (Patel and Da Costa 2022). This is not Donna Haraway's (1988) god trick because it is not a view from nowhere, but a Brahminical trick that theorizes one's complicity in certain imperial and class structures of violence alongside, and sometimes as means of, evading caste reflexivity.

Transnational feminists like Mohanty and Spivak might be attuned to noticing that we are outsider and insider to Western society, but we have much less practice at processing the epistemological implications of our specific caste histories—that is, as insider to the pre-British coloniality of caste, as insider to the consolidation of caste through British coloniality, and as insider to ongoing coloniality of caste in modern India. Thus, when Mohanty treats as analytical and political resource the "lives of marginalized communities of women," we must ask about the prevalence of Brahminical supremacy within transnational feminism and methodological practices of accessing the lives of others.

Indeed, Spivak, Mohanty, Richa Nagar, and others have grounded questions of positionality, reflexivity, and accountability within processes of political education and collaborative knowledge production with activist movements among marginalized communities as crucial to transnational feminist praxis (Alexander and Mohanty 1997: ix; Spivak 2007; Nagar and Swarr; Nagar 2014). Despite these commitments, Anu Ramdas's critique of a "casteless academe" rings true, given the realities of a savarna-dominated academy circulating in India as casteless, secular leftists, and in North America as casteless, racialized, and postcolonial. Mohanty and Spivak are thus far from exceptional in writing castelessly.

Diasporic Brahmin academics like myself sit with a lot of power because the world of caste, class, and imperialism is organized to place us there, dominating what counts as theory and merit, extracting what we need from others, accomplished partly by hoarding academic positions in Brahminical and white institutions (Guru 2002; Subramanian 2015; Madan 2020). For a long time, I too identified as Indian/South Asian, and when asked, I acknowledged being born into a Hindu family—all of which obscured my caste power and named postcolonial, racialized markers instead. I remember my early hesitation with North American campus race politics for obscuring class and caste, indicating my nascent hesitation about entirely erasing caste questions while in the process of becoming a racialized subject. Nonetheless, systematic reflection on my own casteist practices is very recent work for me. Like countless other savarna feminists, even when I wrote about caste, I wrote castelessly. With autobiographical intention, I turn now to specifying the Bengali Brahminical formation of castelessness and savior politics.

Bengali Brahminical Castelessness and Structures of Savior Feeling

In an interview with the transnational feminist scholars Richa Nagar and Sarah Saddler, published in 2019, when asked about my roles and responsibilities in the academy, I noted the following:

My role and responsibility as I see it is primarily to challenge the structures of savior feeling and mentality that inhere in development and progressive politics, at the global, national, local and individual levels. . . . [C]onsider how those of us with privilege might move from the resilient savior mentality deeply structured into our person towards betraying the structures that assure our privilege within and beyond academia.
(Da Costa 2019)

By structures of savior feeling, I am attending to the caste- and class-based version of the white savior–industrial complex and its "helping imperative" grounded in colonial capitalism and institutional development processes (Heron 2007). While I'm recounting histories close to mine using this framework, I want to nonetheless resist methodological/political individualism. The Bengali Brahmin relationship to land, education, and politics shifted under colonial rule, revealing the aligned formations of castelessness and structures of savior feeling as national political projects produced in this period. Tracing regional formations of the post/coloniality of casteism shows Brahminical supremacy as the fabric of Indian nation-state formation.

Raymond Williams's (1977: 130) concept of structure of feeling refers to the emergent forms of lived, practical consciousness that do not neatly map onto "formed and deliberate" ideology. Williams proposes that although different structures of feeling do not simply map on to different classes, new structures of feeling do map onto "rise of a class," or "contradiction, fracture, and mutation" or "when a formation appears to break away from its class norms" (130). Savior feeling transformed into a "formed and deliberate" savarna savior mentality through anti-colonial nationalism appearing to break away from casteist norms without actually doing so. Specifically, savarna savior feeling appears committed to transforming the lives of the caste-oppressed, but it is structurally grounded in preserving Brahminical supremacy and savarna castelessness. Evidently, Brahmins have treated the nation, its resources, and knowledge about it as Brahminical property—ours to appropriate, hoard, sell, distribute, destroy, or share as and when we deem fit. As Deshpande notes, this caste of ownership, however, is eclipsed by the hypervisibility of the caste-oppressed who are granted things by savarna benefactors (Deshpande 2013).

Castelessness takes significantly differentiated form regionally because caste is regionally distinct. Rather than take cover behind caste's complexities, however, I argue that regional class differentiations among Bengali Brahmins actually consolidated Brahminical power (Bhattacharya 2005). Scholars have demonstrated that, in Bengal, casteist state power well preceded British colonial rule (Bandopadhyay 2004). Under British colonialism, savarna grappled with the relative social mobility afforded the caste-oppressed when the British expanded access to education and the Permanent Settlement Act (1793) opened up land markets. Tithi Bhattacharya's history of the *bhadralok* class (Bengali for gentleman) notes that while *bhadralok* is not coextensive with Brahmins, it largely comprises savarna castes—Brahmin, Kayastha, and Baidya. In class terms, however, the *bhadralok* could be as wealthy as absentee landowners, merchants, and traders who held high offices in the East India Company (Bhattacharya 2005: 38). Or they could be teachers, doctors, shopkeepers, and low-level clerks in colonial offices who owned minimal land and lived in what is often described as "genteel poverty" (55–57). This sentimental language of "genteel poverty" for savarna poverty nurtures a casteless class critique.

Bhattacharya notes that the ostentatious wealth of the upper-class Brahmin *bhadralok* was secured through investments in colonial cash crops like cotton and indigo, which later gave them access to high-level jobs in the colonial bureaucracy. By contrast, for the lower-middle-class Brahmin seeking to reproduce some status in the face of colonial political-economic transitions, the precolonial monopoly that Brahmins claimed over education was an absolutely crucial tool to constitute hierarchized difference from subordinated castes despite and because of the relative, mutual proximity in terms of class (85–97). This class took on racially humiliating and monotonous clerical work in the colonial bureaucracy (Sarkar 1997). Bhattacharya's (2005) analysis shows that, despite class differences, the *bhadralok*'s claim to caste distinction was accomplished by consolidating what counted as culture, knowledge, and respectability via cheaply printed novels written by various classes of *bhadralok* nostalgically satirizing the changes wrought by colonialism. My family history aligns with this lower-middle-class strata among Brahmins who jealously guarded exclusive, casteist *bhadralok* control over the meaning of being cultured and educated as one of the only ways to secure distinction in changing times.

Bengali castelessness was cultivated within these shifts under colonialism, obscuring the citadel-protecting work that Brahmins of all classes did to consolidate their control over what counts as education and culture. Over time, this cross-class, cross-savarna-caste control over education produced the idea of a general Bengali affinity for culture and education, still prevalent as a community's stereotype of itself today. This castelessness is powerfully captured in the presumption that bhadralok refers to anyone with culture, even though it is historically grounded in savarna supremacy. These regionally specific processes of consolidating Bengali casteist power animate Satish Deshpande's (2013: 35) striking finding that 98 percent of Hindus who selected the category of "no caste" in the 1931 census were Bengali.[1]

The historian Dwaipayan Sen (2018) further contributes to understanding the formation of Bengal's castelessness by studying the political career (1930s–1960s) of the Bengali Ambedkarite and Dalit leader Jogendranath Mandal and analyzing why Dalit politics failed to gain traction during this time. It is not, Sen argues, because Mandal simply accepted the nationalist resolution of the caste question, which took the caste-oppressed from alienation toward integration. Rather, as Sen shows, Mandal's efforts were actively thwarted by Bengali savarna Congress leaders "to contain autonomous Dalit political organization" (12). Even predominantly Brahmin parliamentary Communists in Bengal (1977–2011) were in denial about casteism, including, as Sen notes, the Communist Chief Minister Jyoti Basu, who called caste a feudal legacy irrelevant to Bengal in the 1980s (Basu cited in Government of India 1980: 46; Sen 2018: 1).

Castelessness was grounded in savarna Bengali resistance to autonomous Dalit-Bahujan politics: a reflection of national-level Gandhi-Ambedkar conflicts. Since separate electorates for Dalit-Bahujan would diminish savarna electoral power considerably, Gandhi pressured Ambedkar through a fast unto death to cede preference for separate electorates to the savarna preference for caste-based reservations in electoral seats, education, and employment (Deshpande 2013: 35). This concession of tremendous import, called the Poona Pact, Deshpande argues, made the numerical savarna minority the "de facto owner of the nation, with power to grant favours to this or that group," principally Dalit-Bahujan (35).

Notably, savarna Bengali resented even the Poona Pact. In Bengal, Dalit-Bahujan and Muslims were on the same side in calling for tenancy reforms in the 1930s, but as predominantly landowning castes, savarna Bengalis resisted such reforms (Sen 2018: 39–41). Deflecting their casteism, savarna portrayed Dalit-Muslim alignments as divisive and not suited to properly encompassing nationalist politics (51). Thus, speaking over Dalit-Muslim alignments, savarna claimed monopoly in defining nationalism. Sen details how prominent savarna Bengali political leaders, professors, writers, and lawyers objected to the Poona Pact as putting "a premium upon inexperience and ignorance" by taking political power from those "who by education, tradition, upbringing, and sacrifice are the best suited to represent Hindu constituencies" and giving it to people "only slowly emerging from obscurity" (50). Sen also notes that the Dalit leader Amulyadhan Ray challenged this "Brahminical fraud" of claiming divisiveness, considering the pact argued for more Dalit-Bahujan seats within a joint, not separate, electorate. Even diluted concessions were intolerable for Bengali Brahmins because holding political space for Dalit-Bahujan could effect structural change via tenancy reform (39–41).

Similarly, in the late nineteenth and early twentieth centuries, Dalit-Bahujan struggled for self-respect by entering public spaces (schools, government buildings, and temples) and holding inter-caste commensality feasts against prevailing casteist norms (Pawar and Moon 2008). These actions against untouchability were popularized in the savarna imagination by Gandhi, who fought untouchability while defending caste as a system of mutual division of labor. Sen (2018: 57) shows that, significantly, liberal and orthodox Bengali Brahmin lawyers claimed that "uplift" of Dalits needs to be accomplished without outraging Hindu society, and that temple entry would cause rioting and disorder. These Brahmin men claimed to not be orthodox because they devoted time and money to "improving the social conditions" of the caste-oppressed (57). They deflected casteism through a claim to castelessness nourished through a structure of savior feeling while staunchly defending Brahminical supremacy. By default on Brahminical terms, such altruism ensured that Brahminical supremacy was consolidated through a liberal modernity of championing the Dalit cause.

Guided by nationalist historiography on the colonial drain of Indian wealth, the predominant framework for nationalist leaders trying to understand poverty was imperial and class analysis. Yet the first prime minister, Jawaharlal Nehru, ultimately failed to compel regional governments to conduct substantial land reforms—a failure that disproportionately affected landless Dalit-Bahujan (Guru and Chakravarty 2005: 137). State officials succumbed to feudal resistance against land reforms and the expropriation of their power base (Kaviraj 1988: 2433). Despite Bengali Dalit legislative efforts calling for agrarian reform, savarna walkouts and denial scuttled legislative change (Sen 2018: 66–67). Ultra-lite Nehruvian socialism amounted to what Sudipta Kaviraj (1988) called "India's passive revolution," which nurtured Indian capitalist development with a focus on steel, dams, and factories for the supposed common good.

This casteless approach to class questions was enhanced in the national popular common sense by sentimental tropes of "genteel poverty" referring to the Brahmin poor, including the Brahmin filmmaker Satyajit Ray's 1950s depictions of Brahmin rural poverty. The "poor Brahmin" remains a stock figure in children's literature and in Brahmin academic self-representation. While inciting empathy for Brahmin poverty, we must ask what we are supposed to feel about "non-genteel" poverty of the caste-oppressed, the predominant form of Indian poverty (Guru and Chakravarty 2005). Even when it appeared that some Brahmin leaders were betraying caste norms by committing to liberal or socialist modernity, they were in fact cementing casteist foundations for post-British India. Ultimately, when Bengal's Left Front took power in the 1970s, a Brahminical leadership reproduced a casteless class politics (Chandra, Heierstad, and Nielsen 2016).

The casteism of nationalism already apparent in Brahminical patriarchy's approach to women's rights in the nineteenth and twentieth centuries (Pawar and Moon 2008) was further consolidated in denying Dalit political determination alongside selective Brahminical altruism. Nehruvian policies chose not to transform casteist capitalism's land and labor relations, and Marxian approaches privileged a casteless class analytic that saw caste as a feudal vestige rather than foundational to modern India (Rawat and Satyanarayana 2016). This interlocking formation of anticolonial nationalism, castelessness, and savior mentality among savarna leaders marked the Indian sociological canon on caste and engendered solidarity research, as I show next.

Caste in the Lives of Others

Given these Brahminical material histories, unsurprisingly, Indian sociological training at Lady Shri Ram College and Delhi School of Economics taught me that caste marked people other than "us" (urban) savarnas. I don't recall being taught to examine my caste position or that of authors to explicitly consider its relationship to knowledge production. Despite "reflexivity" reshaping disciplines at least since the 1980s, my education in Indian sociology (1993–97) evaded caste reflexivity. Canonical norms in sociological methodology effectively taught students how to read, write, and analyze castelessly.

Recent anti-caste scholarly critique (Deshpande 2003; Jangam 2015; Rawat and Satyanarayana 2016) confirms my memories of curricular privileging of Brahmin scholar M. N. Srinivas, Andre Beteille (Bengali Brahmin and French heritage), and others such as G. S. Ghurye, Milton Singer, McKim Marriot, and A. M. Shah. Most were rooted in anthropological methods that conceptualized the caste system as a complex, fluid, and ultimately *"consensual system based on complementarity"* (Deshpande 2003: 103). While Beteille privileged a class analytic, his contribution to Indian sociology is farcical in its violent Brahminical supremacy. In response to Dalit efforts to gain recognition for casteism as racism at the 2001 United Nations (UN) World Conference against Racism in Durban, Beteille (2001) called on the UN to rethink the Dalit view as "politically mischievous" and "scientifically nonsensical." Analytically placing casteism on par with racism, Dalit-Bahujan critique posed a fundamental threat to Brahminical sociology's anti-imperial and anti-oppressive self-conception (Visweswaran 2011: 149).

Savarna scholars conducted "village ethnographies," undertaking decades of research on the everyday complexity of caste evident in rituals, endogamy, electoral processes, social mobility, and social change. For example, Srinivas's celebrated, voluminous writings on caste (1940s–80s) emphasized sub-caste divisions rather than the fourfold caste hierarchy. He conceptualized "dominant caste" to refute synonymity with "upper caste" and characterized "Sanskritization" (assimilation into dominant-caste norms) as social mobility, to reason that the caste system was fluid. In all this, as Dalit scholars such as Kancha Ilaiah and Gopal Guru have pointed out, the fixated valorization of Hindu traditions evaded critiquing Brahminical violence.

The sociologist Veena Das, who taught me about caste, placed considerable emphasis on a critical reading of the French Indologist Louis Dumont's (1966) book *Homo Hierarchicus*. Critiques of Dumont's work were published by professors for the 1971 issue of *Contributions to Indian Sociology*—a journal also edited by prominent savarna scholars such as T. N. Madan and Srinivas. Steeped in savarna discourses, rather than recognizing these revolving doors of knowledge production, at the time, I simply tried to wrap my head around basic terms—*ideology, ethnography, political economy, structuralism*. But I do recall the consternation over Dumont's characterization of hierarchy as the bedrock of Indian society. In an essay entitled "The Elementary Structure of Caste," Das and J. P. S. Uberoi (1971: 39) argued that Dumont sees Hindu society in static, unidimensional terms focused on hierarchy to

the epistemic exclusion of coexisting elements of "equality and reciprocity" apparent from Srinivas's research. While the 1971 debates justifiably
challenge Dumont's "idealistic" Indological methodology that places French
egalitarian society in opposition to Indian hierarchical society, Dumont's
critics demonstrate no parallel self-reflexivity regarding savarna portrayals
of caste as a complementary, dynamic stratification system.

Ironically, Indian sociologists demand a dialectical approach. For
example, Das and Uberoi fault Dumont's focus on Brahmins (ritual power
and status) and Kshatriyas (political and economic power) for focusing on
the top of the caste hierarchy. Instead, they propose that "the bird's-eye
view of the caste system must be complemented by a worm's-eye view, so to
speak, and the dialectical relation between the two explained, before we
can attain a complete sociological understanding" (40). They invisibilize
caste when their argument with Dumont shifts to his national, disciplinary, and methodological locations: conceptual generalizations versus ethnography, Indology versus social anthropology, and French versus Indian.
Yet dialectic and relational methodologies did not inform how Das taught
village ethnographies, considering urban Brahmin students like myself
were not asked to notice caste in our locations, lives, or thinking.

Das and Uberoi insist that the primary opposition of the caste system is
not between purity and pollution, Brahmin and Shudra, as Dumont would
have it, but, rather, between the "principal of asymmetric exchange and the
principal of reciprocal exchange"—the latter located in examples of caste-
based division of labor (41). Reminiscent of Gandhi's argument, they assert
that the caste system is equally about hierarchy and reciprocity—just like
other societies. Thinking with the benefit of Dalit-Bahujan critiques, it is
striking that an essay entitled "The Elementary Structure of Caste" makes
no mention of the caste terror, humiliation, segregation, or sexual violence
needed to secure caste endogamy. Das and Uberoi exhibit a structural
"need to not know" (Mills 2007), the routine violence required to enforce
the division of labor as an elementary structure of caste—and in this way
they wrote, taught, and constructed a casteist sociology as a neutral one.
In Brahminical epistemology, the emphasis on mutuality and reciprocity
represents complexity and nuance, whereas Brahminical violence is not
worthy of complex analysis (Deshpande 2003: 101).

Considering that savarna prioritize the methodology of a lived, complex
view of caste, the deliberate absenting of Ambedkar and other Dalit-
Bahujan theorists in the curriculum is duplicitous and violent. Beteille's
reasoning to students who queried the absence is that "the Delhi School of

Economics pursues sociology as a rigorous discipline, not as activism"—a classic, masculine, imperial partitioning of worthwhile knowledge (Beteille cited in Hebbar 2013). By the 1990s savarna could not claim lack of published Dalit writing as an excuse. The deliberate curricular exclusion reinforced what counts as knowledge, rigorous discipline, theory, and debate. This exclusion is precisely about Brahminical ignorance, a structural group-based interest and need not to know the wide-ranging implications of multifaceted Dalit theorizing of Brahminical violence in knowledge, power, and society.

This exemplifies what Dalit-Bahujan theorist Gopal Guru has characterized as the "pernicious divide between the theoretical Brahmins and the empirical Shudras" in Indian social science, mirroring the caste system in which "some are born with the theoretical spoon in their mouths and the vast majority with the empirical pot around their neck" (Guru 2002: 5003). Even in our classroom in the 1990s, with casteist, Hindutva politics raging around us, there was no acknowledgment that Ambedkar's arguments, made in the 1930s, foregrounded caste violence well before Dumont and without relativizing inequality as Dumont did (Deshpande 2003: 102). Instead, the savarna curriculum could only stomach the caste-oppressed as aspiring for change within the system (e.g., Sanskritization), to the outright exclusion of Ambedkar's theorization of annihilation of caste (Guru 1993).

Unsurprisingly, then, the central figures of Indian sociology stood vehemently opposed to extending reservations (affirmative action) in education and employment to "other backward classes" (castes). In Rawat and Satyanarayana's (2016: 13) words:

> "Invoking modern developmentalism and the constitutional abolition of caste-based discrimination, some social scientists and commentators—such as Srinivas, A. M. Shah, B. S. Baviskar, Andre Beteille, and Veena Das—maintained that caste is an anachronism in modern India and caste-based quotas are a legacy of colonial policies of divide and rule" (see also Deshpande 2003).

Here Ramnarayan S. Rawat and K. Satyanarayana expose the Brahminical logic among savarna professors, in its stunning similarity to Bengali Brahmin objections to the Poona Pact, as divisive. If Bengali Brahmins projected Dalit-Bahujan politics as bad nationalism, savarna sociologists saw it as bad postcolonial modernity.

We must see this Brahminical epistemological training in accessing the lives of the caste-oppressed as a political resource for reproducing savarna castelessness, because making it canonical to study caste as a complex, complementary exchange system in the lives and labor of others offered Brahmins ways to deflect the task of confronting caste supremacy in ourselves, in our definitions and structures of postcoloniality, and in science and modernity. When it comes to caste, the epistemological belief that identity gets essentialized if you name it, and by contrast it exists in fluid, complementary ways if savarna nuance commits to solid or solidarity research, is dangerously pervasive.

Where Is the Line between Solidarity and Savior Research?

The ethnographic approach to caste in the lives of others is a necessary, if not sufficient, condition to nourish savior or solidarity research. After all, if and when the casteless Brahmin academic feels drawn to socialist politics and social movements research as I did, the canonical methodologies ensured microscopic scrutiny of caste-oppressed lives, creativity, and politics, rather than focusing on a Brahminical state, society, and lives in order to dismantle caste's pervasive modern violence in society and knowledge.

As demonstrated above, savarna anti-colonial nationalist leaders had already woven the fabric of this casteless approach into class analytics and nationalism toward a post/coloniality of caste. Brahminical savior feeling was also a specifically patriarchal formation. Although savarna feminism tends to credit nineteenth-century Brahmin men with the origin of Indian feminism, in fact these men had relied on caste-based traditions to counter British views of Hindu society as barbaric. In turn, Brahminical patriarchy's feminism selectively "modernized" its spatial segregation of women by initially granting wealthy Brahmin women access to caste-segregated educational spaces, and eventually cultivating middle-class savarna women as casteless anti-imperial mothers for an incipient nation (Kumar 1993).

In independent India, aligned with Brahminical patriarchy's script of savior feminism within an anti-imperial nationalist mold, savarna socialist feminists ambivalently transgressed the still-powerful relegation of savarna women's work within the home. Savarna feminism focused on the other-projected-as-real-Indian-woman "in the villages, at the wrong end of development, suffering the injustices of the state or the limitations of leftist politics and so on . . . while rendering their own identities within the dominant culture largely transparent" as if their specific relationship to caste injustices did not have to be named (John 1996: 137). In her 1996 book *Discrepant Dislocations*, the feminist Mary E. John notes that, until the 1980s, urban, savarna socialist feminists still normalized the practice of "reaching out to and identifying with their more distant sisters" to build "justice for 'all' women" (141).

The early 1990s manifest a crisis in enacting casteist saviorism in the lives of caste-oppressed others because extant feminist ideological ground was totally destabilized with the demolition of the Babri Masjid, the blatantly anti-socialist liberalization policies, and the increasing prominence of middle-class Hindutva women. As John argues, savarna feminist work shifted "closer to home," as she was haunted by having to admit a spectacularly violent Hindutva woman into the category of feminist and by the possibility that the brazenly Islamophobic Hindutva feminists may just have greater traction in the lives of others than savarna socialist, liberal feminists (139). The progressive savarna feminist thus found herself recoiling from a previously well-worn path (140–41). Now queasy about identifying with Hindutva sisters, savarna "feminists are forced to scrutinize their immediate worlds in a new way" apparent in the turn toward theorizing critical genealogies of the middle-class self (141).

My coming of age happened in this crucial decade. When I applied for doctoral studies in development sociology in 1997, my application anchored my social movement research interests in two personal/political events: (1) traveling in a train out of Bombay while in grade 12, two days after the violent demolition of the Babri Masjid, alongside fleeing Muslims, which prompted a shameful recognition of my own failure at secular thinking; and (2), a woman factory worker in a special economic zone who questioned me in 1996 for bringing my pretentious, rustic ideas of development as an urban middle-class undergraduate student to her space through a research methodologies class. Hindsight tells me that my doctoral application was oriented toward self-reflection about my embodied articulation of Brahminical state violence and feminist saviorism.

But my educational training was stuck in the inertia of methodological colonialities that reached out to distant others. Feeding into earlier education, my doctoral training in development sociology in the United States effectively required a year of fieldwork among subjects of development. Methodologies thus structurally incited through the curriculum, as a Brahmin development sociologist I spent time doing solidarity research with people in rural Bengal. Like other Brahmin scholars, I took the line between solidarity and savior research to be located in my good intentions and anti-capitalist convictions. A casteless appreciation for self-reflexivity and learning from the oppressed oriented my work.

Consider my approach to reflexivity in my first book as evidence of writing castelessly in feminist solidarity research. My purpose is not to engage in guilt-ridden self-flagellation but to notice how methodologies can nurture our skills at deflecting caste. In the book, in accounting for my interest in rural political theatre, I briefly noted the ways that gendered, urban, middle-class experiences prompted me to question reductive development discourses, without noticing that casteism shaped my methodologies. In the acknowledgments, I wrote, "I received a lot of admiration and moral support from my grand-uncles and grand-aunts for the unknown work I did 'in the villages'" (Da Costa 2010: xii). This tells a story about the kind of merit and capital accrued from reproducing solidarity/savior methodologies, affirming savarna in a world made in the virtuous image of Brahminical savior feeling.

Implicitly aligned with transnational feminist sensibilities, my research resisted the totalizing first world power–third world victim binary that sees the former as shaping the latter, in my case, through development discourses. Indian social anthropological methodologies framed my hope that subaltern "histories from below" might offer genuine alternatives. This book foregrounded peasants' and agricultural workers' scripts of development and life worlds they deemed worthwhile, against dominant scripts of development. I believed that subalterns spoke all the time and the privileged had a responsibility to be in solidarity with them, in part, by finding ways to bring subaltern politics to wider audiences. In this regard, the idea of "situated solidarities," conceptualized initially in 1997 by the transnational feminists Richa Nagar and Susan Geiger, directly spoke to me. They argued against perfunctory statements of positionality and reflexivity, and for deeper "situated solidarities," grounding reflexivity in material struggles and "economic, political and institutional processes and structures that provide the context for the fieldwork encounter and shape its effects" (Nagar 2014: 85). Despite alignments with such "situated solidarities," I want to notice how I nonetheless wrote this book castelessly.

For example, I wrote about (Mahishya) middle-caste peasant communities who resisted land acquisition by the chief minister, who defined industrial jobs for farmers as development. The minister's rhetorical question "Should the son of a farmer always remain a farmer?" received the middle-caste peasant response of "No, but that is what I know how to do. Would Buddhadeb [then chief minister] start farming tomorrow?" (Da Costa 2010: 20). I heard the question and the subaltern response in terms of epistemic violence and class relations but ignored its caste politics. I nominally noted caste discrimination in Bengal politics, but I failed to study Brahminical histories of state and society in Bengal, or the Brahminical leadership of the political Left (cf. Chandra, Heierstad, and Nielsen 2016; Nielsen 2016; Sen 2018). I did not ask how *bhadralok* leadership and mostly middle-caste peasant leadership shaped social movement politics. Nor did I scrutinize my desire to study the cultural politics of rural Bengalis and its relation to material histories of Bengali Brahmins and our profound obsession with "culture" as a particularly significant medium of reproducing castelessness.

In all these ways, my research was inclined not to know the evidence of Brahminical domination of the political and social Left in Bengal, even though I was trying to understand political action. Looking back on these methodologies of solidarity research today, my casteless writing stares back at me. I can't help notice that what shaped my solidarity is not as separable from what trained me in savior methodology as I might like to think. I don't claim to entirely know how to pursue rewriting previous projects, but without tracing the specific historical and material grounds of our particular articulation of castelessness, how can we possibly situate our solidarity?

Conclusion

In this article, I traced historical and disciplinary formations to partially explain why savarna like me inhabit structures of writing castelessly, while harboring intentions of anti-caste solidarity. I characterized writing castelessly as obscuring savarna material relations to regional control over education, knowledge production, and power; studying caste but not toward dismantling it; reading, teaching, and reproducing Brahminical knowledge and rarely letting Dalit-Bahujan theory enter the disciplinary canon even about caste; and nurturing the conceit that savior research is clearly separable from solidarity research.

Making apparent the specifics of Brahminical supremacy in our training, writing, and research practices can reek of methodological individualism, navel-gazing, self-flagellation, or badge-of-honor exercises—all of which I have either been accused of or worried about. In closing then, I tentatively offer three implications of the argument above, to an intended audience of Brahmin and white feminists. First, a point about locating personal political purpose with thanks to the reviewer who suggested reading *Discrepant Dislocations* and to Professor Mary John for capturing twenty-five years ago what the shifting methodological proclivities in an increasingly violent political-economic conjuncture of the 1990s meant to savarna feminists. The only qualification I offer is that instead of recoiling, an ethical Brahmin feminist practice, including in North America, might refuse to disidentify with the seemingly uncouth Islamophobic Hindutva feminists and learn to notice our continuities with her, then and now.

The distance afforded by the seemingly polished decorum and respectability of savarna feminism is grounded in class and caste relations that reproduce Brahminical supremacy. Indeed, the affective need for this kind of spatial, subjective distancing is a hallmark of Brahminical castelessness. Making specific Brahminical histories apparent is intended to refuse this segregating distance. We must be able to see our proximity to seemingly distant Hindutva sisters when history makes our Brahminical socialist selves cringe from the lives that we compulsively reached out to in (earlier) methodological proclivities at least because Dalit-Bahujan, Adivasi, Muslim women do not get to distance themselves from the violence of Hindutva.

Second, this argument supports the Dalit-Bahujan demand that savarna foreground our historical-material caste positionality within public spheres such as writing and classrooms; teach, read, and write caste as a problem (not just a system); and learn to stop in our tracks despite compulsions of productivity for neoliberal universities. Whether disciplines like transnational feminism, education, or sociology normalize practicing naming our histories of caste power and holding oneself and community accountable in historical, material (not perfunctory) ways depends on those who squarely shape these fields. Can field-shaping savarna improve on popular caste-evading identity locators such as people of color, postcolonial, South Asian, or Hindu in their writing (Patel 2016)? Might savarna summon gratitude, reflection, and care when we are being held accountable rather than display Brahminical fragility and ignorance? Even as a Brahmin I have witnessed prominent savarna scholars relying on deflection, toxic silence, personal attacks, gaslighting, lying, and trolling while relying on powerful leaders and lawyers from Brahminical and white supremacist networks when critiqued and called to account.

Simultaneously, savarna might be busy packing Dalit-Bahujan writing into our award-winning syllabi. I have caught myself gushing over powerful Dalit-Bahujan theory, silently wondering how and when to use it in teaching or writing. Merely including Dalit-Bahujan voice/writing ultimately amounts to extractive savior altruism for Brahminical supremacy.

Instead, can we ask ourselves questions: Do we know what it means to be prepared, or worthy of teaching Dalit-Bahujan scholarship? Do we have the intellectual, political, ethical capacity to advise Dalit-Bahujan students? Without reading Dalit-Bahujan critique, I doubt I would even raise these questions. When it comes to canonical scholarship by savarna feminists, all feminists can be in solidarity with caste-oppressed feminists by reading and teaching against casteless writing, while being vigilant about not servicing old patterns of imperial white feminism's divide and rule.

Finally, knowledge questions are material questions: complicity talk can reproduce coloniality and casteism (Patel 2021). Moves to innocence are written into articles like this one, even if no innocence is structurally available. "Good" Brahmin feminists rise to the top because the material violence of the Brahminical state and its collusions with imperialism remain, notwithstanding the trials of racism and sexism. What everyday changes can savarna practice so that Dalit-Bahujan academic careers do not remain pervasively tied to extractive Brahminical patronage politics? Can we refuse the seduction of moves to innocence, wherein Brahmin feminists use institutional power to support, include, collect, and possess Dalit-Bahujan and Muslim faculty and students by publicly acknowledging Brahminical aggrandizement through these patronage structures?

White and Brahmin feminist academics and administrators have recently been following the lead of the Dalit feminist organization Equality Labs in making everyday and institutional caste discrimination legible and institutionalizing caste as a protected category.[2] South Asian and gender studies departments are also taking further concrete steps and making deeper curricular changes. Can all academic sectors make commitments like the Ethnic Studies Department (2021) of the University of California, San Diego, which committed to recruiting Dalit and Muslim faculty and students in nontokenizing and nonappropriating ways? Can savarna evacuate boards of journals and granting institutions and make room for Dalit Bahujan feminists?

By collectively, publicly noticing ways in which the structural (Brahminical state) is personal, methodologies of knowledge production and change might also work at chiseling power in specific, personal sites that are close to home, especially academia. Challenging savarna selves not to write castelessly can, I hope, move Brahmins to contribute toward broader sociopolitical reorganizations that denaturalize/demote our merit and institutionally refuse Brahminical monopoly over knowledge. Juxtaposed with situating our solidarities by collaboratively studying the lives and co-scripting the politics of others, thereby sometimes sanctifying extraction, this approach offers another methodology. Of course, the politics of reorganizing knowledge practices does not dismantle caste in society at large. It merely seeks to support the Dalit-Bahujan call that we at least begin with honest scrutiny of our specific caste histories as these shape the limits of our knowledge, power, and solidarity.

. . . .

Dia Da Costa is professor of social justice and international studies in education at the University of Alberta. She is the author of *Politicizing Creative Economy: Activism and a Hunger Called Theatre* (2016) and *Development Dramas: Reimagining Rural Political Action in Eastern India* (2009). Her current research focuses on the relationship of caste, multiple colonialisms, and the reproduction of Brahminical domination within transnational feminism, higher education, and development.

Notes
Original submission date: June 11, 2021
Date revision accepted: July 1, 2022

Over the last three years of writing this article, I have had always-generous conversations with Shaista Aziz Patel on the questions addressed in this article. I am also thankful for the careful feedback on earlier versions provided by Erin Morton, Terri Tomsky, and Alex Da Costa. Finally, I am grateful for the Social Sciences and Humanities Research Council grant, which enabled some of the research on which this article is based.
1   Deshpande (2013: 35) argues that the census of 1931 birthed "'castelessness' as a possibility and as a conscious political and social desire."
2   https://www.equalitylabs.org/press-releases?offset=1667931040865&reverse Paginate=true.

Works Cited
Alexander, M. Jacqui, and Chandra Talpade Mohanty, eds. 1997. Preface to *Feminist Genealogies, Colonial Legacies, Democratic Futures*, ix–xii. New York: Routledge.
Ambedkar, Bhimrao, and Valerian Rodrigues. 2002. *The Essential Writings of B. R. Ambedkar*. New Delhi: Oxford University Press.
Bandopadhyay, Sekhar. 2004. *Caste, Culture, and Hegemony: Social Dominance in Colonial Bengal*. New Delhi: Sage.
Beteille, Andre. 2001. "Race and Caste." *Hindu*, March 10.
Bhattacharya, Tithi. 2005. *The Sentinels of Culture: Class, Education, and the Colonial Intellectual in Bengal*. Delhi: Oxford University Press.
Chandra, Uday, Geir Heierstad, and Kenneth Bo Nielsen, eds. 2016. *The Politics of Caste in West Bengal*. New Delhi: Routledge.
Chatterjee, Piya, and Sunaina Maira. 2014. *The Imperial University: Academic Repression and Scholarly Dissent*. Minneapolis: University of Minnesota Press.

Da Costa, Dia. 2010. *Development Dramas: Reimagining Rural Political Action in Eastern India.* New Delhi: Routledge.

Da Costa, Dia. 2019. "The Perils and Possibilities of Creative Economy: A Conversation." Interview with Richa Nagar and Sarah Saddler. *Agitate!: An Anti-disciplinary Agitation.* https://agitatejournal.org/article/the-perils-and-possibilities-of-creative-economy-a-conversation/.

Da Costa, Dia. 2022. "Brahmanical Ignorance and Dominant Indian Feminism's Origin Stories." In *Routledge Handbook of Gender in South Asia,* edited by Leela Fernandes, 70–84. Abingdon, Oxon: Routledge.

Das, Veena, and J. P. S. Uberoi. 1971. "The Elementary Structure of Caste." *Contributions to Indian Sociology* 5, no. 1: 33–43.

Deshpande, Satish. 2003. *Contemporary India: A Sociological View.* New Delhi: Viking.

Deshpande, Satish. 2013. "Caste and Castelessness: Towards a Biography of the 'General Category.'" *Economic and Political Weekly* 48, no. 15: 32–39.

Dumont, Louis. 1966. *Homo Hierarchicus: The Caste System and its Implications.* Chicago: University of Chicago Press.

Ethnic Studies Department. 2021. "UC San Diego Ethnic Studies Statement against Caste and Caste-Based Discrimination." University of California, San Diego. https://ethnicstudies.ucsd.edu/news-and-events/index.html.

Government of India. 1980. *Report of the Backward Classes Commission, First Part, Volumes I and II.* New Delhi.

Guru, Gopal. 1993. "Dalit Movement in Mainstream Sociology." *Economic and Political Weekly* 28, no. 14: 570–73.

Guru, Gopal. 2002. "How Egalitarian Are the Social Sciences in India?" *Economic and Political Weekly* 37, no. 50: 5003–9.

Guru, Gopal, and Anuradha Chakravarty. 2005. "Who Are the Country's Poor?: Social Movement Politics and Dalit Poverty." In *Social Movements in India: Poverty, Power, and Politics,* edited by Raka Ray and Mary Fainsod Katzenstein, 135–60. Lanham, MD: Rowman and Littlefield.

Haraway, Donna. 1988. "Situated Knowledges: The Science Question in Feminism and the Privilege of Partial Perspective." *Feminist Studies* 14, no. 3: 575–99.

Hebbar, Nistula. 2013. "Another Social Construct." *Business Standard,* February 6. https://www.business-standard.com/article/beyond-business/another-social-construct-105072101042_1.html.

Heron, Barbara. 2007. *Desire for Development: Whiteness, Gender, and the Helping Imperative.* Waterloo, ON: Wilfred Laurier.

Jangam, Chinnaiah. 2015. "Politics of Identity and the Project of Writing History in Postcolonial India: A Dalit Critique." *Economic and Political Weekly* 50, no. 40: 63–70.

John, Mary E. 1996. *Discrepant Dislocations: Feminism, Theory, and Postcolonial Histories.* Berkeley: University of California Press.

Karunakaran, Valliammal. 2016. "The Dalit-Bahujan Guide to Understanding Caste in Hindu Scripture." *Medium,* July 13. https://medium.com/@Bahujan_Power/the-dalit-bahujan-guide-to-understanding-caste-in-hindu-scripture-417db027fce6.

Kaviraj. Sudipta. 1988. "A Critique of the Passive Revolution." *Economic and Political Weekly* 23, nos. 45–47: 2429–44.

Kumar, Radha. 1993. *The History of Doing: An Illustrated Account of Movements for Women's Rights and Feminism in India, 1800–1990.* London: Verso.

Madan, Amman. 2020. "Caste and Class in Higher Education Enrollments: Challenges of Conceptualising Social Inequality." *Economic and Political Weekly* 55, no. 30: 40–47.

Mandal, Dilip. 2020. "Oprah Winfrey Sent a Book on Caste to One Hundred US CEOs but Indians Still Won't Talk about It." *Print*, August 23. https://theprint.in /opinion/oprah-winfrey-wilkerson-caste-100-us-ceos-indians-wont-talk-about-it /487143.

Mills, Charles. 2007. "White Ignorance." In *Race and the Epistemologies of Ignorance*, edited by Shannon Sullivan and Nancy Tuana, 13–38. Albany: State University of New York Press.

Mohanty, Chandra Talpade. 1984. "Under Western Eyes: Feminist Scholarship and Colonial Discourses." *boundary 2* 12/13, no. 3, no. 1: 333–58.

Mohanty, Chandra Talpade. 1997. "Women Workers and Capitalist Scripts: Ideologies of Domination, Common Interests, and the Politics of Solidarity." In *Feminist Genealogies, Colonial Legacies, Democratic Futures*, edited by M. Jacqui Alexander and Chandra Talpade Mohanty, 3–29. New York: Routledge.

Mohanty, Chandra Talpade. 2003. "'Under Western Eyes': Feminist Solidarity through Anticapitalist Struggles." In *Feminism without Borders: Decolonizing Theory, Practicing Solidarity*, 221–51. Durham, NC: Duke University Press.

Nagar, Richa. 2014. "Reflexivity, Positionality, and Languages of Collaboration in Feminist Fieldwork." In *Muddying the Waters: Coauthoring Feminisms across Scholarship and Activism*, 81–104. Urbana-Champagne: University of Illinois Press.

Nagar, Richa, and Amanda Lock Swarr. 2010. "Introduction: Theorizing Transnational Feminist Praxis." In *Critical Transnational Feminist Praxis*, edited by Amanda Lock Swarr and Richa Nagar, 1–20. Albany: State University of New York Press.

Nielsen, Kenneth Bo. 2016. "The Politics of Caste and Class in Singur's Anti-land Acquisition Struggle." In Chandra, Heierstad, and Nielsen 2016: 125–46.

Patel, Shaista Aziz. 2016. "Complicating the Tale of 'Two Indians': Mapping 'South Asian' Complicity in White Settler Colonialism along the Axis of Caste and Anti-Blackness." *Theory & Event* 19, no. 4. https://muse.jhu.edu/article/633278.

Patel, Shaista Aziz. 2019. "Complicity Talk for Teaching/Writing about Palestine in North America." *Critical Ethnic Studies* (blog), June 3. http://www .criticalethnicstudiesjournal.org/blog/2019/6/3/complicity-talk-for -teachingwriting-about-palestine-in-north-american-academia.

Patel, Shaista Aziz. 2021. "Talking Complicity, Breathing Coloniality: Interrogating Settler-Centric Pedagogy of Teaching about White Settler Colonialism." *Journal of Curriculum and Pedagogy* 19, no. 3: 211–30.

Patel, Shaista Aziz, and Dia Da Costa. 2022. "'We Cannot Write about Complicity Together': Limits of Cross-Caste Collaborations in Western Academy." *Engaged Scholar Journal* 8, no. 2: 1–27.

Pawar, Urmila, and Meenakshi Moon. 2008. *We also Made History: Women in the Ambedkarite Movement*. New Delhi: Zubaan.

Ramdas, Anu. 2012a. "Casteless Academes, Name-Calling Dalits?" Pt. 1. *Savari*, October 4. http://www.dalitweb.org/?p=1021.

Ramdas, Anu. 2012b. "Casteless Academes, Name-Calling Dalits?" Pt. 2. *Savari*, October 6. http://www.dalitweb.org/?p=1045.

Rao, Anupama. 1999. "Understanding Sirasgaon: Notes towards Conceptualising the Role of Law, Caste, and Gender in a Case of 'Atrocity.'" In *Signposts: Gender Issues in Post-independence India*, edited by Rajeswari Sundar Rajan, 205–48. Delhi: Kali for Women.

Rawat, Ramnarayan S., and K. Satyanarayana. 2016. "Introduction: Dalit Studies: New Perspectives on Indian History and Society." In *Dalit Studies*, edited by Ramnarayan S. Rawat and K. Satyanarayana, 1–30. Durham, NC: Duke University Press.

Rege, Sharmila. 2000. "'Real Feminism' and Dalit Women: Scripts of Denial and Accusation." *Economic and Political Weekly* 35, no. 6: 492–95.

Sarkar, Sumit. 1997. *Writing Social History*. New Delhi: Oxford University Press.

Sen, Dwaipayan. 2018. *The Decline of the Caste Question: Jogendranath Mandal and the Defeat of Dalit Politics in Bengal*. Cambridge: Cambridge University Press.

Soundararajan, Thenmozhi. 2022. *The Trauma of Caste: A Dalit Feminist Meditation on Survivorship, Healing, and Abolition*. Ohlone Land: North Atlantic Books.

Soundararajan, Thenmozhi, and Sinthujan Varatharajah. 2015. "Caste Privilege 101: A Primer for the Privileged." *Aerogram*, February 10. https://theaerogram.com/author/thenmozhi-soundararajan-and-sinthujan-varatharajah/.

Spivak, Gayatri Chakravorty. 1999. *A Critique of Postcolonial Reason: Toward a History of the Vanishing Present*. Cambridge, MA: Harvard University Press.

Spivak, Gayatri Chakravorty. 2007. *Other Asias*. Malden, MA: Wiley-Blackwell.

Spivak, Gayatri Chakravorty, and Sarah Harasym. 1990. *The Postcolonial Critic: Interviews, Strategies, Dialogues*. New York: Routledge.

Subramanian, Ajantha. 2015. "Recovering Caste Privilege: The Politics of Meritocracy at the Indian Institutes of Technology." In *New Subaltern Politics: Reconceptualizing Hegemony and Resistance in Contemporary India*, edited by Alf Gunnar Nilsen and Srila Roy, 77–100. Oxford: Oxford University Press.

Teltumbde, Anand. 2010. *The Persistence of Caste: The Khairlanji Murders and India's Apartheid*. London: Zed Books.

Visweswaran, Kamala. 2011. *Un/Common Cultures: Racism and the Rearticulation of Cultural Difference*. New Delhi: Navayana.

Williams, Raymond. 1977. "Structures of Feeling." In *Marxism and Literature*. Oxford: Oxford University Press.

Sreerekha Sathi

....

When My Brown Got Colored
Living through/in the Times of White and Brahmanical
Supremacy

Abstract: This essay is a testimonial of the author's experiences, memories, and reflections about becoming a person/woman of color, discovering, and unearthing the meanings of racialization, white privilege, and white supremacy in the contemporary United States. The author gives voice to her new migrant experience as a Brown woman from India, positioning her reflections and learnings amidst the history and politics of colonialism and capitalist development, linking it to contemporary neoliberal academia in the United States. By sharing some events and encounters in her relatively short stint in Charlottesville, Virginia, between 2016 and 2019, the author reviews her attempts to critically analyze concepts like women of color, diversity, colorism, privilege, invisibility, and othering. The article further connects some of the author's experiences of racialization in view of the growing politics of casteism and Brahmanical supremacy in India, locating and reassessing herself in the midst of Trump's hardened propagation of white privilege in the United States and Modi's Hindutva, both emanating a politics rooted in racialization, exploitation, and marginalization of the other.

My Brown

I share here my experiences and thoughts on the process of knowing and becoming a "person/woman of color." It is partly an auto-ethnography, an outcome of my own desire to share and engage constructively with some of my experiences of living in Charlottesville, Virginia, in the United States. There is always more untold than told; however, this story told here involves my living as a privileged Brown and highly skilled salaried

MERIDIANS · feminism, race, transnationalism   22:2 October 2023
DOI: 10.1215/15366936-10637564 © 2023 Smith College

migrant, a teaching faculty member on an annually extended temporary contract in the University of Virginia's Global Studies program. Through an analysis of some select experiences of being part of a workplace that was mostly "white," in an institution inseparable from its legacies of slavery and white privilege, I offer this lived experience to help understand the discourse on colorism, racialization, diversity, white privilege, and white supremacy in Charlottesville, Virginia, extending and connecting it briefly to my own critical understanding of caste privilege and Brahmanical supremacy in India.

In the first part of the article, I talk about my experience of migrating and the initial perceptions in Charlottesville of the process of racialization as a migrant Brown woman. In the second part of the article, taking cues from a few works that helped me in my attempts to understand the history of racialization, slavery, and white supremacy, I discuss my understanding of the term *women of color* in relation to the processes of othering. In the third part, I talk about life in Charlottesville in the period 2016–19, my visit to the Thomas Jefferson home in Monticello in Virginia, my workplace—the Global Studies program at the University of Virginia (UVA), Charlottesville—and the events in Charlottesville in August 2017 in relation to the white supremacist rally and its aftermath. The fourth and the final part of the article briefly reflects my attempt to connect my critical thoughts on the meanings of caste privilege and Brahmanical supremacy in India to racialization, white privilege, and white supremacy. I try to understand how my situation pushed me toward a reassessment of myself as one from a privileged middle-class, middle-caste Hindu background in a Hindu Brahmanical society—moving as a Brown woman to the United States—a society rooted in white supremacy. For me, examining and educating myself through these experiences are illuminating for personal, epistemological, and political purposes.

The Move to the United States

In moving from Narendra Modi's India to Donald Trump's America, I found myself in the midst of a right-wing restoration. Moving to the United States meant experiencing the heightening of racialized right-wing politics, whereas in India I lived in the midst of growing casteism. While Trump was busy with blatant anti-immigrant, anti-Black, and anti-leftist moves (Painter 2017), lynching of Muslims and Dalits became an everyday story under the Modi government and the assertion of Hindu extremism in India.

Born and raised in South India, I lived life between my twenties and forties trying hard to see myself both as an activist and an academic. After teaching in a university in New Delhi for nine years, I moved to the United States in 2016 to take up an academic appointment at UVA in Charlottesville. It wasn't a well-thought-out decision to migrate to the United States. Within a year of moving, my newly adopted city became the site of the largest white supremacist rally in many years, giving a jolt to the new kind of racialization I experienced.

For some of us, there are those moments in our lives when we suddenly realize we have a color. Soon after I arrived in the United States, I had an interesting telephone conversation with my mother who has never lived away from her home in Kerala, India. I said, "They call me a woman of color," and she asked, "What does that mean?" As a feminist, I soon realized it is, of course, a new process, different from the process of becoming a woman, as the other. I had to learn that, in this process, anyone who is not "white" or overwhelmingly of a European-like phenotype becomes "colored"; a process that continuously and consistently contributes to the making of white, the color or not a color—not as an imitation but rather as the original source from which the other colors spring.

I have tried to understand the historical and political significance of the term *people/women of color*, how it came into use, and how it became normalized in a historical context as a way of contesting and resisting the negative racialization of particular groups of people. I learned more about the complex history of the term in the context of immigrants in the United States—of the double consciousness of the Black American and the connection between color, class, and labor. As M. Jacqui Alexander (2006: 269) put it: "We are not born women of color, we become women of color." For me, the phrase *people/women of color* represents the lack of a full person, an absence imposed by its invisibility. It also shows how the invention and construction of that absence is superimposed on the color of a person. The presence of a person comes to be defined through—or fundamentally reduced to—their color. Whiteness meanwhile is construed as the opposite of this reduction, to serve as the universal phenotype. Whiteness, and thus the white community, is created through its own negation—negation of white as a color, while its creation and negation simultaneously negate or diminish the reality of the other. Therefore, defining and naming the community of the other seem to have occurred through bringing them together, collapsing them into an undifferentiated mass as people of color.

Is othering interpreted through an absence, the lack of one or another positively associated phenotype trait? I understand that the power and privilege of whiteness were not simply created from what is assumed to be lacking; rather, they were created through a process of erasure of what existed before, as noted by many decolonial and first nation scholars (Balkenhol 2016; Smith, Tuck, and Yang 2019), and it is these historical processes of othering and erasure that met the needs of colonial capitalism, slavery, and development (Callinicos 1995). For the "colored" or those who become a person/woman of color, it's important to learn these historical processes that are part of the history of colonialism and slavery.

In a world of white supremacy, with its different origins, specifically in the historical context of the United States, I came to understand that these other colors are not merely alterations but can also be constructed as "aboriginal" types that are "naturally" inherited, shaping the otherness. I had much to learn about the invention of "whiteness" through the settler colonial context (Dunbar-Ortiz 2015) and through capitalist slavery (Williams 1994), which in the United States became associated with the one-drop rule that underscores white supremacy and eugenics, especially in the southern states, with claims that separate Black, Brown, yellow, and white bloods exist (Du Bois 1998). I also became aware how white supremacy made people of "Asian," "mixed," or any other background fit into the one-drop rule—which has no biological or scientific basis—and thus created a basis for (a heightened logic of) racism. In other words, I began to understand how, over the course of recent human history, whiteness (and what are seen as common European phenotypical features) became the canvas and the original art form, while other colors (and phenotypical features that are seen as straying from European norms, played out differently in different contexts) were constructed as secondary alterations, the negatively racialized others. Importantly, I began to see clearly how ideologically and politically white supremacy functions as a norm of world order and how it is built—as white privilege—into the institutions, laws, and policies of the global system.

Knowing/Reading Color/Race

Being familiar with feminist literature on heteronormative sex/gender systems and capitalist patriarchy, life in the United States motivated me to learn more about racialization and its relationship with patriarchy, colonialism, and white supremacy. The work of James Baldwin has inspired those who were part of the struggle against racism in the United States from the 1960s onward. His writings helped me bridge the personal and the political through a deeper understanding of race, class, sexuality, and masculinity, within the complexity of these relationships in the context of U.S. imperialism. As a migrant, his experience of the cultivated blindness and delusion around color and whiteness in America resonated with me, and I instantly recognized his description of white privilege and how it "attacked one's sense of one's own reality" (Baldwin [1962] 1993: 18). Baldwin reminded me that the value placed on the color of skin everywhere in white America is a political reality, not just a personal or human one (89–90). Further, his position that "white Americans find it as difficult as white people elsewhere do to divest themselves of the notion that they are in possession of some intrinsic value that black people need or want" (131) made me aware of the near impossibility of the privileged white to see themselves as the other.

Reading the history of the invention of race and the material base of white privilege helped me learn the importance of knowing race as a myth or fallacy of race (Montagu 1997), the problematic interpretations of the relationship between race, whiteness, and racial inequality, and how the invention of race itself has allowed societies to restrict the scope of equality along racial lines (Malik 1996); how the politics of white supremacy informs whiteness as it exists in the United States as a settler colonial society (Mills 1997); and how the processes of racialization need to be seen through a deep, historically informed understanding of capitalism and the rise of imperialism and neoliberalism (Horne 2018; Reed 2013). In addition, I recognized how the invention of race—like the invention of the tribe—led to further inventing, discovering, and colonizing through control, in which the "colored" were put into 'tribes'/colonies and were given the appearance of monolithic entities in need of enlightenment and civilization (Mamdani 1996).

Feminist theorists have explored how women's oppression historically has been constructed through a heteronormative sex/gender system which along with its relationship with capitalism, colonialism, and white supremacy, contributes to local patriarchies (Rubin 1975; Ebert 1996; Mies 1986). As a feminist scholar who has spent most of my life in the Global South, I am interested in the debates in feminist epistemologies on binary thinking in the context of the North-South debate, issues of representation, and the process of othering. I recognize and acknowledge the importance of the relevance of these debates in the individual and community spaces, while I also see the need to go further to connect the knowledge created from these debates to larger structural goals for change.

On the politics of othering and the binary relationship between the privileged and the oppressed, feminist theorists like Linda Alcoff (1991) support the position of a meaningful silence, a retreat and receptive listening by the privileged white community, while also proposing a position of speaking to/with instead of speaking for/about the other. Moving forward from this position, a meaningful silence of the privileged self seems highly problematic. Listening and speaking here has to be a position taken depending on the context in relation to whom you are speaking to or who the audience is. Silence can not be a meaningful position while speaking to the privileged and vice versa. I see as extremely important an attempt to address white privilege by un/learning from history, acknowledging white privilege; joining the struggle to fight white privilege through a dialogue within the white community.

I see herein an attempt to address white privilege by un/learning from history and joining the struggle to fight white privilege; through a dialogue within the white community, a process of seeing, learning from, listening to, and acknowledging white privilege, as extremely important (Harding 1993; Case 2012).

I also appreciate the fact that there are members of the privileged white community, though very few, who consider it their primary struggle to challenge the ideology of white supremacy and its politics of conquest, discovery, and control, as racialized communities should not be expected to fight racialization and white privilege alone.

The irony of becoming "colored" is that you do not initially see whiteness in the way you are expected to see it. However, the experience of becoming "colored" is a shifting terrain, moving between feelings of invisibility, objectification, hypervisibility, or exoticization of yourself. In situations of power struggles, all these become unnerving and sometimes unbearable, as Black feminist thinkers have described (Collins 2000; hooks 1995). I have found these debates on issues of invisibility and hypervisibility very meaningful, especially to explore the multiple locations of invisibility and the link of invisibility to hypervisibility and to otherness. Life in Charlottesville was marked by the external imposition of invisibility, either my own or that of anyone who isn't white, which came very close to the absence or denial of the full person and the occasional hypervisibility, a racially sexualized nature or otherwise. However, addressing this led to the repetitive narrative, that of a commonly assumed response of the so-called race in me, the Brown, which would be angry and desperate, with a hidden deep desire to become one with the white. I have been curious about the debates on the hidden desire to be white—as discussed from Frantz Fanon to bell hooks (1995)—as a yearning in the nonwhite/Black world's imagination. For me, it has always been important to reveal that the imposed invisibility and hypervisibility did not seem to contribute toward any deep or hidden desire in me, and maybe among the other "colored" too, toward becoming white.

Fanon's ([1952] 2008) critical reading of whiteness and his critical interpretation of the self, its subjectivity, and its heightened forms of individualism helped me see how talking of color or experience was shaped to some extent by politics around identity and the individualization process (Fanon [1953] 2004). However, the focus here was on the individual's subjective struggle and the search for the color of one's soul in terms of how the white man would see it. On the one hand, this opens space for the possibility of acknowledging that there is a segment among the other who may not have the slightest desire to be white; it also reminds us that the absence of a desire—conscious or unconscious—to be white does not necessarily come from anger, hate, or despair.

Of course, my experience as a new migrant with a professional position encountering white supremacy doesn't reflect the experience of the working-class Black community's having to live or coexist in a former slave-owning society, nor does it mirror the experience of Indigenous peoples existing in a settler state that dispossessed and murdered their ancestors. I understand the differences in Black and "colored" histories and how these differences provide distinct context to these communities for theorizing racialization and white supremacy. Much of the focus in research on whiteness and white privilege has been toward a deep comprehension of the day-to-day reproduction of whiteness, acknowledging its intentional blindness and its promotion. As Gloria Wekker (2016: 172) describes in the Dutch context, understanding white privilege and whiteness is a process of recognizing and learning the history of "white innocence" founded on an intentional ignorance with its aggressive rejection of the possibilities of knowing. It is, however, also a process of reflecting on white privilege as a symptom, an outcome of the economic and political power and the ideological and cultural landscapes created through it. Further, for me, more than the focus on the individual and the cultural links, a focus on white privilege needs to help contribute to a structural analysis of the roots of racialization and its birth thorough colonial capitalism.

The new experience of racialization brought an unfamiliar level of anger and disgust in me, which perhaps emerged from my inability—the inability of the "colored" to identify and accept the inferiority in one's color. I was born in the 1970s. Much was written in the 1960s and 1970s about the processes of racialization in the mind and language of the colonized. Colonialism had widely ended, at least in its formal political definition, and the discourse on understanding neocolonialism and decolonization contributed to a more thoughtful reading of the politics of race and white privilege. Today I understand white privilege as a dynamic of white supremacy; in most of the world, postcolonial societies are still ruled by people who are invested in global white supremacy, which represses through institutional and cultural forms as the norm of the global capitalist order. This complex location brings me closer to Albert Memmi's ([1965] 1991) conceptual subcategory of the colonial—the colonial who gives up his or her privileges out of choice but still remains a colonizer. Memmi's colonizer/colonized framework helps reflect on the complexity of these binaries and the diverse histories and processes of the colonial and white privilege. A love for the colonized is combined with a pride for the white legacy. Further, Memmi's reflections on the feelings of self-hate and shame among the colonized of the 1960s helped me better understand the self-hate produced through racism/casteism and its impact on the subjectivities of the oppressed.

New migrants are often told that they suffer from a cultural shock. This made me wonder what exactly was cultural about the space in which I found myself. Limitations of language or cultural anguish are used to explain much of the inability of a new migrant to adjust to the developed world. In its simplest form, the elucidation of what is cultural is interpreted within the privileges of the developed world. For me, the local lifeworld in this modernizing capitalist empire of the developed felt mostly as one that was devoid of any culture of its own—an absence of variety or diversity along with an abundance of materiality, conformity, and uniformity. In Charlottesville, I experienced the emptiness of a small white town, a culture borrowed through the processes of colonialism and closely tied to the neoliberal market. However, I understand that this process is not limited to Charlottesville or the Global North; the culture of the local in the Global South is also changing radically with the invasion of neoliberal global capital and the culture that it imposes.

Historically, European colonialists have been successful in producing non-European Black and Brown men and women who fully internalized

European norms and values (Kiernan 1969). For this section of the contemporary non-European elite, not recognizing colorism and racialization
along with the history of racism, slavery, and global capitalism may be an
advantage. Many among the powerful elite in postcolonial countries seem
content to apply colonial standards and policies to local communities in
their home countries. The minds of the elite in postcolonial countries such
as India are recolonized and still enslaved (deSouza 2017). More than the
recolonization of the enslaved minds, most elites in the Global South are
content to enjoy the benefits or profits of supporting such recolonization
through the contemporary neoliberal capitalist system. A better understanding of this recolonization politics has enabled me to learn about and
reflect on the complexities of my racialization in the United States. I am
able to see a caste Hindu becoming Brown in a town like Charlottesville,
and the importance of talking of both racist and casteist practices together
in contemporary times. The privileged among the colonized, the elite
among the Brown and Black communities have mostly invested in global
white supremacy, the norm of global capitalist social order. Personally, I do
separate myself from this colonial elite among the colonized as someone
whose entry into the elite or privileged space is new and limited to my
transition from a student to a skilled immigrant in the Global North.
However, this current position also makes it important for me to face the
challenges produced by white and Brahmanical supremacy and privilege
within Western academia both epistemologically and politically. Here I am
specifically thinking of the privileged who collaborated with the colonial
capitalists for profit, in the world of development or in business, government, the arts, or other fields.

Life in Charlottesville, 2016–2019

I did not know much about Virginia's role in the history of American slavery, with Richmond serving as the capital of the treasonous Confederate
states during the American Civil War (1861–65). I knew nothing about the
history of the University of Virginia and its buildings, which were constructed by chattel slave labor. I had taken a decision to move out of Delhi
in India, and it wasn't important where I was relocating to. So I packed two
suitcases and left, and in the next two to three years, I tried to learn about
the history of UVA as part of the larger history of Charlottesville in the
context of capitalist slavery, racism, gentrification, segregation, and
much more.

Life in Charlottesville was shaped by how I experienced the lifeworld as a highly skilled new migrant entering a particular community. I came with my own understanding and experiences, as a first-generation migrant, limited and skewed in some ways but deeper in others. I had to learn how people are socialized to see things through the racialized order of whiteness, Blackness, and other identities and, in so doing, work to see experiences beyond these monolithic existences and representations. Beyond the status quo understanding, I wanted to learn from the community, how they speak of themselves, within and beyond their own identity and community. Though there would be many attempts to understand the power hierarchies, privileges, and oppression within specific white and Black communities in Charlottesville, in reality, any conversation on racism got stuck on identifying a specific community as Black or white. It seldom went into the deeper politics of racialization. I saw this as a reflection of the binary thinking, processes of othering, and the silence or retreat of the privileged. In many ways I could see how a simplified, straightforward, and dichotomous relationship between racialized communities exists, reflecting the artificial barriers that have been created to separate people from one another (Balibar 1991) and the real-life experiences that occur through a spatial concept of geographical borders (Agnew 2009)—a separation that helps regenerate Black and white communities in Charlottesville.

In 2016 I visited Thomas Jefferson's home at Monticello just outside Charlottesville. It has a relatively new so-called slavery tour. The tour starts at the servants' dwelling (built circa 1793–1830, reconstructed in 2014) for the enslaved Hemmings family (the enslaved woman Sally Hemmings who was raped, had given birth to children by Thomas Jefferson). At the entrance of the dwelling is a placard entitled "Not so bad?" Further on, the note reads as follows: "John and Priscilla Hemmings lived in a cabin similar to—or even better than—the dwellings of the many poorer free whites. . . . " These were words of perhaps both guilt and arrogance. Although the walking tour did serve as a learning process, the placard at the entrance along with the young white lady who gave the tour, with her interpretations of the slave family life, filled me with feelings of sadness, anger, and a sense of humiliation. In response to a question from the audience on the family life of the slaves, the tour guide explained that the selling and buying of slaves were done taking into consideration that slave families should be kept together. Walking with the all-white crowd of tourists, I couldn't help but be furious at myself that I paid or had to pay the

Monticello estate to do a slavery walk and put myself through this experience. As far as I could see, I was the only nonwhite person in a crowd of
around sixty people. Suddenly, at the end of the slavery walk, an older
white woman approached me and said, "I am so sorry!" and walked away,
adding another dramatic and bizarre moment to the slavery walk.

Leaving India, I was already familiar with the proto fascism of its prime
minister Narendra Modi and his Hindu right-wing party, Bharatiya Janata
Party (BJP), with its various tendencies. Now I also became familiar with
contemporary American politics, with Trump coming to power. Often in
the mornings, as I woke up in Charlottesville, I would wonder, "who said
that, was it Trump or Modi?" However, the events of August 2017 made me
see Charlottesville and the United States more clearly. That month, amid
a controversy about the removal of Confederate statues, white supremacists from all over the country organized a "Unite the Right Rally" in
Charlottesville, instilling terror and inciting violence in the Black and
other negatively racialized communities, leaving three dead (one activist
and two state troopers) and many injured (Hart and Danner 2017). Hundreds of armed white supremacists marched through the streets of Charlottesville, violently abusing and attacking those who resisted their presence. That fatal evening, the white supremacist James Alex Fields Jr.
deliberately rammed his car into a crowd of protestors, killing Heather
Heyer and injuring many others. Heyer, a thirty-two-year-old woman, was
on the street to protest the white supremacist presence in her town.

Earlier, on July 8, 2017, I had joined hundreds of counter-protesters
against a rally of around fifty Ku Klux Klan (KKK) members. The KKK was
upset about the city's plan to remove a statue of the Confederate general
Robert E. Lee from a park—one among many, many Confederate statues in
Virginia (Spencer and Stevens 2017). I lived close to the street where the
controversial statue of Lee was located. Weeks before the rally in August,
activists cautioned people in the town to prepare themselves in peaceful
but powerful resistance. I had convinced myself that nothing very volatile
could happen in this university town. But it did. On the evening of August
11, neo-Nazis marched not only through the streets but also through the
corridors of the rotunda of UVA. While students from multiple backgrounds hid for safety, the alt-right marchers shouted, "Jews will not
replace us." A small section of students stood face to face with them,
bravely and peacefully, showing powerful resistance. I had just returned
from my summer break in India. The day before, I was in a local flight from

Charlotte to Charlottesville surrounded by many with white pride T-shirts coming to Charlottesville to join the Nazi rally. While helicopters circled all night, one of my neighbors left milk, bread, and some snacks at my door-step with a note saying it isn't safe to go out. That evening, holding hands with a few of my friends, I stood near the site on the roadside where Heyer was murdered.

The happenings of August 11–12 in Charlottesville have been extensively covered. In its aftermath, I attended meetings, memorials, and events devoted to sharing, thinking together, and healing from the aftereffects of that night. There were two starkly different versions of the events of August 11–12. In the immediate aftermath of August 11–12, in contrast to liberal-minded white people saying, "This town wasn't like this, it was never like this," the Black version ran: "There isn't much new about all of this, if you know the history of this town. Only maybe the intensity of what happened now is new." Like many others, I found that whenever I was in a public space, my Brown became suddenly visible in the eyes of white people and was greeted with a smile. That was new and, of course, it was encouraging to have that expression of sympathy and recognition; it lasted for about two weeks, before things returned to normal. Just two months after the pro-Trump Nazi/Klan/alt-right rally in Charlottesville, to my disbelief, a report was published in the *Washington Post*, listing Charlottesville among the top twenty-five happiest towns in the United States (Hui 2017). The town's real estate market soon stabilized for the positively racialized middle strata and wealthy of Charlottesville. The return to normalcy was greeted with enthusiastic relief. Maybe such incidents do little to alter history.

Every history told, every institution, every public space in Charlottesville has beneath it a legacy of slavery and segregation. Yet the history of post–Civil War Vinegar Hill (Field Studio 2015), once a flourishing Black community, and its transformation into contemporary Charlottesville, with the ever-growing gentrification of the Black community, is still mostly absent from any inquiry into race, racism, and slavery in the history of Virginia and the United States. What is present and visible is the narrative of the colorless white. The white Charlottesville constantly asks you to look at the bright side of this beautiful, tree-lined, quiet town with its moun-tainous landscape, its long chain of nice restaurants and southern archi-tecture. Yet one struggles not to see what is hidden and made invisible. In January 2018 the city elected Nikuyah Walker, its first Black woman mayor. The election of Walker was also a response by the liberal members of the community to the events of August 2017. While the election of Walker set the tone for a progressive step forward, the cloak of invisibility thrown over the active presence of Black women and men in the leadership of resistance remained, except in a few spaces like the Jefferson School of African American Heritage Centre. These resonances were clear if you listened to the Black community in town. For them, there is still a need for collective strength to move forward, learn from the trauma, and seek lessons of tolerance and resistance for the future.

In any public space in Charlottesville, whom you happen to be with makes a big difference. Whether you are with a white man or a white woman, a lesbian/queer/trans white person, a lesbian/queer/trans Black person, another Brown man or Brown woman, a Black man or a Black woman will often result in a different experience. From the waiters at the restaurants who look right through you, to the dogs that bark only at you, the random white people who say how beautiful you look in that Indian dress, the white man who whispers to your white friend "you are with a colorful woman today," followed by a laugh, or some of your white students who feel entitled to get good grades from you—for me, Charlottesville breathed racism. Except of course for a few close friends and the beautiful Rivanna River trail, it was easy to feel isolated. It can sometimes be a paranoia similar to Baldwin's ([1962] 1993: 95) experiencing the inability to distinguish "a real from a fancied injury," in which one believes something happens just as a result of one's color even when that might not be the case.

It is a constant struggle to resist a surface-level reaction, trying instead to clear one's head and consider the deeper structural processes at work. My South Asian friends who were born and brought up in the United States sometimes do not see it the same way; they seem to have become accustomed to it. Was I being paranoid? Perhaps it is real, but you see it only when you are new. Or you could be blinded by the familiar if you are an insider (Bolak 1996). However, it's undeniable that Charlottesville is visibly segregated in racial and class terms. I could try imagining the history of the blood that was spilled in these streets, the segregation endured by the many marginalized, the social apartheid for the poor, the transgendered, and the homeless. I strongly sensed its heavy burden when I spoke to the ordinary working-class people or the activists based there, especially those from the Black community, or through the Black homeless men sitting in the streets of its downtown mall, speaking loudly to themselves.

In the aftermath of August 2017, every event, every memorial I attended affected me deeply. I felt the need to distance myself and found it easier to focus on a primary struggle, connecting with those who have had similar experiences. I do not come from the Black poor or the white poor in Charlottesville, I did not feel I could represent its middle class or elite, or even its low-waged taxi drivers who are often migrants from distant countries. However, I could relate with the particular experiences of the marginalized, the negatively racialized, migrant, and working-class people in Charlottesville and connect these to larger struggles commensurate with experiences from my world.

Many conversations in the aftermath of August 2017, including among UVA students (usually from middle- and upper-strata backgrounds) and activists, focused on white people in Charlottesville, thinking together about how to have a conversation with the white community about white supremacy and racialization, or how to address gentrification in the town. Charlottesville soon became a focal point in political debates nationwide. The town drew much attention as offers of support and solidarity poured in. While this led to some community support projects, inside UVA it led to massively funded projects like its Democracy Initiative or Democracy Labs. While some university students became the voice of the community and were present everywhere, few among the university faculty were also visibly present or vocal in responding to the events of August 2017. Of those who were present, many struggled with the boundaries between their own career interests and their (contradictory) social and political commitment. With millions of dollars flowing into these projects, the relationship between the Charlottesville community and the university and its experiments in democracy would understandably be a complex one to negotiate.

I had been teaching a course on global development in a global studies program, as the only nonwhite faculty at the time, to a majority-white student cohort at UVA, many of whom were from wealthy or middle-class backgrounds. I was constantly reminded by my colleagues of the value of my presence as the only woman of color in the program. For me, it was a gradual learning process to equip myself through my everyday lessons at work, dealing with the white innocence of my colleagues. In my experience, resisting white innocence and challenging white privilege are more difficult with those members of academia who teach the very same subjects like racism or feminist politics in the classroom. During my own experience of teaching, I found my identity often limited to being a woman of color and a new migrant, perhaps ticking the box for the program. For the few students who were from a background similar to mine, or those who were interested in studying India or South Asia, it meant bringing familiar and important issues like caste or patriarchy to the classroom. Since most Brown students in this context would also be from privileged backgrounds, this entailed addressing or challenging caste/class privilege in the classroom, which is extremely relevant in relation to critical theories of development and decolonization. The discipline has witnessed a shift from "international" to "global," and a fundamental challenge in the discipline has been combining the discourse on decolonizing academia at the same time that academic institutions continue to offer international development studies as a career option (Rutazibwa 2019: 158). These debates with their complexity and inherent contradictions help students challenge the myths around development and critically and pedagogically engage with coloniality and Eurocentrism, while shifting the focus from seeing the Global North as a permanent location of good life and solutions (174).

For me, a deeper analysis of the relationship between white privilege, capitalism, and development is reflected in my classroom discussions around student loans, housing loan mortgages, access to health insurance, and other problems facing the vast majority of working people in the contemporary United States. It is imperative for us to rethink especially in the contemporary times what it means to see the United States as a developed country. Many students at UVA come from families in the greater Washington, DC, area, with parents involved in the U.S. imperial state and its numerous apparatuses, intervening constantly around the world. This impacts their worldview. For me, it was easy to connect and contrast the developed and rich United States to a country like India where millions of people lack education or access to basic health care. It helped me open up a space toward a more radical and critical approach in the classroom, unraveling the meaning of development in the context of contemporary United States and its continuing imperial hegemonic power in shaping life in many Global South countries while abusing its own internal poor and marginalized.

It Is a Labyrinth

When I received my first invitation at the university to attend a reception for diverse faculty, I was perplexed. It showed genuine ignorance and newness on my part that I had to find out if I was part of the diverse and if white people would be there too. It took time for me to understand that the diversity reception or diversity week serves a clear purpose in a majority white space. Diversity, like color, is not white, and for many spaces in social and institutional contexts, addressing racial politics is possible only through holding diversity events with a variety of "colored" people. For the "colored," when a place is not diverse, it is like "walking into a sea of whiteness" (Ahmed 2012: 35).

Experiences of racialization in the workplace are subtle and complex, and one is constantly negotiating within the limitations of a safe space between narcissism and the liberal disguise (Goldberg 2009). In my experience, being recognized as part of the diverse community is loaded with patterns of patronization and paternalism that are sometimes difficult to uncover. This has been true even in feminist spaces where white women in academia who discuss unlearning racism could nevertheless be patronizing and condescending (hooks 1984). Furthermore, this recognition and level of consideration demands, in return, unlimited amounts of gratitude (Ghorashi 2014) for being there. There is a need to constantly tell you just how amazing you are (even though you are different) or that your presence is so needed because of who you are (not white). hooks (1984: 12) sees this is an inevitable outcome of being focused on individual attitudes rather than addressing racism in a historical and political context.

This process of being and becoming just exactly what you are expected to be, nothing more, nothing less, makes one vulnerable and cautious. It is also an outcome of the heightened levels of individualism, insecurity, and paranoia within the highly competitive and careerist atmosphere of U.S. academia, which encompasses racialization and works in complex ways between different genders, classes, and nationalities. For institutions like UVA, this paranoia in response to attempts at a deeper conversation on diversity projects and their meaningful implementation reflects the fear that the so-called historical pride and legacy of the institution is being challenged. When you are overwhelmed by good liberal white people with good intentions in good institutions, you tend to lose or forget your own story and doubt your own ability to understand life and the world around you. It is a labyrinth.

Diversity projects are intended to aesthetically erase racism. However, in the process of institutionalizing diversity, in some sense, your simply being there is enough in itself (Ahmed 2012: 22). In implementing projects on diversity, you mostly have to work in the absence of much support for that goal. Sara Ahmed describes the effort to make diversity meaningful in institutions as like "banging your head against a brick wall" (27). Nevertheless, diversity or a focus on differences seems to be seen as a more attractive option than equality; it creates an illusion of equality, though with no historical or material base (Ebert 1996). The possibility of practicing diversity in the absence of decolonizing practices within institutions is not talked about. Thus diversity projects can steer one away from equality and justice while remaining part of the diverse. For Ahmed (2012: 176), "to inhabit a category of privilege is to not come up against the category." What is invisible to the white in a diversity project is visible to the "colored," and vice versa. Are diversity projects within institutions making the "colored" see themselves as lesser beings and then creating a common space for all lesser beings to come together? Diversity projects, much like multiculturalism, are used by liberals to mask racialized social relations, protecting the status quo. Diversity is where the real color of your skin counts, and yet not all diverse people fit in there. As far as the elite-run, majority-white institutions are concerned, in the long run, if you fit in, your smiling face will appear everywhere—in brochures, websites, and the like. But in order to reach that point, you need to be disciplined and trained, made aware of your worth and your place.

The Caste of My Brown and the Exits

Feminist epistemologies argue that it's essential for a feminist subject to be reflexive in order to be free from all binary thinking and oppositional categories (Ramazanoglu and Holland 2002: 88) and to critically locate one's self in a position of strong objectivity (Harding 1993). I have learned, from the complexity around feminist debates on representation, how difficult it is for the privileged to recognize and acknowledge their power and privilege and to put reflexivity into practice (Ramazanoglu and Holland 2002: 119). This has inspired me to attempt a deeper political and epistemological reading of myself, learning from the challenges through a critical reading of my experiences, locating myself in this discourse into the ethic of personal accountability, acknowledging and recognizing myself within the politics of caste. While conceptions of color and phenotype, and colorism, do exist in India, more structurally prevalent are dynamics around caste. A deeper perception of the complexities of colorism and racialization has helped me reflect on my understanding and engagement with the increasing influence of Brahmanical supremacy, Brahmanical patriarchy (Chakraborty 2018), and the caste regime in both contemporary India and the United States. Similar to white supremacy, Brahmanical supremacy as an idea and as politics functions as a norm, supporting caste privilege by influencing societal norms and state institutions, through laws and policies in India. It represents a way of life leading to the hegemony of a Hindu caste-based regime, supporting the creation of a Hindu nation through Hindutva, a political ideology to propagate an extreme version of Hindu nationalism.

The rise to power of the right wing in India, which supports the ideology of Hindutva, an extreme version of Hindu nationalism, has seen a large-scale increase in lynchings and police brutality against Muslims and Dalits, and in incidences of killings associated with inter-caste marriages (wrongly termed *honour killings*) (Grewal 2013) or of love jihad (Sarkar 2018). Recently, India has also witnessed a redefining of its constitution through an amendment to the Citizenship Act, which has been followed by brutal organized violence against dissenting voices. In contemporary times, there has been a widespread growth among the South Asian diaspora of Hindu nationalism and support for the politics of Hindutva in India. The BJP-led government in India has extensive support from the non-resident Indian (NRI)/South Asian community abroad. In the past few decades, the NRI community in parts of the United States, UK, and Europe has played an important role, financially and culturally supporting the growth of the Indian right wing in India and the rest of the world. In the same period, Hindu extremist groups like the Rashtriya Swayamsevak Sangh have been promoting the ideology of Hindutva, using the power and sentiments of dominant cultures, traditions, and nostalgia and interpreting and linking these with the virtues of a spiritual orientation against the Western materialist world. Decolonization thoughts in recent times have been more easily (mis)used in the Indian context, replacing colonialism with Hindu nationalism (Sharma 2019) to support the right-wing agenda. There is also growing investment in research within social science academia especially in the Global North, in the name of Hindu ecology, Hindu economy, and so on. Multiple academic approaches to decolonization within ecofeminist and other ecological and climate movements are being appropriated, misinterpreted, and infiltrated by Hindu right-wing ideology. Along with securing large-scale funding to support themselves, these Hindu extremist organizations have successfully propagated the need for a process called re-Hinduization (Bose 2008; Jaffrelot and Therwath 2007). The solidarity expressed between Modi, Trump, and the NRI community in their enthusiastic support for a right-wing alliance was seen in the Howdy Modi event in the United States in 2019 and the Namaste Trump event in India in 2020.

Indeed, there is a similarity in the erasure or silencing of the history of colonialism and slavery in the Western world to the erasure of the history of caste atrocities under Brahmanical supremacy and Hindutva rule in India. Like the ethnically cleansed Indigenous population in the United States, Dalits (the casteless untouchables of Hinduism) were among the original inhabitants of the country (Joseph 2018) whose history of continuing economic, social, and political oppression also has been erased. For thinkers like B. R. Ambedkar (1916), who contributed immensely to resisting casteism and Brahmanical supremacy, caste is like "an artificial chopping of the population into fixed and definite units, each one prevented from fusing into another through the custom of endogamy." Caste Hindus imposed casteism on people who historically have been an integral part of their lives and communities, leading to centuries-long discrimination, oppression, torture, and lynching. Sadly, knowledge production both in the Western and Indian academia on the ideology and practice of caste has been problematic and limited.

Similar to Baldwin's thoughts on race, Ambedkar saw caste and untouchability imposed by Hindu religion as a confiscation of the human persona. Ambedkar believed that Brahmanism created, enclosed, and fortified communities, imposing a caste order, wanting Indians to believe that caste is produced and reproduced through these communities. There is a history of international solidarity between Black movements and Dalit movements, and conversations by scholars like W. E. B. Du Bois discussing the caste system in the context of racism. However, for Ambedkar, Europeans wrongly emphasized the role of color in caste. He argued that caste is fundamentally linked to, and has evolved through, class, division of labor on the basis of occupation, and enforced endogamy, all of which define a Hindu social order (Ambedkar 1916, 1979: 18–22).

It is particularly important to point out that, ironically, while the Indian/ South Asian diaspora in the United States experiences racism and may even resist it, few have tried to recognize and unlearn their own caste practices and privileges that they transplanted from India. It's a historical reality that

India's migrant Hindu community spread casteism wherever they went. There is a vital need to educate students from the Indian diaspora on casteism, so that they can consciously connect to the painful history of racism in the United States. One of the challenges is to remind them that the dynamics of racism and colorism go beyond North America and to show the similarities between the struggle against racialization and white privilege and fighting casteism. This is further linked to the realization and acceptance that people from the Global South have their own role in reproducing racialization, anti-Blackness, and anti-Dalitness. Such racism is manifest, for instance, in frequent violent assaults on people of African descent in many Indian/South Asian societies (Adibe 2017), which is best understood through what Sureshi M. Jayawardene (2016) calls a history of "racialized casteism," linking race, caste, and colorism.

Stories of South Asians migrating to the United States are multiple, plural, unfinished, and ongoing. Many who migrated earlier were privileged, representing the landowning, upper strata of Indian society. There are many experiences and stories of the struggles that their parents went through as first-generation migrants. However, these stories tend to lack a critical analysis of their own privileges both in India and in the United States. While the fear of migrants has grown in the United States, it has also provoked questions around understanding colonialism, slavery, and imperialism, and the response "we are here because you were there" (Mehta 2019). Recent research shows increasing caste-based discrimination and caste violence among South Asians in the United States (Equality Lab n.d.; Public Radio International n.d.). In India Hindu nationalists seek to impose a rigid caste system, while denying it even exists, and in the Western world their leaders present Hinduism as a pure spiritual universal religion reflected in symbolic representations such as yoga and vegetarianism.

Over the past decade, I have seen many in my middle-caste/class family who were leftist, progressive, or secular becoming Islamophobic and supporting the Hindu right wing in India. This has led to heated arguments and conflicts within the family. When my ties with my family fell apart for political reasons, I tried to seek the support of those outside my family and community, especially among my Dalit activist friends. An interesting and tough lesson for me during this process was that it was suffocating and frustrating for them to hear of my struggles. It reminded me that I had also found it suffocating to be forced to listen to progressive white members of the Charlottesville community talking of the dangers and the threats they had to face in fighting white supremacy. It helped me understand why the Dalit community does not want to hear caste Hindus sharing their stories about fighting casteism, demanding a larger share of recognition and appreciation in the name of experiencing the pain and price paid for resistance.

It's a Journey
Ethical and political questions around the hierarchy and privileges of the upper/middle-caste and upper/middle-class Brown people and the denial of the centrality of the oppressive caste system in Indian society are yet to be reckoned with by the majority of privileged Brown people in India and in the United States. Today, more than ever, there is an urgent need for solidarity between progressive anti-racist and anti-casteist movements. Solidarity needs to be renewed between the others, between and among the marginalized and exploited. Discourses that justify neutrality and silence for the privileged and the dominant must be directly challenged, while silence must be recognized as an intentional strategy to maintain the status quo. New migrants are always in need of resources, time, and experience to learn strategies necessary to survive white supremacy. Within the professional world of academia, a small minority of successful, established Black and Brown people—who in many ways belong now to the Global North and who have often earned their academic degrees and skills from the so-called best universities—learn to master the strategies of careerism or survival. I feel the pressure to join these ranks all around me. However, for me, like many others who are caught up in the shifting roles of othering and marginalization within the academic world, it is not easy to disconnect myself from my own path and move where I originally do not belong. I am uncomfortably placed amid this process, and I hope to someday have my own separate space within it.

○ ○ ○

. . . .

Sreerekha Sathi joined the International Institute of Social Studies (ISS) in January 2020. Prior to ISS, she taught at the University of Virginia, in its Global Studies Program, and at the Department for Women's Studies at Jamia Millia Islamia in New Delhi, India. Her areas of academic interest span theories of gender and political economy, capitalist globalization, feminist theories of development, women social welfare workers in South Asia, feminist research methodologies and epistemologies, caste politics in India and South Asia, Adivasi land rights in India, and the Kerala model of development. In the past, she has been involved in the struggles for the rights of women, landless communities, and slum dwellers and has engaged with issues pertaining to caste, race, sexuality, displacement, and Indigenous land rights in India. Her book *State without Honour* was published in 2017.

Note

I would like to thank former students at the Multicultural Student Center, University of Virginia (2017–18) for inspiration. I would like to acknowledge my sincere gratitude to Hilbourne Watson, Jeb Sprague, Wendy Harcourt, Rosalba Icaza, and the anonymous readers at *Meridians* for helping with their suggestions and comments on this testimonial piece.

Works Cited

Adibe, Jideofor. 2017. "Impact of Xenophobic Attacks against Africans in India on Afro-India Relations." *Journal of African Foreign Affairs* 4, nos. 1–2: 85–97.

Agnew, John. 2009. *Globalization and Sovereignty.* Lanham, MD: Rowman and Littlefield.

Ahmed, Sara. 2012. *On Being Included: Racism and Diversity in Institutional Life.* Durham, NC: Duke University Press.

Alcoff, Linda. 1991. "The Problem of Speaking for Others." *Cultural Critique*, no. 20 (Winter): 5–32.

Alexander, M. Jacqui. 2006. *Pedagogies of Crossing: Meditations on Feminism, Sexual Politics, Memory, and the Sacred*, edited by Judith Halberstam and Lisa Lowe. Durham, NC: Duke University Press.

Ambedkar, B. R. 1916. "Castes in India: Their Mechanism, Genesis, and Development." Paper presented at an Anthropology Seminar taught by Dr. A. A. Goldenweiser, May 9, Columbia University.

Ambedkar, B. R, and Vasant Moon. 1979. *Dr. Babasaheb Ambedkar, Writings and Speeches: Ḍô. Bābāsāheba Āmbeḍakara Lekhana Āṇi Bhāshaṇe.* Bombay: Education Department, Government of Maharashtra.

Baldwin, James. (1962) 1993. *The Fire Next Time.* New York: Vintage.

Balibar, Etienne. 1991. "The Nation Form: History and Ideology." In *Race, Nation, Class: Ambiguous Identities*, edited by Etienne Balibar and Immanuel Wallerstein, 86–106. London: Verso.

Balkenhol, Markus. 2016. "Silence and the Politics of Compassion: Commemorating Slavery in the Netherlands." *Social Anthropology* 24, no. 3: 278–93.

Bolak, Hale C. 1996. "Studying One's Own in the Middle East: Negotiating Gender and Self-Other Dynamics in the Field." *Qualitative Sociology* 19, no. 1: 107–30.

Bose, Purnima. 2008. "Hindutva Abroad: The California Textbook Controversy." *Global South* 2, no. 1: 11–34.

Callinicos, Alex. 1995. *Race and Class.* London: Bookmarks.

Case, Kim A. 2012. "Discovering the Privilege of Whiteness: White Women's Reflections on Anti-racist Identity and Ally Behavior." *Journal of Social Issues* 68, no. 1: 78–96.

Chakraborty, Uma. 2018. *Gendering Caste: Through a Feminist Lens.* Theorizing Feminism. Los Angeles, CA: Sage.

Collins, Patricia Hill. 2000. *Black Feminist Thought: Knowledge, Consciousness, and the Politics of Empowerment.* Rev. 10th ann. ed. New York: Routledge.

deSouza, Peter Ronald. 2017. "The Recolonization of the Indian Mind." *Revista crítica de ciências sociais*, no. 114: 137–60.

Du Bois, W. E. B. 1998. *Black Reconstruction in America, 1860–1880.* Detroit, MI: Free Press.

Dunbar-Ortiz, Roxanne. 2015. *An Indigenous Peoples' History of the United States.* Boston, MA: Beacon.

Ebert, Teresa L. 1996. *Ludic Feminism and after: Postmodernism, Desire, and Labor in Late Capitalism.* Ann Arbor: University of Michigan Press.

Equality Lab. n.d. http://www.equalitylabs.org/castesurvey.

Fanon, Frantz. (1952) 2008. *Black Skin, White Masks.* New York: Grove.

Fanon, Frantz. (1953) 2004. *The Wretched of the Earth.* New York: Grove.

Field Studio. 2015. "That World Is Gone: Race and Displacement in a Southern Town." Vimeo video, 20:00. http://vimeo.com/ondemand/thatworldisgone.

Ghorashi, Halleh. 2014. "Racism and 'the Ungrateful Other' in the Netherlands." *Thamyris/Intersecting*, no. 27: 101–16.

Goldberg, David Theo. 2009. *The Threat of Race: Reflections of Racial Neoliberalism.* Malden, MA: Blackwell.

Grewal, Inderpal. 2013. "Outsourcing Patriarchy: Feminist Encounters, Transnational Mediations, and the Crime of 'Honour Killings.'" *International Feminist Journal of Politics* 15, no. 1: 1–19.

Harding, Sandra. 1993. "Rethinking Standpoint Epistemology: 'What Is Strong Objectivity'?" In *Feminist Epistemologies*, edited by Linda Alcoff and Elizabeth Potter, 49–82. New York: Routledge.

Hart, Benjamin, and Chas Danner. 2017. "Three Dead and Dozens Injured after Violent White Nationalist Rally in Virginia." *Intelligencer*, August 13. www.nymag.com/intelligencer/2017/08/state-of-emergency-in-va-after-white-nationalist-rally.html.

hooks, bell. 1984. *Feminist Theory: From Margin to Center.* Boston, MA: South End.

hooks, bell. 1995. *Killing Rage: Ending Racism.* New York: Henry Holt.

Horne, Gerald. 2018. *The Apocalypse of Settler Colonialism: The Roots of Slavery, White Supremacy, and Capitalism in Seventeenth-Century North America and the Caribbean.* New York: Monthly Review.

Hui, Mary. 2017. "'Blue Zones' Author Ranks Charlottesville, Va., No. Three on His List of Twenty-Five Happiest U.S. Cities. Here's Why." *Washington Post*, November 30. www.washingtonpost.com/news/inspired-life/wp/2017/11/30/bestselling-blue-zones-author-just-ranked-charlottesville-va-3-on-his-list-of-the-25-happiest-cities-in-the-u-s-heres-why/.

Jaffrelot, Christophe, and Ingrid Therwath. 2007. "The Sangh Parivar and the Hindu Diaspora in the West: What Kind of 'Long-Distance Nationalism'?" *International Political Sociology* 1, no. 3: 278–95.

Jayawardene, Sureshi M. 2016. "Racialized Casteism: Exposing the Relationship between Race, Caste, and Colorism through the Experiences of Africana People in India and Sri Lanka." *Journal of African American Studies* 20, nos. 3–4: 323–45.

Joseph, Tony. 2018. *Early Indians: The Story of Our Ancestors and Where We Came From.* New Delhi: Juggernaut Books.

Kiernan, Victor G. 1969. *Lords of Humankind: European Attitudes towards the Outside World in the Imperial Age.* London: Weidenfeld & Nicolson.

Malik, Kenan. 1996. *The Meaning of Race: Race, History, and Culture in Western Society.* London: Palgrave Macmillan.

Mamdani, Mahmood. 1996. *Citizen and Subject: Contemporary Africa and the Legacy of Late Colonialism.* Princeton, NJ: Princeton University Press.

Mehta, Suketu. 2019. *This Land Is Our Land: An Immigrant's Manifesto.* New York: Farrar, Straus and Giroux.

Memmi, Albert. (1965) 1991. *The Colonizer and the Colonized.* Boston, MA: Beacon.

Mies, Maria. 1986. *Patriarchy and Accumulation on a World Scale: Women in the International Division of Labour.* London: Zed Books.

Mills, Charles W. 1997. *The Racial Contract.* Ithaca, NY: Cornell University Press.

Montagu, Ashley. 1997. *Mankind's Most Dangerous Myth: The Fallacy of Race.* Walnut Creek, CA: AltaMira.

Painter, Nell Irvin. 2017. "The Trump Era: The Politics of Race and Class. How Donald Trump Made 'Working Class' White." *Princeton Alumni Weekly,* March 1. www.paw.princeton.edu/article/trump-era-politics-race-and-class.

Public Radio International. n.d. "Caste in America Series." *World,* www.pri.org/categories/caste-america.

Ramazanoglu, Caroline, and Janet Holland. 2002. *Feminist Methodology: Challenges and Choices.* London: Sage.

Reed, Adolph Jr. 2013. "Marx, Race, and Neoliberalism." *New Labour Forum* 22, no. 1: 48–57.

Rubin, Gayle. 1975. "The Traffic in Women: Notes on the 'Political Economy' of Sex." In *Toward an Anthropology of Women,* edited by Rayna R. Reiter, 157–210. New York: Monthly Review.

Rutazibwa, Olivia U. 2019. "On Babies and Bathwater: Decolonizing International Development Studies." In *Decolonization and Feminisms in Global Teaching and Learning,* edited by Sara de Jong, Rosalba Icaza, and Olivia U. Rutazibwa, 158–80. New York: Routledge.

Sarkar, Tanika. 2018. "Is Love with Our Borders Possible?" *Feminist Review* 119, no. 1: 7–19.

Sharma, Shalini. 2019. "India: How Some Hindu Nationalists Are Rewriting Caste History in the Name of Decolonization." *Conversation,* May 9. https://theconversation.com/india-how-some-hindu-nationalists-are-rewriting-caste-history-in-the-name-of-decolonisation-114133.

Smith, Linda Tuhiwai, Eve Tuck, and K. Wayne Yang, eds. 2019. *Indigenous and Decolonizing Studies in Education: Mapping the Long View*. London: Routledge.

Spencer, Hawes, and Matt Stevens. 2017. "Twenty-Three Arrested and Tear Gas Deployed after a K.K.K. Rally in Virginia." *New York Times*, July 8. www.nytimes .com/2017/07/08/us/kkk-rally-charlottesville-robert-e-lee-statue.html.

Wekker, Gloria. 2016. *White Innocence: Paradoxes of Colonialism and Race*. Durham, NC: Duke University Press.

Williams, Eric. 1994. *Capitalism and Slavery*. Chapel Hill: University of North Carolina Press.

Grace L. Sanders Johnson

....

Picturing Herself in Africa
Haiti, Diaspora, and the Visual Folkloric

Abstract: This essay explores the relationship between imaging, archival cataloging, and African diasporic belonging through the developed and undeveloped photography of Haitian anthropologist Suzanne Comhaire-Sylvain. Using her family correspondences and research on folklore to contextualize her image-based archive on Haiti, the Belgian Congo, and Nigeria, the author proposes that Comhaire-Sylvain's visual catalog is rendered legible through her undeveloped images taken in Africa. Tracing Comhaire-Sylvain's contortions in front of and behind the camera, the author shows that her undeveloped and unpublished imaging practices of play and experimentation exemplify a medium of scholarly and personal reflexivity that troubled the authority of her professional research practice and enlivened the range of her diasporic expression. With particular attention given to photos taken during her time in the Belgian Congo between 1943 and 1945 and her long-stay return to Haiti in 1957, the author argues that Comhaire-Sylvain's imaging catalog is most provocatively read as an assemblage bound by her use of folklore as a unique technology for crafting meaning between overlapping sites of diasporic belonging and intellectual inquiry.

....

I am also interested in teaching, especially experimental research on questions of methods.
—Suzanne Comhaire-Sylvain, letter to Pierre Ryckmans, Governor General of Belgian Congo, August 28, 1943.

....

MERIDIANS · feminism, race, transnationalism   22:2 October 2023
DOI: 10.1215/15366936-10637681 © 2023 Smith College

In 1944 Suzanne Comhaire-Sylvain posed for a picture in the Belgian Congo. It was the first and only developed headshot of the first Haitian woman anthropologist, in her collection of over two hundred photos from her residency in the colonized central African region between 1943 and 1945. As her archive reflects, Comhaire-Sylvain's lens was often focused on the subjects and landscapes of her ethnographic studies in Haiti, the Belgian Congo, and Nigeria. In these locations, and later in East Africa, her images were extensions of her research on urban and rural family networks, folklore, and linguistic continuities between Haitian Kreyòl and African languages.

Comhaire-Sylvain was indoctrinated into the professionalized science of early twentieth-century anthropology through her studies at La Sorbonne, the London School of Economics, and a brief tenure at Columbia University. Her scholarship garnered collaboration with and acclaim among international circuits of anthropologists, folklorists, linguists, and historians, including Melville Herskovits, Bronislaw Malinowski, Alfred Métraux, and Carter G. Woodson (1937), who praised Comhaire-Sylvain as "one of the most intellectual people of Haiti." As a colleague of the elder Haitian ethnographer Jean Price-Mars, she studied the field of ethnography and produced research that documented and argued for the significance of African survivals in Haitian culture and thinking. Comhaire-Sylvain did not make any explicit claim of pan-Africanist scholarship, but she wrote in a 1943 job application, "I have always been interested in the question of African cultures and their influence on negroid groups of the new world."[1] Comhaire-Sylvain's diasporic research sensibility was deeply informed by her social scientific training and by her exchanges with disciplinary kin like Price-Mars and Herskovits, who emphasized intellectual and cultural recovery and recognition of Africa in the diaspora. But her perspective was also punctuated by her own movement between these "new world" African diasporic communities and her practice of documenting the quotidian qualities of Black women's belonging in these spaces. For example, in the 1930s her studies of women's and girls' work, education, and leisure practices in Port-au-Prince were championed by early twentieth-century Haitian feminists as a model for their movement (Perez 1937).[2] Charged with inspiring the intellectual agenda of Haitian women's political thought, her research provided unprecedented documentation of working-class and peasant women through close analysis of national folklore and family rituals.[3]

In the Belgian Congo, Comhaire-Sylvain rehearsed similar celebrated research practices. But when Comhaire-Sylvain arrived in Léopoldville (current-day Kinshasa) in the middle of 1943, she had no official fellowship or line of study and was excited by the opportunity to freely experiment in her "pet fields" of linguistics and musicology. She was also navigating several intersecting diasporic realities of her own. Most notably, she was a Black Haitian woman anthropologist stationed in the Belgian Congo with her white Belgian husband who was a fellow anthropologist and member of the colonial occupying army in the middle of World War II. She was also unemployed and experiencing chronic sickness that left her immobilized for weeks at a time. Thus she filled her periods of rest with frequent letter writing to her family in Haiti, seeking to remain abreast of her home country's most current news.[4]

In this layered transnational context, Comhaire-Sylvain probed her social and political place through photography. Eventually working on her own self-guided studies, Comhaire-Sylvain, when able, went on "field trips" throughout the country. On these trips, Comhaire-Sylvain produced an extensive visual record of quotidian pre-independence Congo—women braiding hair, young boys playing in the "Léo" city pool, women selling produce in the urban marketplace, men carrying lumber in the forest, a ritual dance, pregnant women, houses, and furniture. Unlike her photographs of the everyday in Haiti, these photographs were produced alongside a new subject—herself. In her pre-Congo photography Comhaire-Sylvain rarely appeared in front of the camera. However, in central Africa she slowly emerges: first, in a few sightseeing images with her figure framed by vast open fields, then in images of her visiting with friends, and finally, in a series of images mimicking the familiar cranial and "type photography" of nineteenth- and early twentieth-century race science. One frame captures the back of her head; the next, a left-side profile; and another two are front-faced photos (fig. 1). The images resulted in four undeveloped proofs. And then again. The three shots are repeated, this time with her in a different dress, resulting in two undeveloped proofs and a single, just out of focus, developed photo.

Observed within the ensemble of professional and personal photographs in Comhaire-Sylvain's archive between 1943 and 1945, the anthropologist's presence in front of the camera is unexpected and provocative.[5] The developed image is out of place. First, it is a photo of Comhaire-Sylvain, of which few exist. Second, it is a headshot. It is the only of its kind in her archive. The image not only reveals proximity, but the angle and focus are askew. This is in contrast to the field and family photographs in her collection that are focused, staged in groups, or stylized as landscapes. Third, the developed photo is most peculiar because of the numerous undeveloped

Figure 1. Suzanne Comhaire-Sylvain, Congo River, Belgian Congo, 1944. Courtesy of Stanford University Special Collections, Stanford, CA.

images that accompany it. The photo was taken in a rapid, photo-booth-like pace—a fact that becomes clear only when reviewing the negative sheets. Perhaps the images were taken by her travel companion, fellow anthropologist, Belgian military member, and husband, Jean Comhaire, in a private moment between two researchers. In her archive, the occasional changes in handwriting and notation on the backs of the photos suggest that the research partners passed the lens back and forth between them.

But the photo also conveys the aesthetic markers of a twenty-first-century selfie—"the spontaneous self-portrait, taken with a range of consumer-based devices . . . [including] film cameras" (Murray 2015: 491). Comhaire-Sylvain had, after all, bartered images of the Congo with fellow anthropologists and research institutions in the United States to acquire research equipment, including a new Kodak Argoflex seventy-five-millimeter film camera for herself during her first days in Léopoldville. She (or they) could have been practicing with her new research instrument. And yet the novelty of Comhaire-Sylvain's presence in front of the camera and the question of who took the image are dwarfed by the evidence that on multiple occasions she placed and posed her body in front of the camera in an aesthetic that was well known and used to scientifically classify "the other."

By the time Comhaire-Sylvain arrived in Léopoldville, she was open about her enthusiasm for multimethod and experimental research, even when it was not well received. As one critic later commented on her published work from the Congo, "Her attempt to combine qualitative with statistical techniques in these fields is rare and enterprising" (Sofer 1953: 81). But for this critic, her interdisciplinary work was so unique that it could not be fully trusted; as they concluded, "It would be wise to regard with caution those conclusions based upon, or inferred from, the statistical data" (Sofer 1953: 81). Yet as the epigraph above offers, Comhaire-Sylvain desired to expand the general knowledge about field approaches stating that she was interested in "experimental research on questions of methods."[6]

Comhaire-Sylvain's record of methodological bending and experimentation sets the scene for reading her archive and contextualizing her self-imaging. Among the developed images in the same sequence of her undeveloped photos are ones taken with the same camera of Congolese women and men in the same racial categorizing poses. Considering Comhaire-Sylvain's interest in tinkering with methodological boundaries and her physical, political, and social location in the Belgian Congo, what do Comhaire-Sylvain's decisions to pose, take, and catalog, but not develop, these signifying images of herself and others communicate about her practice and her lines of inquiry about racial belonging? The collection that is framed within an orderly narrative, partitioned in thematic folders—"Family Photos," "Kenscoff 1943," "Congo 1944," "Haiti 1957"—is messied by her images that are aesthetically different and not seen at all. There is, using Tina Campt's (2012: 128) phrase, a "thingyness" in and between the undeveloped and developed photos that communicates an emerging narrative about Comhaire-Sylvain's articulation of racial, intellectual, gendered, and diasporic belonging that materializes visually and also in the tactile curation of the collection. These photos, then, are not only a historical record of her research but also a catalog of choices, intentions, and projections of Comhaire-Sylvain's present and possible futures (6). In particular, I offer that the undeveloped photographs exist beyond their "negative" status and serve as a reflexive technology that binds to and haunts a larger visual tale of diasporic affiliation and intellectual experimentation.

Developing Family Images

There are other images of Comhaire-Sylvain in her Africa archive. Most were taken during her time in the Belgian Congo, and later in Nigeria, and shared with her family to account for her days and health abroad. In her correspondences to family and colleagues throughout the Americas, Comhaire-Sylvain framed the unique context of her time in the Congo: "I have not come here to do any research on folklore, although I may bring back a good collection. I was called by my husband who, as you know, had been mobilized in the Belgian forces. They transferred him from England to Africa and he got permission from the Civil and Military authorities to have me join him."[7] In 1936 Comhaire-Sylvain married Jean Comhaire, a Belgian social scientist whom she met during her research at the University of London. In adherence with Haitian constitutional law, which revoked citizenship of women who married foreigners, her union with Comhaire, an immigrant and noncitizen, meant that she lost her Haitian citizenship when she married. Thus, when Comhaire-Sylvain landed in Léopoldville, she arrived as a Haitian-born Belgian national accompanying her husband as a member of the Belgian colonizing project.

Because Comhaire-Sylvain was a direct descendant of nineteenth-century Haitian revolutionaries who fought French colonial rule, and the daughter of twentieth-century anti–U.S. occupation organizers, Georges and Eugenie Sylvain, the irony of arriving in the Congo to contain and govern over Black people could not have been lost on her. In fact, in 1943 she produced a résumé for the governor general of the Belgian Congo that started with a unique section about her revolutionary past. Where in previous résumés she had simply put her birthplace as Port-au-Prince, for her 1943 résumé she presented another section entitled "Haitian family and Catholic religion." In this section she described herself as the "daughter of Georges Sylvain (1865–1925), minister of Haiti to Paris, founder of l'Union Patriotique and man of letters, direct and legitimate descendant of the knights of Vallières, who took part in the Haitian Revolution and fought for 15 years in the armies of Toussaint-

Louverture and Bolivar."[8] This addition to her résumé and its location before her multiple degrees, publications, and job qualifications suggests that she was both announcing her esteemed ancestry and claiming a distinctly Haitian orientation to the world during her time in the Belgian Congo. From this new section her probable employer at least knew that, although she married into the Belgian colonial project and would work for it, Comhaire-Sylvain came from a line of people who fought against the types of occupation practices upheld in the Congo.

In addition to her anti-colonial family history, Comhaire-Sylvain also described her research as investigations into the grave consequences for communities when they "have been abruptly put in contact with European elements or completely Europeanized." Her study of Haitian folklore and language, for example, addressed the damaging cultural erasures and misrepresentations of African-descended people as a result of colonization (Comhaire-Sylvain 1938). Like many folklorists of the 1930s and 1940s, Comhaire-Sylvain's intellectual interests were buttressed by a disciplinary impulse and training at institutions like Columbia University to preserve, store, and catalog cultures perceived to be distant from white European and Western norms that were at risk of erasure. Yet Comhaire-Sylvain's presence as a woman of African descent from a predominantly Black, formerly colonized country in a colonized African country meant that she had to physically and intellectually reconcile her study of "not-so-different Others" and her entanglement with colonization (Cotera 2008: 38). Although her Belgian status afforded her certain privileges in the Congo, under colonial racial segregation laws, women's curfews, and work prohibitions between "African" women and "European" men, Comhaire-Sylvain was subject to policing. In her letters to her family in Haiti she bemoaned that in addition to frequent sick spells that limited her mobility, her freeform research agenda and travel throughout the country was also "badly handicapped by . . . [a] segregation policy" that limited Congolese women's movements and likely hampered hers as well.[9] The conditions of Comhaire-Sylvain's first months in Léopoldville incited questions about her place in the country, and from her siblings this included their repeated insistence that she send pictures of herself.

In response to her family's longing, the early objective of Comhaire-Sylvain's photography in the Congo was to provide evidence of her wellness and assuage her siblings' concerns about her safety and health as she navigated her new home. Her images both captured the mundanity of the comings and goings of her life as seamlessly integrated into Congolese

Figure 2. Suzanne Comhaire-Sylvain, Belgian Congo, 1944. Courtesy of Stanford University Special Collections, Stanford, CA.

society and simultaneously provided a lens into a landscape and cultural experience foreign to her siblings.[10] The photos uniquely captured Comhaire-Sylvain's mobility on roads and in towns, evidence that she was moving about the country. In a photo that was staged twice, Comhaire-Sylvain marked herself as part of and yet distant from the world around her—posed on the side of a dirt road with an open parasol and a vast grassland behind her (fig. 2). In the image, she looks like a tourist, standing too far off the road to be walking along it, but not far enough into the grass to convince viewers that she "knew" the environment. Yet, in the context of her photography, the image affirmed her goal to amuse her family, who were "happy to know that [she had] acclimated well to the Congo," as well as to locate her in a shifting physical and political African landscape.[11] As reflected in her sister's comments on the photos that "Léopoldville truly has the air of a beautiful city, fresh and well mapped out," Comhaire-Sylvain transferred familial becalm and spatial cosmopolitan connectivity through her images and transatlantic sharing.

Merging with Africa

While Comhaire-Sylvain used images to connect to loved ones and colleagues across national boundaries, she also used photography to establish connection within the Congo and among the Congolese. Comhaire-Sylvain spent "a few hours per week" assisting her husband who was "doing a good bit of research work on culture contacts and race relations in the Native city in his spare time."[12] And as she explained, "I am helping him as much as I can." Additionally, she continued to organize several "field trip[s]" throughout the country where she hoped to record music and learn "mixed languages."[13]

During these early field trips she combined her adherence to her siblings' requests for photos with her intellectual inquiry, but also with her desire to establish kinship relations. In a 1965 interview in the Congolese newspaper *L'courrier d'Afrique*, Comhaire-Sylvain (1965) recounted, "As soon as I arrived [in the Congo] I wanted to mingle with the native population. I spent my days in what was called at that time, 'the native zone.'"[14] Her reflective assertion of a merged life with the Congolese could invoke the familiar late nineteenth- and early twentieth-century anthropological practice of "going native." Yet in the context of her photography the desire for proximity was apart from the brand of performative mimicry in dress, comportment, or culture; rather, her photography suggests a desire to engage, situate, and even showcase her life and work among and within an African kinship frame. She was not only a scholar, she was a member of a shared African story of belonging that had by the time of the interview evolved over twenty years. And as the headline of *L'courrier d'Afrique* intimated, she was "a dear friend to the African woman."[15]

Hints of this evolving familiar relation between Comhaire-Sylvain and the Congolese emerge in Comhaire-Sylvain's photographs of families and ritual ceremonies during her trip to the Kasai region in 1944. The photos engage her subjects and welcome their gaze in a manner that was only scattered throughout her previous work. The eyes of the subjects and the camera connect. The images close in on women weaving baskets and preparing meals, and they move alongside men transporting goods from town to town. The images of men carrying lumber throughout the Congolese forest and women at work in the Léopoldville market continue to reflect a particular physical distance, suggesting that the photographer does not completely abandon the wide-angled aesthetic of an observer. However, in this context of labor another image of Comhaire-Sylvain appears. She is also at work. She is dressed in pants and a white blouse and stares directly at the camera while forcefully leaning toward the photographer. In the canon of Black women anthropologists of the early twentieth century, the image resonates with pictures of African American anthropologist Zora Neale Hurston in the field, staring down a camera and posing authoritatively over her research domain (Kali Films 2013). Like the gripping images from the late 1920s through the 1940s of Hurston with wide-brimmed hats and styled outfits that reveal her crafted identity to blend into the communities that she studied, Comhaire-Sylvain's stance conveys a disciplined command over her appearance in the space and the environment behind her. In her study of Hurston, who similar to Comhaire-Sylvain "drift[ed] in the borderlands between multiple discourses, ideologies, and allegiances," the feminist theorist María Eugenia Cotera (2008: 17) argues that Hurston used her clothing and comportment to signal kinship between herself and the familiar, but different, Black folk that she studied.

Comhaire-Sylvain did not mimic the appearance of those she studied, recognizing, as Hurston did, that this performative measure would make her presence suspicious. Instead, she framed her presence in a way that highlighted points of Black diasporic connection. For Comhaire-Sylvain, this meant demonstrating that she was working in community and that ultimately her research was, despite her colonial affiliations, in the interests of the Congolese people.[16] This was a long-standing relationship-building project that would in the 1950s incorporate her sister, the gynecologist Yvonne Sylvain, who established a women's health center in the independent Democratic Republic of the Congo. But in the 1940s Comhaire-Sylvain's images convey that she used her body as a tool to mitigate her location as an "insider-outsider" in the field and merge her reality with that of the Congolese. Similar to Hurston, Comhaire-Sylvain performed "ethnographic research as an aesthetic exchange" (Cotera 2008: 95). Her longing for connectivity in the Congo, her research trips, and the images of her throughout the country invite the viewer to visualize her work as part of the Black experience in the colonized Congo. This relationship was not only defined by spiritual affiliation or by the political pan-Africanist impulse that sent hundreds of Haitians to the independent Democratic Republic of the Congo to support the newly free country in the 1950s. Rather, Comhaire-Sylvain figured an additional relation between her

Figure 3. Suzanne Comhaire-Sylvain, Belgian Congo, 1944. Courtesy of Stanford University Special Collections, Stanford, CA.

African and Caribbean histories that considered herself and her body of work as a link between the two spaces.

This aesthetic exchange moved along the hyphenated space between insider and outsider, blurring the gaps between Comhaire-Sylvain's ability to claim insider status as a person of African descent in the Belgian Congo and her well-situated location as an outsider from Haiti, academically trained to encounter the Congolese as culturally and aesthetically distant. In this way, both the roadside and work photos reflect an imbalance around Comhaire-Sylvain's (in)ability to "fit" into the country. The Congo remained foreign even as she became familiar with and was pictured within the frame of Africa. This discord is evident in her letters home and to colleagues as she framed the country and people as "unevolved" and categorized the Congolese as either "progressive or primitive natives."[17]

While her qualifying word choices were often used in professional correspondences and reflected the vocabulary of her disciplines, the disso-
nance between her aspirational connection to Africa and her professional
practice appears most clearly in Comhaire-Sylvain's use of "type" photography during her time in the Kasai region. In the late nineteenth century,
the "type" style focused on cranial measurements and helped scientists
draw racist conclusions based on the physiognomy and phrenology of
populations. By the early twentieth century the style had moved beyond
science into an anti-Black art aesthetic popularized on postcards and in
magazines that claimed to "document all contemporary aspects of life" in
Africa, an aesthetic that all the while was used to "classify and control
colonial subjects" (Geary 2003: 17, 18). In the 1930s a growing body of cultural anthropologists frowned on this practice; however, throughout the
twentieth century, anthropologists in the Congo region were central to the
circulation of "type photography" (19).

In central Africa these images were captured and most popularized by
the Russian photographer Casimir Zagourski. A Zagourski postcard became
a staple of gifting among tourists, scholars, and residents alike.[18] During her
time in the Belgian Congo, Comhaire-Sylvain participated in the circulation of these images by sending the postcards to friends and colleagues.
Remarking on two postcards that accompanied a letter Comhaire-Sylvain
sent in early 1944, her friend and semiotics scholar Thomas Sebeok replied,
"I was simply delighted to receive your card. The photo on the back was certainly interesting. I tried it out on my anthropological colleagues here, and
got rather amusing guesses."[19] As Sebeok passed around the images of Black
people for intellectual sport, Comhaire-Sylvain capitalized on the race discourse infused into the exchange and continued to circulate more images.
Responding to Sebeok's enthusiasm, she sent more images and wrote:

> As you like pictures, I am sending you two more. In these Bukawu people
> it is easy to trace the Arab mixture, although they are jet black with very
> kinky hair. In my opinion, many Bantu tribes now classified as Negro
> because of their complexion and hair texture ought to be termed
> "Negroid" as the amount of white blood averages probably 25%. As the
> mixture is not recent, they think themselves "pure blood," but my experi-
> ence of mixed bloods in my country (where the mixing took place during
> the last two or three centuries and where the grand father and great
> grand father are generally known) has shown me that such types occur
> only within a certain range of mixture.[20]

As Comhaire-Sylvain volleyed new images into play, her facility with racialized dissecting, aligned with polygenist undertones, seemed to impress her friend. In her letters, she went on to describe other women whose bloodline mixture did not match their racial categorization. Her comments about blood percentages and origins reflected an investment in theories of race and racial categorization that often led to racist and eugenic conclusions about Black people in a global context in the early twentieth century. By the 1940s, the Boazian turn in anthropology that challenged polygenetic thought with cultural studies was well circulated and accepted within the field. Comhaire-Sylvain was familiar with and largely subscribed to this approach in her own practices of African diasporic cultural study. Yet, as Comhaire-Sylvain's use of images reflects, the actual unhinging of scientific racist methods from twentieth-century anthropological practice was negotiated well into the mid-twentieth century by the same anthropologists who were actualizing the intellectual turn.

Coupled with her postcard trafficking and correspondence, her discussions about Black Congolese people are disquieting and echo what Laura Wexler calls the "tender violence" of colonial exchange (Wexler 2000: 7). Pairing them with friendly pleasantries, Comhaire-Sylvain assessed the epidermic, physiological, and somatic features of the women in the photos in order to describe them as atypical on the continuum of modernity. Comhaire-Sylvain used the photographs as intellectual currency, participating in what Krista A. Thompson (2015: 3) calls the "visual economy of people as images." Most puzzling, though, is that Comhaire-Sylvain also used the images as literal currency when she agreed to send Sebeok more photos if he committed to sending her several "Portra lenses and a Kodak adapter ring" for her camera.[21] Comhaire-Sylvain's potential material acquisition through the trade of African images revealed the contradictions of her presence and work in the colonized space. At the same time, Comhaire-Sylvain's reference to her "experience of mixbloods in [her] country" points toward her diasporic navigation of Blackness. Haiti appears as referent and anchor for her knowledge in the Congo. While she asserts the Bantu are 25 percent white, the salient truth that displaces this "sanguine" percentage is that the Bantu women thought of themselves as "pure" Black African. Her lived experience in Haiti paralleled this thinking as she explained that, even "where the grand father and great grand father are generally known" to be white, the mixed-raced population in Haiti claimed African descendancy and were nationally defined as Black. Her conjuring of Haiti in this context nods toward differences among Haitians regarding color and culture. It also points to the fallacies of methodologies that erased African-descended people's experience of Blackness in relation to colonization as well as differences among one another. Comhaire-Sylvain's navigation of her personal experiences and connections to Haiti and the Congo, combined with official and unofficial research practices, offered the ideal scene for methodological experimentation to understand the contours of Black belonging. This was most evident in her undeveloped images from the Kasai region.

(Un)developed Belonging

During her time in southern central Congo, Comhaire-Sylvain experimented with crafting "type" pictures. The pictures from these trips include a dozen profile and forward-facing images of Kasai women and men. It is among the developed profile photos of the Kasai that the undeveloped photos of Comhaire-Sylvain in the same poses appear. In this series, as stated above, there are five undeveloped photographs: three front-facing photos taken at varying distances, one left-profile photo, and one photo of the back of Comhaire-Sylvain's head (figs. 4 and 5).

In an unexpected depiction of bodily classification, Comhaire-Sylvain was fused into the subject position and marked as a member of the available people inserted into the science of this imaging practice. Her image, joined with those of the Congolese in the archive, blurs the historical understandings of her subjective and political sympathies. In the photos, her already alienated body, as noncitizen (of either Haiti or the Congo), was placed into the larger spectrum of racialized and gendered global othering. Appearing in the archive only a few images away from the type photographs of Kasai men, these photographs frame her presence as deeply intertwined with, and even blended with, the moments of colonization, race science, and anthropology in the Belgian Congo.

In particular, her undeveloped photos reveal a haunting pleasure in her play with imaging. In the first undeveloped photo Comhaire-Sylvain looks straight into the camera, with no smile (figs. 6 and 7). In the second photo, her cheekbones are risen and her lips are turned upward. She is smiling at the camera. Comhaire-Sylvain certainly engaged the camera differently over time, yet in her archive of developed self-authored or independent photographs from her teenage years through her later adult years, she was rarely captured smiling. However, in this negative she is not only smiling,

Figures 4–5: Suzanne Comhaire-Sylvain, Negatives, 1944. Courtesy of Stanford University Special Collections, Stanford, CA.

Figures 6–7: Suzanne Comhaire-Sylvain, Negatives, 1944. Courtesy of Stanford University Special Collections, Stanford, CA.

but the movement captured in the image's blurriness suggests laughter. Perhaps she was toying with her camera. Yet, even in tinkering, the photograph suggests a possibility that she too could be, and maybe should be, the subject of her intellectual gaze. Thus in the blurred negative, Comhaire-Sylvain not only is looking at the camera but also might be considered extending herself to the camera, to the person behind the camera (perhaps Jean), and to her own interrogation of her subject positioning.

Comhaire-Sylvain's posing as researcher and research subject engages and refuses the spectacle of Blackness and race science on which the legibility of type photography depended. Here, her undeveloped and expressive images echo an ethnographic reflexivity that the anthropologist Gina A. Ulysse (2007: 6) argues "interrupt[s] the problem of ethnographic authority that arises when the focus is only on the subject" and "shift[s] or expand[s] the ethnographer as well as the subjects' gaze on the researcher to cause a paradigm shift that has the potential to influence a symbolic change." Thus, when Comhaire-Sylvain cast her body and laughter into the type style, as herself (subject-researcher) focusing on herself (researcher-subject), she rendered the spectacle of Blackness strange. Her smile breaks out of the dehumanizing parameters of the technology that othered, alienated, and ignored Black people's emotion and critical self-theorizing, and offered entrée into reading Comhaire-Sylvain's stated amusement with experimentation.

In particular, Comhaire-Sylvain's play hides within the undeveloped photos and begs the future viewer, somewhere in a far-off archive, to seek. This laughter, which is accessible only through her intentional archival dodging, also reminds the viewer that Comhaire-Sylvain was a folklorist.[22] She drew methodological and theoretical insight and clarity from this creative aesthetic. It was through studying the details of syntax, narrative cadence, character construction, and story rehearsal and repetition in myth and lore that Comhaire-Sylvain identified theories of understanding and knowing. And in her written scholarship she even framed the folkloric practices of Haiti and the Congo together, naming Kenscoff, Haiti, a "Kongo beyond the seas" because of the similar storytelling forms (Comhaire-Sylvain 1973; Comhaire 1984). Her research notes include folktales, images of mythical characters in these tales, and her own musical notations to visually document the sounds in the stories that she heard. She was familiar with visualizing and hearing the folkloric. But more importantly, she was familiar with the contours and operations of what

Kaiama L. Glover (2010: 209) describes as the "discourses of subversion [that] are camouflaged by the playful stylistics of a folk aesthetic." In her own interrogation of Haitian folklore, Comhaire-Sylvain (1933: 98) identified it as an "enigma," "sometimes poetic and of a captivating charm, with its fables and humorous tales" that often contradicted the assumed totalizing melancholy around mourning, loss, or daily life.

In the negatives, Comhaire-Sylvain's smile puzzles and consorts with the camouflaging components of the folkloric form. Animated by the stark whites and shades of black, the negatives in their total inversion of color and light reflect translucent images. Yet beyond the visual science, these images mark a presence that Avery F. Gordon (2008: 8) might characterize as "ghostly matter," reflecting "something lost, or barely visible, or seemingly not there to our supposedly well trained eye." The haunting quality of the images, like folklore, "draws us affectively . . . always a bit magically, into the structure of feeling of a reality we come to experience, not as cold knowledge, but as a transformative recognition" (8). This feeling of recognition is present in Price-Mars's (1951: 51) articulation of Haitian folklore as "the faithful mirror of a life that is tormented, unstable, but infused nevertheless with optimism and infectious candor." Reflected back to the viewer, the negative images catch Comhaire-Sylvain, and some ghosts, in the mirror. Peeking through her poses and smile are also the proofs of the Black Congolese men hauling lumber from the forest, walking under a Belgian flag, whose labor would ultimately create vast deforestation in the country—a similar environmental violence that was enacted on her home country when it was occupied by the United States (1915–34).

The layered images organized in individual photo sleeves are beset by Comhaire-Sylvain's ambiguous affiliation with the Belgian empire and her location in the Congo. But as Gordon (2008: 8) explains, "If haunting describes how that which appears to be not there is often a seething presence, acting on and often meddling with taken-for-granted realities, the ghost is just the sign, or the empirical evidence if you like, that tells you a haunting is taking place." Comhaire-Sylvain's visual matter—the negative images, her poses, and her laughter in (and likely at) the type aesthetic—signal the haunting. They are the ghosts. But the meddling, the seething presence, is taking place and felt in the residue of her decision making. It is the tension between Comhaire-Sylvain's choices to take, but not develop the images, and her choices to store and preserve these images. It is the sentience of the tale that emerges when Comhaire-Sylvain's visual archive is read not as distinct images of locations or by the degree of development, but as an ongoing reflexive practice of methodological experimentation in which her overlapping worlds do not quite afford her unification with Africa or Haiti.

Where traditionally these negatives would be marked as appendages, excess, and marginal to the developed work, Comhaire-Sylvain's folkloric play within the undeveloped photos, and their physical proximity to the "type" photographs in her archive, invite a relook at the effects of the developed, visibly catalogued images and their circulation. For example, during her field trips in 1944, Comhaire-Sylvain posed for a second set of headshots in type form. The developed photo from this series is the unfocused headshot discussed above (fig. 1). The image was sent home to Haiti and served as an account of Comhaire-Sylvain's self-care. It also carried the residue of experimentation.[23] It carried the disconnection as well as intersecting truths of her personal and professional well-being and desire for greater proximity with the Congolese that Comhaire-Sylvain actively revealed and concealed. In this regard, the developed photo is not so significant for its technical components as it is provocative as a trace of thought, choices, and sometimes conflicting articulations of connectivity within and between African diasporas.

The resonant space between Comhaire-Sylvain's circulated and cataloged images in the Belgian Congo and Haiti recall Brent Hayes Edwards's (2001) often cited analysis of *décalage* as a model for understanding the uneven, disconnected, and untranslatable contours of diaspora. Considering the effects of African-descended people's making meaning of their relation, Edwards invites an analysis of diaspora that, "instead of reading for the *efficacy* of the prosthesis"—in this case the political, scientific, photographic, and aesthetic claims of shared racial connections that "prop up" (*calé*) diasporic affiliation—"look[s] for the *effects* of such an operation, for the traces of such haunting, reading them as constitutive to the structure of any articulation of diaspora" (66). Here the negatives are part of the developed whole of the archive, not as leftovers, but as morsels (something delectable and pleasing) of Comhaire-Sylvain's experimentation with diasporic belonging. Comhaire-Sylvain's presence in the images in Africa, and particularly in the type form, presents evidence of African-descended people's lives being impacted by global anti-Black science and colonization, but the undeveloped images also expose "the points of misunderstanding, bad faith, [and] unhappy translation" in her play (66). The opaque process hidden in Comhaire-Sylvain's undeveloped photos reveals the misgivings of her scientific technologies to do the work of establishing an infallible sameness among Black people, as well as the uneven relationships to power experienced by Black people within intersecting diasporas. And still these discrepancies and undeveloped excess are, as Edwards argues, "necessary" to the articulation of diaspora.

Comhaire-Sylvain's imaging in Africa undoes, blurs, and remixes her configurations of Black belonging. The effects or traces of Comhaire-Sylvain's photographs are in the ongoing archival choices of development and cataloging that occur in and after her time in central and western Africa. In this way, the work of the undeveloped images comes into greater relief when zooming out to look at the ensemble of images in Comhaire-Sylvain's collection and one image just beyond her archive when she returns to Haiti.

The Congo Framed in Haiti
Comhaire-Sylvain's long-term return to Haiti coincided with the 1957 election season. The political theater that ultimately resulted in François Duvalier's presidency (1957–71) brought the labor movement, women's rights organizers, Black nationalists, the working poor, and the merchant elite into the streets singing campaign jingles and waving banners with words and images that relayed various aspirations for Haiti's future. Surprisingly, Comhaire-Sylvain did not photograph any of the city's overt political activity. Rather, along with several pictures of classic architecture and monuments in Port-au-Prince, she took photographs of her sister Yvonne Sylvain's medical office. She captured Haitian women sitting in the waiting room and her sister at work. Like the quotidian photographs that she took in the Congo, she inserts women into her image of modern Haiti.

The photos of Yvonne's office made space for images of women, curated by women, in her visual archive of Haiti (fig. 8). In the photos of the office waiting area, for example, the physical staging of the artwork on the walls enclosed the clientele and the historical observer in a uniquely Haitian space with images of peasant farmers and the bold tones of the nation's traditional visual art.

Scanning the walls of Yvonne's office through Comhaire-Sylvain's archive, one can observe her folkloric play and reflexivity from the Belgian Congo inhabiting the space through traces of her experimental practices. The collection of office photos communicate the intentional amplification of the self and shared community. Although she does not appear in the

Figure 8. Suzanne Comhaire-Sylvain, photo of Yvonne Sylvain's doctor's office, 1956. Courtesy of Stanford University Special Collections, Stanford, CA.

office images, she is capturing her life in Haiti. As reflected throughout her archive, Comhaire-Sylvain and her sister Jeanne Sylvain (also pictured in some office photos) often supported Yvonne in her work. Thus, again Comhaire-Sylvain turns the camera onto her life through documentary methods of anthropology. But the images invite a look within and just beyond the political moment, the science, the anthropological lens, or even the promise of a women's space to witness Comhaire-Sylvain's visual experimentation. In this collection of images, there is one image of Yvonne Sylvain's reception area that resonates most poignantly. In the waiting area three people are shown (fig. 8). Unlike the other office photos in which the people are physically engaged and perhaps caught in some aspect of the waiting room performance (reading, working, or sitting in exhausted anticipation of being served), in this image the type style reemerges. The woman closest to the frame is in a right-side profile, the woman in the center looks straight ahead, and the man to the right is positioned in a left-side profile. Their faces are curiously unengaged and posed. This is made clear from other images of the same people in other photos of the office. The composite visual of the people in the photo is a type scene. Again, Comhaire-Sylvain's image announces a haunting and calls attention to and consideration of something "barely visible" (Gordon 2008: 8).

In the same photo of Yvonne Sylvain's reception area a collection of faint images are seen on the back wall (fig. 8). The images recall Jeanne Sylvain's words to her sister in 1944. After receiving images of Comhaire-Sylvain in Africa, Jeanne celebrated the images of the tropical Belgian Congo. Her pleasure was attached to the images' utility. Referring to Yvonne decorating her new medical office, she suggested to Comhaire-Sylvain, "She [Yvonne] should use your photos from the Congo. Léopoldville truly has the air of a beautiful city, fresh and well mapped out. . . . For the coolness and freshness; after your description we understand that it is only an illusion, but it is the affect that is suggested from all of the big trees and flowers."[24] The affect ascribed to the photos as conduits between the spaces amplifies the use of archival images to establish diasporic affiliations, even while acknowledging the illusions of sameness. Were the images on the back wall the same images that Jeanne Sylvain referenced? We cannot know. But if so, Comhaire-Sylvain's Haiti quite tangibly merged with that of the Congolese, locating Haitian women within an African frame.

Yet Jeanne Sylvain's suggestion also reveals the cognitive work these Congolese images evinced. In the context of Krista Thompson's (2007: 5) use of "place images" to define "tropicalization" of the Caribbean, Jeanne's suggestion to decorate this Haitian women's space with the affect of Africa through the "vision and visual representation in the imaginative geography" of the Belgian Congo would have reproduced colonial imaging that locked the country in a narrative of a timeless and uninterrogated Africa, holding the affective pull of a place nestled securely in the past only to be consumed. Taking into account Comhaire-Sylvain's complex relationship to Belgian colonization in the Congo, Jeanne's décor suggestion to choreograph tropicalization is disconcerting. However, in her work, Thompson also considers Black Caribbean uses of tropicalization to engineer and frame diasporic perspectives. In this regard, the inference of Congolese-Haitian topographical sameness presented more questions even as I navigated the archive. As I tried to distinguish unmarked photographs of Haiti, the Congo, and Nigeria, much of my ability to discern the pictures' locations relied not only on Comhaire-Sylvain's notations and the dates, dress, or architectural clues but also on the geography and topography of the landscape that provided essential hints. This process was further complicated by several superimposed images that mapped pictures from the Congo, Nigeria, and 1950s Haiti on top of the other. My desire to place these photographs and tease the images apart from one another attuned me to the humor of Comhaire-Sylvain's archive in the Congo and after. The chronological and regional categorization of the archive both by Comhaire-Sylvain and later by archivists only further accentuates the gaps in the carefully curated record. Either by picturing the nations within the other or by storing Congo-Haiti superimposed photographs together, Comhaire-Sylvain's visual archive—the complete practice of taking, developing (or not), storing, and cataloging—toys with any claim or desire for clarity. Moving between the similarities, distinctions, and satire of the photographic exchange, Comhaire-Sylvain's archive parallels her practice and study of "the nocturnal world of the storyteller, a world that necessarily presents a certain opacity" (Glover 2010: 211).

Conclusion

Balking at scholars' and even archivists' efforts to catalog and contain narratives, the superimposed and undeveloped photographs in Comhaire-Sylvain's archive tell a story of alternative imaginings and framings of national and global Black belonging. Her experimentation is visually announced in her Belgian Congo archive, but it is replayed and rehearsed in hers and that of her peers' imaging. For example, four years after her time in the Belgian Congo, Comhaire-Sylvain joined the United Nations Educational, Scientific and Cultural Organization (UNESCO) research project with her mentor and colleague, Alfred Métraux, in the Marbial Valley of Haiti. This project had the explicit goal of building a monogenetic argument of one human race with particular ethnic and cultural uniqueness. Thus it did not incorporate type photography and its accompanying systems of analysis. But in Métraux's archive of this two-year project from 1948 to 1950, another picture of Comhaire-Sylvain appears and expands the provocative quality of her presence in her archived photography.[25] In a photo of a peasant family in the Marbial Valley, Comhaire-Sylvain sits to the left of the frame (fig. 9). And in the background, should to shoulder with the woman next to her, she nearly blends in. Her desire for merger articulated in the Belgian Congo is developed in Haiti.

Figure 9. Suzanne Comhaire-Sylvain sitting with a family in Maribial Valley, Haiti. UNESCO 1948–50. Courtesy Musée du Quai Branly, Paris, France.

This blending and blurring of Comhaire-Sylvain, her methodologies, and ideas from her time in the Congo echoed in this family photo in Haiti returns us to Ulysse's (2007) analysis of reflexivity. In her theorizing of her own ethnographic work in the African diaspora, but outside her home country Haiti, she writes, "Reflexivity also allows me to unmask the political content of my encounter—I am there to learn about the region because of Haiti" (6). Ultimately, Comhaire-Sylvain's archive communicates a diasporic coupling that refashions her claims on Haitian citizenship, her health, and her definition of and proximity to family, as well as reflects her culpability and vulnerability in the colonizing process through her labor and the labor around her. Comhaire-Sylvain's visual archive holds the aperture of interrogation open long and wide enough for both the self-indulgence of the technical and the scholarly authority that accounts for her presence as both agent and subject of Belgian colonization, while interrogating her otherness and inviting a realm of experimentation that allows her to play in her desires about national and regional belonging. The traces and candor of which, as Comhaire-Sylvain's words state, were meant to teach.

....

Grace L. Sanders Johnson is assistant professor of Africana studies at the University of Pennsylvania. She received her PhD in history and women's studies at the University of Michigan where she specialized in modern Caribbean and Latin American history, transnational feminisms, oral history, and African diasporic studies.

Notes

1   Suzanne Comhaire-Sylvain Curriculum Vitae, August 1943, Correspondences 1942–1943, Comhaire-Sylvain Collection, Special Collections and University Archives, Stanford University, Stanford, CA (hereafter, CSC).
2   "Bienvenue," *La Voix des Femmes* 11, no. 19 (April 1937): 4.
3   Jacques Roumain and Jean Price-Mars wrote about the condition of peasant life; however, no periodical shared peasant women's daily lives with the nation. See Roumain 1941 and Price-Mars 1928. Comhaire-Sylvain's conclusions often reflected the tensions of early Haitian feminists who sought to extend a practice and philosophy that represented "all" Haitian women, yet were entangled in their own classed critique of respectable behavior and sociability. For more on the early Haitian women's movement, see Johnson 2023; Charles 1995; and Chancy 1997.
4   In email correspondences with Kathleen Gyssels and Jean Félix, Comhaire-Sylvain's son, December 7, 2016.
5   My use of *ensemble* is inspired by Tina Campt's (2012) attention to the musicality of photographic collections in the African diaspora.
6   Suzanne Comhaire-Sylvain, letter to Pierre Ryckmans, Governor General of Belgian Congo, August 28, 1943, CSC.
7   Comhaire-Sylvain, letter to Thomas Sebeok, February 9, 1944, Comhaire-Sylvain Collection, CSC.
8   Curriculum vitae, 1943, CSC.
9   Comhaire-Sylvain, letter to Edwin W. Smith, August 7, 1945, CSC
10   Yvonne Sylvain, letter to Suzanne Comhaire-Sylvain, April 19, 1944, CSC.
11   Yvonne Sylvain, letter to Suzanne Comhaire-Sylvain, April 19, 1944, CSC.
12   Comhaire-Sylvain, letter to Thomas Sebeok, February 9, 1944, Comhaire-Sylvain Collection, CSC.
13   Comhaire-Sylvain, letter to Henry Allen Moe, September 29, 1943, CSC.
14   "Dès mon arrive, j'ai voulu me mêler à la vie des autochtones, je passais mes journées dans ce que l'on appelait à cette époque, la 'cite indigene.' " "Suzane [sic] Sylvain, notre grande amie à toutes . . . " *L'courrier d'Afrique*, 1965, CSC.
15   "Nous avons recontré une grande amie de la femme africaine" (Comhaire-Sylvain 1965).

16 For Hurston, this included showing that she knew work songs in Florida and learning to serve the *lwas* in Haiti. For more on Hurston's research in Florida and Haiti, see Hurston 2008, 2009. There is no evidence to suggest that Comhaire-Sylvain and Hurston ever met. Comhaire-Sylvain was in Europe when Hurston was in Haiti. And over the course of Comhaire-Sylvain's time in the United States neither mention meeting the other.

17 Comhaire-Sylvain, letter to Sebeok, 1944.

18 Zagourski's full collection, *L'Afrique qui disparait!*, is located at the Yale University Library and Special Collections.

19 Thomas Sebeok, letter to Comhaire-Sylvain, November 16, 1943, CSC.

20 Comhaire-Sylvain, letter to Sebeok, February 9, 1944, CSC.

21 Comhaire-Sylvain, letter to Sebeok, February 9, 1944, CSC.

22 Dodging is a technique used during photograph development when an opaque object is held between the photographic paper and the enlarger lens to block the light, making an image lighter.

23 It is unclear whether the photo was sent in response to her siblings' concern, but, as her sisters wrote in a joint letter, "We received a photo and it made us very worried. We can see in your face that you need to care for yourself." Madeleine and Jeanne Sylvain, letter to Comhaire-Sylvain, 1944, CSC.

24 Jeanne Sylvain, letter to Comhaire-Sylvain, 1944, CSC.

25 Curiously, many of the images around this photo are duplicated in Comhaire-Sylvain's and Métraux's archives, but this developed picture is found only in Métraux's collection.

Works Cited

Campt, Tina. 2012. *Image Matters: Archive, Photography, and the African Diaspora in Europe.* Durham, NC: Duke University Press.

Chancy, Myriam J. A. 1997. *Framing Silence: Revolutionary Novels by Haitian Women.* New Brunswick, NJ: Rutgers University Press.

Charles, Carolle. 1995. "Gender and Politics in Contemporary Haiti: The Duvalierist State, Transnationalism, and the Emergence of a New Feminism (1980–1990)." *Feminist Studies* 2, no. 1: 1–30.

Comhaire, Jean. 1984. "Vie et oeuvre d'une folkloriste haïtienne en Afrique." *Folklore in Africa Today/Folklore en Afrique d'aujourd'hui* 11: 1–4. African Research Project, Budapest.

Comhaire-Sylvain, Suzanne. 1933. "Contes Haïtiens," *Revue de folklore Français et de folklore colonial* 2, no. 4 (March–April): 97–111

Comhaire-Sylvain, Suzanne. 1938c. "La femme dans le proverbe Créole." *La voix des femmes,* March.

Comhaire-Sylvain, Suzanne. 1940. *Le roman de Bouqui.* Port-au-Prince: Imprimerie du Collège Vertières.

Comhaire-Sylvain, Suzanne. 1965. "Suzane Sylvain, notre grande amie à toutes . . . " *L'courrier d'Afrique.*

Comhaire-Sylvain, Suzanne. 1973. *Qui mange avec une femme: Contes zaïrois et haïtiens.* Bandundu, Zaïre: Ceeba.

Cotera, María Eugenia. 2008. *Native Speakers: Ella Deloria, Zora Neale Hurston, Jovita González, and the Poetics of Culture.* Austin: University of Texas Press.

Dash, Michael J. 1981. *Literature and Ideology in Haiti, 1915–1961.* New York: Palgrave Macmillan.

Edwards, Brent Hayes. 2001. "The Uses of Diaspora," *Social Text* 19 (1 (66)): 45–73.

Geary, Christraud M. 2003. *In and Out of Focus: Images from Central Africa 1885–1960.* Washington, DC: Smithsonian National Museum of African Art in association with Philip Wilson Publishers.

Glover, Kaiama L. 2010. *Haiti Unbound: A Spiralist Challenge to the Postcolonial Canon.* Liverpool: Liverpool University Press.

Gordon, Avery F. 2008. *Ghostly Matters: Haunting and the Sociological Imagination.* Minneapolis: University of Minnesota Press.

Hurston, Zora Neale. 2008. *Mules and Men.* New York: Amistad/Harper Perennial.

Hurston, Zora Neale. 2009. *Tell My Horse: Voodoo and Life in Haiti and Jamaica.* New York: Harper Perennial.

Johnson, Grace Sanders. 2023. *White Gloves, Black Nation: Women, Citizenship, and Political Wayfaring in Haiti.* Chapel Hill: University of North Carolina Press.

Kali Films. 2013. *Resurrecting Zora Neale Hurston, Alice Walker: Beauty in Truth.* Kali Films LTD and Kali8 Productions LLC.

Murray, Derek Conrad. 2015. "Notes to Self: The Visual Culture of Selfies in the Age of Social Media." *Consumption Markets & Culture* 18, no. 6: 490–516.

Perez, Jeanne. 1937. "Bienvenue." *La voix des femmes: Revue mensuelle* 2, no. 19: 4.

Price-Mars, Jean. 1928. *So Spoke the Uncle (Ainsi parla l'oncle, Essais d'ethnographie).* Paris: Imprimerie de Compiègne.

Price-Mars, Jean. 1951. "Haitian Folklore." In *An Introduction to Haiti*, edited by Mercer Cook, 51–52. Washington, DC: Pan American Union.

Roumain, Jacques. 1941. *Masters of the Dew (Gouverneur de la Rosée).* Port-au-Prince.

Sofer, Cyril. 1953. "Review." *Africa* 23, no. 1: 80–81.

Thompson, Krista A. 2007. *An Eye for the Tropics: Tourism, Photography, and Framing the Caribbean Picturesque.* Durham, NC: Duke University Press.

Thompson, Krista A. 2015. *Shine: The Visual Economy of Light in African Diasporic Aesthetic Practice.* Durham, NC: Duke University Press.

Ulysse, Gina A. 2007. *Downtown Ladies: Informal Commercial Importers, A Haitian Anthropologist, and Self-Making in Jamaica.* Chicago: University of Chicago Press.

Wexler, Laura. 2000. *Tender Violence: Domestic Visions in an Age of U.S. Imperialism.* Chapel Hill: University of North Carolina Press.

Woodson, Carter G. 1937. "Review of *Le Creole Haitien* and *Les Contes Haitien* by S. Comhaire-Sylvain." *Journal of Negro History* 22 (July): 369–372.

Cherise Fung

In the Name of Sovereignty
Rethinking the "Tiger Bitch" and the Terrorist Bomber
in Nayomi Munaweera's *Island of a Thousand Mirrors* (2012)

Abstract: In a post-9/11 world, the figure of the female suicide bomber has
emerged as a contentious figure in global discourse. Through the character
of Saraswathi, Nayomi Munaweera's novel *Island of a Thousand Mirrors*
(2012) foregrounds how the construction of this subaltern figure hinges on
her susceptibility to rape. This relationship between rape and suicide
bombing is deployed differently by the counterterrorist institutions that
target her and the ethnonationalist movements that recruit her to make
her speak as both victim and agent while silencing her. This article thus
argues that we need to move away from the framework of victimhood and
agency, which assumes subjectivity without accounting for how the body of
the female subaltern is excluded from inhabiting subjecthood as a construct
of bounded national sovereignty. Using Jasbir Puar's theory of queer assemblage, the author explains how Saraswathi's suicide bomber in ITM is constructed as a figure of antinormative subjectivity through a discourse of U.S.
exceptionalism in opposition to a normative U.S. national identity and
sovereignty. The author builds on Puar's insights, which draw on affect theory, to rethink Saraswathi's violent protest as a moment that destabilizes
these normative identities and their related social scripts. The author further posits alternative visions of antinormative subjectivity in the novel that
allow for Saraswathi's survival after her rape.

In a post-9/11 world, the figure of the female suicide bomber has emerged
as a contentious figure in global discourses on counterterrorism and
national security. As a figure that defies gendered norms of domestic

MERIDIANS · feminism, race, transnationalism   22:2 October 2023
DOI: 10.1215/15366936-10626350 © 2023 Smith College

passivity, she inspires both interest and fear in members of the general public and security experts alike: "Burqaed and belted-up to the nines, she is the ultimate Other, transgressing not only civilizational prohibitions against murder and suicide, but also deeply ingrained assumptions about what it means to be a woman in patriarchal societies where women are accorded lesser status" (Cottee and Bloom 2017). The idea of rigid gender roles and gender oppression in regressive patriarchal societies hinges on an Orientalist worldview that structures understandings of the female suicide bomber. Her path to political agency through violence is read as resistance to an Orientalized patriarchy (Brunner 2007: 964). This paradigm extends to not just female suicide bombers in the Islamic world but also those beyond it, as in the case of the Liberation Tigers of Tamil Eelam (LTTE) during the Sri Lankan civil war. The LTTE's use of women fighters and suicide bombers has been described, in words that reveal similar presumptions, as extraordinary and effective, considering that women are culturally valued in Sri Lanka for their "quiet passivity" (Filkins 2000).

Nayomi Munaweera's debut novel, Island of a Thousand Mirrors (2012), shows the persistence of this kind of narrative in delimiting the representational parameters of the female suicide bomber through the figure of Saraswathi, a Tamil woman who joins the secessionist fight of the LTTE, during the Sri Lankan civil war from July 1983 to May 2009. This war was a result of conflict between the Sri Lankan government, then controlled by the dominant Sinhalese majority, and the LTTE, a militant separatist group that represented the interests of the minority Tamil population in pursuing political independence and a separate state (Jayasuriya 2012: 8–11; Nadarajah and Sriskandarajah 2005: 94). We first meet Saraswathi as a relatively carefree girl and a bright student who is hopeful about the prospects of her future despite the daily horrors of war-torn northern Sri Lanka. Her dreams of becoming a teacher, however, are punctured when she is gang-raped by a group of Sinhalese soldiers who mistakenly accuse her of being a "Tiger Bitch" (Munaweera 2012: 152). Rape disqualifies her from fulfilling her role in her community as a chaste Tamil woman and brings shame on her and her family. As a result, her mother presents only one bleak path for her survival, which is to join the Tamil Tigers: "You must go. Show people that you are a good girl. If you don't go, no one will believe that you were taken by force. They will say, she is not even angry. There is a checkpoint close to the house and she must have encouraged them in some way. We will lose face with everyone. You must go. It is the only way" (160). Pressured by her family, Saraswathi joins the LTTE after her rape to wreck vengeance on Sinhalese communities. Her only other option appears to be committing suicide, a lesson she observes from the tragic death of her friend, Parvathi, who drowns herself in a well after she is raped by a soldier and shunned by her community (143).

Saraswathi's narrative culminates when she commits the ultimate honor of suicide bombing for her people's cause at a political rally of a Tamil politician-turned-traitor (195). Her act of self-other destruction releases her from the shame that has plagued her since her rape, transporting her into a realm of spiritual transcendence in a flash of "blinding light" and "cleansing pain" (216). Gayatri Spivak (2004: 96) contends that such suicidal resistance is the only means of communication when discourse is structured to preclude subaltern expression so that it "is both execution and mourning, for both self and other, where you die with me for the same cause, no matter which side you are on, with the implication that there is no dishonor in such shared death." Yet her act of agential protest is eclipsed by the end of the novel as her identity is reduced to an "unnamed, unloved assassin" in the eyes of the surviving relatives of Lanka Rajasinghe, a Sri Lankan American and ethnic Sinhalese woman who is killed during the attack (Munaweera 2012: 236). The image of Saraswathi blasting her body apart is negated by the novel's closing scene, which depicts Lanka's sister, Yasodhara, imagining her daughter emerging from an ocean in Sri Lanka as a wholesome product of peace with the "waves lick[ing] away her footsteps, the sand retaining no record of what came before her" (237).

Given this representational elision, how might we understand the female subaltern and her act of protest in ways that move beyond this injurious silencing? How might we make sense of the female suicide bomber in this novel as a figure who is both highly visible as an object of national security interests yet silent in her various representational iterations? In this essay, I demonstrate how the causal relationship between rape and female suicide bombing proffered by security studies—a field that is dominated by the national security interests of the United States and its allies (Brunner 2007: 968)—creates harmful binary assumptions regarding the victimhood and agency of female suicide bombers. In doing so, these national security interests come to stand in for the voices of female suicide bombers such as Saraswathi. Scholarly assertions of agency for this figure are predicated on her alignment with masculinized ethnonationalist struggles, which fail to account for her constitution as the antithesis of agency by virtue of her preclusion as a subject of a sovereign masculinized nation within the Orientalist framework of the global war on terror. *Island of a Thousand Mirrors* (ITM), in particular, foregrounds the limitations of recovering agency for Saraswathi as a subaltern figure against the narrative dominance of the novel's Sri-Lankan American characters in justifying the expansion of U.S. empire.

Given these representational limitations, I argue that we need to shift the discursive terrain from the victim/agent binary by turning to Jasbir Puar's (2005) theory of the suicide bomber as queer assemblage. This approach challenges the assumption of subjects as preconstituted whole, bounded bodies tied to sovereign nation-states; instead, it attends to the forces that construct these bodies in relation to the environment in different moments. I illustrate how the U.S. characters in the novel uphold U.S. identity as the normative embodiment of this national subjectivity through a discourse of exceptionalism against the subaltern figure of Saraswathi as an emblem of antinational (and thus antinormative) identity.

I apply Puar's (2005) framework to destabilize the limited social scripts of normative national subjectivity. Building on Puar's (2005) insights, which draw from affect theory, I then identify other possible modes of antinormative subjectivity in the novel that depart from the demands of sovereign subjectivity through the works of Susan J. Brison (2002) and Veena Das (2006); these works address the remaking of the self after sexual trauma and gendered postcolonial trauma, respectively. By articulating the possibility of Saraswathi's bodily continuity through social connectivity, I challenge the seemingly inevitable conclusion of the rape-to-female-suicide-bombing trajectory that demands her death. My goal is not to speak for the subaltern but to identify other possible modes for her survival in the aftermath of sexual trauma that do not reproduce the battle for her recruitment in the service of masculine empire or ethnonationalism. In doing so, I offer an alternative understanding of cross-ethnic and transnational feminist solidarities that move beyond normative sovereign subjectivity.

The sexual violation of women like Saraswathi is deployed by both the counterterrorist organizations who study them and the militant movements who recruit them, in their respective masculinist terms of U.S. hegemony and ethnonationalism. Rape is often cited as a causal factor in these women's decisions to undertake suicide bombing within a security studies framework driven by U.S. national security interests (Bloom 2011: 237; Stack-O'Connor 2007: 55; O'Rourke 2009: 712). Sexual trauma is central to her discursive construction in a security studies narrative to undergird the necessity of Western masculine rescue against Islamic or Third World patriarchy (Deylami 2013: 178). While there has been a heightened perception of the Middle East as a hotbed of Islamic terrorism in a post-9/11 milieu, I would argue that a similar Orientalist discourse operates for the LTTE as an organization that has been blacklisted by many in the international community for its use of terrorist violence even though it is not religiously motivated (Yass 2014: 72–73). Sri Lankan society and its Tamil community are susceptible to similar charges of patriarchal oppression, which circumscribes the Islamic Middle East in the eyes of the West. Such charges of patriarchal oppression have been used to justify direct U.S. military intervention in the Middle East. While Sri Lankan patriarchal values did not result in direct U.S. military intervention in the Sri Lankan civil conflict, I contend that this assessment of patriarchal oppression remains relevant for female suicide bombers in the LTTE, who are often grouped together with those from other geographic regions including the Middle East in scholarly discussions of counterterrorism (O'Rourke 2009: 706–7; Bloom 2011: 137). The causal trajectory of these women from victims of sexual violence to perpetrators of terrorist violence substantiates the narrative of U.S. masculine hegemony against an infantilized, feminized other who paradoxically presents a threat to the former's national security.[1]

On the other side of the equation, national liberation groups—or terrorist organizations and illegitimate political actors according to a security studies perspective—such as the LTTE view these women as martyrs for their ethnonationalist cause (De Mel 2001: 223). The LTTE emerged in 1972 as an extremist faction of the Tamil independence political movement, a response to "institutionalized racism and violence against the Tamil people by a Sinhala-dominated state" (Nadarajah and Sriskandarajah 2005: 88–89). Sri Lanka's highly charged postindependence ethnic relations is commonly understood to be a product of British colonization.[2] Resentful of the privileges conferred on the Tamils, who are predominantly Hindus, by the British colonial administration, the Sinhalese exercised their power as the majority group to establish political dominance on gaining independence from Britain in 1948. The Sinhalese-dominated government subsequently implemented exclusionary constitutional principles and policies such as the Ceylon Citizenship Act to exclude Tamils (and their language and religion) from the project of nation building (Jayasuriya 2012: 9–11).[3] Although the group is antinationalist in relation to the Sri Lankan state and the Sinhalese-dominated government, it nonetheless subscribes to a nationalist view of ethnic Tamil identity in its stated goals for an independent state called Tamil Eelam (Nadarajah and Sriskandarajah 2005: 88). Instead of "a mere 'non-state actor' in Sri Lanka's conflict or the peace process," the LTTE presented itself as a "'regional state' of the 'Tamil nation' or a 'state in the making'" (Uyangoda 2010: 30).

Gender appeared to be irrelevant for the LTTE in advancing political goals as leaders set aside more traditional understandings of women's roles out of political necessity (De Mel 2001: 215). Women were thus viewed equally with their male counterparts in their capacity to wield violence in the service of Tamil ethnonationalism (223). At the same time, gender remained salient for the LTTE's recruitment and retention of female fighters against a common enemy force. The LTTE reportedly cited the sexual assault of Tamil women by Sri Lankan and Indian soldiers as evidence of systemic state brutality against the Tamil people, thereby shoring up support for their cause (Stack-O'Connor 2007: 56). The symbolic equating of women's sexual integrity with ethnic or national loyalty by the LTTE in the context of the Sri Lankan civil war is not unique. As Janet Halley (2008: 108) illustrates in her reading of *A Woman in Berlin*, sexual relations with enemy forces, even ones that are consensual, are vilified as acts of national disloyalty. We see this gendered investment in national identity play out with Saraswathi, whose sexual violation at the hands of enemy forces is intertwined with discourses of political and ethnic allegiance to present only two choices for her narrative: Parvathi's way of death or a reassertion of selfhood through masculinized violence in pursuing the LTTE's quest for political sovereignty. The options outlined for Saraswathi respond to her rape within this patriarchal structure as a fate akin to or "worse than death," thus foreclosing any possibility for survival (112).

Both these discourses work to delimit the female suicide bomber as either victim or agent, "an object of homoterritorial contestation between two ostensibly masculinist enterprises: empire and terror" (Deylami 2013: 178).[4] Shirin S. Deylami (2013) argues that these competing narratives work to silence the female suicide bomber, thus indexing another instance of how the "subaltern cannot speak" (Spivak 1994: 104).[5] The voice of the female suicide bomber is claimed so unequivocally by both imperial and ethnonationalist forces that even her attempts to rewrite the script would be made to represent agendas that are not her own (Deylami 2013: 188). These discursive constraints overdetermine the portrayal of Saraswathi's act of suicide protest in *ITM*:

The bus lurches to a stop and I am in another place, a bullet-splattered cement room open to a perfect square of sky, and I cannot tell where the walls end and the sky begins—Tiger bitch—and where the voices begin and the hands end, and where I begin or end, and I am tearing into shreds and something buried deep is erupting like a land mine, like rage buried in my flesh, something settled—Tiger bitch—and burrowed under my heart like a fetus raising its head. Tiger bitch Tiger bitch Tiger bitch! (Munaweera 2012: 216)

Disguised as a pregnant woman, she boards a bus to reach her target but is thwarted by an unexpected security check en route and detonates her bomb prematurely. Although we see her speak in this passage, I contend that we need to keep Spivak's (1994) argument in mind in evaluating this speech as an approximation of her voice. If we read this scene according to the parameters set by a counterterrorist framework, we see Saraswathi doubling down on her identity as a Tiger bitch, the derogatory term that first makes her a target of the Sinhalese soldiers but which she has now apparently reclaimed by joining the Tamil Tigers. The "bullet-splattered cement room" is a direct reference to the scene of her rape, which reinforces the relationship between sexual victimization and suicide violence detailed by counterterrorist studies to feed the security apparatus of the global war on terror. Conversely, this act of protest is conceived by the LTTE as the ultimate expression of commitment and sacrifice to advance the LTTE's fight against Sinhalese oppression. Saraswathi internalizes the notion that aligning herself with masculinized ethnonationalism is the only way to escape the shame of rape, thus calcifying her identity as an enemy in relation to the Sinhalese. Given this alignment with ethnonationalism, I will demonstrate how Saraswathi is effaced as a female Tamil insurgent not only by the struggle between empire and nation but also within the national history of the Sri Lankan government's condemnation of the LTTE's terrorist violence "as a challenge to its authority, unity and territorial integrity" (Nadarajah and Sriskandarajah 2005: 88).

Security studies, however, has unfortunately set the terms of discussion for literary analyses of female suicide bombers in Sri Lanka. Literary readings unwittingly affirm this paradigm by reproducing the discursive terms of patriarchal structures that can only result in mutually exclusive assignments of victimhood or agency, while obscuring U.S. national security interests that define such identity constructs. Neloufer De Mel (2004: 79) contends that the patriarchal structures of the LTTE and the Sri Lankan state appropriate the female suicide bomber's narrative authority as an agent. Maryse Jayasuriya (2013) traces representations of the female suicide bomber in literature and film according to the same gendered tropes established by counterterrorist experts through her identification and examination of the effects of rape, the pursuit of family vengeance, and the draw of motherhood in selected works. While she gestures toward a literary reading that moves beyond these gendered tropes toward the end of her essay, she quickly drops this line of argument and concludes that more work needs to be done in creating "a more nuanced understanding of these women's motivations, fears, and desires" (146).[6] These critical works, although helpful in uncovering the possibilities and limits of feminist agency within an androcentric national discourse, do not attend to the interaction of the female suicide bomber with larger geopolitical forces. In doing so, the scholarly project of recuperating agency by creating a more nuanced understanding of these women's motivations also reproduces the theoretical constraints of security studies in speaking for this figure.[7]

Ascriptions of agency to female suicide bombers ignore their fundamental preclusion from the masculine frameworks of imperialism, anti-colonialism, and ethnonationalism, as evidenced by ITM. The presence of two U.S. citizens in the novel, Yasodhara and Lanka Rajasinghe, elucidates the collusion between these forces in constructing Saraswathi as a subaltern figure and co-opting her act of protest. Though born as ethnic Sinhalese and raised partly in Sri Lanka, Yasodhara and Lanka Rajasinghe emigrate with their family to the United States after the 1983 racial riots. The lives of these three characters intersect when the Rajasinghe sisters return to Colombo as adults for a visit. Saraswathi detonates her bomb on the same bus that Lanka is riding after work, thus killing her and the other passengers in a moment of subaltern protest. Yet in Yasodhara's retelling of the war, Saraswathi becomes an unknown entity in contrast to her dead sister, Lanka: "I dream of the one that I can give a name to: my sister, Lanka Rajasinghe. And that other, her unnamed, unloved assassin" (Munaweera 2012: 236). Yasodhara's description of Lanka in this instance humanizes her sister by giving her a name while dehumanizing Saraswathi as a nameless antagonist unworthy of love. The radical nature of Saraswathi's acts of militancy and violent self-other dissolution falters, and eventually dissipates, in the aftermath of her death as she is discursively silenced by the U.S. citizens in the novel. The remaining pages of the novel shift back to Yasodhara's experience after the suicide bombing, thus reshaping Saraswathi's story through her eyes.

The sisters' narrative dominance extends the dynamics of masculine imperialism by relegating Saraswathi's suicide bomber to silence. Existing scholarship on ITM, however, does not address these dynamics as wielded in the novel through Yasodhara and Lanka as Sri Lankan, Sinhalese women who are also U.S. citizens. The (small) body of scholarly work on the novel often situates it in terms of Sri Lankan diasporic women's writing either to analyze the continuing trauma of the Sri Lankan civil war or to critique the circumscription of the female suicide bomber within patriarchal nationalism; neither approach situates this figure within the context of counterterrorist discourse driven by U.S. national interests (Jayasuriya 2016: 146; Heidemann 2019: 387). For example, Birte Heidemann (2019: 12) argues that, "by employing two female protagonists from across the ethnic divide, the novel succeeds in presenting a balanced perspective on Sri Lanka's polarized political identities at different stages of the war." Heidemann's reading places Yasodhara's and Saraswathi's identities and perspectives on an equal plane in ways that ignore how the former's attainment of U.S. citizenship changes her relationship to her native country and the trauma of civil war. Similarly, while Shamara Ransirini (2017: 35–38) argues that Saraswathi's suicide illustrates a more fluid political self-conception beyond a victim/perpetrator binary, she does not fully explore how this ambiguous subjectivity interacts with Yasodhara's status as a U.S. subject.

The distinctions between the Rajasinghe sisters as U.S. citizens and the local Sri Lankans are emphasized repeatedly throughout the novel. After their family uproots to the United States to escape the unfolding chaos of civil war, the sisters grow up in relative prosperity as they assimilate into American culture, becoming more adamant with each passing year in maintaining their distance and difference from their newly arrived Sri Lankan counterparts. They are duly rewarded with the bestowal of American citizenship, becoming the "most privileged and God-blessed persons on the planet" (Munaweera 2012: 161). While this statement alone could be excused as tongue-in-cheek, the sisters' subsequent actions and attitudes during their return to Sri Lanka make such a dismissal more difficult. As U.S. citizens, they are at once part of the chaotic scene of civil conflict, but also shielded from the worst of it. Passing a military checkpoint at nightfall, a privilege denied local people, is easily done with a careless wave of

Lanka's American passport—"Don't look so shocked, Akka. We have these magic things after all. They keep us protected from all this madness" (198).

As such, the Rajasinghe sisters settle quickly into a comfortable rhythm of life, teaching at the school during the day and walking leisurely along Galle Road and the beach in the evenings. Daily news of bloodshed does little to disrupt this idyllic existence because in Colombo, away from the epicenter of the fighting in the north, "it is possible to pretend that all of it is happening somewhere else . . . while the only thing affected here is the price of shrimp coming from the northern lagoons" (205). They vacation along the southern coast at Hikkaduwa, their father's home village, reveling in the pleasures of sun and sea while laughing at the other tourists even as they are acutely aware that they are only "a different shade of tourist" from these white Europeans, having themselves abandoned local customs (207). Neither one of them seems to feel particularly distressed by this awareness, safe in the knowledge that they are inoculated in certain ways from the reality of violence in Sri Lanka. For them, Sri Lanka is a means of escape. When Yasodhara decides to return to America toward the end of the novel, she expresses how the demands of her students, studies, and estranged husband will quickly eclipse her time in Sri Lanka: "By the time I reach LAX, it will be a faint memory, washed away by the dryness of the air, the loud questioning of immigration officials, and the glare of the desert sun" (209).

The relative ease with which the Rajasinghe sisters navigate material violence compared to Saraswathi is especially evident in the novel's treatment of their respective bodies in relation to the trauma of war. Though Lanka and Saraswathi both perish in the explosion, the former's body is depicted as relatively whole and unmarred, whereas the latter's remains comprise bloodied fragments. Yasodhara can still discern her sister's facial features and imagine her last acts of consciousness as she lies dead, "eyes focused on the ceiling in wonder, mouth puckered. As if she were seeing it happen" (222). In contrast, Saraswathi's head is severed from her body and mutilated into "wisps of ribboned flesh" and scarlet "jellyfish tentacles" from the blast (219). The police officer at the morgue confirms the singularity of Yasodhara's situation, telling her that she is "lucky. A lot of the other people have no body. Only pieces of flesh to burn or bury" (224). Yasodhara's blue U.S. passport allows her to invoke the power of the American Embassy in speeding up the process of identifying Lanka, a privilege that further distinguishes her from the locals and causes some resentment (221). Saraswathi's remains, on the other hand, are dumped unceremoniously into a plastic bag by policemen, and Saraswathi herself is described by Yasodhara as a "vanquished Medusa, death dealer, and serial killer" (219). The differences between how these two bodies are treated in the novel cannot be examined apart from the geopolitical structures that delineate the humanity and legitimacy of certain bodies as proper subjects over others.

The image of Lanka's whole, unblemished body as a U.S. citizen is significant in relation to Saraswathi's unidentifiable bodily fragments as a subaltern. The function of U.S. identity here serves to uphold a form of dominant masculinist ideology that necessitates the preservation of bodily coherence as an index of national sovereignty in geopolitical relations. Recognitions of state sovereignty form the bedrock of modern international politics and depend on bounded, stable state borders (Weber 1995: 1; Wilcox 2014: 68–69).[8] Lauren Wilcox (2014: 68) contends that the illusion of bounded bodies and states is mutually constituted by sovereignty as an expression of "unity and agency, the ability to self-govern and act autonomously" in this global order. She explains that representations of the sovereign state as a masculine body (as in the "body politic") are not merely metaphorical but produce states and the bodies of their citizens as objects with distinct borders (69–70). Abjection is crucial to this exercise of sovereign production in preserving the illusion of coherent bodies (68).[9] Female bodies, which are already configured as abject in relation to normative "white, heterosexual, able-bodied men" (70), elicit further horror and disgust when embodied by female suicide bombers in relation to the nation-state. Their acts of bodily annihilation threaten the concept of bounded bodies and the security apparatus of bounded states that are central to the existence of modern statehood (71–72). The predominance of this model of coherent national sovereignty in structuring the international political milieu thus informs the novel's preservation of Lanka's bodily coherence as a subject in relation to Saraswathi's subaltern figure.

This discursive silencing of female suicide bombers reveals a deeper foundational assumption of security studies regarding state sovereignty and how their terrorist acts threaten this global order. Given its role in spearheading counterterrorism initiatives, the U.S. state is especially invested in maintaining its bodily integrity and those of its citizens by systemically manufacturing and managing female suicide bombers as the antithesis of sovereignty. Puar's (2005) theory of queer assemblage is especially useful in considering how bodies themselves are constituted as subjects in relation to political sovereignty within a geopolitical hierarchy.

In contrast to identitarian frameworks that assume subjectivity as a corollary of bound bodies, Puar (2005: 127–28) draws from Gilles Deleuze and Félix Guattari's (1987) assemblage to focus more on how various social forces "merge and dissipate time, space, and body" against the fiction of stable, coherent identity across linear space and time.[10] Attending to these forces, she argues, allows us to examine how the body of the suicide bomber is constructed as not only a nonsubject but also an anti-subject by U.S. geopolitical supremacy as a complex social articulation of race, gender, sexuality, empire, and globalization (Puar 2005: 123).[11] Queerness as an identity category is deployed in the service of U.S. imperialist expansion in the war on terror (123). The (white) gay American community's condemnation of the Abu Ghraib sexual scandal as homophobic oppression serves to uphold "an orientalist notion of 'Muslim sexuality,'" while allowing the United States to project itself as the exceptional space of sexual liberation (124). Queer exceptionalism allows the United States to articulate itself as the normative space of identity in opposition to the terrorist figure (125). Consequently, queerness as an identity category is subsumed under the rubric of U.S. national citizenship, thereby allowing queerness to be redefined and reassembled as antinational in the figure of the terrorist (131). Saraswathi embodies this redefined queerness as a terrorist and subaltern figure in the case of ITM.

I would argue that Puar's theory helps us understand the operation of American exceptionalism through the diasporic figures of Yasodhara and Lanka. Like queer identity in the case of the Abu Ghraib scandal, the sisters' gender and racial diversity are recruited by the same normativizing function of U.S. citizenship to allow for the expansion of its identity categories through the discourse of American exceptionalism. As Puar (2017: 165) asserts in her reading of the Lawrence and Garner v. Texas (2003) case and its role in decriminalizing sodomy, "citizenship remains a critical yet undertheorized facet of sexual regulation in the United States" in relation to the war on terror. By extending citizenship to bodies that would typically be excluded from normative whiteness, the United States is able to utilize a logic of multicultural pluralism to produce and patrol homonationalism (92). The purpose of American exceptionalism in recruiting these diverse bodies is to project them as the normative standard for identity, as is the case with the production of queer identity as normatively white, U.S. subjects (Puar 2005: 123).

Under the aegis of U.S. exceptionalism, the Rajasinghe sisters are reconfigured as proper national subjects with whole, coherent bodies in relation to the queer subalternity of Saraswathi as an antinational terrorist—a nameless, faceless villain and murderer, and the antithesis of normative identity, thus exemplifying how "queerness is always already installed in the project of naming the terrorist" (127). My goal in highlighting the sisters' role in perpetuating American exceptionalism is not to dismiss the violence that directly affects them in the 1983 riots or Saraswathi's suicide bombing, but to point out how their attainment of U.S. citizenship shifts their relationship both materially and discursively with their native country and people. The fact that Lanka's bodily and narrative integrity escapes Saraswathi's self/other annihilatory act speaks to the difficulties of subverting the exceptionalized status of U.S. national identity.

Considering the salience of Yasodhara's status as a U.S. citizen in ITM, her celebration of peace and reconnection with her Sri Lankan roots consequently enacts a neocolonial erasure of the extent and depth of trauma resulting from this interethnic conflict. Though she acknowledges the magnitude of death caused by the war after her sister's death (Munaweera 2012: 236), it is overshadowed by her hopes for connecting her American-born daughter, Samudhara, to her Sri Lankan heritage. At the close of the novel, she expresses a desire for Sam to know the contours of the island and take part in its pleasures, from the depths of its ocean with its "blue-green moods" and "finned creatures" to the "bare-chested fishermen" who will "teach her their songs" (237). She will show Sam how to dive so that the water becomes one with her pulse, and how she can "claim this submerged world as her own" (237). Yasodhara imagines Sam emerging from the ocean, confident in her claim on the island:

> She drips seawater. She has grown so tall, into a young woman . . . [h]er skin is shining dark, polished by sun and salt.
>
> She walks in purpose and self-knowledge, a long, rolling walk that unfolds from the hip. She is a child of the peace, the many disparate parts of her experience knit together in jumbled but peaceable unity. The waves lick away her footsteps, the sand retaining no record of what came before her. (237)

This passage positions Sam as a subject whose identity is enriched and serviced by Sri Lanka—along with its people and culture—as an object for her to know and derive pleasure. Such a positioning constructs Sam in similar terms to a U.S. tourist. Yasodhara's hopes are further disconcerting because the self-assurance she projects in the seamless interweaving of Sam's mixed heritage as the daughter of a Sinhalese mother and a Tamil father effaces the material history of interethnic violence and fracture that has engendered her existence. The language of claiming she uses in this passage to describe Sam's relationship to the island is also problematic, given the ongoing exercise of U.S. imperialism across the globe. In this final image, the supremacy of U.S. national identity as embodied by Sam is upheld as a symbol of normative bodily coherence and sovereignty against Saraswathi's self-dissolution as the epitome of antinormative bodily incoherence. In doing so, the unified body of the U.S. subject not only erases the fractured history of Sri Lanka's bloody interethnic conflict but also projects itself as the canvas on which the roots of Tamil-Sinhalese enmity can be reconciled. Whatever claims of agential resistance we can make for Saraswathi dissipates in the confluence between the androcentrisms of U.S. empire and ethnonationalism that insist on her silence.

Queer assemblage's elucidation of U.S. supremacy in delimiting the antinational subaltern, however, is not a concession to its inevitable hold on Saraswathi's constitution. Puar (2005: 131) additionally contends that the political utility of assemblage lies in its ability to untether our understandings of identity from the seemingly immutable scripts of race, gender, sexuality, nationality, and empire. In the context of the female suicide bomber, the body itself is blasted apart as the corporeal container of subjectivity, the ultimate resistance against the hegemonic demands of Western, heteronormative, and state-sanctioned identity (131). We return to the earlier scene of Saraswathi's self-other annihilation not as a re-instantiation of sides in the Sri Lankan conflict and the larger context of the War on Terror that produces bodies along established lines of gendered and racialized national identity, but one that foregrounds the assemblage of these bodies as a state of "always becoming" (136). This revised formulation of bodies in relation to the nation-state is crucial in resisting "narratives of U.S. exceptionalism that secure empire, challenging the fixity of racial and sexual taxonomies that inform practices of state surveillance and control, and befuddling the 'us versus them' of the war on terror" (128).

In contrast to assuming the roles of the bodies on the bus as a given according to identitarian frameworks (i.e., evil terrorist and innocent civilian), Puar's queer assemblage reading of the turbaned terrorist is instrumental here in highlighting the affective, tactile, and other intangible elements that precede and shape the construction of the female suicide bomber in any given moment (134). In her last moments on the bus, affect displaces identity as Saraswathi's sense of spatial and temporal ordering begins to unravel and she and her environment blend into each other—"I cannot tell where the walls end and the sky begins—Tiger bitch—and where the voices begin and the hands end, and where I begin or end" (Munaweera 2012: 216). Panic, fear, and rage condense in a potent affective cocktail to bring her back to the scene of her rape even as her body is both blasted apart by, and blends with, the metallic explosive device, creating what Puar (2005: 129) calls a "queer temporality" that transmits "affective information between and amid beings." The force of the explosion upsets our artificial organization of time, space, and matter by dissolving the coherence of bodies along the register of national identity categories, reducing both self and other to bloodied and blackened bits that fuse indiscriminately with the iron entrails of the bus (Munaweera 2012: 219). In this moment, Saraswathi's act of self/other dissolution allows us to glimpse how the materiality of the body itself is converted into an event, thus challenging the notion of events as a set of discrete acts perpetuated by coherent bodies with sovereign wills (Massumi 2002: 14–15).This unraveling of the self in relation to others and the environment offers a powerful image of how the "Tiger Bitch" is not a stable, preexisting identity but its antithesis as a subaltern figure continuously constructed by various political forces.

In challenging coherent bodies as a natural representation of state-sanctioned identities, I contend that a queer assemblage reading of Saraswathi's suicide bombing provides the conditions for a rereading of the female suicide bomber beyond the identities of victimhood and agency circumscribed by patriarchal Orientalism or ethnonationalism. Her death confirms neither the rape-victim-to-suicide-bomber trajectory of security studies nor its counternarrative of agential reclamation; instead, it allows us to identify other possible modes of subaltern being even though they are foreclosed and submerged in the novel. In this sense, I am extending the conclusions of Puar (2005) in locating the political utility of the suicide bomber in her moment of bodily dissolution; I argue for the possibility of employing queer assemblage to detach the notion of bodily survival from the violence of maintaining sovereign subjectivity.

Such a rereading requires that we revisit the aftermath of Saraswathi's rape. Deeply traumatized after the attack by the Sinhalese soldiers, Saraswathi spends weeks in seclusion in the back room of her house. She describes a dissociation from her body, recognizing her emaciated image in the mirror yet struggling to acknowledge it as her own:

> In Amma's cloudy mirror, I catch a glimpse of a girl. I know she is me, only because there is no one else in the room. . . .
>   The flesh has dripped from me. The hair that Amma combs every day hangs limp like oily curtains on either side of my face. I want to draw them shut. Close off the view of this terrified, wide-eyed creature who looks out of my eyes. (157)

In this moment, we can see how sexual trauma shatters the notion of a sovereign coherent subject, which is already a myth of (Western) normative subjectivity, but even more so for her as a subaltern antinational. However, Saraswathi is unable to conceive of survival with the vision and feeling of herself wasting away. The script of rape-as-death—which is informed by existing gendered norms within ethnonationalist discourses of loyalty and pre-installed in Saraswathi by the rape of her friend, Parvathi—intensifies her disgust toward the corrupted nature of her flesh (158). This disgust is reinforced by her parents, who see her as a source of shame and ruin. Rape shatters not only her social conception of self as a chaste, marriageable Tamil woman but also her relation to others. This loss of a coherent self as a future wife in the script of Tamil patriarchy also jeopardizes her family's social status within that script (159).

If we employ queer assemblage to examine this period of isolation, however, we can attend to the affective conditions generated by this "event-space" to heighten Saraswathi's relation to her body, thus uncovering identity formation as a continual process in contrast to the inevitability of her death according to existing scripts of Orientalized patriarchal oppression or ethnonationalist loyalty (Puar 2012: 63). The appearance of Saraswathi's teacher, Miss Rajasingham, some weeks later introduces an element of uncertainty into these scripts. Still ashamed at the smell of men buried in her skin, Saraswathi refuses to see her teacher. But Miss "stays for so long that I start to think maybe she wouldn't mind so much about the smell" (Munaweera 2012: 158). Saraswathi finds herself raising her head and "willing [her] legs to move" in response to the promise of a life of learning and teaching she harbored before the attack (158). The fact that her teacher might still accept her as a person worthy of survival despite being "spoiled" by men provides a crucial counterpoint to the shame and dishonor she now represents to her family.

The scene with Miss Rajasingham thus presents a third option for subaltern being and self-other relationality that challenges the two seemingly
inevitable choices of committing suicide like her friend, Parvathi, or fighting for the Tamil Tigers and committing suicide bombing. Both these
choices culminate in death and are born out of a commitment to the prevailing masculinized logic of coherent bodily and national boundaries that
cannot accommodate the notion of harm and trauma. However, her
teacher leaves just as Saraswathi begins accepting the imprint of harm on
her body, thus signaling a "closing off of one becoming, routed into
another assemblage" (Puar 2012: 61). The path of survival, of living with a
shattered self through her teacher's support without turning to violence,
vanishes in that moment for Saraswathi: "I see her ride away in my mind's
eye. I watch her until she is only a streak of vermilion against the green
banana trees and tall, waving palmyras, and then she is gone and I am truly
alone" (Munaweera 2012: 158). Left alone to contend with the weight of
shame, Saraswathi cannot bring herself to engage with the books her
teacher has left her. She looks hopelessly at the numbers on the page, now a
"blurring, messy heap" that she can no longer make sense of and realizes
that her dream of pursuing a teaching career "has slipped through [her]
fingers" (159). Though this moment of reclaiming survival is short-lived
and ultimately suppressed, it remains pivotal in highlighting the potential
for rupture in a seemingly closed circuit of coherent identities and scripts.
Such a potential does not claim to resolve the stain of "Tiger bitch" as a
subaltern figure; it merely proffers a glimmer of another form of antinormative subjectivity, one that encompasses survival in the wake of sexual
harm and challenges the inevitable violent conclusions of the subaltern
suicide bomber.

The possibility of undoing the subject/nonsubject dichotomy presented
by this scene resembles the concept of empathetic witnessing outlined by
Brison (2002). While Brison's framework cannot account for Saraswathi's
situation in a postcolonial context, I am interested in exploring how her
vision for reconceptualizing the self through her own brutal rape experience and attempted murder might offer some insight for my rereading of
the female suicide bomber. Brison's notion of empathetic witnessing supports this reconceptualization by acknowledging the self as inherently
relational, and thus both vulnerable to being violated by others but also
capable of being remade in social connection (xi). This interdependency is
especially crucial in the wake of sexual trauma in which a self-concept

invested in sovereignty or autonomy is injured, thereby necessitating a need for the surviving self to be "known and acknowledged in order to exist" (62).

Brison's (2002) conception of self-other relationality thus offers us a way to build on Puar's (2005) insights regarding the queerness of the female suicide bomber as an assemblage of affective, tactile, and sensory elements to chart an alternative framework that allows for the possibility of Saraswathi's survival after sexual trauma. Developing such a framework for subaltern survival is important in challenging the discursive violence wrought by the victim/agent binary—and its demands for allegiance to sovereign statehood—in suturing the female suicide bomber to a fate of death. Subaltern survival for Saraswathi dovetails with Brison's (2002: 110–11) experience of surviving rape in that it not only entails an acceptance of a coherent self as a myth but also holds onto the potential to be heard by a listener who is "stable and reliable enough to bear witness" to her project of revising an "unfolding narrative" of trauma and recovery. The presence of Saraswathi's teacher as a potential empathetic witness could have mitigated her turn to self-other destruction by elucidating how her loss of cohesive subjectivity does not have to come at the expense of her survival.

Brison's model of self-reconceptualization, however, inevitably hinges on her status as a white American woman by virtue of its basis on her own experience, a limitation that she acknowledges herself (94). Any practice of empathetic witnessing for Saraswathi thus needs to account for the aftermath of colonial trauma and the discursive aporia of the female subaltern. Das's (2006) work is especially informative here in addressing the limitations of Brison's (2002) model by highlighting the inadequacy of narrative alone for the process of remaking the self in the wake of sexual trauma in the context of postcolonial national trauma.

Unlike Brison, Das (2006: 58) cautions against the ability of speech afforded through narrative in breaking this gendered silence; in the context of mass rapes and abductions of women during the partition of India in 1947, she argues that this speech remains circumscribed within the prevailing discourses of national honor and sovereignty.[12] Instead, Das demonstrates how survival for women in the aftermath of the partition is not voiced "as a spectacular, defiant creation of the subject through the act of speech" as in the case of Antigone in Western lore (62), but is both voiced and shown through complex negotiations "between body and language" (59). The "poisonous knowledge" of the partition is simultaneously destructive and productive in that it unsettles seemingly established social relationships, thus providing opportunities for the articulation of other selves beyond the demands of sovereignty. These articulations do not manifest in a triumphant transcendence of the self and its everyday existence, but in a "descent into the ordinary world . . . in a gesture of mourning" by patiently repairing frayed relationships (77). To be a witness in this case is to be an objective conveyor of not events but a complex experience of (gendered) self-formation through said events (5, 74).[13] Granted, the historical context of India differs from that of Sri Lanka, as do the situations of the women Das describes in her study from Saraswathi's predicament in ITM, in that they do not turn to insurgency and suicide bombing. Nonetheless, her argument, coupled with Brison's, enables us to envision what subaltern being might look like if we decouple an understanding of the body from its conception as a container for state-sanctioned identities under the dictates of coherent sovereign subjectivity.

Identifying this first glimpse of an alternative subaltern being allows us to pinpoint another fleeting moment of solidarity between two different women earlier in the novel before the 1983 riots: Visaka, the mother of the Rajasinghe sisters, and the unnamed wife of Ravan Shivalingam, whose family rents the upper floor of the Rajasinghe house in Colombo. These two women initially see each other as rivals because Visaka was Ravan's previous lover; however, they experience pregnancy and undergo labor at the same time. The pain of labor and giving birth makes them "forget enmity so that they grip each other's hands white and scream in unison," a shared experience that establishes one potential ground for feminist solidarity across ethnic lines (Munaweera 2012: 59). Munaweera describes the connection between Visaka and her Tamil counterpart from Yasodhara's perspective as such:

> In those early years, our mothers take pleasure in each other. Who else can understand Visaka's bloated breasts, her ripped innards, her strange and unaccountable moods better than another woman who has just performed the same impossible feat? We are breastfed at the same time, our mothers nodding over our tiny heads, chatting in a mixture of Tamil, Sinhala, and English that makes them laugh often. . . . The strange timing of our birth allows us entry into each other's families in the most intimate of ways since the two women, previously rivals, now seek out the comfort each other's company. (61)

This passage illustrates how the process of maternity and birth blurs the distinctions between the self and other as sovereign, coherent entities tied to the demands of statehood and ethnonationalism. The violent tearing apart of these two women's bodies through pregnancy simultaneously creates an opportunity for bonding not just with their respective children but also with each other—a breaking down that engenders a building up.[14]

Rethinking the framework of victimhood/agency and its consequences for the rape-to-suicide-bombing trajectory through the work of Puar (2005), Brison (2002), and Das (2006) thus allows us to see how Munaweera (2012) offers an image of cross-ethnic, self-other relationality that counters our initial reading of Saraswathi on the bus and her determination regarding the impossibility of repair in ethnic conflict. In that scene, the explosive device fuses with her body in a simulation of pregnancy but with the opposite intent of creating carnage and a calcification of interethnic enmity, thereby reinforcing the imperatives of national security. Waiting in line to board the bus with a male cadre in disguise, she notices Lanka, who is but a stranger to her: "She wants to look in my eyes and feel sisterhood. She wants me to smile at her. But she cannot see what is buried in my heart, or the strange fruit that lies just beneath it. Like the rest of her people, she sees nothing" (215). The depiction of Saraswathi's response here as a refusal to see Lanka beyond a member of the Sinhalese community that has harmed her and her people, though justified, nonetheless perpetuates the cycle of interethnic violence and the war on terror that erases her. But where the implications of Saraswathi's bodily destruction are lost under the governing logic of U.S. exceptionalism and ethnonationalist loyalties in the Sri Lankan civil war, they are now reframed as a critical opening by queer assemblage. Rather than assuming that bodies are always accorded subjectivity, queer assemblage allows us to trace how certain bodies like the female subaltern are excluded from inhabiting the space of identity even as she is deceptively ascribed identities of victimhood and agency to fuel competing masculinist logics. A queer assemblage reading enables us to decenter the violence of her protest as the target of a global counterterrorist apparatus and, instead, foreground the critical fissures it produces across dominant scripts of identity through a turn to alternative theories of self-other relationality that do not revolve around the sovereign subject.

Therefore, although the novel ultimately shuts off possibility in the scenes between Saraswathi and her teacher as well as the two mothers, the fact that it does allow these brief windows into other modes of alternative subjectivities highlights the fact that our material flesh and bodies are not irrevocably subject to the totalizing control of normative ideologies of coherent sovereignty that undergird imperial and nationalist projects.

Recognizing such moments of possibility is as equally imperative as the mapping of networks that produce normative subjectivity in the context of subaltern protest against exclusionary frameworks. What this reading of ITM contends, then, is that U.S. national subjectivity inevitably espouses a politics of coherence in the name of sovereignty to reproduce the disciplinary demands of normative identity, subject and national sovereignty, and the moral epistemologies of empire. The female suicide bomber as the embodiment of queer antinationality thus stands in stark contrast to this model of coherence as an embodiment of a politics of incoherence. To practice such a politics of incoherence, however, is not to insist on bodily annihilation, for such acts cannot guarantee the integrity of the antinational subaltern's protest in the face of empire and ethnonationalism. Instead, queer assemblage remains crucial despite these risks of re-inscription within dominant discourses of power because it serves to attenuate the tenacious hold of rigid identitarian constructs on our conception of bodies. As such, this essay retains the utility of Puar's (2005) queer assemblage theory by building on the female suicide bomber's act of exploding the binary of normative subjectivity and antinormative subjectivity, and taking this act as a point of rupture to identify alternative routes of embodying antinormative subjectivity in social connectivity.

In light of this alternative reading, our re-conception of rape in relation to suicide bombing also changes in ways that affect how we envision feminist solidarity. Indeed, the novel seems to challenge the possibility of feminist alliances based on coherent, sovereign identities. In contrast to a security studies reading that posits rape as a cause of suicide bombing and a threat to the integrity of U.S. national security, its boundaries, and the bodies of its subjects, this form of antinormative subjectivity brings together queer assemblage and empathetic witnessing in conversation with postcolonial trauma to offer a paradigm of survival that disrupts its enmeshment in cycles of violence. Such a paradigm entails the relinquishment of the sovereign nation-state, its twin concept of sovereign subjectivity, and, with them, our attendant notions of gender as an essentialized identity category that operates in a geopolitical vacuum.

....

Cherise Fung, she/her/hers, is a PhD candidate in literary studies at the University of Wisconsin–Madison. Her research focuses on contemporary Asian American literature, transnational feminism, and transnational queer theory.

Notes

1   For Mia Bloom (2011), female suicide bombers are simultaneously victims of patriarchal gender violence and perpetrators of such violence against other women. Despite their victimization, she ultimately paints these women as unique threats to "innocents" (237) and the national security of countries worldwide, more specifically, the United States: "But we need to understand the women better to fully understand the threat" (234).

2   Sri Lanka was fully colonized by the British in 1815 (Wickramasinghe 2014: 28). See chapters 1 and 2 of Wickramasinghe (2014) for a detailed historical account of British colonialism in Sri Lanka.

3   The 1972 constitution enshrined Sinhala and Buddhism as the official language and religion of the Sri Lankan nation-state (Jayasuriya 2012: 10). Other exclusionary policies such as the 1948 Ceylon Citizenship Act had already precluded Tamil plantation workers brought over from India by the British from acquiring Sri Lankan citizenship (10). These policies employed racial and national modes of categorization that were created for British administrative purposes and further retained by Sri Lankan politicians after independence to strengthen group identities (9–11).

4   Deylami (2013: 178) defines homoterritoriality as "the perpetuation of territorial conquest through masculine/male relationships in which women are rendered as objects of contest." Homoterritorialism extends beyond geographical control here to include the dominance of a masculinist worldview (178).

5   Spivak's (1994) case study of the 1829 British abolition of sati, the Indian practice of widow sacrifice, powerfully illustrates the struggle between white imperialism and native paternalism in representing the female subaltern. She challenges Western feminists' ascriptions of agency to this figure by recuperating her voice when it is lost to history (90–91).

6   Talal Asad (2007) asserts that questions of motivation for the suicide bomber are unproductive. What Western commentators take to be an explicit indicator of interior motive is more accurately described as a particular condition or effect (41–42). Discussions regarding motives are thus equivocal and can only remain at the level of speculation.

7   Julie V. G. Rajan (2011: 5), for example, critiques both Western and anticolonial or rebel conceptualizations of this figure; instead, she aims to reassign political agency to these women bombers through empirical data, interviews, biographical information, and "factual information about their missions."

8   Cynthia Weber (1995: 1) clarifies that while the specific meaning of sovereignty is contested within international relations, theorists remain committed to the term as an undeniable "ground or essential modifier" of modern statehood. Historical variations in the meaning of the term are glossed over by referencing post–World War II Western industrial states as the standard for a universal concept of sovereignty (2).

9   Julia Kristeva (1982: 3–4) defines the abject as that which "does not respect borders, positions, rules" and must be expelled to define the bounded self.

10 See Delueze and Guattari (1987: 8) on the multiplicity of the rhizome in relation to the subject.

11 Assemblage resists the notion of bodies as ultimate agents that act on other objects in their environment; instead, it emphasizes the reconception of bodies as both organic and inorganic matter, and the affective conditions by which they possess equal reactive qualities on each other at the (Deleuzian) molecular level (Puar 2012: 61).

12 See Das (2006) for an illustration of how sexual violence was deployed as a weapon in ethnic and religious conflict during the partition of India and Pakistan.

13 Das (2006: 77) goes on to characterize this process of subject formation in terms of "a complex agency made up of divided and fractured subject positions." While I view Das's form of agency as distinct from the kind of masculine, nationalist agency that Saraswathi tries to wield in the novel, I nonetheless refrain from using this term in my analysis because of its ubiquity in discourses of identity recuperation. In doing so, I hope to chart other terms and ways of self-constitution that do not tap into existing notions of agency as a necessary component of subjectivity.

14 Brison (2002: 66) describes a similar regenerative effect of childbirth in living with her shattered self: "While I used to have to will myself out of bed each day, I now wake gladly to feed my son whose birth, four years after the assault, gives me reason not to have died. He is the embodiment to my life's new narrative and I am more autonomous by virtue of being so intermingled with him."

Works Cited

Asad, Talal. 2007. *On Suicide Bombing*. New York: Columbia University Press.

Bloom, Mia. 2011. *Bombshell: Women and Terrorism*. Philadelphia: University of Pennsylvania Press.

Brison, Susan J. 2002. *Aftermath: Violence and the Remaking of a Self*. Princeton, NJ: Princeton University Press.

Brunner, Claudia. 2007. "Occidentalism Meets the Female Suicide Bomber: A Critical Reflection on Recent Terrorism Debates; A Review Essay." *Signs: Journal of Women in Culture and Society* 32, no. 4: 957–71.

Cottee, Simon, and Mia Bloom. 2017. "The Myth of the Isis Female Suicide Bomber." *Atlantic*, September 8.

Das, Veena. 2006. *Life and Words: Violence and the Descent into the Ordinary*. Berkeley, CA: University of California Press.

Deleuze, Gilles, and Félix Guattari. 1987. *A Thousand Plateaus: Capitalism and Schizophrenia*. Translated by Brian Massumi. Minneapolis: University of Minnesota Press.

De Mel, Neloufer. 2001. *Women and the Nation's Narrative: Gender and Nationalism in Twentieth Century Sri Lanka*. Lanham, MD: Rowman & Littlefield.

De Mel, Neloufer. 2004. "Body Politics: (Re)Cognising the Female Suicide Bomber in Sri Lanka." *Indian Journal of Gender Studies* 11, no. 1: 75–93.

Deylami, Shirin S. 2013. "Saving the Enemy: Female Suicide Bombers and the Making of American Empire." *International Journal of Feminist Politics* 15, no. 2: 177–94.

Filkins, Dexter. 2000. "In Sri Lanka, Dying to Be Equals." Los Angeles Times, February 21.

Halley, Janet. 2008. "Rape in Berlin: Reconsidering the Criminalisation of Rape in the International Law of Armed Conflict." Melbourne Journal of International Law 78: 1–47.

Heidemann, Birte. 2019. "The Symbolic Survival of the 'Living Dead': Narrating the LTTE Female Fighter in Post-war Sri Lankan Women's Writing." Journal of Commonwealth Literature 54, no. 3: 384–98.

Jayasuriya, Maryse. 2012. "Sri Lankan Anglophone Literature and the Problem of Publication." In Terror and Reconciliation: Sri Lankan Anglophone Literature, 1983–2009, 8–28. Lanham, MD: Lexington Books.

Jayasuriya, Maryse. 2013. "Exploding Myths: Representing the Female Suicide Bomber in the Sri Lankan Context in Literature and Film." Journal of Postcolonial Cultures and Societies 4, no. 1: 133–47.

Jayasuriya, Maryse. 2016. "Legacies of War in Current Diasporic Sri Lankan Women's Writing." Asiatic: IIUM Journal of English Language and Literature 10, no. 1: 145–56.

Kristeva, Julia. 1982. Powers of Horror: An Essay on Abjection. Translated by Leon S. Roudiez. New York: Columbia University Press.

Massumi, Brian. 2002. Parables for the Virtual: Movement, Affect, Sensation. Durham, NC: Duke University Press.

Munaweera, Nayomi. 2012. Island of a Thousand Mirrors. New York: St. Martin's Griffin.

Nadarajah, Suthaharan, and Dhananjayan Sriskandarajah. 2005. "Liberation Struggle or Terrorism? The Politics of Naming the LTTE." Third World Quarterly 26, no. 1: 87–100.

O'Rourke, Lindsey A. 2009. "What's Special about Female Suicide Terrorism?" Security Studies 18, no. 4: 681–718.

Puar, Jasbir K. 2005. "Queer Times, Queer Assemblages." Social Text 23, nos. 3–4 (84–85): 121–39.

Puar, Jasbir K. 2012. "'I Would Rather Be a Cyborg than a Goddess': Becoming-Intersectional in Assemblage Theory." Philosophia 2, no. 1: 49–66.

Puar, Jasbir K. (2007) 2017. Terrorist Assemblages. Durham, NC: Duke University Press.

Rajan, V. G. Julie. 2011. Women Suicide Bombers: Narratives of Violence. New York: Routledge.

Ransirini, Shamara. 2017. "Excessive Becomings: Rethinking Women and Militancy." Hecate 43, nos. 1–2: 20–42.

Spivak, Gayatri Chakravorty. 1994. "Can the Subaltern Speak?" In Colonial Discourse and Post-colonial Theory: A Reader, edited by P. Williams and L. Chrisman, 66–111. New York: Columbia University Press.

Spivak, Gayatri Chakravorty. 2004. "Terror: A Speech after 9-11." boundary 2 31, no. 2: 81–111.

Stack-O'Connor, Alisa. 2007. "Lions, Tigers, and Freedom Birds: How and Why the Liberation Tigers of Tamil Eelam Employs Women." Terrorism and Political Violence 19, no. 1: 43–63.

Uyangoda, Jayadeva. 2010. "Government-LTTE Peace Negotiations in 2002–2005 and the Clash of State Formation Projects." *Conflict and Peacebuilding in Sri Lanka: Caught in the Peace Trap?*, edited by Jonathan Goodhand, Benedikt Korf, and Jonathan Spencer, 16–38. New York: Routledge.

Weber, Cynthia. 1995. *Simulating Sovereignty: Intervention, the State, and Symbolic Exchange.* Cambridge: Cambridge University Press.

Wickramasinghe, Nira. 2014. *Sri Lanka in the Modern Age: A History.* Oxford: Oxford University Press.

Wilcox, Lauren. 2014. "Explosive Bodies and Bounded States: Abjection and the Embodied Practice of Suicide Bombing." *International Feminist Journal of Politics* 16, no. 1: 66–85.

Yass, Shlomi. 2014. "Sri Lanka and the Tamil Tigers: Conflict and Legitimacy." *Military and Strategic Affairs* 6, no. 2: 65–82.

Rosetta Marantz Cohen and Doris H. Gray

···

A Conversation with Doris H. Gray on the Power and Limitations of Restorative Justice across History, Culture, and Gender

Abstract: This interview with Doris H. Gray, author of *Leaving the Shadow of Pain: A Cross-cultural Exploration of Truth, Trauma, Reconciliation, and Healing*, explores the impact of political trauma across time, and the strategies for healing and justice. The conversation with Gray focuses on the ways in which her own experiences, as the child of a traumatized German Jew, intersect with those of formerly persecuted and incarcerated Tunisian women before and after the Arab Spring. What are the possibilities and limitations of restorative justice for those haunted by history?

Befriending the author of any book that deals with personal trauma obviously opens you to the subject in a new way. When I first met Doris Gray at a party in Northampton, Massachusetts, she was a visiting scholar through Smith College's Global Studies Center; professor of women and gender studies at Al Akhawayn University in Ifrane, Morocco; and former director of the Hillary Clinton Center for Women's Empowerment. At the time, she was midway through her manuscript *Leaving the Shadow of Pain: A Cross-cultural Exploration of Truth, Trauma, Reconciliation, and Healing*. During that first social conversation, Doris spoke to me—a stranger—about her personal life and suffering in a way that enacted, I later realized, the very thesis she was in the process of exploring in her book, that is, the ways in which spoken truth can heal, the limitations of that truth telling, and the power of individual friendship to move beyond simple binaries of pain and forgiveness.

MERIDIANS · feminism, race, transnationalism   22:2 October 2023
DOI: 10.1215/15366936-10637573 © 2023 Smith College

In *Leaving the Shadow of Pain*, Gray draws a powerful and persuasive comparison between two seemingly disparate examples of trauma and its aftermath. The first is the experience of Gray's own father, a German Jew, who continued to keep hidden his Jewish identity long after the Nazi defeat, and who remained haunted and privately embattled throughout his life, inflicting his fears and dysfunction on his daughters. The second documents the experiences of formerly incarcerated or persecuted Tunisian women, victims of Tunisia's cruel and oppressive regime under the dictator Zine El Abidine Ben Ali. Like Gray's father, these women carry their past trauma into the present, even after the 2011 regime change of the Arab Spring, when the state sought to recognize and redress past wrongs.

Gray's book uses these two examples to demonstrate the often-unacknowledged complexity of any strategy designed to foster forgiveness and healing in those victimized by state violence. Her particular focus here is on the 2013 creation in Tunisia of the Truth and Dignity Commission, a group formed to encourage formerly victimized Tunisian women to unburden themselves through public accusations and truth telling. Gray's argument complicates the idea that truth telling and revelation is a universal key to healing. Though we cannot know what strategies, if any, would have helped Gray's father heal from the fear that haunted his life, we do know that for many of the Tunisian women with whom Gray spoke, to make public the nature of their persecution would be to create new kinds of stigma, a fact that is too often overlooked when states seek to redress past abuse. In acknowledging this, her book looks at the nature of reconciliation through a lens that is personally intimate, psychologically nuanced, and culturally specific.

In the interview that follows, I ask Gray to explain the dangers of holding secrets, the value of confessing one's truth, and the complicated nature of healing. I also ask her to speak about the ways in which bringing one's own story into this kind of work can deepen one's empathy and understanding.

My Interview

Rosetta Marantz Cohen: Your book begins with the story of your father, a German Jew who had to keep his identity a secret during World War II, and how that secrecy impacted his relationship with you and your sister. It's a sad but fascinating way in to this study of how personal pain—secret pain—has generational implications. Can you begin by talking about that cross-generational trauma? What are some ways in which your father's secrets impacted your own childhood and your early adult life?

Doris Gray: So many ways. There always was an aura of secrecy in our home. Like many survivors of the Holocaust, we had no relatives on our father's side, no grandparents, no aunts, no uncles, no cousins and were not allowed to ask why. Our dad put us through strenuous—sometimes cruel—survival trainings, and our mother, a highly accomplished and out-spoken woman, who in today's parlance would be called a feminist, silently looked on. Knowing about our father's background, she became complicit in his secret which kept her distant as well. I felt we never could touch our father, not his body and not his soul. As a result of this, and other manifestations of his secret past, I never had a clear sense of identity or belonging. As soon as I was able to, I left Germany and would not return until almost forty years later.

RMC: Much of your work and research as an academic has focused on issues of trauma and healing. How did your own experience with your father's "secrets" help you understand the lives of the Tunisian women you were working to help and support? Can you explain the connection you make in the book between the buried trauma of your father's life and the efforts of these women in Tunisia to heal after they were persecuted prior to the Arab uprising in 2011, the uprising that resulted in a regime change.

DG: I started my research before my father revealed his secret Jewish identity. In my encounters with women who were either prisoners of conscience or relatives of someone imprisoned under the previous dictatorships, I always impressed upon them the need to come forward with their stories of torture, extreme social isolation, discrimination, and often also rape. My position was that a nation could not heal if the routine wrongs committed in the name of the state did not come to light.

However, after hearing why my father kept quiet about his Jewish heritage, namely, because he was afraid even in postwar Germany, I began to reflect on the theme of who has a right to the truth. My father was afraid that anti-Semitism had not disappeared despite Germany's defeat in World War II and the subsequent change in political system. He wanted to build a new life for himself and his family and did not want to pass on the burden of his Jewish identity to his children. He felt he had a right to conceal the truth about his background. However, once I found out, I felt that I had a right to the truth too because his secrecy had clouded our childhood and cast a shadow long into adulthood. The conflict between national reckoning and an individual's right to speak out or to be silent is not easily reconcilable.

RMC: The book creates an arch between autobiography and scholarship. Why did you choose this format?

DG: As a scholar, I felt that I could not ask my interview partners in North Africa to do something—come forward with the truth about their torturous past—if I was not willing to do the same with my own story. Plus, I realized that there is a connection between my personal experiences and my professional life that I needed to acknowledge and come to terms with. Commonly referred to as "positionality," my goal here was not to point out the relative differences between me and my interlocutors but rather to search for commonalities. In doing this, I hoped to make a contribution to transnational feminist scholarship.

RMC: You speak about healing as a "collective endeavor," but you acknowledge that not everyone wants or needs to tell their stories in the same way. Can you speak about some of the inherent problems in a survivor "telling her story," and why speaking about torture or injustice is always complicated—politically, culturally, and in other ways.

DG: First of all, there is the potential of being revictimized when feeling forced to bear one's soul about trauma. This is particularly the case when the victim does not have assurance of structures that address the wrong such as counseling as well as legal procedures that aim at offering justice.

On a national level, wrongs of the past and their enduring effects must be acknowledged so that a need for justice can be understood and supported by a majority of the population. Crimes committed in the name of a political system are not abstract but were carried out by fellow citizens. Though not on the same scale, in Germany after World War II and in Tunisia, victims and perpetrators continue to live in the same country, towns, or even neighborhoods. Certainly, in Germany few victims of the Shoah survived, so my father was an exception and his sense of being vulnerable was acute. In Tunisia, because there were many more survivors, this added a different level of complexity to reintegrating victims and perpetrators.

Just because someone chooses not to tell their story of trauma, does not mean they are not in need of healing. A person has many reasons to speak or to remain silent. It is a precarious balance between the one who carries a burden and the one who feels they have a right to know. For my father, the risk of revealing himself was greater than the pain he inflicted on himself and his children with his secrecy. And while I wish he would have found a way to let us know about what happened to him, it was his right to speak out or to remain silent.

RMC: Why might this be particularly hard for women?

DG: There are several issues here: violence against women often involves sexual violence. In some cultures, the reputation of a family lies in the perceived sexual virtue of the women. A sexually violated woman brings shame not only on herself but also on her entire family—hence women may not want to come forward with horrific crimes they endured when they are of a sexual nature.

What I learned from women in Tunisia applies more broadly, namely, that victims of violence often experience a sense of feeling abandoned by the state and betrayed by their families and a culture that holds that violated women dishonor their family. The law did not protect them, nor did authorities attempt to ensure their safety. In spite of a regime change, they did not feel they could trust the new state because some of the same people remained or regained positions of power.

Women are often taught to be mild, kind, and forgiving. Therefore, openly to demand accountability can be viewed as not becoming of a woman. This demand for justice can be denounced as shrill, "bitchy," and disturbing the peace—an aggressive, assertive attitude is more acceptable in men.

RMC: You speak about the difference between "truth" and "facts" and how those two concepts, as they were inadequately distinguished from each other, impacted the possibility of healing for the Tunisian women you interviewed. What is the difference between truth and facts, and can you explain how this distinction might have broader implications for other victims of state violence?

DG: I found the distinction between fact and truth useful, but it is not a scientific or scholarly differentiation. For example, my dad hid the fact that he was Jewish and had survived the Holocaust as a Jew inside Nazi Germany. But the truth that something was awry with our father was clear to my sister and me from early childhood. He could not hide his immense sadness and abiding mistrust of people, especially people in positions of authority. Likewise, the women who suffered torture and persecution in Tunisia often did not speak about the facts of their cruel mistreatment, but they could not hide their bitterness and resentment. And this truth gets passed on and consequently, trauma is multigenerational, even when detailed facts are not revealed.

RMC: What is the role of "remorse" in the process of forgiving, reconciling, and healing?

DG: Again, these are lessons [that] I learned but may not be applicable to others. In the case of routine acts of violence, that is, politically sanctioned violence, subsequent governments must acknowledge the wrongs of the past in a clear, unequivocal manner. That is, victims must hear from someone in a trusted position of authority: "This should not have happened to you. You have been wronged." Plus, there has to be an official assurance that all efforts will be undertaken to rectify past wrongs and with a view of nonrecurrence. However, though countries may engage in acts of public contrition, on an individual level, there often is a "don't ask, don't tell" attitude so that individual perpetrators are not held accountable. For the sake of a harmonious living together as a nation, some victims choose to reconcile, others feel forced to reconcile via truth and reconciliation commissions. I have found that expressions of remorse are eminently important in the process of healing. All too often the emphasis is on the victims and what they should do for collective healing to occur: they have to forgive, they have to reconcile for the greater good. In addition to their own trauma, the burden for future success of their family and the state is placed on their shoulders as well.

RMC: Toward the end of the book, you tell powerful stories of two victims of torture and imprisonment, Moncef and Amina, who are permanently changed in surprising ways as a result of their experiences—changes that involve new understanding about the brutalities of class and power. Can you speak about their transformations, the implications of it, and the role of "courage" in this process.

DG: Moncef and Amina are the only two people I cite in the book, but there were several more like them. They feel the revolution had vindicated them. The dictatorship had been overthrown, and a democratic system installed. They felt that their suffering had paid off. The country they loved but had mistreated them had changed in profound ways. People who still clung to the old regime were now the ones left behind. The national narrative had changed; people who previously were despised as enemies of the state were now admired as martyrs of the revolution.

While there were separate facilities for male political prisoners, women political prisoners shared cells with common criminals. They could only survive by helping each other. Islamist women (who constituted the majority of those persecuted) who had considered themselves morally superior depended on thieves and sex workers to get them a bar of soap or food. This sense of solidarity endured after their release.

Neither Moncef nor Amina mentioned forgiveness toward their former torturers; rather, their time in prison had freed them from conventions and allowed them to embrace life on their own terms. Their suffering and steps toward self-care, their rejection of deeply entrenched cultural mores, led them to embrace a common humanity with others who also suffered.

I consider these changes in outlook acts of courage. Forgiveness keeps perpetrator and victim entangled, while the acts of courage I observed in some Tunisians—and also my dad—allowed them to emerge from their ordeals with a hopeful focus on the future. Hope, borne of trauma, is not the same as cheery optimism or faith in an imminent good outcome. In hoping, one puts faith in some transcendental goodness—and that takes courage.

RMC: The pain and trauma of your own life—the difficulties of your childhood, the death of your daughter, the terrible physical attack you survived—these experiences seem to have made you more acutely sensitive to the complexities of healing as an individual, but also as a culture. You offer no easy solutions at the end of the book, but appeal to readers to use their own pain as a way to find common humanity in others. Can you give some examples of how that might work in other parts of the world and other conflicts?

DG: A saying in German goes: the shortest way is the one from victim to perpetrator. This is to say that victims can turn into perpetrators when circumstances allow it. It is often merely an accident of history, not a matter of a deliberate choice, on which side we end up. This rather trite insight should help us to understand that as humans we are more similar than we are different.

The events in my own life that you mention in your question must have left a noticeable mark. When I was conducting my interviews in Tunisia, women would ask me if I was one of them. I am not Arab, not Muslim, not born into a dictatorial system where the simple act of voicing a word of criticism can land you in prison, so why did they think we had something in common? Still, they sensed that I could relate to their pain, to their outrage, to their difficulty in articulating what had happened to them. I felt sure that I presented myself in an "objective, professional" way to my interlocutors. Yet to these victims of trauma, it was obvious that I too carried a burden. This understanding created an atmosphere of trust in which women told me of atrocities they had endured that they had not shared with anyone else. I had nothing to offer them in return, no redress of grievance, no assurance of nonrecurrence, and so forth. But we would sometimes just sit, hold hands, and cry. The experience of being heard, of having their trauma acknowledged and taken seriously, was profoundly affirming—and an experience that transcended culture, religion, language. Every time I return to Tunisia, I receive phone calls where people ask if I am still listening to testimonies. What started out as a scholarly research project turned into an experience of shared humanity that was comforting.

RMC: How have you, as a teacher, tried to communicate these lessons to your students?

DG: I don't talk much about myself in class. Students feel obliged to listen and pretend to be interested. Instead, I ask them to describe a moment in their life where they personally experienced an act of discrimination, cruelty, or violence and how they felt about it. Then I ask them to reflect on an incident where they committed an act of discrimination, cruelty, or violence and reflect on this experience. They do this in writing but do not have to put their name on the paper if they wish to tell their story in confidence. Which act changed them and how? After this exercise we start from the presumption that all—to various degrees—have been on the receiving and giving end of injustice. I have found that this creates a safe environment in which students are open not only to absorbing new knowledge, but learning that is transformative. What is true on the individual level also applies to the national level; we are all—to different degrees—victims and perpetrators. Inasmuch as we learn to become numb to injustice, we can unlearn our indifference. In the process, we rediscover our humanity, and this feels eminently empowering and creates a sense of connection to others. I believe without feeling connected, we cannot heal.

....

Doris H. Gray is professor emerita of women and gender studies, Al Akhawayn University in Ifrane, Morocco, and Honorary Professor at Roskilde University, Denmark.

Rosetta Marantz Cohen is Myra M. Sampson Professor Emerita at Smith College.

Work Cited

Gray, D. H. 2020. *Leaving the Shadow of Pain: A Cross-cultural Exploration of Truth, Trauma, Reconciliation, and Healing*. Berlin: Logos Verlag.

Nancy Kang

Bruise Blue

They had swarmed, expectant,
in the back bleachers, ripping skirt and shirt
her legs kicking up, catching wild hands
bucking like a rodeo pony, prodded electric
the frantic powdering of moth's wings
mouth stopped by mitt upon mitt of salted slaps
arched backs, pounding fists on keyboards
mad jazz, tympanic torsion
hamburger grinding and all the belching
oil spills and dumb eruptions then—
the blue stillness of the left-alone.
She fetus-rolled and went blank
sinking through gel, catching each edge
with a rough palm in passing
a red meditation
a serration.

Without the hard shell to clutch back all
that had been pulled out wildly and stuffed back neatly
with barbed-wire stitches and scotch-tape salves
she had to relearn balance, love the slant
of light going gentle there, mend hips and ego,
numb the grins and whispers that
swaggered by, accept prayers lingering
in wet, kind eyes like river-smoothed stones.

MERIDIANS · feminism, race, transnationalism   22:2 October 2023
DOI: 10.1215/15366936-10637654 © 2023 Smith College

She cauterized dreams of tangled amber,
body's newness, thoughts of princely things
once promised in dabs of pink gloss, sticky
glitter, and a snow-globe's gilded carousel.
She marked a calendar cross for every day
that followed the one bruised blue, like
strolling a graveyard lit full
of luminol kisses.

It hurt, the sad sag of Dad's shoulders,
the tv's curt clicks and cold trigger
of Mum's tongue, volleying blame, spitting disbelief.
Under words flung like a gnarled net, she sat
dog-dejected, inert as a snoutful of quills.
She would seek then hide the pills, hoard
an arsenal of sugar, stir the sediment of drinks and sigh
Healing is as gusty and oceanic as time.

Sleep is her suspension, a whale-belly bed
knobbed by barnacles and the deep embrace
of ribs so heavy, curved, and mute yet
buoyant like a breath in winter.
She vows next time to be vengeful, agile,
and kinetic, so as never to be caught
surrounded again
without weapons.

....

Nancy Kang is Canada Research Chair in Transnational Feminisms and Gender-Based Violence and associate professor of women's and gender studies at the University of Manitoba. She was coeditor of *The Culture and Philosophy of Ridley Scott* (2013) with Adam Barkman and Ashley Barkman. More recently, she was coauthor, with Silvio Torres-Saillant, of *The Once and Future Muse: The Poetry and Poetics of Rhina P. Espaillat* (2018). The book won honorable mention for best book (2017–20) from the Society for the Study of American Women Writers in 2021. Her research and creative work are made possible in part through the support of the Canada Research Chairs Program.

Saher Ahmed and Amrita Hari

. . . .

Young Afghan-Canadian Women's Negotiations of Gendered Cultural Scripts and Hybrid Cultural Identities

Abstract: A hybrid identity is neither a happy nor an undesirable mixture; it involves negotiating sometimes two contrasting cultural identities of the home and host nations. Research on post-migratory negotiations of gender identity, roles, and expectations has found that partner selection and marriage are significant cultural practices in a diasporic context. In this study, the authors contribute to two sets of literatures: studies on the lived experiences of Afghan-Canadian migrant and refugee women and postcolonial debates on cultural hybridity. The authors employ in-depth feminist interviews to reveal second-generation Afghan-Canadian women's gendered negotiations of partner-selection practices and marital ceremonies, including their resistance and conformity to these practices through the mobilization of their hybrid diasporic identities. Overall, the study design allows the authors to situate the voices of young Afghan women at the forefront.

Second-generation Afghan women's negotiations of subjectivity have been and continue to be determined by gendered cultural scripts maintained by the diaspora (Khanlou, Koh, and Mill 2008; Sadat 2008; Shakya, Guruge, and Hynie 2010; Hynie, Guruge, and Shakya 2012; Abbasi-Shavasi et al. 2012; Abbasi-Shavasi and Sadeghi 2014). In this article, we reveal the agency exercised by a select group of young, self-identified second-generation Afghan-Canadian women to challenge (and in some instances reinforce) existing gendered cultural scripts in the Afghan diasporic community in Canada. We draw on two sets of literatures: studies on the lived

MERIDIANS · feminism, race, transnationalism   22:2   October 2023
DOI: 10.1215/15366936-10637627 © 2023 Smith College

experiences of Afghan-Canadian migrant and refugee women and postcolonial debates on cultural hybridity. We employ in-depth interviews to contextualize young Afghan-Canadian second-generation women's negotiations of partner-selection practices and marital ceremonies to reveal instances of their resistance and conformity to gendered marital practices.

Research on gendered negotiations in a post-migratory context has found that marriage is a significant cultural practice that secures women's cultural identity (Gupta 1997; Dasgupta 1998; Dwyer 2000; Handa 2003; Sundar 2008; Abbasi-Shavazi and Sadeghi 2014). In particular, scholars emphasize the significance of marital ceremonies and partner-selection practices (Khanlou, Koh, and Mill 2008; Sadat 2008; Shakya, Guruge, and Hynie 2010; Hynie, Guruge, and Shakya 2012; Abbasi-Shavasi et al. 2012; Abbasi-Shavasi and Sadeghi 2014). Based on these literatures, we focus on Afghan-Canadian second-generation women's gendered expectations related to marriage. There are few studies that highlight young Afghan women's voices to understand how they interpret and negotiate these gendered cultural expectations within their diasporic community, while simultaneously adapting to more mainstream cultural gender expectations of the society they reside in.

There is limited but insightful scholarship that employs a gender lens to address the migratory experiences of Afghan migrant and refugee women in Canada (Stack and Iwasaki 2009; Dossa 2005, 2014; Nourpanah 2014). Similar to previous studies, we adopt a gendered and racialized lens to situate the narratives of Afghan-Canadian second-generation women at the forefront to understand their dynamic, situational, and hybrid cultural identities. More specifically, we tell the stories of how ten women construct these identities through their choice of marital partners and engagement in marital ceremonies with their immediate and extended family members, as well as their friendship networks.

Theoretically, we engage with postcolonial definitions of cultural hybridity offered by the theorists Homi K. Bhabha, Stuart Hall, and Avtar Brah to explain identity formation in relation to cultural practices of marriage. Using participant narratives, we uncover that a hybrid identity is neither a happy nor an undesirable mixture of two contrasting cultural identities (Hall 1990; Bhabha 1994; Brah 1996). Participants engage in gendered marital practices while also expressing their disapproval of cultural beliefs that reinforce unequal gendered roles within the Afghan diaspora in Canada. Overall, the study design allows us to center the voices of second-generation Afghan women to understand the complex and ongoing construction of their hybrid identity.

The next two sections outline the current theoretical debates on diasporic identity and gendered cultural practices, and the conceptualization and application of the term *second generation*, followed by a discussion of the Afghan-Canadian diasporic context. Building on these sections, we provide an overview of the research design. The next section highlights the significant research findings, specifically how Afghan-Canadian women strategize to (re)negotiate marriage practices and selecting their spouses. We conclude that Afghan-Canadian women are autonomous social actors who are reconceptualizing gendered cultural practices and provide recommendations to broaden our limited understanding of the Afghan diaspora in Canada.

Postcolonial Frameworks of Diasporic Identity

Homi K. Bhabha, Paul Gilroy, and Stuart Hall coined the term *cultural hybridity* to resist narratives of cultural hegemony. In his influential collection of essays in, *The Location of Culture* (1994), Homi Bhabha describes cultural hybridity as two contradictory cultures that meet and combine to create a third space of identity. Similarly, Stuart Hall (2005) identifies the hybrid subject as one who traverses cultures, and is both negotiating and mediating differences within a space that is in-between. These definitions provide a useful framework to study the dynamic and situational identities of second-generation Afghan women in Canada.

Cultural hybridity was originally introduced to challenge traditional claims posed by diaspora theorists such as William Safran (1991), who argued that there is only one type of diasporic identity: an original diasporic identity, which constitutes memories and desires to return to one's homeland. Bhabha (1994), Gilroy (1993), and Hall (1990) argued against the rigid nature of Safran's conceptualization—they proposed that cultural diasporic identities are not fixed; on the contrary, they are manipulated, created, and maintained in diverse ways within and among diasporas. Moreover, they firmly critiqued conceptualizations of an original diasporic identity, which inevitably reduces identity to an essentialist category of sameness.

Bhabha (1994: 9) asserts that hybridity can help address the complex dynamics between the self and the other; the space we construct as hybrid is the third space—the "in-between" in which hegemonic narratives of cultural identity are disrupted. The construction of hybrid identity involves a "sense of the relocation of home and the world"—the unhomeliness—that is the condition of "extra territorial and cross-cultural initiations." Bhabha's (1994) conceptualization of hybridity denotes elements of seemingly two contradictory cultures that meet and combine to create a third space of identity. Hall (1990: 235) builds on hybridity theory to argue that identity "lives with and through, not despite, difference by hybridity."

By using the term *hybrid identities*, we can resist claims of stagnated or fixed identities and identify the ambivalent site where cultural meanings and representations have no "primordial unity or fixity" (Bhabha 1994). The hybrid subject is traversing cultures and is both negotiating and mediating similarities and differences within the space that is "in-between." The ambivalence within this third space also works as a strategic mode of articulation for new forms of cultural identities that subvert the concept of an authentic origin or identity, as proposed by earlier scholars of diaspora such as Safran (1991).

The theoretical framework of cultural hybridity also requires that we pay attention to how gender influences the formation of cultural identities. Avtar Brah (1996, 2003) argues for a gendered lens to deepen our understanding of the heterogeneity of diasporic women's construction of cultural identity. We adopt the framework of gendered cultural hybridity to examine how Afghan women's identities are continuously reproducing themselves anew, through transformation and difference. Inspired by Brah (1996), we employ a gendered lens to build on postcolonial definitions of cultural hybridity offered by Bhabha (1994), Gilroy (1993), and Hall (1990) and draw on investigations into Afghan women's strategic negotiation of and resistance to gendered cultural practices. In particular, we examine how the processes of identity (re)formations and negotiations of gendered roles and expectations involve a fluid and complex interplay of culture, environment, and communities.

Defining Second Generation
In this article, we extend this dynamic, malleable, messy, and ambivalent conceptualization of hybrid identity to the term *second generation*. Shifting away from existing definitions of the term discussed below, we contend that the category second generation can also be manipulated, created, and maintained in different ways. Definitions of *second generation* have relied primarily on large-scale data (Portes and Zhou 1993; Rumbaut 2002).

Alejandro Portes and Min Zhou (1993: 75) defined *second generation* as having at least one foreign-born parent or children who were born in a foreign country and have settled in a new host country before the age of twelve. Rubén G. Rumbaut (2002, 2004) made further generational distinctions: 1.75 generations are those who arrive between one and five years old; 1.5 generations include those who arrive between six and twelve years old; while 1.25 generations include those who arrive between thirteen and seventeen years old (Rumbaut 2002, 2004). These studies show that second generation is not conceived as a singular entity; however, the study design prevented opportunities for self-identification.

Our research design allowed participants to self-identity as second generation, and their narratives show that the process of defining second generation is more nuanced, complex, and ongoing than the traditional definitions proposed by Portes and Zhou (1993) and Rumbaut (2002). A significant factor in defining the category of second generation for participants is the visibility of their difference as opposed to country of birth or age of arrival. While identifying as second generation, participants were simultaneously challenging fixed and imposed definitions of their gender, racialized, and cultural identities. We found that participants continually redefined or reformulated the term *second generation* to make sense of their own identities as Afghan-Canadian women.

Gendering Afghan Migrant and Refugee Experiences in Canada

There is broad consensus among scholars, activists, and policy makers that migration and refugee experiences are gendered (Dwyer 2000; Dossa 2008). Scholars have also discussed the unequal treatment of women in flight, exile, resettlement, and repatriation. Gender often determines where people are displaced, their vulnerability to human rights abuses, and their access to services and economic livelihoods. Young women are more likely to have negative experiences of seeking asylum and face greater challenges to integration and settlement (Khanlou and Crawford 2006).

In Canada, ethnographic research of Afghan refugees found that Afghan women experience tremendous distress during migration and settlement (Dossa 2005; Stack and Iwasaki 2009; Kohistani 2012; Nourpanah 2014). Parin Dossa (2014) writes in her book *Afghanistan Remembers* that Afghan refugee women continuously recall the gender-based violence they experienced when fleeing Afghanistan, as well as the extreme violence and repression they were subjected to prior. Dossa (2014) explains that social barriers such as lack of access to health and social services when in Canada exacerbate feelings of isolation and alienation among Afghan refugees, especially Afghan women. Despite the obstacles that Afghan refugee women encounter when integrating in Canada, these women are also constantly adapting and formulating strategies to mitigate their premigration trauma, overcome barriers to settlement, and integrate into the Canadian economy and society.

Dossa (2014) and Shiva Nourpanah (2014) discuss Afghan refugee women's resilience and agency in developing a sense of belonging in Canada, through food, friendship, parenting, religion, and education. For instance, for Afghan women the act of praying is a quest for healing the wounds that are deeply embedded within their memories of displacement. These scholars demonstrate the interconnectedness of migration, gender, and identity in everyday lives. Afghan women therefore rebuild their lives by overcoming adversities, testimonies of which are passed down to their daughters. We predict that this process infuses different meanings for the various generations of Afghan diasporic women, contributing to their sense of belonging and construction of identity. Although gender has been employed as a dynamic and constitutive lens that helps researchers understand the cultural hybrid identities of Afghan women, there are still gaps in this existing scholarship, which we discuss next.

Gaps in Scholarship on Gender Socialization
in the Afghan Diaspora

Scholars writing on the intersections of gender and migration processes draw attention to how gender imbues social relations and complicates the formation of a cultural identity (Gupta, Akhil, and Ferguson 1997; Dasgupta 1998; Dwyer 2000; Curran et al. 2006; Donato 2006). Second-generation women, often expected to be the "good daughter" within their families (Dwyer 2000; Handa 2003; Sundar 2008; Rajiva 2013), are "disproportionately burdened with the preservation of culture in the form of religion, language, dress, food, and childrearing" (Gupta, Akhil, and Ferguson 1997: 386). These expectations lie between parents' cultural values and the culture of the "adopted home" (585). Second-generation women, to a greater extent than their male counterparts, are the reproducers of culture. Marriage therefore remains a significant symbolic cultural practice that young women are expected to adhere to (Handa 2003).

Scholarship specific to second-generation Afghans in Canada also addresses gendered expectations, in particular the cultural practices related to marriage (Khanlou, Koh, and Mill 2008; Sadat 2008; Shakya, Guruge, and Hynie 2010; Abbasi-Shavasi et al. 2012; Hynie, Guruge, and Shakya 2012). However, these are comparative studies, which tend to represent racialized newcomer and diasporic youth as a relatively homogenous group. For instance, some studies rely on the experiences of Afghan men and racialized second-generation women from different ethnic/national groups to speculate on the experiences of young second-generation Afghan women. As a result of this selection bias, the personal narratives of second-generation Afghan women that present their lived experiences in their own words have remained under-explored. I provide three examples below to demonstrate this particular lacuna in research: Michaela Hynie, Sepali Guruge, and Yogendra B. Shakya (2012); Nazilla Khanlou, Jane G. Koh, and Catriona Mill (2008); and Shakya, Guruge, and Hynie (2010).

Hynie, Guruge, and Shakya's (2012) research is on the acculturating experiences of Afghan adolescents in Canada in addition to those of Sudanese and Burmese adolescents. While the scholars divided their participants by ethnicity, age, and gender, their analysis does not demonstrate and explain if participants' experiences varied based on ethnicity/nationality. Additionally, the study design did not allow for the individual and personal narratives of the Afghan female participants to emerge, which would provide a richer understanding of how these young women interpret unequal cultural practices, how these practices shape their experiences of integrating into a new society, and more generally the ways in which young women from differing ethnic/cultural/national backgrounds might resist such gendered expectations.

Khanlou, Koh, and Mill (2008) use similar research methods to explore the experiences of Afghan and Iranian youth. The focus of their study is the shared challenges faced by Afghan and Iranian youth when integrating into Canadian society; however, the authors provide little to no comment on how the experiences of Afghans and Iranians may also differ. As a result, the researchers inadvertently homogenize the experiences of two groups of youth based exclusively on their shared religious identity rather than considering distinctions such as gender, education, or social class (Khanlou, Koh, and Mill 2008). Shakya, Guruge, and Hynie (2010) also continue to present similarities rather than differences in participant responses and focus on family-level responsibilities for second-generation women (70). In this way, the comparisons evoked by Shakya, Guruge, and Hynie (2010), Khanlou, Koh, and Mill (2008), and Hynie, Guruge, and Shakya (2012) resulted in a homogenization of Afghan women's experiences based on their shared religious or racialized identities with other ethnic groups of second-generation youth.

There are few scholars who have exclusively examined the experiences of second-generation Afghans in different diasporic contexts. Abbasi-Shavasi et al. (2012) studied sociocultural adaptation patterns among Afghan adolescents in Iran. While the authors did conclude that gender is an important conceptual lens, their finding that Afghan women are more likely to marry outside the Afghan culture justified the limited attention paid to their experiences of integration, as compared to Afghan men (124).

Despite the limited analysis of how women navigate social and cultural terrains to shape their negotiations with their families, friends, and romantic partners, one exception is the work of Mir Hekmatullah Sadat (2008), who relies on an ethnographic survey to determine Afghan cultural practices across North America, Europe, and Australia. Sadat demonstrates that arranged marriages and traditional gendered customs associated with the practice are common within the Afghan diaspora. Young men's social activities include late-night partying and dating. In contrast, young Afghan women are expected to avoid these social activities, as their parents require them to act modestly and represent their family honor, thus preserving their reputation as "marriageable." Despite the invaluable research insights brought forward by Sadat, the surveys cannot account for how these women negotiate such distinctive cultural practices.

In summary then, the existing scholarship on second-generation Afghan women (Khanlou, Koh, and Mill 2008; Sadat 2008; Shakya, Guruge, and Hynie 2010; Abbasi Shavasi et al. 2012; Hynie, Guruge, and Shakya 2012) has a tendency to homogenize the experiences of racialized youth adhering to similar (not the same) cultural responsibilities and in relation to Afghan patriarchy and masculinity with little in-depth explanation of gendered expectations, attitudes, and behaviors, as understood by Afghan women. Arguably, the shortcomings of these studies reveal a relative gap in scholarly understandings of how self-identified second-generation Afghan-Canadian women interpret and negotiate cultural expectations. We add to scholarship on second-generation immigrant youth and to the understandings of intergenerational experiences of Afghan refugee women (Dossa 2005, 2014; Stack and Iwasaki 2009; Kohistani 2012; Nourpanah 2014).

Research Design and Participants

Qualitative Interviews and Research Identities

Interviews have become an invaluable methodological tool in feminist research. Researchers maintain an overall structure of the interview session, while allowing for flexibility in probing with follow-up questions. Feminist researchers (Harding 1986; Reinharz and Davidman 1992; Chase 2003; Fonow and Cook 2005) contend that qualitative interviews help researchers identify the social reality of their participants' lives, while also creating a welcoming space for engagement. Qualitative interviews actively challenge the common misunderstandings of those who are socially marginalized (Fonow and Cook 2005). Previous research on migration and gender demonstrate that semistructured, in-depth interviews allow for the creation of a space in which participants can share their individual experiences (Dwyer 2000; Kirk 2006; Stack and Iwasaki 2009; Kalvir 2011; Kohistani 2012; Nourpanah 2014;).

We employed ten qualitative, semistructured interviews to capture how gender influences the formation of a hybrid cultural identity and identification as second generation for Afghan women in Canada. The interview process accounted for participants' experiences and feelings—although predetermined, the open-ended and additional free-flowing questions provided participants with the opportunity to share their personal stories. Questions were divided into three main sections, with sub-questions under each heading: introduction and demographic, second generation (hybrid identity), and transnationalism and cultural identity.

The exploratory design of this study serves as a vehicle for learning more about cultural hybridity and identity and to provide directions for future qualitative research on second-generation Afghan women. We collected unique and empirically rich testimonies shared by second-generation Afghan-Canadian women describing how they construct, maintain, and negotiate their cultural identity, and the meanings they inscribe to their hybrid subjectivities and being second generation within the Afghan diaspora and the broader Canadian society. We should note a limitation of the study design: a relatively small sample. Additionally, an inevitable outcome of participants' self-identification as second generation was the heterogeneity of the sample with respect to birth country (Afghanistan or Canada) and age of arrival in Canada.

Although the study is limited in scope, the primary objective was to develop a thick description of young Afghan women's experiences, that is, provide a detailed account of explicit patterns of cultural and social relationships and put them in context. These interviews highlight the processes of meaning making and decision-making, and how participants' everyday lived experiences are understood and negotiated. These processes include marriage and partner-selection practices and conversations with family and friends on such matters. We noted a point of theoretical saturation when participants discussed similar strategies/negotiations of the small number of marital practices being discussed (Crabtree and DiCicco-Bloom 2006). Similar to approaches employed by qualitative social researchers (Guest and Johnson 2006; Creswell 2011), we included phenomena to our analytical map as they emerged; however, after ten interviews, we felt it was unlikely that any new phenomena would emerge.

The majority of studies on immigrant Muslim women use face-to-face, in-depth interviews. The stories that naturally emerged in the interview setting provided a space for Muslim women to share their experiences in their own words (Dossa 2009). In-depth interviews also reveal themes that continue to be missing from broader scholarly research on Arab Muslim immigrants (Khatib 2013). Researchers who belong to minority cultural diasporas similar to that of the research participants can more easily establish rapport with their participants because the interview situation allows the researcher to acknowledge their identities and engage with participants more closely and learn their stories (Kalvir 2011).

This study is informed by the researchers' own diverse cultural identities as diasporic members of Canadian society. More specifically, the lead researcher's identification as a second-generation Afghan-Canadian woman served as a constant reminder of their social location and positionality as a supposed insider. Participants spoke about a shared sense of familiarity, comfort, and safety, throughout the interviews, especially as disclosures became personal and sensitive; they felt that their stories were more readily understood. For instance, participants often used words such as *us* or *we* to include the interviewer within their narratives. Similarly, Sherry-Anne Butterfield (2004: 81), who studied second-generation West Indian immigrants in New York City, reported that her respondents related to her in culturally specific ways after sharing that she too was also "from a yard" (Jamaica).

Insider status, however, is neither rigid nor exclusive; the unfettered release of personal stories from participants led us to reflect on the narratives that were not shared owing to the simultaneous outsiderness the researcher holds. Ultimately, the researcher was neither fully an insider nor outsider but, rather, occupying an in-between or hybrid position—an ideal position to discuss the topic under study. It is the hybridity of the researchers' and participants' identities and the complexity of research as a coproduction that helped us present the voices, stories, and experiences of second-generation Afghan-Canadian women. Their narratives illustrate the complexities of identity construction, transformation, and preservation, all of which resonate deeply with the researchers' cultural identities and the ongoing, dynamic, and intersubjective nature of qualitative social research.

Research Participants

A predetermined sampling frame was used to identify study participants: self-identified as second-generation Afghan woman who were either born in or arrived at an early age. All participants were at least eighteen years old, thereby able to provide individual consent to participate in this research study. All participants live in Ottawa or the surrounding area.[1] Because of the small population of Afghan women living in Ottawa, our research relied heavily on snowball sampling to recruit more participants. In addition, we used recruitment posters and letters that were distributed to universities, student organizations, nongovernmental organizations who worked with Afghan women, and Facebook. Participants were asked to introduce themselves and were given the option to share their age, marital status, education, and religious beliefs. All ten participants were university educated. Participants emphasized their social progressiveness, educational attainments, and partner, family, friendship, and kinship relations. In particular, participants discussed their relationships as mothers, partners, and daughters as defining social markers.

All participants signed a consent form, including a brief statement explaining the research and informing them of their rights, such as being able to withdraw from the study before the withdrawal date, confidentiality, and anonymity. Participants were also informed of the intended length of interviews (one hour). All interviews were recorded and transcribed verbatim.

Data Analysis

One of the problems inherent within the richness of interview data is that analysis is impractical without a reduction of this large amount of information. Data analysis constitutes this meaningful reduction to draw

Table 1 Selected information on study participants

Pseudonym	Age	Education	Marital status	Roles	Age of arrival	Transit country (Yes/No)
Afia	18	First year—bachelor's degree	Single	Daughter	Born in Canada	No
Salma	19	Second year—bachelor's degree	Married	Daughter Wife	Born in Canada	No
Maryam	22	Advanced diploma	Single	Daughter	Born in Canada	No
Sharbat	23	Second year—bachelor's degree	Single	Daughter	10	Yes (Pakistan)
Sabrina	27	Bachelor's degree— master's degree	Married	Daughter Wife	9	Yes (Saudi Arabia)
Afsoon	26	Bachelor's degree	Single	Daughter	2	No
Parisa	20	Second year—bachelor's degree	Single	Daughter	9	Yes (France)
Tamana	27	Bachelor's degree First year—master's degree	Engaged	Daughter Fiancé	15	Yes (Russia)
Sarah	27	Second year—bachelor's degree	Married	Daughter Wife	12	Yes (Pakistan)
Alia	33	Bachelor's degree	Married	Daughter Wife Mother	20	Yes (Pakistan)

conclusions. A grounded theory approach was used to systematically analyze the interview transcripts. We grouped sections of the transcript based on themes and constructed descriptive and explanatory accounts set within the theoretical framework and social context of the study. NVivo was used to store and code interviews. Using NVivo query, we analyzed the intersections between themes, participant characteristics, and common concepts or phrases.

In analyzing the transcripts, we uncovered various themes such as goals and accomplishments, gendered cultural expectations and beliefs, incidents of racism or alienation from community (either Canadian or Afghan), and issues related to national events in Canada and Afghanistan. When participants discussed these themes, their stronger emotions—tears, contagious laughter, and other physical gestures that depicted their frustration or anger—were also recorded. Coding also took into account the themes that participants spoke more passionately or emotionally about, indicating that they wanted these stories to be heard. The following section will discuss the meaningful findings that emerged.

Becoming Second Generation

The category of second generation, by definition, ascribes some form of outsider status, exemplified in the traditional definitions proposed by Portes and Zhou (1993) and Rumbaut (2002, 2004). Moreover, these definitions removed the capacity for immigrants to define for themselves the meaning of this ascribed outsider status. We asked participants to define and explain what it means to be second generation.

Several participants associated the term with access to opportunities that were previously restricted, such as education and employment—they spoke of their aspirations to "go far with education, work, and life" (Sharbat). Sharbat, who arrived in Canada in 2002, explains how she understands belonging as second generation:

> What's important to me is that through everything, [migrating] to Canada and the stuff I witnessed with my family . . . going to Afghanistan to Pakistan because there was war . . . one of the most important things for me is being able to give back . . . to my mom and do well in school and work hard.

Sharbat distinguished her migratory experiences from that of her family, particularly her mother, to further explain what it means to be second generation. This specific need to "give back" to their mothers through their work ethic and academic performance was a prevalent theme among all participants when defining second generation.

Previous conceptualizations of second generation, including the segmented assimilation theory, exclusively measured outcomes and achievements rather than meanings and aspirations. For example, Portes, Zhou, and Rumbaut refer to socioeconomic opportunity structures to determine economic and educational attainments (Portes and Zhou 1993), with no discussion of how such opportunities may be perceived by the second generation they studied, the systemic barriers to attainment, sense of belonging, or satisfaction with their immigration outcomes.

To further complicate traditional definitions of second generation, Alia, Sarah, and Tamana, all of whom arrived in Canada after the age of twelve, drew our attention to the limitations of using fixed geographic or temporal definitions of second generation. Previous definitions do not account for people who have experienced transnational mobility[2]—multiple migration countries. Prior to arriving in Canada in 2002, Alia and her family moved to Pakistan where they lived for ten years. Born in Afghanistan, Alia was only nine years old when she and her family had to leave their home country. Similarly, Sarah and her family moved from Afghanistan to Pakistan in 1992 when she was three years old and eventually settled in Canada in 2002 when she was thirteen years old. Tamana and her family left Afghanistan and moved to Russia in 1998 and were sponsored to move to Canada in 2001 when she was thirteen years old.

In consequence, all three women had formed identities as refugee children growing up in other countries before they settled in Canada. Their experiences of migrating from Afghanistan to Canada reveal that the temporary location of settlement is where their identity as second-generation Afghan women began to develop. All three women emphasized how their cultural identities are reconstructed through their everyday life in these multiple homes. Their narratives of becoming second generation are also reflected in their discussions of negotiating gendered cultural practices within the Afghan diaspora in Canada.

Negotiating Gendered Cultural Practices in the Diaspora

As previously discussed, the broader literature on second generation has shown that women are often expected to conform to gendered cultural roles to preserve their cultural identity and familial honor (Dwyer 2000; Handa 2003; Sundar 2008; Rajiva 2013). Gendered cultural practices such as arranged marriages are emblematic of how second-generation women are situated as the reproducers and bearers of culture (Khanlou, Koh, and Mill 2008; Sadat 2008; Shakya, Guruge, and Hynie 2010; Abbasi-Shavasi et al. 2012; Hynie, Guruge, and Shakya 2012). Within Afghan culture, daughters are expected to marry someone who is also of Afghan descent. Also prevalent within the Afghan diaspora is the practice of consanguineous marriages, otherwise understood as marriage within the family. Traditionally, arranged marriages have been practiced to ensure that marriages remain consanguineous to maintain stronger kin relations (Sadat 2008).

Second-generation women in the study described in detail the gendered cultural expectations of the diaspora, in particular the first generation, through subtle acts of resistance and reformation. Participants revealed their diverse experiences, perceptions, and understandings of marital expectations and ceremonies and how they exercise agency during these familial negotiations. What is particularly significant is that, in the process of negotiating gendered cultural practices relating to marriages and partner selection, second-generation Afghan women are also continuously reconstructing their hybrid cultural identities. Among the married women in our study, three participants indicated that their marriages were arranged. On further probing, they explained in detail how they negotiated the gendered customs and traditions within their arranged marriages to exercise their agency and exert their independence.

Resistance to and Reformations of Transnational Arranged Marriages

Arranged marriages within the Afghan diaspora involve two significant events that occur prior to marriage: *khastegari* and *lavs-dadan*. *Khastegari* refers to an "honorable request" in which the suitor or his family asks for the woman's hand in marriage. *Lavs-dadan* translates to "the word of approval," which is the response that the woman and her family would deliver to the suitor if they approve of the proposal. It is during the moments before the *lavs-dadan* when a woman decides whether she consents to the marriage. She can meet the suitor only after her *lavs-dadan*. Depending on whether the family patriarch agrees to an "unsupervised" meeting between his daughter and the suitor, the social interactions between the two are usually chaperoned until they are married. In addition, women who have intimate relations with their suitor before marriage are considered to bring shame and dishonor to their family because they are seen to have participated in immodest activity (Bhopal 1999). Salma draws our attention to these traditional elements of arranged marriages and her deviation from the traditional practices:

> [My husband] asked for my hand in marriage, the *khastegari*, two years ago. I always follow my parents' decisions . . . but this time I [told them] if you want me to marry him you have to buy my flight to go to [Tajikistan] to see him . . . we lived together before getting engaged . . . I really liked him so that's why I said yes to him.

Salma approved her parents' decision for a transnational arranged marriage while resisting the practice of not meeting or knowing her potential husband before marriage. Salma's ultimatum is her defiance of traditional gender scripts and exemplifies her agency in the marital negotiation process.

Salma's story is emblematic of the negotiations of traditional marital practices in the Afghan diaspora. The participants' narratives reveal young women taking an increasingly active role in decision-making; however, this should not be read as a dismissal of traditional gendered cultural practices but, rather, a reformation or renegotiation that is more closely aligned with their hybrid sense of self. In many ways for Salma, agreeing to an arranged marriage was not only desirable but also consistent with her beliefs. Salma also shared that the arranged marriage was consanguineous in nature, as the *khastegari* was from her "cousin's son." Salma explicitly demanded of her parents that if they "choose a guy" for her to marry, she does not "want him to be from [Canada]":

> I wanted to be with someone who lives in Afghanistan because they culturally and personally respect me. I don't want my kids to be white washed like I am. I want them to be somehow involved with their community as well, and by having a husband from there helps.

Salma felt that her decision to have a transnational arranged marriage in Afghanistan would help her align her hybrid cultural identity with that of her future children, by marrying someone who has similar "beliefs and ideologies." Simultaneously, Salma expressed guilt for adopting a cultural identity that is not fully Afghan—a subjectivity that also explains her caution with the type of Afghan man she marries. In providing her *lavs-dadan* to a transnational consanguineous marriage, Salma accepts her Afghan cultural obligations in preserving kin relations and cultural values, while also exercising her agency, by adding the condition that she and her suitor live together before agreeing to the arrangement.

Salma's story also sheds light on how transnational marriages have evolved to include a shift in gender roles; women are not the only ones crossing territorial borders to settle in their husband's host country. Men are also becoming "migrant" husbands who are dependent on their spouses to sponsor and support them. Not all members of the Afghan community in Canada are sympathetic to this trend, exemplified in the following quote from Sarah, who also had a transnational arranged marriage:

> I have to explain to my friends about the sponsorship and they get shocked [and ask] "How do you live like that? How can you do that? Why is it taking so long?" They get suspicious about my husband. . . . It's frustrating . . . and the second question [they ask me is] "how come it's taking so long to bring him, what's wrong with Canadian immigration?" but there is no Afghan embassy that issues visas in Afghanistan . . . unfortunately we have to process it to Pakistan . . . we applied in 2012 the next

time we heard from them was March 2014 and [were notified] that the
case is transferred to India. So our case was just sitting there collecting
dust for two years . . . it's all frustrating, my friends think it's a scam.

Sarah's quote demonstrates how transnational arranged marriages within
Afghanistan are viewed with hostility and uncertainty among some
second-generation Afghan women. They presume that marrying an
Afghan man in Afghanistan is a decision that will "ruin" your life, based on
the perceived socioeconomic and cultural differences between the diaspora
and those "left behind" in Afghanistan. These perceptions emerged clearly
in the interviews with Maryam and Parisa.

Maryam said that she wanted "someone who is on the same level" as
her, "both educated and have good jobs." She views herself as an educated
and self-determined Afghan woman looking for an equal partner who is
self-sufficient. Commonly held beliefs in the diaspora, however, dictate
that a transnational husband who lives in Afghanistan is less likely to be on
the same social level as an Afghan-Canadian woman. Parisa adds to this by
characterizing Afghan men in Afghanistan as having an "old-school mentality" that is "not compatible" with second-generation Afghan women.

While arranged marriages are desirable as an authentic traditional cultural practice, the ambiguity surrounding this practice and not knowing
one's husband before marriage also caused some participants to resist
transnational arranged marriages altogether. Maryam shares:

I also don't want an arranged marriage because of my mom's
[experience] . . . she [agreed] to an arranged marriage [to my dad]
because his brothers [wives] were so happy, and she's the least happiest.
She didn't know my dad before [and that he] smoked, drank [and] gam-
bled. I saw my mom suffer . . . I saw how much it hurt my mom . . .
when me and my brother were four and five years old, she would wake us
up and we would go pick up my dad on the street because he was so
drunk . . . and that was really hard on my mom because she didn't know
my dad was like that.

Maryam describes her anxieties about the lack of compatibility with a
potential partner through a traditional arranged marriage. Notably, Maryam's perception of her mother's experiences has fostered a sense of
resentment against this specific cultural practice. She further shares that
although she is unsure whether her father's drinking habits began before
migrating to Canada, her mother told her that she found out about his

drinking habits only after she arrived in Canada and when the marriage began with them living together:

> My mom came from Afghanistan to Turkey to Canada. She shared that the moment she came to Canada [to be with him] . . . she saw bottles everywhere. She's seen pictures of Dad with ladies on his lap. She had to rip everything . . . and because of that I am mostly against arranged marriages.

In the Afghan diaspora, when arranging marriages, the family's reputation is used to evaluate whether the male suitors who are matched to the daughters are "good people" who come from "respectable families" (Shaw 2001). Maryam's mother consented to the proposal because of the "good" impression Maryam's father's brothers gave to her mother. Maryam strongly emphasized the importance of "getting to know the person and not just the family" before marrying. Her comments fit with established research on intimate and familial relationships in the diaspora (Dasgupta 1998; Dwyer 2000), which finds that when compared to men, women's bodies are more often policed by family members as an extension of familial honor; women are viewed as sole representatives of their families' reputation.

Maryam adds that individuals entering a marital arrangement should get to know one another and not just their family members. This demand also points to a more egalitarian and transparent process in forming a marital union. Her resistance to an arranged marriage is grounded in the interpretation of arranged marriages as an obscure and outdated cultural practice that often places women at a disadvantage. What remains prevalent throughout the interviews with participants is that while the type, extent, and outcomes of negotiations of gendered cultural practices varied, these negotiations are indeed examples of how women in the Afghan diaspora exercise agency and assert more control over the gendered cultural scripts they are expected to adhere to. These women developed innovative ways to attain and maintain independence, agency, and autonomy.

Marital Ceremonies, Gender Policing, and Second-Generation Ambivalence
The Afghan diaspora is representative of the transformation of Afghan cultural identity (Sadat 2008), while simultaneously being a space of tension wherein second-generation Afghan women enact their hybrid cultural

identities. In this section, we will discuss this complex interplay of culture and community, using the lens of marriage ceremonies and revealing instances of gender policing. Salma provided her *lavs-dadan* to the *khastegari* from her cousin's son, thereby agreeing to the marital cultural practice that reinforces gendered cultural scripts in the Afghan diaspora. She used a popular proverb to explain her decision and provide more context to the gendered cultural beliefs surrounding women's bodies: "A girl is like a mirror. If there is one crack in the mirror, no one would want it. [Similarly] if a guy touches a girl, she is broken, and no one would want her." This proverb is passed down through generations of Afghan women. In partic-ular, mothers and grandmothers are seen as responsible for ensuring that their daughters remain virgins until the night of the wedding (Kargar 2012). Researchers on the topic of virginity in Islamic cultures, including the Afghan culture (Amer, Howarth, and Sen 2007), found that the cultural subordination of women through the policing of women's sexuality is seen as integral to preserving familial honor, a practice that continues to operate even now. Virginity, when employed within cultural narratives, has relied on traditional patriarchal tropes ingrained within religion and cultures surrounding the "modest" Muslim woman (Amer, Howarth, and Sen 2007). This is further exemplified in our interviews with Salma, during which she revealed the significant role cultural scripts relating to virginity play in Afghan culture.

More specifically, Salma speaks about the *takht-jami*, meaning, the night of the wedding. As mentioned earlier, Salma decided to live with her now-husband in Tajikistan before she provided him with her consent for mar-riage (*lavs-dadan*). During that time, she recalls that her husband's mother called them every day to tell them: "Make sure you guys don't have sex, because I and [the grandmothers] want [Salma] to bleed at the night of the wedding and we need to look at the cloth." Traditional Afghan customs dictate that a bride's hymen must remain intact until the night of her wed-ding. A displaying of a handkerchief or a cloth on which the new bride must bleed on during sexual intercourse on the night of her wedding often proves this—a test of her virginity. This display of honor is presented to the older women in the groom's family as proof of her virginity and in turn purity.[3] Despite the growing consensus that resists such a custom (Coyne 2000; Vincent 2006), it continues as a cultural practice in the Afghan dias-pora as proof of women's purity. Salma also shared her fear that she will not bleed the night of her wedding:

I don't want my parents to be ashamed of me . . . my Mom told me [that] if I lose my virginity my value will go down and in the future if I wanted a big wedding reception my in-laws would [respond with], "No, why the hell would you want a big wedding if you're not a virgin." . . . My mom [tells me] that if she spoke to my future in-laws and asked that they pay for my wedding to be $5,000 or $10,000 dollars, for example, they would [respond with]: "No, your daughter is not a virgin why she would want a big wedding? $2,000 is enough for her.

Salma's primary concern was bringing shame to her family. She found herself caught between negotiating her choice to live with her partner before marriage and also maintaining her parents' honor and her own values as an Afghan woman in the eyes of her husband and her extended family. She reconciled this dilemma by translating her parents' traditional expectations into a "vernacular" that represents her diasporic identity as an Afghan-Canadian. In the book entitled *Dear Zari: Hidden Stories from Women of Afghanistan*, Afghan author Zarghuna Kargar (2012) finds that cultural discussions surrounding virginity and women's sexuality were considered taboo if discussed by men. Salma, however, also recounted that after a brief intimate moment when both she and her then-fiancé were close to having intercourse, her fiancé immediately stopped the act and reminded her that "her aunts (his mother and grandmother) want to see the bloody cloth, because [she's] from [Canada] and [is] dirty." Salma recalled feeling shame and guilt in almost committing an act that would prove her fiancé's mother's beliefs that Afghan-Canadian girls are "dirty." In an effort to maintain her "Afghanness" and abstain from any activity that may rupture her hymen such as "sitting a certain way," Salma attempts to safeguard her virginity to avoid being perceived by her husband as just a "Canadian girl." This was not the only driving force of her fear; she wanted to also uphold her familial honor, as Salma's virginity is also a reflection of her mother. Therefore, failure would be read as her mother's inability to raise a "good Afghan daughter."

Salma's situation also exemplifies the ambivalence that is characteristic of the experiences of second-generation Afghan women when faced with managing the competing norms of Afghan and Canadian culture—the in-betweenness or third space that results from their hybrid cultural identity (Bhabha 1994). The process of renegotiating gendered cultural practices within the Afghan diaspora also involves self-mediation, to calm the anxieties that arise from constructing a hybrid identity. Salma's anxiety is evident in the lengths she plans to go to mitigate not bleeding on the night of her wedding (*takht-jami*). She shared that she would resort to faking the rupture of her hymen by "staining the cloth with fake blood." Salma's narrative of anxiety demonstrates how she can exert some agency, afforded to her by her status as an Afghan-Canadian; however, her sense of self remains significantly linked to how other Afghans in Canada and beyond perceive her.

Another significant but complementary finding that emerged in the participants' discussion was their effort to engage in autonomous decisions related to virginity. For instance, Maryam's approach to customs related to arranged marriages is to be vigilant:

> I do want an Afghan cultural [wedding] . . . But no *takht-jami*. I'm against that stuff . . . not everyone has to bleed on the night of the wedding. But we [are] required to keep our virginity until the night of our wedding. . . . I follow that but it's also a choice maybe that changes.

Maryam is willing to conform to practices such as her decision to remain a virgin until she is married; however, she is also opposed to traditional ceremony to display it: the *takht-jami*. Maryam also shares that she does not consider being a virgin to be important, and she may also change her mind about keeping her virginity until she is married, maintaining autonomy and the right to decide about her body. What remains clear is that despite the ambivalence that arises in the third space of negotiating a hybrid culture identify, participants such as Maryam continue to exercise agency to regulate their own sexuality while reforming gendered cultural practices and choosing the personal, familial, and cultural values that she will adhere to. In this way, by resisting the cultural tradition of the virginity test and by conceding to cultural tropes that expect women to remain "chaste," Maryam attempts to balance her two cultures, Afghan and Canadian, without fully complying with the customs and beliefs of either.

The idea of an unsteady straddling between two cultures while negotiating gendered marital cultural practices is further complicated when the renegotiation of identity is formed outside the liminal spaces within the Afghan diaspora, that is, not free from the family gaze or homeland cultural norms. Parisa alludes to this in the following quote:

> My dad never put pressure on me. But I do know a lot of Afghan girls who have lived here their whole lives and [have experienced] pressure, [such as] to be "Sangeen" [to be decent] . . . you have to be shy when you're

sitting around men. . . . So I feel like [Afghan] women they struggle to reach out . . . because of that pressure at home . . . there are Afghans who have that old mentality and then there are Afghans who have a mixture of Afghan traditions and Western ones.

Parisa uses the word *pressure* to describe the experiences of second-generation Afghan girls who are expected to conform to traditional practices. While she does not feel pressured by the patriarch within her family, Parisa demonstrates her own ambivalence in navigating her cultural identity. For example, she shares that even though her parents allow "interactions with men," it is not "to the extent where they can come over and hang out." In conceding to Western social practices, such as interactions with the opposite sex, Parisa also knows there are limits to what her parents consider appropriate and remains careful in ensuring that these social interactions remain outside the boundaries of her parents' home. By implying that she does not feel pressured and yet is conforming to what is expected of her, Parisa demonstrates how she navigates her two cultural identities through self-regulation and regulating her social interactions. This self-regulation also demonstrates the ambivalence that remains part of the experiences of many second-generation Afghan-Canadian women in the diaspora when desiring premigration ideas of gendered cultural norms while at the same time asserting themselves as autonomous.

Cautionary Tales Circulating in the Afghan-Canadian Diaspora

Within the Afghan diaspora, discussions on gendered cultural scripts also included challenging and difficult conversations related to extreme cases of gendered expectations that lead to acts of gendered violence. Parisa briefly discussed the horrific killing of three teenage Afghan sisters—known as the Shafia sisters—that took place in 2009 in Kingston, Canada (Jiwani 2014), which received unrelenting coverage from Canadian media and also caused uproar in the diaspora.

The Shafia sisters and their step-mother were killed by their parents and their eighteen-year-old brother because they believed that the three girls were participating in activities that were not compatible with their family's cultural and religious values—such as having non-Afghan boyfriends, wearing revealing clothing, and possibly engaging in sexual activities. This event was characterized as an honor killing,[4] a term often used interchangeably to discuss honor-based violence within minority ethnic groups, especially in Muslim and South-Asian cultures (Gill and Aujla 2014: 161). Parisa mentions the Shafia killings to explain the power and fear associated with patriarchs in traditional Afghan families and their complicity in restricting women's mobility (specifically their engagement in what are considered Western social activities) and policing their bodies. As Parisa states:

> I see Afghan boys . . . they have been brought up in a house that allows them to [have more freedom] and the [Shafias] I feel like that's the perfect example . . . the father had money, had a good job, and two wives . . . he didn't care about [his daughters], and then when they would go have boyfriends, he and his son went and killed them.

Parisa's statement addresses the gendered dynamics that can exist within an Afghan home, in which Afghan men have more freedom to exercise their desires compared to Afghan women. Within the Shafia household, the parents and their male sibling aggressively pursued these gendered dynamics. Not only was the Shafia brother given extra privileges to impose his own household rules onto his sisters, but the family patriarch also freely practiced traditional gendered customs, such as having a polygamous marriage. Parisa argues that the family were "not proper Westerners and not proper Afghans either." She explains that a "proper" Afghan-Canadian is someone who integrated "the best of both worlds [instead] of the worst of each sides." Parisa, however, also expressed her uncertainty when asked what these two worlds looked like and, specifically, what cultural elements were to be resisted or reinforced in both.

The killing of the Shafia sisters circulated in the diaspora as a cautionary tale, resulting in many young Afghan-Canadian women remaining cautious and in some ways fearful of deviating from their parents' Afghan cultural values. Afsoon shares that during this time, her parents were quite strict in the type of social relationships and interactions she could have. In the aftermath of the event, her parents added a number of household rules, which made Afsoon fearful of deviating in the slightest from her Afghan cultural values:

> I was never allowed to have boyfriends; I was never allowed to go out, not even to my friend's birthday parties. . . . But [during a school trip] . . . something really bad happened and I told the teacher, if my parents find out about this, they are literally going to kill me; literally, I'll invite you to my funeral.

Afsoon's quote above illustrates her fears in participating in social activities that her parents did not approve. Her comment about being killed, even though she revealed it to be an exaggeration through humor, speaks to her fears. Afsoon's narrative also reveals how efforts to navigate two distinct cultures can be disrupted by social groups—in this case, her parents, the Shafia family, and Canadian media—to create an identity that favors traditions in one culture over the other. Her parents' imposition of cultural values resulted in conflict, ambivalence, and fear in constructing her hybrid cultural identity.

Parents were not the only source of the pressure that many of the participants felt when either resisting or conceding to specific cultural practices of their Afghan heritage; they also felt it from the broader Afghan community. This became evident when participants discussed incidents of gendered violence in Afghanistan. Some participants drew attention to the event that took place on March 19, 2015—the tragic death of a twenty-seven-year-old Afghan woman, Farkhunda Maikzada, who was brutally attacked and set on fire by a mob of Afghan men in Kabul after she was falsely accused by a religious leader of burning the Koran, the holy book of Islam (Faizi 2016). The slaying of Farkhunda stunned the nation and caused social upheaval among Afghan people (Faizi 2016). Afghan women took to the streets of Kabul and rallied to demand justice for Farkhunda. A pivotal moment during this event was that the Afghan women in Kabul collectively carried Farkhunda's casket to the burial ground without allowing any Afghan men to touch it. This significant gesture and moment marked the first time in Afghan history that women carried a casket to the grave to finish the burial ceremony.

In discussing this event, Parisa said that she is uncertain about "how these men [in Afghanistan] are raised," and that she feels there is a possibility that Afghanistan's ongoing "political instability" and "violence has [caused] them to [have] psychological or mental issues." From her comment, it is apparent that the murder of Farkhunda and the ongoing violence against women within Afghanistan has instilled in her a sense of fear that influences her attitudes toward men in Afghanistan. Other participants discussed their fear of visiting the homeland and in particular fears of being confined or witnessing violent incidents and mechanisms used by Afghan men to coerce women to adhere to traditional gendered cultural scripts.

While addressing gendered practices and expectations within Afghan culture, it is imperative to remain mindful of how second-generation Afghan women negotiate fulfilling their own desires and meeting diasporic cultural demands. While some of the participants shared varying narratives that addressed their fears, anger, guilt, and resentment, all participants revealed their ambivalence in navigating the contrasting worlds they are simultaneously living within. The preservation of an Afghan identity for second-generation Afghan women includes an ongoing negotiation and conscious decision to internalize gendered expectations at different life stages.

Conclusion

As expressed by Salma, this study is "a moment where second-generation girls [came to] share their stories and stick together." Our research sought to demonstrate the ways in which second-generation Afghan-Canadian women exercise agency and resilience when negotiating gendered cultural scripts, roles, and expectations in a diasporic cultural context. Their expressions and mobilizations of their hybrid cultural identities were not a mere tracing [of] "two original moments from which the third emerges" (Bhabha 1990: 211). Participants described their identities as being in constant flux, continuously transforming in relation to the interplay of individual desires, familial duties and expectations, the sociocultural context of the diaspora, and incidents of gender-based violence in Afghanistan and Canada.

Young women described instances of conformity and resistance; however, most importantly, they described their agency, autonomy, and independence. They shared their disapproval of particular gendered cultural practices and gender policing within the Afghan-Canadian diaspora, while at the same time symbolically aligning themselves with their parents' cultural values (the tension and ambivalence of inbetweenness/the third space). We found that scholarly discussions on Afghan-Canadian women's experiences are often extrapolated from young Afghan men's experiences or that of other groups of young racialized Muslim women (South Asian, Iranian, etc.). In this study, we placed young second-generation Afghan-Canadian women's voices at the forefront, and as a result, we found that these women are not passive but rather strong actors in their own right.

Although not directly questioned on these topics in the interviews, participants hinted at social class, religiosity, and other cultural practices as significant and relevant to their negotiations of gendered roles, expectations, and identities. The research design could be expanded in two important ways: (1) a larger sample size to derive broader sociological patterns; and (2) direct questions about social class (i.e., using proxy measures

beyond education, such as occupation, incomes, lifestyle, self-
identification), religious practices, influences, affiliations, cultural practices (including food, consumption of pop culture), as well as familial,
kinship, and friendship networks. Direct questions on these topics asked
from a larger and perhaps more homogenous group would provide a fuller
understanding of the intersections with gender, race, and social class in
negotiations of hybrid cultural identities of second-generation youth. Furthermore, future research on these topics could nuance current understandings and discourses of the Afghan diaspora, and in particular Afghan
women in Canada. Overall, this study provides valuable insights into adopting an intersectional lens to explore the interrelatedness of migration, settlement, and identity. As researchers, we are indebted to our participants
with whom we created "a safe space where we can talk about our struggles"
(Salma). We hope that this social space for dialogue can continue.

....

Saher Ahmed is a doctoral student in global studies at the University of British
Columbia. Her research is situated at the intersections of migration and asylum, pay-
ing specific attention to spatiality, surveillance, and the geopolitics of migration
management. Her previous research focused on the geographic displacement of
people, transnationalism, and identity.

Amrita Hari (DPhil, Oxon) is associate professor in and director of the Feminist Institute of Social Transformation at Carleton University. She examines global migrations, transnationalism, diaspora, and citizenship, and has published in *Signs* and
Gender, Work, and Organization, among others. She is funded by multiple grants and
teaches on feminism, post- and de-coloniality, and social research methods.

Notes

1   Ottawa is a secondary settlement area for immigrants, and it was a location of
    convenience for the researchers.
2   *Transnational mobility* in this context refers to a person migrating from one coun-
    try to another (Sirkeci 2009). Transnational mobility also includes liminal
    space(s), such as the location of temporary residence that is between the origin
    country and country of destination. This liminal space is often occupied by
    those who leave their origin countries to seek immediate human security and
    those who are avoiding the root causes of human insecurity (7).
3   Within Afghan culture, it is common for the bride and groom to have their reli-
    gious marital ceremony before the Afghan cultural wedding, particularly in the
    case of marriages that are arranged transnationally. In such cases, the *takht-
    jami* takes place after the Afghan cultural wedding; however, the couple are con-
    sidered married after the religious ceremony.

4   We use the term *honour killing* with extreme caution and remain mindful of the
colonial, Oriental, and biased depictions in most Western media outlets. We
also recognize the ongoing work of feminist scholars such as Yasmin Jiwani
(2014) and Aisha Gill and Wendy Aujla (2014) who argue that the term denies
victims a voice and cloaks the larger social structures of patriarchy that perpetuate all types of violence against women.

Works Cited

Abbasi-Shavazi, Mohammad Jalal, and Rasoul Sadeghi. 2014. "Socio-Cultural Adaptation of Second-Generation Afghans in Iran." *International Migration* 53, no. 6:
89–110.

Abbasi-Shavazi, Mohammad Jalal, Rasoul Sadeghi, Hossein Mahmoudian, and Gho-
lamreza Jamshidiha. 2012. "Marriage and Family Formation of the Second-
Generation Afghans in Iran: Insights from a Qualitative Study." *International
Migration Review* 46, no. 4: 828–60.

Amer, Amena, Caroline Howarth, and Ragini Sen. 2015. "Diasporic Virginities:
Social Representations of Virginity and Identity Formation amongst British Arab
Muslim Women." *Culture & Psychology* 21, no. 1: 3–19.

Bhabha, Homi K. 1990. *Nation and Narration*. New York: Routledge.

Bhabha, Homi K. 1994. *The Location of Culture*. London: Routledge.

Bhopal, Kalwant. 1999. "South Asian Women and Arranged Marriages in East London."
In *Ethnicity, Gender, and Social Change*, edited by Rohit Barot, Harriet Bradley, and
Steve Fenton, 117–34. London: Palgrave Macmillan.

Brah, Avtar. 1996. *Cartographies of Diaspora: Contesting Identities*. London: Routledge.

Brah, Avtar. 2003. "Diaspora, Border, and Transnational Identities." In *Feminist Postcolonial Theory: A Reader*, edited by Reina Lewis and Sara Mills, 613–34. Edinburgh:
Edinburgh University Press.

Butterfield, Sherry-Anne. 2004. "Being Racialized Ethnics: Second Generation West
Indian Immigrants in New York City." In *Race and Ethnicity in New York City*, edited
by J. Krase and Ray Hutchison, 107–36. Research in Urban Sociology 7. Bingley,
UK: Emerald Group.

Chase, Susan. E. 2003. "Taking Narrative Seriously: Consequences for Method and
Theory in Interview Studies." In *Turning Points in Qualitative Research: Tying Knots in
a Handkerchief*, edited by Yvonna S. Lincoln and Norman K. Denzin, 273–96.
Walnut Creek, CA: AltaMira.

Coyne, Kathleen. 2000. *Performing Virginity and Testing Chastity in the Middle Ages*.
London: Routledge.

Crabtree, Benjamin F., and Benjamin DiCicco-Bloom. 2006. "The Qualitative
Research Interview." *Medical Education* 40, no. 4: 314–21.

Cresswell, John W. 2011. *Educational Research: Planning, Conducting, and Evaluating Quanti-
tative and Qualitative Research*. New York: Pearson.

Curran, Sara R., Steven Shafer, Katharine M. Donato, and Filiz Garip. 2006. "Mapping Gender and Migration in Sociological Scholarship: Is It Segregation or Integration?" *International Migration Review* 40, no. 1: 199–223.

Dasgupta, Shamita Das. 1998. "Gender Roles and Cultural Continuity in the Asian India Immigrant Community in the U.S." *Sex Roles* 35, nos. 11–12: 953–74.

Donato, Katharine M. 2006. "A Glass Half Full? Gender in Migration Studies." *International Migration Review* 40, no. 1: 3–26.

Dossa, Parin. 2005."'Witnessing' Social Suffering: Testimonial Narratives of Women from Afghanistan." *BC Studies*, no. 147 (Autumn): 27–49.

Dossa, Parin. 2008. "Creating Politicized Spaces: Afghan Immigrant Women's Stories of Migration and Displacement." *Affilia* 23, no. 1: 10–21.

Dossa, Parin. 2009. *Racialized Bodies, Disabling Worlds: Storied Lives of Immigrant Muslim Women*. Toronto: University of Toronto Press.

Dossa, Parin. 2014. *Afghanistan Remembers: Gendered Narrations of Violence and Culinary Practices*. Toronto: University of Toronto Press.

Dwyer, Claire. 2000. "Negotiating Diasporic Identities: Young British South Asian Muslim Women." *Women's Studies International Forum* 23, no. 4: 475–86.

Faizi, Fatima. 2016. "Afghanistan: 'Farkhunda Will Not Be Forgotten.'" *Al Jazeera*, March 18.

Fonow, Mary Margaret, and Judith A. Cook. 2005. "Feminist Methodology: New Applications in the Academy and Public Policy." *Signs: Journal of Women in Culture and Society* 30, no. 4: 2211–36.

Gill, Aisha, and Wendy Aujla. 2014. "Conceptualizing 'Honour' Killings in Canada: An Extreme Form of Domestic Violence?" *International Journal of Criminal Justice Science* 9, no. 1: 153–66.

Gilroy, Paul. 1995. *The Black Atlantic: Modernity and Double Consciousness*. Cambridge, MA: Harvard University Press.

Guest, Greg, Arwen Bunce, and Laura Johnson. 2006. "How Many Interviews Are Enough? An Experiment with Data Saturation and Variability." *Field Methods* 18, no. 1: 59–82.

Gupta, Akhil, and James Ferguson.1997. *Cultural, Power, Place, Explorations in Critical Anthropology*. Durham, Duke University Press.

Gupta, Monisha Das. 1997. "What Is Indian about You? A Gendered, Transnational Approach to Ethnicity." *Gender & Society* 11, no. 5: 572–96.

Hall, Stuart. 1990. "Cultural Identity and Diaspora." In *Identity: Community, Culture, Difference*, edited by Jonathan Rutherford, 392–403. London: Lawrence & Wishart.

Handa, Amita. 2003. *Of Silk Saris and Mini-Skirts: South Asian Girls Walk the Tightrope of Culture*. Toronto: Women's Press.

Harding, Sandra. 1986. *Feminism and Methodology*. Bloomington: Indiana University Press.

Hynie, Michaela, Sepali Guruge, and Yogendra B. Shakya. 2012. "Family Relationships of Afghan, Karen, and Sudanese Refugee Youth." *Canadian Ethnic Studies* 44, no. 3: 11–28.

Jiwani, Yasmin.2014. "Honour on Trial: The Shafia Murders and the Culture of Honour Killings by Paul Schliesmann." *Canadian Ethnic Studies* 46, no. 2: 150–60.

Kalvir, Giti Eghbal. 2011. *Iranian Women in Beautiful British Columbia: Economic Security among Iranian Immigrant Lone Mothers.* Vancouver, BC: Simon Fraser University Library.

Kargar, Zarghuna. 2012. *Dear Zari: Hidden Stories from Women of Afghanistan.* London: Chatto & Windus.

Khanlou, Nazilla, and Charmaine Crawford. 2006. "Post-migratory Experiences of Newcomer Female Youth: Self-Esteem and Identity Development." *Journal of Immigrant and Minority Health* 8, no. 1: 45–56.

Khanlou, Nazilla, Jane G. Koh, and Catriona Mill. 2008. "Cultural Identity and Experiences of Prejudice and Discrimination of Afghan and Iranian Immigrant Youth." *International Journal of Mental Health and Addiction* 6, no. 4: 494–513.

Khatib, Maissa. 2013. "Arab Muslim Women's Experiences of Living in the United States: A Qualitative Descriptive Study." PhD diss., University of Texas at El Paso.

Kirk, Jackie. 2006. "Transferring Cultural Knowledge and Skills: Afghan Teachers for Afghan Students in Montreal." *Refuge: Canada's Journal on Refugees* 23, no. 1: 45–50.

Kohistani, Venos. 2012. "Identifying Cultural Strengths of Afghan Refugees as a Source of their Resiliance." *Theses and dissertations.* Paper 1533.

Nourpanah, Shiva. 2014. "A Study of the Experiences of Integration and Settlement of Afghan Government-Assisted Refugees in Halifax, Canada." *Refuge: Canada's Journal on Refugees* 30, no. 1: 45–57.

Portes, Alejandro, and Min Zhou. 1993. "The New Second Generation: Segmented Assimilation and Its Variants." *Annals of the American Academy of Political and Social Sciences* 530, no. 1: 74–96.

Rajiva, Mythili. 2013. "Better lives: The Transgenerational Positioning of Social Mobility in the South Asian Canadian Diaspora." *Women's Studies International Forum* 36 (February): 16–26.

Reinharz, Shulamit, and Lynn Davidman. 1992. *Feminist Methods in Social Research.* New York: Oxford University Press.

Rumbaut, Rubén G. 2002. "Severed or Sustained Attachments? Language, Identity, and Imagined Communities in the Post-immigrant Generation." In *The Changing Face of Home: The Transnational Lives of the Second Generation,* 43–95. New York: Russell Sage Foundation.

Rumbaut, Rubén G. 2004. "Ages, Life Stages, and Generational Cohorts: Decomposing the Immigrant First and Second Generations in the United States." *International Migration Review* 38, no. 3: 1160–1205.

Sadat, Mir Hekmatullah. 2008. "Hyphenating Afghaniyat (Afghan-ness) in the Afghan Diaspora." *Journal of Muslim Minority Affairs* 28, no. 3: 329–42.

Safran, William. 1991. "Diasporas in Modern Societies: Myths of Homeland and Return." *Diaspora: A Journal of Transnational Studies* 1, no. 1: 83–99.

Safran, William. 2004. "Deconstructing and Comparing Diasporas." In *Diaspora, Identity, and Religion: New Directions in Theory and Research,* edited by Waltraud Kokot, Khachig Tölölyan, and Carolin Alfonso, 9–30. London: Routledge.

Shakya, Yogendra B., Sepali Guruge, and Michaela Hynie. 2010. "Aspirations for Higher Education among Newcomer Refugee Youth in Toronto." *Canada's Periodical on Refugees* 27, no. 2: 65–78.

Shaw, Alison. 2001. "Kinship, Cultural Preference and Immigration: Consanguineous Marriage among British Pakistanis." *The Journal of the Royal Anthropological Institute* 7, no. 2: 315–34.

Sirkeci, Ibrahim. 2009. "Transnational Mobility and Conflict." *Migration Letters* 6, no. 1: 3–14.

Stack, Julie A. C., and Yoshitaka Iwasaki. 2009. "The Role of Leisure Pursuits in Adaptation Processes among Afghan Refugees Who Have Immigrated to Winnipeg, Canada." *Leisure Studies* 28, no. 3: 239–59.

Sundar, Purnima. 2008. "To 'Brown It Up' or to 'Bring Down the Brown': Identity and Strategy in Second-Generation, South Asian-Canadian Youth." *Journal of Ethnic and Cultural Diversity in Social Work* 17, no. 3: 251–78.

Vincent, Louise. 2006. "Virginity Testing in South Africa: Re-traditioning the Postcolonial." *Culture, Health & Sexuality* 8, no. 1: 17–30.

Michaela Django Walsh

Between Skin and Stone
A Letter to My Son, Lienzo

Abstract: This piece, written in the form of a letter to my son, explains the meaning of his name. In Spanish the word *lienzo* is a type of drystone wall. Spanning rural areas of Mexico, the lienzo has—for centuries—been a way to gently delineate space. I frame the composition of this hand-stacked structure, which is designed to accommodate movement in relation to the biopolitical technology of the U.S.-Mexico border fence, migrant dispossession, and my own family's experiences navigating borders and cleaved spaces.

Lienzo,

At some point you will ask me about your name, and I will share this letter with you, which is also about my own experiences navigating borders and cleaved spaces. Even though you are only sixteen months, I write this letter to initiate an opening, not only of me to you, but you to me. It is an invitation into conversations about place and belonging, levity and resistance that I imagine us having. This letter, which is a beginning, is the reason for your name.

I named you for the drystone walls that span rural areas of Mexico. From an aerial view they look like veins weaving through the countryside. They are layered as skin is layered. For centuries, lienzos have been used to gently delineate space. They are unlike the different types of cement and steel barriers that scrape toward sky as they jut burial-deep into portions of the land west from the playas of Tijuana, east to the Gulf of Mexico. The *lienzo* is only

MERIDIANS · feminism, race, transnationalism   22:2 October 2023
DOI: 10.1215/15366936-10637636 © 2023 Smith College

as tall as the human body alone can build. It is made of stones that have been hugged to the chest, hoisted from the stretch of thighs and torso, and arranged to press into and against one another. One day when we are walking to the pueblo I will tell you that it can take two days to complete three yards of wall, and then I will show you what three yards is, and you will marvel at how many years it took to create this small stretch of your namesake. The process of building is as slow as it is deliberate.

One day I will point out the hundreds of heart- and fist-sized stones that fill the gaps in the wall, and I will tell you that the Spanish word for this process is *hilar*, which means to weave and spin, to thread or string together. We don't usually think of walls in terms of the intricate softness of tapestry. Nor do we think of them somatically—as capable of arterial contraction and expansion, inhalation and exhalation, as accommodations for the shifting nature of the land through their own movement. As the ground settles or heaves, the lienzo flexes, adjusts, and yields in relation. Unlike the binding force of mortar or the impenetrability of steel, this wall is semipermeable. The small gaps between the stones filter the ungraspable movement of dust-flecked sunlight. They are a conduit of rain. A place of passage for small animals. Lienzo, I named you for a way of imagining space that isn't premised on terror or woundedness, but on the possibility of bodies being able to touch and merge across place and time.

The Latin root for the word *territory* can mean land, but it can also mean to terrorize, to make tremble, to exclude (Elden 2009: xxiv). While the lienzo is a form of bordering that is connective and live, the ruling of land by a settler nation operates through terror. It's a force that severs people from place. It's a force that severs people from one another. Materially, borders and walls impose a claim to land. Along the San Diego–Mexico border the beach, sand rippled by wind, looks like stretch-marked skin—the pillars of the fence that mark the first international borderline, like sutures. Past the fresh and saltwater marshes that rise and fall with the expansion and contraction of tides, the metal posts extend toward horizon. The practice of terrorization extends deep into the currents of the Pacific where the physical border reappears and disappears with the swell of the ocean. Along the San Diego–Mexico border terrorization is manifested in the performative flex of sovereign might. Migrant movement is directed into spaces of threshold by towering steel and cement fences, tumbleweeds of concertina wire, and the thrust and thrum of aerial and terrestrial surveillance. In the scorch and chill of the desert, fluctuating extremes of temperature short-circuit the human body. When pushed further from shore, into the weight of the Río Bravo, or toward precipice, precarity is felt in marrow and breath. *Náufrago*,[1] the migrant is (the) cast/away. The refuse/d. But you are too young to know these words. Now, you say mama, *luna*, *leche*. You say dog and belly. It will be years before terror enters your lexicon, before you know the tremble of loss or ache.

One day you will make choices about what to carry with you and what to leave behind, and I will tell you about the intimacy and intrusion of searching migrant bodies and belongings. I will tell you about how I learned that folding clothes is an act of dignity. Before they arrived at the deep spaces where land and water form natural borders they transited the entirety of Mexico, which is itself a cat's cradle of defensive designs to halt migrant movement into the United States. When morning turns the color of a bruise, I would catch a bus to Guadalajara to volunteer at a *casa de migrante*.[2] It was here that people sought momentary stasis before continuing north. The majority arrived via El Diablo, the cargo train that runs the Pacific route of the country. A condition of their entry was a physical search of their bodies and an interview.

In the foyer of the shelter that smells like instant coffee and sweat I felt the burn of heat and chill and exhaustion through the fabric of their clothing. It formed a thin boundary between the bareness of our skin as I moved my hands down their backs, ribs, and calves. Some swayed as though still seasick from riding the rails. Everything they carried with them—the carefully folded shirt, identification protected in a Ziplock bag, a toothbrush and a bar of soap, the thumb-sized toy car or palm-sized bible—they removed from their backpacks. I could feel the storm and the soil of their journey now on my hands as I returned their belongings. Later they would be asked about their experience migrating. The responses formed part of a database shared among shelters across the country. Among all the questions that migrants are asked, Lienzo, it's not the harrowing reasons for why they are migrating, or what they've endured en route that gave me pause, so much as the one where they share distinguishing marks on their bodies. The information is used to help identify them if they go missing, or should they die along the way. I would input the location of their birthmarks and moles, their scars, tattoos, and burns, the in/visible wounds of missing body parts. We think of the land as palimpsest, but what of skin?

When I was pregnant with you I would swim in a lake to find relief from the summer heat, from the weight of your being in my body. Your movement within me like a ripple, a throb without the ache, I could sometimes trace the outline of your arm or leg bowed against the tautness of my belly, the boundary of my skin enfolding you. What marks of my own being, the birthmarks, the shape of my eyes would touch you, Lienzo? What traces of your grandmother, *en paz descanse*,[3] would become physically manifest on you, so that in you I would be able to see her once again? In Spanish the word *lascar* when used in reference to skin means to graze or bruise. When used in reference to rock it means to chip off. The lienzo is also made from these fragments, bits and pieces of stone that form the wall's interior. If stone is part of the earth's memory, what of the anatomy of water, which also forms a skin?

That summer a photo of a young Salvadoran man who drowned with his twenty-three-month-old daughter while trying to cross the Rio Bravo made headlines. What made the image unbearable was not the man lying face down in the silt, but the little girl whose body was protectively tucked underneath her father's T-shirt. At first glance it looks like they are just sleeping. She has her arm draped around his neck. Her face is burrowed in his shoulder. In the months before you were born I imagined the tiny droplets from the surfaces of the Rio Bravo and the lake where I swam traveling skyward as the air became warmer. I thought about the merging of this vapor like breath and wondered about the possibility of these two bodies of water touching across time and space to form clouds. I thought about how the clouds eventually become too heavy to remain in the atmosphere. Released from the sky in the form of rain and hail, graupel and snow, they return to the soil. They return to bodies of water. As you stretched inside of me I imagined the little girl and her father as connected to the cycle of falling and rising, their last breaths in the river a continuation of clouds.

Lienzo, one day I will also tell you about searching for the missing. The arroyos where San Diego and Mexico touch used to form the migrant path. Now that path leads to mountain summits where the clouds look tidal, like they could drown the earth. Spatial disorientation—the inability to distinguish up from down—horizon from earth, or the necessary direction to surface from the depth of water, happens in the void of visual reference. It can cause the pilot to crash, the diver to sink. Typically experienced in air or water, can it also take place on the land? Does the person who is marooned have a heightened awareness of nature? Do they notice the way the desert flowers bend, yielding fragrance to the heat? Do they feel the forgiveness of shadows cast by boulders at the height of day, notice how the stone holds warmth into the night, or how the moon moves from scythe, to billowing sail, to pregnancy? Beyond a primal drive to live, Lienzo, what propels the body forward? I joined searches for those who were shipwrecked on land to recover them from dispossession, to intervene in their dry drownings, to at the very least bear witness, even if only by leaving jugs of water and pop-open cans of tuna.

When will it ever be the right time to tell you about the Honduran mother? I can't possibly tell you, and I can't possibly not tell you . . . But when, if not now or never? She made it to Tijuana with her three children, one of them only a little older than you. She was fleeing the barbarity of a man who tried to set them on fire. It wasn't the imposition of the wall that stopped her from trying to cross into the United States—they traversed Guatemala and the entirety of Mexico, a feat of endurance and hope. What propelled her to turn around was the possibility of being separated from her children at the border. The law came into effect while they were in transit. Some walls are invisible. You hit them psychically and they halt you physically and if you can you find a way to endure. Even though they made it to the brink of crossing, the threat of having her children taken from her was so hopeless and hollow a prospect that she would have rather died. That was her wall.

In the quietest part of night when I hold you to my chest, Lienzo, the small weight of your body against mine is pure, our connection is primal. In the quietest part of night, I listen to the warmth of your sleep and feel the palimpsest of our skin connecting us backward and forward across time and space, and I think about the un/imaginable. The physical ache of the breasts of the woman who has her infant taken from her. How the ache of s/welling signals his absence. How she kneads her breasts to release the pressure and to sustain milk flow in anticipation of his return, how she kneads and kneels, releasing her milk to the cold floor like a prayer (Walsh 2021: 34). I think about the famine I would feel if I had my uterus taken, the possibility of your being foreclosed to me. Along the U.S.-Mexico border the wall now extends beyond land into the territory of the corporeal. It is physically incised into the bodies of women. It is meant to ravage.

Lienzo, I named you for the walls that form the boundaries of the fields leading into the pueblo. They are made of stone the size of thighs and small torsos, curved shoulders and bowing backs. They are the color of elephants, of earth, of skies weighted with rain. One day when we are traveling through Mexico you will notice that the lienzo is arterial, forming a circuitry across *campos*, how it extends through *cerros* and *valles*, and I will tell you that I named you Lienzo to remind you of your connection to the pueblo. It is the smell of wood smoke early in the morning, the way the mountains look like shadows against sky. It is the tingle of lime and salt on your tongue, the flight sounds of the *garza* like sighs. I named you for a way of embodying space that is connective, intimate, ancient. I named you for strength and yield. Lienzo, you are a continuation of me. You belong to a family of people marked by movement in between and through geographies. Your name, which also means canvas, is my acknowledgment that your life will be shaped by your own movement, and that there may be times when you struggle to distinguish soil from sky, depth from surface. Whether from the toll of weather, the seismic sighs of the earth, or vulnerabilities in its composition, like the clouds that eventually become too heavy to remain in the atmosphere, it is inevitable that the lienzo will one day buckle. What I want you to know is that what makes this structure like none other is that when it does fall the same stones can be repurposed to build anew. Today you are sixteen months. Your hands knead my skin as you nurse. It took thousands of years for you to arrive, first by construction, then by name, then by touch. Thousands of years, and now you are sixteen months and I am imagining the day we walk the path to the pueblo and I point out to you the beauty of your name.

. . . .

Michaela Django Walsh is assistant professor of ethnic studies at Bowling Green State University. Her creative writing and research focus on the U.S.-Mexico border and transnational productions of belonging.

Notes
1   Shipwrecked.
2   Migrant shelter.
3   Rest in peace.

Works Cited
Elden, Stuart. 2009. *Terror and Territory: The Spatial Extent of Sovereignty.* Minneapolis: University of Minnesota Press.
Walsh, Michaela. 2021. "Paso Libre," *New Letters: A Magazine of Writing and Art* 87, nos. 1–2: 129–37.

Julie Torres

···

"We Are Orlando"
Silences, Resistance, and the Intersections
of Mass Violence

Abstract: The 2016 shooting at Pulse Nightclub in Orlando, Florida, was mourned as an unspeakable act of violence against the lesbian, gay, bisexual, transgender, and queer (LGBTQ+) community. But what was perhaps less audible was the fact that Latinxs, particularly Puerto Ricans, who represent more than one million of the state's population, were disproportionally affected. In the wake of the tragedy, a group of Puerto Rican women came together to demand translation and mental health services for survivors and their families. This article details their public refusals to be silenced from the public imaginary of mourning and loss. It also considers how the multiple subject positions of Puerto Ricans shape belonging both locally and across transnational borders. In doing so, the author makes the case for an intersectional analysis of mass violence, mourning, and resistance, in order to generate inclusive spaces and a more just vision for the future.

On June 12, 2016, at 4:17 a.m., I awoke to the sound of a BBC alert on my phone that read: "Florida police confirm multiple injuries from shooting at Orlando's Pulse gay nightclub, warn people to stay away."[1] My eyes were heavy. I sighed and went back to sleep. Gun violence has become increasingly normalized in the United States. Since 1966 there have been 190 public mass shootings in the United States, including several high-profile cases, such as Sandy Hook, Aurora, San Bernardino, Sutherland Springs, Charleston, Las Vegas, Parkland, El Paso and, more recently, Buffalo and Uvalde (Peterson and Densley 2021).[2] It was not until later that morning

MERIDIANS · feminism, race, transnationalism   22:2 October 2023
DOI: 10.1215/15366936-10637600 © 2023 Smith College

that I realized the magnitude of the shooting: forty-nine dead and fifty-three wounded.[3] The news that the gunman was Muslim and used an assault rifle proliferated discourses of terror that surround racialized populations in the post-9/11 moment (Rana and Rosas 2006) and reignited debates around gun reform. But while the event was rightfully condemned as an act of violence against the LGBTQ+ community, there was little to no mention in those early reports that it also happened to be "Latin Night."[4] As the images and names of victims flashed across the television screen, I felt the uneasy transition from grief to anger. Eighty percent of the victims were Latinx, and nearly half, twenty-three of the forty-nine, were Puerto Rican. If you had any doubts, all you needed to do was walk around the city in the days following the attack. Symbols of Puerto Rican and Latinx identity covered the expansive lawn of the Dr. Phillips Center for the Performing Arts and adorned the path to Orlando Regional Medical Center, where victims and survivors were treated (fig. 1; see also Torres 2016). The Puerto Rican flag tied around the bark of a tree, the prayer candle to a patron saint lit near a beloved's photograph, and messages of love and solidarity chalked on the sidewalk in Spanish—these material expressions at once disidentified with the whiteness of queer identity and stood in stark contrast to the erasure of queer Brown and Black lives from the public stage of loss and mourning.

On the day of the shooting, I came across a post on the blog *Orlando Latino* titled "Latinas Translate for Victims' Families" (Padilla 2016b). It described how a "group of Latinas" came together within hours of the tragedy to coordinate translation and mental health services for victims' families and survivors. The core group of women, whom I would later learn were primarily Puerto Rican, drew on their networks to form a coalition of Latinx organizations, which led to the eventual founding of "*Proyecto Somos Orlando*" (We Are Orlando Project).[5]

Drawing on feminist scholarship, particularly that of Black, Indigenous, and Women of Color feminists, this article describes the conditions that led to its creation and details the activist efforts of these women. In her introduction to *Living a Feminist Life*, Sara Ahmed (2017: 1) describes feminism as a word that "brings to mind loud acts of refusal and rebellion as well as the quiet ways we might have of not holding on to things that diminish us. It brings to mind women who have stood up, spoken back, risked lives, homes, relationships in the struggle for more bearable worlds." Historically, Latinas in the United States have done just that—from labor organizing (Ruiz 1998; Zavella 1987) and involvement in organizations such as the Young Lords (Fernández 2020; Morales 2016; Wanzer-

Figure 1. Memorial outside the Orlando Regional Medical Center. Photo by author, 2016.

Serrano 2015) to quotidian claims to human dignity and respect grounded in family and community (Benmayor, Torruellas, and Juarbe 1997; Bermudez 2020; Hardy-Fanta 2002; Pardo 1998; Segura and Facio 2008). Latina feminisms have also attended to the intersections of race, gender, and sexuality, providing counternarratives to Latinx heteronormativity (Acosta 2013; Blackwell 2011; Moraga and Anzaldúa 1983; Baca Zinn and Zambrana 2019).

This article is about Puerto Rican women who have "stood up" and "spoken back." It is about the continued salience of intersectionality—a framework for understanding how human experiences of oppression and privilege are shaped by a variety of interwoven factors, including race, gender, class, and sexuality (Crenshaw 1989; Collins and Bilge 2016)—for projects located at the crossroads of migration, mourning, and activism. I argue that the language of crisis—what I refer to as the silences surrounding catastrophic events and moments of violence, chaos, and disorder—generates public refusals that speak to the ways that those at the margins contest intersecting forms of oppression. I begin by providing a brief overview of the migration of Puerto Ricans to the Orlando metropolitan area. I then engage in an analysis of the intersections of race, sexuality, and gender, pointing to the institutional and cultural factors that reify heteronormative whiteness and create the desire for "safe spaces" such as Pulse. Lastly, I conclude by foregrounding the activism of Puerto Rican women in Orlando, who refused to be silenced.

As Monica, one of Somos' cofounders put it, "The Latino voice was not part of the narrative and *no nos dio la gana* [we didn't feel like it] to keep quiet."[6] Ultimately, Somos emerged as a critical response—a reminder that we, too, are Orlando.

Field Site and Methods

"We know that it didn't have to be Latin night for it to be mostly Latinos in that club," said Mariana, one of the cofounders of Somos, as we sat outside a Dunkin' Donuts not far from where Pulse stood, now shuttered. To understand the depth of Mariana's statement, we must understand something of the history of Puerto Rican migration, given the effects of U.S. imperialism on labor, the economy, and other facets of social life. Puerto Ricans have been colonial subjects of the United States since 1898. The passage of the Jones Act of 1917, which conferred U.S. citizenship on Puerto Ricans, and economic changes resulted in increased migration from the archipelago to the United States following World War II. While Puerto Rican migration to the United States has been well documented in traditional diasporic locations, such as New York and Chicago (Fernández 2012; Pérez 2004; Ramos-Zayas 2003; Rúa 2012; Sanchez-Korrol 1983; Whalen 2005), less attention has been paid, until recently, to the diaspora of Puerto Ricans to the U.S. South and central Florida.

The migration of Latinxs to the South has led some scholars to refer to the region and its changing demographic landscape as the "New South";

however, the migration of Latinxs to the South is not new. The movement of Latinxs into the South spans back to the early twentieth century with the recruitment of workers for agriculture, manufacturing, and other industries (N. Rodriguez 2012; Weise 2012).[7] Puerto Ricans were similarly recruited for positions in the agriculture, factory, and garment industries, as well as the cigar-making industry in Tampa (Duany and Matos-Rodriguez 2006). But there were other push-and-pull factors that contributed to the migration of Puerto Ricans to Florida, including the recruitment of Puerto Ricans for the military as early as the 1940s and of Puerto Rican engineers by NASA in the mid-1970s (Silver 2010). Orlando also experienced a surge in migration from Puerto Rico with the opening of Walt Disney's theme park in 1971, which brought jobs and increased real estate speculation in the area (Delerme 2014). By 1980 the Puerto Rican population in Florida had tripled (Duany and Silver 2010). More recently, the economic crisis in Puerto Rico, which is characterized by a $74 billion debt, and Hurricane Maria have contributed to a population loss on the archipelago, which is arguably experiencing its largest exodus to the United States since the Great Migration of the post–World War II period.[8]

Florida, and central Florida in particular, has emerged a top diasporic destination for Puerto Ricans. There are approximately 1.2 million Puerto Ricans currently residing in the state and over 300,000 living in the Orlando metropolitan area, where my fieldwork was conducted (Noe-Bustamante, Flores, and Shah 2019). While the recent important works by Simone Delerme (2020) and Patricia Silver (2020) have provided much-needed insight into the racial and political landscapes, respectively, of Puerto Rican Orlando, this article is part of a larger ethnographic project that examines the activist efforts of Puerto Ricans in Orlando around moments that are conceptualized in the public imagination as crisis. It draws on data collected through traditional anthropological methods, such as participant observation of town halls, vigils, and grassroots and nonprofit organizational meetings and other events, as well as select conversations from forty-eight semi- and unstructured interviews with Orlando activists and residents.

According to Salvador Vidal-Ortiz (2016), "Queer-Orlando-América is an extension of so many Latin American cities as sites of contention, where to be LGBT is both celebrated and chastised—no more, or less, than homophobia in the US." In other words, to say that "we know that it didn't have to be Latin night for it to be mostly Latinos in that club" is to say that Pulse was a diasporic tragedy—not only in the overwhelming number of Latinxs and Puerto Ricans affected in Orlando, but also in the ways it revealed the transnational linkages to Puerto Rico, particularly with regard to sometimes harmful conceptions of gender and sexuality.

The Queering of Sexuality and Gender

Following the shooting, proclamations of solidarity and denouncements of homophobia were heard around the world. But less audible were stories like that of a father in Puerto Rico who refused to accept his son's body from the morgue because he was gay (Padilla 2016a). These stories are far from exceptional, as are the increasing incidents of violence against LGBTQ+ people, especially trans People of Color (Rodríguez-Madera et al. 2017). In 2020 alone, at least six trans or gender-nonconforming people were murdered in Puerto Rico, prompting calls from activists for the declaration of a state of emergency on the archipelago (Jackson 2020). Their names were Michellyn Ramos Varga, Alexa Negrón Luciano, Penélope Díaz Ramírez, Serena Angelique Velázquez, Layla Pelaez, and Yampi Méndez Arocho. Nearly a decade before, a teenager by the name of Jorge Steven López Mercado was found decapitated, burned, and dismembered on the side of the road in Cayey, Puerto Rico (El nuevo dia 2009).[9] While such instances of brutal violence capture the everydayness of homophobia and transphobia, they also demonstrate the need for intersectional transnational and translocal perspectives that take into account these and other forms of oppression beyond a U.S. context (Torres 2016).

The growing and diverse field of Puerto Rican queer studies has much to offer in this area, engaging with the various dimensions of discrimination and queer identity formation, activism, cultural production, gender, as well as their connections to colonialism, both in Puerto Rico and its diaspora (Crespo Kebler 2003; La Fountain-Stokes and Martínez-San Miguel 2018; Negrón-Muntaner 1999; Rivera-Velázquez and Torres Narváez 2016; Torres 2008).[10] For instance, in his recent book, Lawrence La Fountain-Stokes (2021) employs the term transloca to capture the movements, displacements, and disidentifications of Puerto Rican drag and trans performers and activists across local and global contexts. Such approaches enrich a queer reading of sexuality in gender and migration research, uncovering the various ways and geographies in which "sexuality is disciplined by social institutions and practices that normalize and naturalize heterosexuality and heterosexual practices including marriage, family, and biological reproduction by marginalizing persons, institutions, or practices that deviate from these norms" (Manalansan 2006: 225), as well as how these conventions are resisted. In dialogue with this body of research, this section introduces the narratives of two young people, Alejandra and Xan, to discuss how sexuality and gender are disciplined, given the negotiation of identities in movement (Carillo 2004; Povinelli and Chauncey 1999).

Alejandra was a soft-spoken, colored-pencil artist from Ponce. While she lived most of her life in Puerto Rico, she previously spent brief periods of time in Boston and in other parts of Florida because of her parents' employment. She was studying at a Catholic university in Puerto Rico, when she decided to leave for the United States out of fear of being outed as a lesbian. Although devastated by the tragedy at Pulse, Alejandra posited that, while there was still more work to be done, it had opened the door for more dialogue regarding sexuality in Puerto Rico.

"It's still very old-fashioned, like back in my grandma's days," Alejandra explained, when we met outside for coffee before her shift at work. "You're a failure if you're not married by a certain age and have kids by a certain age. The concept of making it as an adult, especially for women, is to find a husband and have kids before thirty. So, if you don't have a boyfriend or a husband, they always have that saying of like, '*Te vas a quedar jamona,*' which means—I don't know how to translate it in English."

"Like an old maid?" I asked.

"Exactly. It's a little bit more unfair for the women in the community and that goes even deeper as Women of Color in our community. There are things that I didn't go through because of my light skin, that my dark-skinned friends went through. But then that coin flipped at some point because of traveling back and forth, I wasn't able to belong to just one. I kind of like meshed both cultures and I was seen as the *gringa* back home and not American enough over here. . . . But when it comes to the gay community, growing up that was a big no-no."

The term *jamona*, referenced by Alejandra, is the equivalent of a spinster or old maid. Translated literally as "ham," it is used to refer to a woman who is unmarried and "old," and oftentimes perceived to be unattractive or overweight. The figure of the jamona appears in Esmeralda Santiago's (1994) autobiographical book, *When I Was Puerto Rican*. In a chapter titled "Why Women Remain Jamona," the protagonist Negi (Esmeralda) takes a trip with her father to visit her grandmother in Santurce. Along the way, they stop at a market where Negi sees a woman with a "long, mournful face, horselike, her large eyes almond shaped, the corners pointed down as if weighed by many tears" (88). She notes a "cold" change in the atmosphere. After whirling around on a counter stool at an *alcapurria* (stuffed fritter) stand, Negi falls to the ground. "Jesus doesn't love children who don't behave," the woman tells her, as the man behind the counter shoos her away. He turns to Negi's father to say, "That's what happens to women when they stay jamonas" (88). After finishing their meals, Negi and her father speak, as they continue their journey:

> "Papi, what's a jamona?" I asked as we left the market, our bellies full.
>   "It's a woman who has never married."
>   "I thought that was a señorita."
>   "It's the same thing. But when someone says a woman is jamona it means she's too old to get married. It's an insult."
>   "How come?"
>   "Because it means no one wants her. Maybe she's too ugly to get married. . . . Or she has waited too long. . . . She ends up alone for the rest of her life. Like that woman in the mercado."
>   "She was ugly for sure."
>   "That's probably why she stayed jamona."
>   "I hope that never happens to me."
>   "No, that won't happen to you. . . . There's our publico. Let's run for it."

We dodged across the street holding hands, avoiding cars, people, and stray dogs sunning themselves on the sidewalk.

"What do they call a man who never marries?" I asked as we settled ourselves in the front of the publico.

"Lucky," the driver said, and the rest of the passengers laughed, which made me mad, because it felt as if he were insulting me in the worst possible way. (89)

Later, after her father had left Negi at her grandmother's house for more than a week to have an affair with another woman, Negi's mother arrives to pick her up. Negi observes her mother's tear-stained face and listens to the quiet whispers coming from the adjacent room. She wonders whether being a jamona is such a bad thing after all: "It seemed to me that remaining jamona could not possibly hurt this much," Negi ponders. "That a woman alone, even if ugly, could not suffer as much as my beautiful mother did . . . I would just as soon remain jamona than shed that many tears over a man" (104).

A queer reading of the figure of the jamona offers the reader another perspective—one that goes against the grain of the heteronormative and sexist gendered expectations revealed by the statements "te vas a quedar jamona" (you're going to stay jamona) and "that's what happens to women when they stay jamonas" in the narratives above. In many ways, the jamona can be read as a border subject "caught between the racism of the dominant society and the sexist and heterosexist expectations of their own communities" (Espín 1996: 82). This parallels Alejandra's reflection on not being "American enough," coupled with the pressures of marriage and childbirth. The figure of the jamona ultimately embodies queerness in their rejection of these norms. But Alejandra's mention of her light-skinned privilege also reminds us of the multiple subject positions that intersect to shape oppression and privilege and are oftentimes mediated by processes such as migration.

Unlike Alejandra, Xan's memories of Puerto Rico were more limited, having moved from San Juan to Florida at a young age. Xan, who identified as genderqueer and trans-masculine, explained the difficulties of negotiating their ethnic, sexual, and gender identities across different social spaces:[11]

> Navigating it, it's interesting because it's pretty similar as before I came out as trans as when I'm trans. The only difference is it's more hyped, more of a hyper thing. When I came out as a lesbian, I was a butch lesbian. I identified as a bull dyke at one point and then I identified as just a dyke for a while, but my presentation was always more masculine. In Spanish circles I would automatically be lumped into the boy's club and there was always an expectation of that same kind of machismo. . . . Like once I came out, even in those safe spaces, you had the adult men who knew I was gay and would make jokes about women thinking I would just laugh along, play along objectifying women—that kind of thing. Or make jokes about how that woman's crazy or how that woman looks fine. It's something that exists in the white masculinity culture, but it's something unique to the Spanish culture because it's more than just a misogyny thing, it's a culturalism almost. To reject it is rejecting both my masculine currency and my Hispanic currency.

Xan's discomfort of occupying spaces where their Puerto Rican and trans identities come into friction underlies the ways that gender and sexuality can work in tandem with other identities to shape diasporic belonging. Their framing of their interactions with Latino men as characteristic of machismo or a "culturalism" aligns with how several others described their experiences with sexism or homophobia on the archipelago or in central Florida. Machismo is a concept associated with Latino masculinity. It denotes a set of prescribed beliefs or expectations, including that Latino men are the heads of households, proud, physically strong, sexually dominant, independent, and aggressive (Hondagneu-Sotelo 1994; Perilla 1999).

But there is a danger in reducing these ideas to "cultural masculinity" (Bilmes 1992), which can have the consequence of reinforcing culture-of-poverty stereotypes. Rather, hegemonic masculinity is not exclusive to Latinx cultures and, as Aida Hurtado and Mrinal Sinha (2008: 337) remind us, "is embodied at the specific intersections of race, class, and sexuality" across various societies.[12]

Safe Space

For some, Florida represented a departure from these gendered expectations and the homophobia they faced back in Puerto Rico.[13] Places like Pulse nightclub became a safe haven for many LGBTQ+ Latinxs, including Alejandra. Pulse was the first gay nightclub she visited when she first arrived in Orlando. She recalled sitting in the nightclub after a particularly painful breakup and quietly watching others dance:

> Sometimes I would just enjoy seeing how everybody else had a blast and that was enough for me because I wasn't ready to be on the dance floor. I was depressed. I was sad but seeing them and seeing couples how they looked at each other gave me *esperanza, como* (hope, like) it is real. What I'm feeling now is not permanent, love does exist, I see it right now. Losing Pulse was awful because every club has its own vibe, even though they might all be gay clubs, they all might celebrate Latin night. I don't know what it was about Pulse that it just felt different and it felt like being in a safe place.

Juana María Rodríguez (2016) contends that sites like Pulse are about more than just dancing—they represent "a space of queer Latinx affirmation and possibilities."[14] The feeling of belonging to a "safe place," as Alejandra calls it, and the hope of a different future, captures the emotive experiences generated by expressions of queer *latinidad* that are free from the constrains of heteronormative society (Rivera-Servera 2012).[15]

While the idea of "safe space" has recently become ubiquitous with debates around free speech, especially on college campuses, the term has a deeper history. The concept of safe space originates in the 1960s gay and lesbian bar scene of Los Angeles, New York, and other urban centers, where discrimination, policing, and anti-sodomy laws were in effect (Ellison 2019; Kenney 2001). Safe spaces were effectively places to "permit and affirm one's own way of being" (Kenney 2001: 10). Over the years, the term has also been used by Black feminist scholars in reference to "social spaces where Black women speak freely" (Collins 2000: 100) and has been associated with the emergence of ethnic studies and cultural houses (Rosaldo 1993). These spaces of free discourse and belonging are a focal point of community building and resistance, particularly for those located at the intersections race, gender, sexuality, and other identities.

But what happens when safe spaces become unsafe? Historically, "safe" spaces have not been entirely free of violence, as evidenced by events such as Stonewall, school shootings, and Pulse. Yet the loss of safe space also manifests itself in other ways, as Emmanuel, a survivor of Pulse who credited the tragedy with transforming him into an organizer and activist, explained:

> A lot of people came out because they were plastered all over the news, as they were there, they were there. It was all over on camera. We had people whose families found out because they saw them on the news and they're calling them. And other people can't tell their family they were there, even though they want to be able to talk to somebody about it because they tell us that they might as well be one of the victims because their families would not—

Emmanuel paused, searching for the words to continue:

> So it brings out the rampant *machista* homophobia that's still there no matter all the progress that we can achieve on one side, there's still, for some people it's more difficult. All of that was put out there. Bright spotlight.

These instances of forced outing, like the father who refused to accept his son's body from the morgue, represent various forms of displacement— from society, the archipelago, and supposedly safe spaces where individuals were once free to live out their intersectional identities. But out of displacement and marginalization may also rise the "counter-hegemonic cultural practice to identify the spaces where we begin the process of re-vision" (hooks 1989: 15). In what follows, I detail the creation of such a space—one that directly responded to that early catchphrase, or rather misnomer, *Orlando United*.

The Crisis of Language and the Language of Crisis
OneOrlando Fund

The news vans were already lining up in front of the Amway Center in downtown Orlando, when I arrived to serve as a translator for the first of two OneOrlando Fund town hall meetings on the morning of August 4,

2016.[16] The OneOrlando Fund was created by Orlando's mayor, Buddy Dyer, to provide financial support to victims' families and survivors. The expressed purpose of the town halls was to explain the process of filing claims and the allocation of funds. After joining the group of other volunteers for a tour of the facility and a rundown of our roles for the day, I headed to the main arena where I would serve as a "greeter," directing attendees in English and Spanish on where they were to sit and making sure to let them know that there was a designated seating area for those who did not want to appear on camera.

People began to enter the arena. Some wore T-shirts printed with images of loved ones lost that night, while others had more visible signs of injury, supported by the use of canes or wheelchairs. There were also survivors and victims' families from other mass shootings, such as Aurora and Santa Barbara, present. Throughout the morning, many left the room in tears, escorted by a friend, family member, or empathetic stranger. There was a noticeable change in the atmosphere at the Amway Center that day.[17] The air felt thick and heavy. Not even the sharpness of the lawyer and fund administrator Ken Feinberg's words could cut through it. Feinberg, who had also presided over the dispensation of funds for the September 11th Victim Compensation Fund, explained very matter-of-factly that the monies would go to four different groups: (1) the families of those killed, (2) individuals injured that required overnight hospitalization, (3) individuals who received emergency out-patient care, and (4) those who were in the nightclub who did not suffer physical injuries (OneOrlando Fund 2016). As he continued, there were murmurs around the room. Would survivors who escaped but immediately fled the scene, never seeking medical attention or contacting law enforcement officials, be eligible to receive the funds? Perhaps it was the adrenaline, or the fear of being outed for their sexual orientation or documentation status. Either way, it became clear during the audience question-and-answer period that the question would remain unanswered.

The town hall meeting that morning was conducted almost entirely in English. While headsets were available for speakers of other languages to listen to live translations, not everyone grabbed a headset or was even aware of their existence. It was almost an hour and a half into the meeting when Mariana approached the microphone that was set up in the center aisle for audience questions. She announced in both Spanish and English that free resources, including bilingual legal and mental health counseling, would be provided through Proyecto Somos Orlando. Only then did one of the moderators tell the audience that they were free to pose questions in Spanish. I thought back to those early responses by the city of Orlando, as told by my interlocutors. The blind spots were almost too glaring to ignore.

"More Than Just an LGBTQ Tragedy"

When I arrived at Monica's home, in a gated community in East Orlando, she was finishing up some work at her kitchen table while her two children watched cartoons in the adjacent living room. Monica, who was born in New York, moved to Puerto Rico when she was eight years old and remained there into adulthood, eventually returning to New York where she enjoyed a successful career in advertising and marketing. On moving to Orlando and subsequently losing her job, Monica started her own consultation business, which provided cultural competency trainings for corporations, among other things.

I scrambled to turn on my tape recorder, as Monica immediately began recalling the events of that morning after she first heard the news of the shooting:

> I was feeding the kids just like today and already by 10:30 my husband's like, "Monica, you got to go right?" And I said, "Yeah, I got to go." He says, "Where you going?" And I said, "I don't know where I'm going, but I need to get out of here." . . . And I got in the car and, all of a sudden, my girlfriends start calling me, "Monica, Monica, hey, where you going? I'm on my way." I'm like, yeah, I don't know where to go. I'm going to go to the LGBT Center. . . . I got there and I bumped into another colleague, a leader. We were all Boricuas too and all women. . . . [18] She's like, no, there's no one here, in the sense of the families. . . . I think all the families are at the Hampton Inn. So, we rushed over there. I called the other girls and I told them don't even bother coming here, go to the Hampton Inn. We went over there and that's when we realized, it was confirmed just by walking in and seeing all the brown faces that this was more than just an LGBTQ tragedy—it was a Latino tragedy. When you have law enforcement making announcements about how the families are going to be moving from there to another center and they only do it in English, we're like, "Excuse me, you need to repeat all that" . . . La gente estaba como, "Que fue lo que dijo" [People were like, "What did they say"?]. Like lost. In the midst of their anguish, to add insult to injury, they were completely lost and confused.

While a bilingual police officer eventually stepped in to serve as a translator, it was only after Monica and others demanded that the information
be repeated in Spanish. Yolanda, another cofounder of Somos, painted
a similar picture. She was on her way to church when she heard the
news and decided to head to the hospital and LGBT+ Center Orlando
(The Center).

"There were very few people who looked like me at The Center and all
you kept hearing was LGBT, LGBT," Yolanda recalled, as we sat in the newly
opened office space of Proyecto Somos Orlando. I could still smell the paint
on the walls as she continued:

> For me having been in both spots it's like, no, Latino LGBT, Latino LGBT.
> My head was exploding, my hair was on fire angry. Not even in the hospi-
> tal in 2016, you can't find someone to talk to these people in Spanish and
> in English. Both languages are urgent. And when I asked the only Latino
> commissioner for the city why isn't anything being said in Spanish—why
> aren't they mentioning the Latino community—the answer was because
> we weren't the only ones there.

The privileging of English by the city of Orlando and other first
responders, described by Monica and Yolanda above, speaks to the existence of linguistic borders that ultimately inhibit access to key information
and resources. Taken together, they point to the ways that language marks
public spheres of belonging, positioning Spanish as "out of place"
(Urciuoli 1996: 35). These narratives also signify the importance of intersectionality in times of crisis. Yolanda's experience as a Puerto Rican lesbian woman and the exclusion of Queer of Color voices at the Center and
the Hampton Inn demonstrates the centrality of whiteness in queer
spaces—an idea that has been discussed at length by queer studies scholars
(Eng, Halberstam, and Muñoz 2005; Hames-García and Martínez 2011;
Manalansan 2003; Muñoz 1999; Perez 2005). But as Patricia Hill Collins
(2019: 2) underscores, "Intersectionality is not just a set of ideas. Instead,
because they inform social action, intersectionality's ideas have consequences in the social world." Thus we must recognize the potentiality of
intersectionality to not only understand inequality but also inspire resistance and social change, as in the case of Somos.

"There were two things that happened," Mariana, the Florida director of
a national Latinx nonprofit organization and one of the first people
Yolanda called, explained:[19]

One is that the mainstream media and local officials here really weren't talking about the fact that it was Latin night—they weren't talking about the fact that it was a primarily Latino population and, then later on we learned, mostly Puerto Rican. We got together to help change the narrative and make sure that not only the entire world at that point, since all eyes were on Orlando, understood that this was mostly a Latino community but that there were very specific needs and strengths to that.

Mariana, Yolanda, and Monica, along with a handful of other Latina leaders from the community, eventually all ended up at the Hampton Inn.[20] While they concluded that the immediate needs would most likely be met by the city, they began to discuss what they believed would be the long-term needs of the Latinx LGBTQ+ community. Yolanda described that initial meeting:

We were sitting at a table trying to decide what to do and I said let me tell you about trauma. It took me seven years of treatment to learn to deal with my PTSD because you never cure PTSD [post-traumatic stress disorder], you live with it for the rest of your life, but you learn to live with it. Whatever they do with the million they raised overnight, whatever they do with that money is never going to be enough. . . . Five years from now, when there is abuse, suicides, no one is going to ask did you have something to do with Pulse.

Yolanda was a 9/11 first responder who was standing by the foot of one of the towers as it came down. By bringing up her own personal struggle with PTSD, she points to other gaps beyond issues of language and short-term monetary responses like the OneOrlando Fund. While survivors and first responders are grappling with the long-lasting effects of PTSD (Aboraya 2017; Contorno and Herndon 2019; Hadad 2017), others like Alejandra, who lost her driver's license and was unable to accompany her friend who died in the club that night, struggle with survivor's guilt, asking: "Why the hell am I here for? Why did he not make it and I did?"

According to the Mental Health America (2021), Florida ranks forty-eighth in terms of access to mental health care. The rankings are based on measures such as access to insurance and treatment, as well as costs. However, according to my interlocutors, there is another obstacle that hinders the accessibility of mental health care, specifically for Latinxs in the state.

It was captured by one key term that came up time and time again: *cultural competency*. Alexis, a social worker and reproductive rights activist who identifies as both Puerto Rican and part of the LGBTQ+ community, explained the realization she came to after the shooting:

> I didn't realize how much people didn't understand the culture, because we think about what cultural competency is and it's like a buzzword. It doesn't mean anything. Go to a one-day training and somehow you're culturally competent. That's how they make that happen. I made this connection later on, especially when I started to do this work. I'm like this is a checkbox because all these people are saying they're culturally competent. . . . I'm finding more and more like the intricacies of what it means to be culturally competent and what my role and how important it is for me to have a seat at the table, for me to be involved in the conversation that affects the community that I'm a part of.

Alexis's assessment of cultural competency as little more than "a checkbox" underscores the superficiality of cultural competency approaches within organizational settings. Like the discourse of "multiculturalism" (Hale 2005; Melamed 2006) and diversity (Bell and Hartmann 2007), the liberal move to become "culturally competent," without any real investment in equity and inclusivity, does little more than reinforce capitalist and racial projects.

Elena, who migrated from Puerto Rico to Orlando over two decades ago and was now the director of a local Latinx counseling center that opened its doors as a crisis intervention center following Pulse, painted a much more nuanced picture of cultural competency. She advocated for a "cultural competency model" for Latinx families in a mental health capacity. "What exactly do you mean by cultural competency?" I asked Elena, who did not hesitate to explain:

> Cultural competency is, for example, a family whose mother calls me because her son was there. I get to the house and I have to spend two hours talking with the mother and the survivor doesn't want to see you. . . . You have to go a second time. You have to go a third time, until the person sees you and then you're in—after you've drank ten coffees, after various sessions in the house, after you've spoken with the mother, after you've spoken with the aunt, after you've spoken with the cousin, after you've spoken with the neighbor, and finally that person gives you the opportunity to work with him. And you've demonstrated to him that you are really there because you want to work with him and not because you want to write a report, not because you want to expose them, but

because you want to help that person. That's what I mean. . . . These are
people that have gone through a very difficult moment, very critical, very
different, that will need long term care . . . not only for those survivors
but for the families that are dealing with those survivors. For us as a community, I think that we are impacted too. All the Hispanics I know either
know someone or they know somebody who knows somebody. [21]

The scenario Elena describes of a counselor drinking more than her weight
in coffee while meeting several members of a potential client's family before
finally being let in by the client is in stark contrast to approaches that reduce
cultural competency to language or a set of other skills that can be learned
(Kleinman and Benson 2006). Elena's understanding of cultural competency
aligns more closely with Maureen H. Fitzgerald's (2000: 184) as "the ability to
analyze and respond to the 'cultural scenes' (Spradley and McCurdy 1972)
and 'social dramas' (Turner 1974) of everyday life in ways that are cultural
and psychologically meaningful for all the people involved."

In addition to providing culturally competent mental health-care services, the women of Somos decided that bilingual legal counsel was also
needed in the community. While Puerto Ricans did not have to grapple with
issues of documentation, there were other Latinxs who were affected by
the tragedy that did. As Mariana explained during one of our conversations:
"We wanted to . . . make sure that people understood that there were going
to be funerals and burials abroad, so people were going to need visas . . .
and that you needed to know what rights people have as undocumented."

It was from these conversations that night at the Hampton Inn that
Somos Orlando was born. The women immediately began to reach out to
their contacts and organized over twenty Puerto Rican and Latinx organizations under the moniker. The very next morning they called a "Unity
Press Conference" outside the offices of Hispanic Federation to demand
attention to the significance of the tragedy for the Latinx LGBTQ+ community.[22] Their ultimate goal was to create a center that would house
bilingual services for Orlando Latinxs. "Here in central Florida, *con tan
grande población Hispana* [with such a large Hispanic population]," Monica
exclaimed, "and there is not one place where people can go to as a safe
haven where they can get in-culture, in-language, and now LGBT-friendly
services too, all under one roof."

However, there were challenges to creating such a center. While Puerto
Ricans were disproportionately affected by the shooting at Pulse nightclub,
not all Puerto Rican– and Latinx-led organizations and activists in the area

rushed to get involved with Somos with the same enthusiasm as they did in
the aftermath of other tragedies, such as Hurricane Maria in 2017. Mariana
was critical of this, confronting several Puerto Rican activists at a meeting.
"It's really interesting how the same folks that I would say are the leaders of
the Latino and Puerto Rican community, not many of you have been involved
with Somos, and that says a lot about LGBTQ issues," she said. "Everybody
was like, 'Ok.' And I'm like, yes, it has to be said because those are our issues
as well, as is gun violence and all the issues that affect our community."

During their early meetings, it also became clear that not everyone
agreed with the vision of the project, arguing that they first needed to
secure a "seat at the table" within existing institutions that have historically excluded Latinx knowledges.

"It got really heated," Monica said, recalling one such meeting. "They
are like . . . we need a place at the table, a place at the table. They got
heated. There were maybe like thirty organizations represented. And I got
up and I said, 'You know what? *Olvidate de esa mesa* [forget about that table].
Forget about it. Look at this table that we're creating here.'"

Despite these struggles, Somos Orlando did come to fruition. The
women of Somos came up with a preliminary budget of $600,000 for
securing a space and equipping it with resources and personnel. Because of
professional ties with Hispanic Federation, they were able to secure the
initial funds needed to lease a building on S. Orange Blossom Trail. Almost
a month later, they received more support in the form of the song "Love
Make the World Go Round" by Jennifer Lopez and Lin-Manuel Miranda. For
the first three months, the artists committed to donating the song's pro-
ceeds from iTunes to the Somos Orlando fund.[23]

By the time I departed Orlando, the women were no longer running the
organization, which was subsumed by its largest funder, the Hispanic
Federation. But while the future of Somos remains unclear, its establishment is significant, as it is the material embodiment of a refusal to be
erased and represents the potential for new spaces of belonging across
intersectional identities. Alejandra captured this best, when she said:

> It [Somos] was the start of my own healing. And I started doing art nights
> with Proyecto Somos Orlando. . . . I started meeting survivors. It felt like
> being at home or when you get together for a *bautismo* [baptism] or a
> Christmas dinner and you're just talking with your family. It was so pain-
> ful at first but it felt so much better. . . . Everything is different, even the
> way I breathe feels different.

Figure 2. Interim Memorial around what once was Pulse nightclub. Photo by author, 2018.

Her words at once reminded me of Ahmed's (2013) words on the importance of thinking "about how to protect ourselves (and those around us) from being diminished" and of "create[ing] spaces of relief, spaces that might be breathing spaces." Ultimately, Somos not only provided a physical space for LGBTQ+ Latinxs and their families to receive essential services, but it also created a space to breathe.

Conclusion

Almost two years after the shooting, I walked alongside the temporary memorial (fig. 2) at the site of the Pulse nightclub with my eight-month-old

son. The sound of cars speeding down Orange Avenue faded into the distance as I followed the contours of the curved wall—a giant collage of photographs capturing the vigils, memorials, art, and faces of Orlando. Behind a clear glass section of the wall, I came across the names of the forty-nine:

Stanley Almodovar III	Antonio Davon Brown
Amanda L. Alvear	Darryl Roman Burt II
Oscar A. Aracena Montero	Angel Candelario-Padro
Rodolfo Ayala Ayala	Juan Chavez Martinez

Luis Daniel Conde

Cory James Connell

Tevin Eugene Crosby

Deonka Deidra Drayton

Simón Adrian Carrillo Fernández

Leroy Valentin Fernandez

Mercedez Marisol Flores

Peter Ommy Gonzalez Cruz

Juan Ramon Guerrero

Paul Terrell Henry

Frank Hernandez

Miguel Angel Honorato

Javier Jorge Reyes

Jason Benjamin Josaphat

Eddie Jamoldroy Justice

Anthony Luis Laureano Disla

Christopher Andrew Leinonen

Alejandro Barrios Martinez

Brenda Marquez McCool

Gilberto R. Silva Menendez

Kimberly "KJ" Morris

Akyra Monet Murray

Luis Omar Ocasio Capo

Geraldo A. Ortiz Jimenez

Eric Ivan Ortiz-Rivera

Joel Rayon Paniagua

Jean Carlos Mendez Perez

Enrique L. Rios, Jr.

Jean Carlos Nieves Rodríguez

Xavier Emmanuel Serrano-Rosado

Christopher Joseph Sanfeliz

Yilmary Rodríguez Solivan

Edward Sotomayor Jr.

Shane Evan Tomlinson

Martin Benitez Torres

Jonathan A. Camuy Vega

Juan Pablo Rivera Velázquez

Luis Sergio Vielma

Franky Jimmy DeJesus Velázquez

Luis Daniel Wilson-Leon

Jerald Arthur Wright

On my way out, I stopped to read the sign at the entrance. Written in both English and Spanish, the inscription read: "On June 12, 2016, 49 angels sought the joy, love and acceptance of Pulse Nightclub. Instead, they found hatred. And they never came home. They were gay. They were straight. Latin, black, white. Mothers. Brothers. Sisters. Daughters. Sons. Lost forever."

But in the wake of Pulse, there was another tragedy—one that erased queer Brown and Black bodies from the public stage of mourning, loss, and recovery. The founding of Somos was a deliberate refusal to be silenced by the normativity of whiteness within the umbrella term LGBTQ+. As the late bell hooks (1989: 20) reminds us, "Marginality [is] much more than a site of deprivation. . . . [I]t is also the site of radical possibility, a space of resistance."

hooks's words resonate today, as mass shootings continue to shake our everyday lives. In August 2019 a gunman opened fire at an El Paso Walmart, killing twenty-three people and wounding over two dozen others, and in 2022 nineteen children and two teachers were killed at an elementary school in Uvalde, Texas.[24] In both cases, the victims were overwhelmingly Latinx. And in the year between, on March 2021, a shooter killed eight, the majority Asian women, at an Atlanta massage parlor.[25] Such acts of violence inspire mourning, rage and, as in the case of Somos, activism. But these incidents are about more than gun violence. They are about xenophobia, sexism, racism, classism, and homophobia—forces that together with other forms of discrimination compound to capture the urgency of intersectionality in our personal, social, and academic worlds. And yet resistance to intersectionality grows in a sociopolitical climate in which there are those that reduce intersectionality to identity politics and attack anti-racist education. The present is, in more ways than one, a struggle for survival. In his conceptualization of queer futurity, José Esteban Muñoz (2009: 1) ascertained that "queerness is essentially about the rejection of a here and now and an insistence on potentiality or concrete possibility for another world." If we are to take this claim a step further and believe that intersectionality is more than a word or idea (Collins 2019; Crenshaw 2015), then to imagine a "possibility for another world" we must also recognize how the "here and now" we seek to reject is manufactured by the various social constructs that shape human experience and oppression.

....

Julie Torres is assistant professor of women's and ethnic studies at the University of Colorado Colorado Springs. Her research and teaching focus on Latinx communities in the United States, diaspora, social activism, and transnational feminisms.

Notes

1   Pulse was a gay nightclub located on South Orange Avenue, not far from downtown Orlando, which opened its doors on July 2, 2004. It was founded by Barbara Poma and Ron Legler, in memory of Poma's brother John, who died in 1991 from HIV-related illnesses.

2   A mass shooting is defined as an incident of gun violence in which four or more people are killed (Krouse and Richardson 2015).

3   This number does not include the gunman who was killed by police.

4   For additional reflections on this omission, see La Fountain-Stokes 2016; Quiroga 2016; J. M. Rodríguez 2016; Torres 2016; and Vidal-Ortiz 2016.

5   Throughout this article, I refer to Proyecto Somos Orlando as Somos, as it was called by my interlocutors.

6   All names are pseudonyms, except in the case of public officials.

7   See the 2012 special issue, "Latino/as in the South," in the *Latino Studies Journal* (Oboler 2012), for more in-depth histories and analyses of these migrations.

8   From 2017 to 2018 alone, Puerto Rico's population decreased by 4.4 percent (Glassman 2019).

468 MERIDIANS 22:2 · October 2023

9   While Mercado's murderer was convicted and sentenced to ninety-nine years in prison, he was not charged with a hate crime.

10 Luis Aponte-Parés and colleagues (2007: 4) describes the field of Puerto Rican queer studies as "the crystallization of diverse forms of scholarship in the humanities and social and natural sciences focusing on the production of sexualized identities, divergent gender expression, and how sexualized identities and practices form a part of and challenge dominant notions of Puerto Rican culture and society."

11 I use the preferred gender pronouns of my interlocutors.

12 Raewyn W. Connell (1995: 77) defines *hegemonic masculinity* "as the configuration of gender practices which embodies the currently accepted answer to the problem of the legitimacy of patriarchy which guarantees (or is taken to guarantee) the dominant position of men and the subordination of women."

13 La Fountain-Stokes (2008) refers to this phenomenon of sexual migration and exile as "sexile." Several interlocutors expressed leaving Puerto Rico because of homophobia and made the decision not to return for that reason. It is important to also note that same-sex marriage was not legalized until 2015, following the U.S. Supreme Court decision in *Obergefell v. Hodges*.

14 See also J. M. Rodríguez 2003.

15 While *latinidad* is a contested term, here I apply Frances Aparicio's (2003: 93) definition of *latinidad* as "a concept that allows us to explore moments of convergences and divergences in the formation of Latina/o (post)colonial subjectivities and hybrid cultural expressions among various Latina/o subjectivities."

16 The Amway Center is an indoor arena and the home of the National Basketball Association team the Orlando Magic.

17 Kathleen Stewart (2011: 452) describes an atmosphere as "a force field in which people find themselves."

18 *Boricua* is another term for Puerto Rican. It originates from the Taíno word *Boriken*.

19 Mariana and Yolanda were scheduled to be at Pulse the night of the shooting to run a voter registration event. The event was canceled because of unrelated reasons.

20 There was another cofounder of Somos, whom I did not have the opportunity to speak with prior to her departure from Orlando.

21 Translated from Spanish by the author.

22 Hispanic Federation is a national nonprofit organization with offices in New York, Washington, DC, Connecticut, and Florida.

23 Lin-Manuel Miranda, known for the Broadway musicals *Hamilton* and *In the Heights*, is the son of the Hispanic Federation's founder, Luis Miranda Jr. While the song had fifty-four thousand downloads in the first week alone, it is not clear how much of the profits were actually received.

24 In a reflexive essay on the El Paso shooting, Gilberto Rosas (2021: 117) contends that the attack exemplifies the role of white nationalism as part of a "global system of white supremacy." The same can be said of the 2022 shooting at a Buffalo supermarket that killed ten Black people. Exclusions of queer People of Color also serve to maintain white hegemony.

25 Maria Cecilia Hwang and Rhacel Salazar Parreñas (2021) analyze the gendered and racial dimensions of Asian women's experiences in the context of the massage parlor shooting, noting how xenophobia, hypersexualization, and attitudes around sex work intersect to shape the disposability of Asian women's bodies.

Works Cited

Aboraya, Abe. 2017. "A Pulse Nightclub Responder Confronts a New Crisis: PTSD." NPR, June 12. https://www.npr.org/sections/health-shots/2017/06/12/531751457/a-pulse-nightclub-responder-confronts-a-new-crisis-ptsd.

Acosta, Katie L. 2013. Amigas y Amantes: Sexually Nonconforming Latinas Negotiate Family. New Brunswick, NJ: Rutgers University Press.

Ahmed, Sara. 2013. "Feeling depleted?" Feminist Killjoys (blog), November 17. https://feministkilljoys.com/2013/11/17/feeling-depleted/.

Ahmed, Sara. 2017. Living a Feminist Life. Durham, NC: Duke University Press.

Aparicio, Frances. 2003. "Jennifer as Selena: Rethinking Latinidad in Media and Popular Culture." Latino Studies 1, no. 1: 90–105.

Aponte-Parés, Luis, Jossianna Arroyo, Elizabeth Crespo-Kebler, Lawrence La Fountain-Stokes, and Frances Negrón-Muntaner. 2007. "Puerto Rican Queer Sexualities: Introduction." Centro: Journal of the Center for Puerto Rican Studies 19, no. 1: 4–24.

Baca Zinn, Maxine, and Ruth Enid Zambrana. 2019. "Chicanas/Latinas Advance Intersectional Thought and Practice." Gender & Society 33, no. 5: 677–701.

Bell, Joyce M., and Douglas Hartmann. 2007. "Diversity in Everyday Discourse: The Cultural Ambiguities and Consequences of 'Happy Talk.'" American Sociological Review 72, no. 6: 895–914.

Benmayor, Rina, Rosa Torruellas, and Ana L. Juarbe. 1997. "Claiming Cultural Citizenship in East Harlem: 'Si Esto Puede Ayudar a la Comunidad Mia. . . .'" In Latino Cultural Citizenship: Claiming Identity, Space, and Rights, edited by William V. Flores and Rina Benmayor, 152–209. Boston: Beacon.

Bermudez, Rosie. 2020. "Chicana Militant Dignity Work and Politics: Building Coalition and Political Solidarity in the Los Angeles Welfare Rights Movement." Southern California Quarterly 102, no. 4: 420–55.

Bilmes, Murray. 1992. "Macho and Shame." International Forum of Psychoanalysis 1, nos. 3–4: 163–68.

Blackwell, Maylei. 2011. ¡Chicana Power!: Contested Histories of Feminism in the Chicano Movement. Austin: University of Texas Press.

Carillo, Héctor. 2004. "Sexual Migration, Cross-Cultural Sexual Encounters, and Sexual Health." Sexuality Research and Social Policy 1, no. 3: 58–70.

Collins, Patricia. 2000. Black Feminist Thought. New York: Routledge.

Collins, Patricia Hill. 2019. Intersectionality as Critical Social Theory. Durham, N.C: Duke University Press.

Collins, Patricia, and Sirma Bilge. 2016. Intersectionality. Malden, MA: Polity.

Connell, Raewyn W. 1995. Masculinities. Berkeley: University of California Press.

Contorno, Steve, and Monica Herndon. 2019. "Three Years after Pulse Shooting, Psychological Wounds Still Raw. 'This Isn't Something That's Going to Heal Itself.'" *Tampa Bay Times*, June 12. https://www.tampabay.com/florida-politics/buzz/2019 /06/12/three-years-after-pulse-shooting-psychological-wounds-still-raw-this -isnt-something-thats-going-to-heal-itself/.

Crenshaw, Kimberlé. 1989. "Demarginalizing the Intersection of Race and Sex: A Black Feminist Critique of Antidiscrimination Doctrine, Feminist Theory, and Antiracist Politics." *University of Chicago Legal Forum* 1: 139–67.

Crenshaw, Kimberlé. 2015. "Opinion: Why Intersectionality Can't Wait." *Washington Post*, September 24. https://www.washingtonpost.com/news/in-theory/wp/2015 /09/24/why-intersectionality-cant-wait/.

Crespo-Kebler, Elizabeth. 2003. "'The Infamous Crime against Nature': Constructions of Heterosexuality and Lesbian Subversions in Puerto Rico." In *The Culture of Gender and Sexuality in the Caribbean*, edited by Linden Lewis, 191–210. Gainesville: University Press of Florida.

Delerme, Simone. 2014. "Puerto Ricans Live Free: Race, Language, and Orlando's Contested Soundscape." *Southern Spaces*, March 24. http://www.southernspaces .org/2014/puerto-ricans-live-free-race-language-and-orlandos-contested -soundscape.

Delerme, Simone. 2020. *Latino Orlando: Suburban Transformation and Racial Conflict.* Gainesville: University Press of Florida.

Duany, Jorge, and Félix V. Matos-Rodríguez. 2006. "Puerto Ricans in Orlando and Central Florida." *Centro* Policy Report 1, no. 1 (Spring). https://www .latinamericanstudies.org/puertorico/Puerto_Ricans_in_Orlando.pdf.

Duany, Jorge, and Patricia Silver. 2010. "The 'Puertoricanization' of Florida: Historical Background and Current Status: Introduction." *Centro: Journal of the Center for Puerto Rican Studies* 22, no. 1: 4–31.

Ellison, Treva. 2019. "From Sanctuary to Safe Space: Gay and Lesbian Police-Reform Activism in Los Angeles." *Radical History Review*, no. 135: 95–118.

El nuevo día. 2009. Confiesa asesinato de joven homosexual. November 17. https:// www.elnuevodia.com/noticias/locales/nota/confiesaasesinatodejoven homosexual-638687/.

Eng, David L., Jack Halberstam, and Jose Esteban Muñoz. 2005. "What's Queer about Queer Studies Now?" *Social Text* 23, nos. 3–4: 1–17.

Espín, Olivia M. 1996. "Leaving the Nation and Joining the Tribe: Lesbian Immigrants Crossing Geographical and Identity Boundaries." *Women and Therapy* 19, no. 4: 99–107.

Fernández, Johanna. 2020. *The Young Lords: A Radical History.* Chapel Hill: University of North Carolina Press.

Fernández, Lilia. 2012. *Brown in the Windy City: Mexicans and Puerto Ricans in Postwar Chicago.* Chicago: University of Chicago Press.

Fitzgerald, Maureen H. 2000. "Establishing Cultural Competency for Mental Health Professionals." In *Anthropological Approaches to Psychological Medicine*, edited by V. Skultans and J. Cox, 184–200. London: Jessica Kingsley.

Glassman, Brian. 2019. "A Third of Movers from Puerto Rico to the Mainland United States Relocated to Florida in 2018." United States Census Bureau, September 26. https://www.census.gov/library/stories/2019/09/puerto-rico-outmigration -increases-poverty-declines.html.

Hadad, Chuck. 2017. "Officer Who Developed PTSD after Pulse Massacre to Lose Job." CNN, December 7. https://www.cnn.com/2017/12/06/health/pulse-shooting -ptsd-officer/index.html.

Hale, Charles R. 2005. "Neoliberal Multiculturalism: The Remaking of Cultural Rights and Racial Dominance in Central America." *Political and Legal Anthropology Review* 28, no. 1: 10–28.

Hames-García, Michael, and Ernesto Javier Martínez. 2011. *Gay Latino studies: A Critical Reader.* Durham, NC: Duke University Press.

Hondagneu-Sotelo, Pierrette. 1994. *Gendered Transitions: Mexican Experiences of Immigration.* Berkeley: University of California Press.

hooks, bell. 1989. "Choosing the Margin as a Space of Radical Openness." *Framework: The Journal of Cinema and Media,* no. 36: 15–23.

Hurtado, Aida, and Mrinal Sinha. 2008. "More than Men: Latino Feminist Masculinities and Intersectionality." *Sex Roles: A Journal of Research* 59, nos. 5–6: 337–49.

Hwang, Maria Cecilia, and Rhacel Salazar Parreñas. 2021. "The Gendered Racialization of Asian Women as Villainous Temptresses." *Gender & Society* 35, no. 4: 567–76.

Jackson, Jhoni. 2020. "Puerto Rico's Rising Femicide Problem: Twenty-One Women and Girls Missing and Twenty-Nine Killed This Year." *Remezcla,* September 22. https://remezcla.com/culture/21-women-girls-gone-missing-29-killed-puerto -rico-year/.

Kenney Moira. 2001. *Mapping Gay L.A.: The Intersection of Place and Politics.* Philadelphia, PA: Temple University Press.

Kleinman, Arthur, and Peter Benson. 2006. "Anthropology in the Clinic: The Problem of Cultural Competency and How to Fix It." *PLoS Medicine* 3, no. 10: 1673–76.

Krouse, William J., and Daniel J. Richardson. 2015. "Mass Murder with Firearms: Incidents and Victims, 1999–2013." Washington, DC: Congressional Research Service.

La Fountain-Stokes, Lawrence. 2008. "Queer Diasporas, Boricua Lives: A Meditation on Sexile." *Review: Literature and Arts of the Americas* 41, no. 2: 294–301.

La Fountain-Stokes, Lawrence. 2016. "Queer Puerto Ricans and the Burden of Violence." *QED* 3, no. 3: 99–102.

La Fountain-Stokes, Lawrence. 2021. *Translocas: The Politics of Puerto Rican Drag and Trans Performance.* Ann Arbor: University of Michigan Press.

La Fountain-Stokes, Lawrence, and Yolanda Martínez-San Miguel. 2018. "Revisiting Queer Puerto Rican Sexualities: Queer Futures, Reinventions, and Undisciplined Archives—Introduction." *Centro: Journal of the Center for Puerto Rican Studies* 30, no. 2: 6–41.

Manalansan, Martin F. 2003. *Global Divas: Filipino Gay Men in the Diaspora.* Durham, NC: Duke University Press.

Manalansan, Martin F. 2006. "Queer Intersections: Sexuality and Gender in Migration Studies." *International Migration Review* 40, no. 1: 224–49.

Melamed, Jodi. 2006. "The Spirit of Neoliberalism: From Racial Liberalism to Multicultural Neoliberalism." *Social Text* 24, no. 4: 1–24.

Mental Health America. 2021. "The State of Mental Health in America." October 20. https://www.mhanational.org/research-reports/2021-state-mental-health -america.

Moraga, Cherríe, and Gloria Anzaldúa. 1983. *This Bridge Called My Back: Writings by Radical Women of Color*. New York: Kitchen Table Women of Color.

Morales, Iris. 2016. *Through the Eyes of Rebel Women: The Young Lords 1969–1976*. New York: Red Sugarcane.

Muñoz, José Esteban. 1999. *Disidentifications: Queers of Color and the Performance of Politics*. Minneapolis: University of Minnesota Press.

Muñoz, José Esteban. 2009. *Cruising Utopia: The Then and There of Queer Futurity*. Durham, NC: Duke University Press.

Negrón-Muntaner, Frances. 1999. "When I Was a Puerto Rican Lesbian: Meditations on *Brincando El Charco: Portrait of a Puerto Rican*." *GLQ* 5, no. 4: 511–26.

Noe-Bustamante, Luis, Antonio Flores, and Sono Shah. 2019. "Facts on Hispanics of Puerto Rican Origin in the United States, 2017." Pew Research Center, September 16. https://www.pewresearch.org/hispanic/fact-sheet/u-s-hispanics-facts-on -puerto-rican-origin-latinos/.

Oboler, Suzanne, ed. 2012. "Latino/as in the South." Special issue, *Latino Studies Journal* 10, nos. 1–2.

OneOrlando Fund. 2016. "OneOrlando Fund Draft Protocol." July 13. https://www .oneorlando.org/wp-content/uploads/2016/07/Draft_Protocol_EN_071316.pdf.

Padilla, Maria. 2016a. "Father Refused to Claim Pulse Nightclub Shooting Victim." *Orlando Latino* (blog), June 22. http://orlandolatino.org/2016/06/father-refused -claim-pulse-nightclub-shooting-victim/ (URL defunct).

Padilla, Maria. 2016b. "Latinas Translate for Victims' Families." *Orlando Latino* (blog), June 12. http://orlandolatino.org/2016/06/latinas-translate-victims-families/.

Pardo, Mary S. 1998. *Mexican American Women Activists: Identity and Resistance in Two Los Angeles Communities*. Philadelphia, PA: Temple University Press.

Pérez, Gina M. 2004. *The Near Northwest Side Story: Migration, Displacement, and Puerto Rican Families*. Berkeley: University of California Press.

Perez, Hiram. 2005. "You Can Have My Brown Body and Eat It, Too." *Social Text* 84, no. 85: 171–91.

Perilla, Julia L. 1999. "Domestic Violence as Human Rights Issue: The Case of Immigrant Latinos." *Hispanic Journal of Behavioral Sciences* 21, no. 2: 107–33.

Peterson, Jillian, and James Densley. 2021. The Violence Project Database of Mass Shootings in the United States, 1966–2019. The Violence Project. https://www .theviolenceproject.org.

Povinelli, Elizabeth, and George Chauncey. 1999. "Thinking Sexuality Transnationally: An Introduction." *GLQ* 5, no. 4: 439–50.

Quiroga, José. 2016. "Straw Dogs: On the Massacre at Club Pulse." *Bully Bloggers*, June 27. https://bullybloggers.wordpress.com/2016/06/27/straw-dogs/.

Ramos-Zayas, Ana Y. 2003. *National Performance: The Politics of Class, Race, and Space in Puerto Rican Chicago*. Chicago: University of Chicago Press.

Rana, Junaid, and Gilbert Rosas. 2006. "Managing Crisis: Post-9/11 Policing and Empire." *Cultural Dynamics* 18, no. 3: 219–34.

Rivera-Servera, Ramón. 2012. *Performing Queer Latinidad: Dance, Sexuality, Politics*. Ann Arbor: University of Michigan Press.

Rivera-Velázquez, Celiany, and Beliza Torres Narváez. 2016. "Homosociality and Its Discontents: Puerto Rican Masculinities in Javier Cardona's Ah mén." In *Blacktino Queer Performance*, edited by E. Patrick Johnson and Ramón H. Rivera-Servera, 264–74. Durham, NC: Duke University Press.

Rodríguez, Juana María. 2003. *Queer Latinidad: Identity Practices, Discursive Spaces*. New York: New York University Press.

Rodríguez, Juana María. 2016. "Voices: LGBT Clubs Let Us Embrace Queer Latinidad, Let's Affirm This." *NBC News*, June 16. www.nbcnews.com/storyline/orlando -nightclub-massacre/voices-lgbt-clubs-let-us-embrace-queer-latinidad-let-s -n593191.

Rodriguez, Nestor. 2012. "New Southern Neighbors: Latino Immigration and Prospects for Intergroup Relations between African-Americans and Latinos in the South." *Latino Studies* 10, nos. 1–2: 41–59.

Rodríguez-Madera, Sheilla, Mark Padilla, Nelson Varas-Díaz, Torsten Neilands, Ana C. Vasques Guzzi, Ericka J. Florenciani, and Alíxida Ramos-Pibernus. 2017. "Violence against Transgender/Transsexual Persons: An Underestimated Problem in Puerto Rico." *Journal of Homosexuality* 64, no. 2: 209–17.

Rosaldo, Renato. 1993. *Culture and Truth: The Remaking of Social Analysis*. Boston: Beacon.

Rosas, Gilberto. 2021. "Grief and Border-Crossing Rage." *Anthropology and Humanism* 46, no. 1: 114–28.

Rúa, Mérida M. 2012. *A Grounded Identidad: Making New Lives in Chicago's Puerto Rican Neighborhoods*. New York: Oxford University Press.

Ruiz, Vicki L. 1998. *From out of the Shadows: Mexican Women in Twentieth-Century America*. Albuquerque: University of New Mexico Press.

Sanchez-Korrol, Virginia E. 1983. *From Colonia to Community: The History of Puerto Ricans in New York City, 1917–1948*. Westport, CT: Greenwood.

Santiago, Esmeralda. 1994. *When I Was Puerto Rican*. New York: Vintage Books.

Segura, Denise A., and Elisa Facio. 2008. "Adelante Mujer: Latina Activism, Feminism, and Empowerment." In *Latinas/os in the United States: Changing the Face of América*, edited by Havidán Rodríguez, Rogelio Sáenz, and Cecilia Menjívar, 294–307. Boston: Springer.

Silver, Patricia. 2010. "'Culture Is More than Bingo and Salsa': Making Puertorriqueñidad in Central Florida." *Centro: Journal of the Center for Puerto Rican Studies* 22, no. 1: 57–83.

Silver, Patricia. 2020. *Sunbelt Diaspora: Race, Class, and Latino Politics in Puerto Rican Orlando*. Austin: University of Texas Press.

Spradley, James P., and David W. MacCurdy. 1972. *The Cultural Experience: Ethnography in Complex Society*. Chicago: Science Research Associates.

Stewart, Kathleen. 2011. "Atmospheric Attunements." *Environment and Planning D: Society and Space* 29, no. 3: 445–53.

Torres, Julie. 2016. "Mourning in Orlando." *Anthropology News* 57, nos. 11–12: 14–17.

Torres, Lourdes. 2008. "Queering Puerto Rican Women's Narratives: Gaps and Silences in the Memoirs of Antonia Pantoja and Luisita López Torregrosa." *Meridians: Feminism, Race, Transnationalism* 9, no. 1: 83–112.

Torres, Lourdes. 2016. "In Remembrance of the Orlando Pulse Nightclub Victims." *Latino Studies* 14, no. 3: 293–97.

Turner, Victor. 1974. *Dramas, Fields, and Metaphors: Symbolic Action in Human Society.* Ithaca: Cornell University Press.

Urciuoli, Bonnie. 1996. *Exposing Prejudice.* Boulder, CO: Westview.

Vidal-Ortiz, Salvador. 2016. "Queer-Orlando-América." *Society Pages*, June 17. thesocietypages.org/feminist/2016/06/17/queer-orlando-america/.

Wanzer-Serrano, Darrel. 2015. *The New York Young Lords and the Struggle for Liberation.* Philadelphia, PA: Temple University Press.

Weise, Julie. 2012. "Dispatches from the 'Viejo' New South: Historicizing Recent Latino Migrations." *Latino Studies* 10, nos. 1–2: 41–59.

Whalen, Carmen T. 2005. "Colonialism, Citizenship, and the Making of the Puerto Rican Diaspora: An Introduction." In *The Puerto Rican Diaspora: Historical Perspectives,* edited by Carmen Whalen and Víctor Vázquez-Hernández, 1–42. Philadelphia, PA: Temple University Press.

Zavella, Patricia. 1987. *Women's Work and Chicano Families: Cannery Workers of the Santa Clara Valley.* Ithaca, NY: Cornell University Press.

Erika G. Abad

....

Farm of Forgetting

Mamá,
As the earth shudders, you open your eyes.
Your eyes take in the cold gray sky hovering behind palm trees that
    survived
Hurricane Maria, the hurricane that split your cabinets.
Earthquakes cracked your walls.
You hear your name. Feel fingers smoothing
Against your brow. Gray sky, quaking earth, persistent palm trees
Begin preparing for your return.

From your bed, your frail voice calls out to
Your Amados, your beloveds. Amado Sr.,
Your beloved husband, sits by you.
He takes remnants of your hands still filled with flesh and warmth
    into his.
Amado Jr., the younger beloved, brews your coffee in the kitchen.

The aroma of Cafe Rico wafts past decaying cabinets.
The paint crumbles off the walls.
you revisit memories of las nenas de Mamá.
They crawl into bed with you as coffee percolates.
Their knobby knees, your gnarled, knuckled hands
share warm hugs and giggles.
They squeal and hum and hug into you how much they love you.

MERIDIANS · feminism, race, transnationalism   22:2 October 2023
DOI: 10.1215/15366936-10637645 © 2023 Smith College

They never outgrow the words and the hugs girls need to grow up to
   give to men.

                              Mamá, if you only knew how long I never wanted to love them.

The elder Beloved asks what else you need.
The younger Beloved adds milk and sugar before bringing you coffee to
   your bedside.

                                    I still remember you bringing it to mine, Mamá

The elder lifts your lip up to the cup as his son sits.
They don't know, among other things, what the graying sky, the weathered trees, the shuddering earth have come to do;
they do not yet know of your homegoing.
Café con leche is the last bit of sweetness to touch your lips.
After it has coated your throat, with a cough
and a squeezing of hands, your soul follows the graying sky, weathered
   trees, the shuddering earth home.
You leave your body behind surrounded by the ones you insisted see
   you through this end.
And you, Mamá, are grateful.
The younger beloved throws himself on what's left of your skin and
   bones
while the elder beloved weeps. Their cries, ride the Caribbean winter
   breeze,
bringing providence in to call an ambulance.
You inform the gray sky, the quaking earth, and the stubborn palm
   trees—
You tell them—that you and your God have prepared.
You bought your coffin, your plot, you bought the nameplate your life
   never allowed you to read.
You reserved the funeral home.
Las nenas need only worry about the planes.

              Mamá, I worry about fading. I worry about the tumor returning. Mamá, I still worry
                                                      about COVID-19.

As others' souls slip through them, the gray sky, the trembling earth,
    tell you
There's never enough. Resistant tears, and youthful hearts
Are never prepared.
Never wanting,
Never wanting to lose your hands.
You remind the earth, the sky, and the silent trees
your love doesn't die with your body.

    Mamá, how can I agree when forgetting to love me was necessary for your surviving?

All the secrets, all the unnamed wounds, the palm trees hiss,
Get left behind.
They linger, the quaking earth says, *longer than it takes your body to join me.*
Those scars flounder, the palm trees persist, *before you become the earth that*
    feeds me.
The unnamed hurt, the gray sky spits, *gets pulled out of me . . .*

    Aye, Mamá, I tire of hiding

Your wounds are the roots that bind us.
Aye, you say, *they'll forget—*
No, the sky and trees, and earth insist, not the women you birthed to
    carry us.

    I never wanted to remember you as anything but warm, Mama.

Erika G. Abad is assistant professor of communications in the Department of Data, Media, and Design at Nevada State University. Their poetry has been published in *Dialogo, Sinister Wisdom,* and *Red Rock Review* and featured in the 2018 show *Women/ Transition* at Left of Center Gallery. They've been featured on podcasts like *The Art People Podcast, Seeing Color Podcast,* and *Latinos Who Lunch* for their research and teaching on LGBTQ Indigenous, Black, and Latine representation in television, film, and visual arts. "Farm of Forgetting" complements the emotional impetus behind "Two Cultures, One Family," an art show they curated at the University of Nevada Las Vegas's Marjorie Barrick Museum in the fall of 2022. Abad can be followed on Instagram and Twitter @prof_eabad.

Kami Fletcher

Black Women Undertakers of the Early Twentieth Century Were Hidden in Plain Sight

Abstract: This essay foregrounds Black women in the very narrative of under-taking that they helped create and develop. It was the wives who helped start the country's oldest undertaking firms, and it was the wives, sisters, and daughters who sustained and professionalized the funeral home leg-acy. The article follows women from the American South and mid-Atlantic regions, illustrating how, with their skills and capital, they labored not just as funeral directresses, embalmers, and undertakers but also as book-keepers, hairdressers, accountants, caterers. These women were "race women," college-educated Black women who were trained to uplift the race. And as race women in the death trade, they brought their skills and education to a field that created generational wealth and civic empowerment.

Conducting a meeting of the National Negro Business Men's League (NNBML) in August 1908, Booker T. Washington, founder of Tuskegee University and arguably the most influential African American of the late nineteenth and early twentieth centuries, intently listened to testimonials of financial success from African American men in the undertaking trade. The *Afro-American* (1908) newspaper reported that, on hearing how under-takers from Baltimore and throughout the country were grossing $5,000 to $150,000, "frequently [Washington] exclaimed 'That's fine!'" Washington knew the success story of the Reconstruction-era undertaker and touted it

MERIDIANS · feminism, race, transnationalism   22:2 October 2023
DOI: 10.1215/15366936-10637582 © 2023 Smith College

in his famed *The Negro in Business*, published 1902, where he devoted two chapters to the turned-nothing-to-something undertaking businesses of six southern men. But just as in his book and at the NNBML sessions, the African American women who too labored to make the business a success were there and not there—hidden, I argue, in plain sight. In *The Negro in Business*, Washington writes of a wife's "efforts" and "knowledge" as just presumed spousal support. The journalist in the *Afro-American* cites one undertaker's success story, writing, "He told his story in a characteristic way, and said his wife was responsible for much of his success," yet she was not present at the meeting, nor was she identified as a co-owner of the funeral business or even coworker in the death trade. In both instances men in the undertaking trade were foregrounded, while women, whose efforts were known and even stated, were still backgrounded in plain sight of their contributions and skill set.

In this essay, I argue that Black women undertakers during the early twentieth century were hidden in plain sight but not invisible or even actively erased; all one has to do is look for the early trades workers in death work and they are right there in the records. This is precisely what I did when I first sought out the 100 Black Women of Funeral Service (100BWFS), an international professional organization that positions Black women and embalming as foundational to undertaking by situating Queen Nefertiti and Egyptian death practices and ideology as the foundation to understanding and practicing funerary work. Ever since founder Elleanor Starks started the 100BWFS in San Antonio, Texas, in 1993, she was adamant about locating the women in death work in order to highlight their accomplishments as well as insert them back into their rightful place as important historical actors in the development of the modern funeral. In one effort, the 100BWFS in 2010 commissioned an anniversary booklet that included the histories of African American funeral homes throughout the nation.[1] These histories were written by the funeral home owners, their descendants, or current owners, making them important pieces of Black history that oftentimes get lost. Women are all over these histories as founders and owners of funeral homes, significant to the industry's growth and development. I mined these twenty-six histories for women's contributions, origin stories, and death work identities.

	Year founded	Name of funeral home	City and state
1	1837	Locks Funeral Home	Baltimore, MD
2	1882	Patton Brothers Funeral Home	Franklin, TN
3	1861	Carl Miller Funeral Home	Camden, NJ
4	1874	J. M. Wilkerson Funeral Home	Petersburg, VA
5	1886	Jarnigan and Son Mortuary	Knoxville, TN
6	1891 (earliest record located)	Charbonnet-Labat-Glapion Funeral Home	New Orleans, LA
7	1885	Gray's Funeral Home	Cape Charles, VA
8	1899	Davenport & Harris Funeral Home	Birmingham, AL
9	1899	James E. Churchman Funeral Home	Orange, NJ
10	1900	Cox Brothers Funeral Home	Atlanta, GA
11	1900	Elliott Funeral Home	Albany, GA
12	1900	Hutchings Funeral Home	Macon, GA
13	1900	Stewart Funeral Home	Washington, DC
14	1901 (charter established)	Kansas City Embalming and Casket Company (now named Mrs. J. W. Jones Memorial Chapel)	Kansas City, KS
15	1903	Collins Funeral Home	Jackson, MS
16	1905	Berry & Gardner Funeral Home	Meridian, MS
17	1905	Daniels & Sons Funeral Home	Harlem, NY
18	1905	Diehl-Whittaker Funeral Service	Columbus, OH
19	1905	E. F. Boyd & Son	Cleveland, OH
20	1905	Scarborough and Hargett Funeral Home	Durham, NC
21	1907	Larkin and Scott Funeral Home	Demopolis, AL
22	1909	Gertrude Geddes Willis Funeral Home	New Orleans, LA
23	1909	Lewis Funeral Home	San Antonio, TX
24	1909	Murray Henderson Undertaking Company	Algiers, LA
25	1910	Scott's Funeral Home	Richmond, VA
26	1913 (charter established)	Rhodes Funeral Home	New Orleans, LA

I then turned to my own decade-long research on Baltimore's Mount Auburn Cemetery and asked, Where are the women? The cemetery patronized a dozen or so male undertakers in the 1870s, but as the patriarchs died, wives, who were already skilled funeral directresses, embalmers, and morticians, took over the businesses. In some cases it was the sister or daughter-in-law who became the owner. So I began to use the *Afro-American* newspaper to learn how they represented themselves and the businesses that were now solely under their control. In advertisements for their funeral businesses, they did not use their first names. The vast majority of the ads led with their married name followed by their titles as "funeral directress" or "embalmer," declaring them as

Figure 1. September 10, 1927, ad in the Afro-American newspaper announcing Mrs. Ida Snowden as successor to deceased husband, Charles B. Johnson. Mrs. Ida Snowden is daughter of Bettie and Robert Elliott of Elliott Undertaking, started in Baltimore in 1902.

"successor" to the undertaker (fig. 1). The rest of the ads listed the names and addresses of their undertaking businesses. Listing themselves as successors is key in that it established them as professional and skilled undertakers and not incompetent widows. Therefore, I followed the trail the 100BWFS laid out before me and coupled it with my own mid-Atlantic research, enabling me to historicize women from various backgrounds around the country.

It was my intent to keep the scope between 1910 and 1950 because before 1910 women were layers out of the dead within the funeral service trade and not generally identified as funeral directors, although there were exceptions to this rule. In nineteenth-century Philadelphia, for example, there is a clear demarcation between male undertakers and female layers out of the dead. Women made the burial shrouds. Burial shrouds were material goods sewn and stitched together—a gendered skill passed down the female line. Between the 1910s and the 1950s women were accepted into the occupation of undertaker because the trade of undertaking shifted to the funeral home profession during this forty-year period. At the same time, and owing to the inception of Historically Black Colleges and Universities (HBCUs), many Black women obtained higher education, propelling them to professional careers, which then further allowed them to contribute to the shifts in funeral home professionalizing and modernizing. This higher education gave Black women the skill sets and freedom to thrive in the burgeoning funeral home business.

What has hidden Black women in plain sight of their contributions to early twentieth-century death work are (1) the patriarchy that attached itself to undertaking as the labor developed from trade to professional work and (2) the gender division of labor ever present in U.S. culture, in which men not only worked outside the home but were also propelled out front in business, leaving women unvalidated. By outlining the beginnings of African Americans' involvement in the death trade and discussing how this Black experience with death work produced what I call "Black undertaking," death work that prioritized and fused Black cultural norms in death care, I show how Black women in undertaking were accepted. Black undertaking was tied to the community uplift work that Black women were already doing and definitely spearheading. However, patriarchy intersected with the Black experience to force Black women undertakers to the margins—indeed, the very name of the funeral business was that of the father, husband, or brother.

Black Experience Intersects with Undertaking

Undertaking, the process by which the deceased is prepared for last rites, intersects with the Black experience in complicated ways in the United States. One most apparent is that, although it is assumed that the dead, regardless of status, will be respectfully and properly disposed of at the end of life, this assumption of funeral rites (or funeral rights) was negated within a society that institutionalized slavery. Slavery—a system based on white supremacy and the complete social and cultural subordination of Black persons—dehumanized Black life, which made it nearly impossible to respect Black death. There was no space for remembering three-dimensional Black people. There was only space for remembering so-called devoted slaves but only in reference to benevolent slaveholders.[2] Black culture pushed back and positioned death, particularly the act of organizing and conducting last rites, as a route to freedom.[3] One scholar speaks explicitly of the transformative power of the Black funeral:

The American community transformed individuals upon death into symbols of freedom. . . . Despite the conflicting ideas about the social standing of African Americans in the United States, through death they
became elite sacred symbols. In their desperate search for dignity,
embracing death rituals was natural for African Americans because of
the powers of transformation contained in death rituals. (Plater 1996: 87)

Slavery shaped death for Black people in such a way that last rites became a
communal experience. It was the family, assisted by the broader enslaved
community on the plantation, that prepared the bodies for last rites. Black
undertaking was important cultural work in the face of white supremacy
because it continued the rituals the enslaved brought from their home-
lands that were later recreated for transmigration or the afterlife. In 1837
Charles Ball, a man enslaved in western Maryland, wrote about helping a
mother and father to undertake their infant: "[We] buried with it . . . a
piece of white muslim, with several curious and strange figures painted on
it in blue and red, by which, he said his relations and countrymen would
know the infant to be his son, and would receive it accordingly, on its arrival
amongst them" (Ball 1837). In death, the body/soul was disassociated from a
slave status and prepared to be directly associated with its kinship within its
true African homeland. By washing and dressing the body, what scholars
term corpse care, as well as adorning the coffin, Black women played a particularly important role in transmigration. The historian Jamie Warren
(2014) argues that corpse care was an important way for enslaved women to
confirm kinship bonds, empower themselves, and carry out proper last rites
along cultural norms. In doing so, Black women participated in ritual
washing, an act of body preparation performed by their foremothers, born
free in Africa. This ritual washing allowed the ancestral chain to remain
unbroken even when one died in the African Diaspora; a prevalent African
belief is that upon death, one is born into the family of the ancestral spirits,
and ritual washing is key to this type of rebirth (Brookman-Amissah 1986).
Warren (2014: 110–30) writes: "Washing the dead body . . . held metaphysi-
cal importance, as bathing the body of the dead symbolically washed away
the soil of life and sickness and prepared the individual to be reborn in
death." Washing the body was gendered death work performed predominantly by women. It took on an added component in the antebellum South
because it was a way for Black women to (1) hold tight to perhaps the last
remaining part of their African culture and (2) empower themselves in a way
that the institution of slavery denied in life.

Undertaking within the Black experience became an act of resistance, a step toward publicly claiming humanity. Charles Ball's account was not as common as we would like to think. Funeral rights were not guaranteed to enslaved Black people. Too many times enslaved bodies were given an "open air" burial in which the dead were not interred and instead disrespectfully left to the open air to be desecrated by animals, or a rushed grave was dug and the body simply put in the ground. Black undertaking took on a form of remembering life. What scholars refer to as "second burial"—funerals held at night when the deceased could be properly buried according to death cultural norms and with his or her kin and community present—ensured a proper burial and was a way for bonded Black peoples to choose the land where they knew the deceased would rest in peace.[4] Sometimes called slave cemeteries, these were spaces near the edges of the property amid the trees and beside the nearby running stream/lake/river. By manipulating and claiming ownership of this slave landscape, the enslaved gained a measure of autonomy and were able to use nature to funeralize their kin (Jones 2011).[5]

Fundamentally, Black undertaking resisted slavery. Frequently, bonded Black women and men used undertaking as a method to actively seek freedom. Henrietta Smith Bowers Duterte, the first female undertaker in Philadelphia and believed to be the first practicing female mortician in the country, used her funeral home as a safe house (Lawrence 1988; "Henrietta S. Duterte," n.d.). She was said to have hid people escaping slavery in her coffins ("Henrietta S. Duterte," n.d.). Duterte came from a family that engaged in antislavery activism. "The [Bowers and Duterte families] worked for the abolition of slavery at least 15 years before the Civil War and for women's rights more than 100 years before the equal rights movement" (Lawrence 1988). Her brother, John C. Bowers Jr., held leadership positions in numerous antislavery organizations like the Wilberforce Settlement, a colonization project aimed at settling an area of Canada that would grant Black Americans self-autonomy, freedom, and self-determination; the Citizens Improvement Association; and the State Convention for Colored People in 1848 (Philadelphia Inquirer 1892; Liberator 1835, 1836).[6] Henrietta's husband Francis, a Haitian immigrant, was a member of the Moral Reform Retreat, which supported the abolition of slavery and equal rights for women. For Black peoples, death work was truly the work of serving the living.

African Americans who became undertakers had learned carpentry skills during slavery. It was commonplace for enslavers to have enslaved Africans learn a trade, so that they could hire them out for further economic gain and have a skilled crafts person always present on the plantation whom the slaveholder did not have to pay (McIlwain 2003; Fox-Genovese 1988). As the historian Daina L. Ramey Berry reminds, the trades on a plantation were highly gendered (Ramey 1998, 2007). Enslaved men occupied the trade positions of mechanic, shoemaker, blacksmith, and carpenter, while enslaved women were relegated to cook, nurse, seamstress, and midwife. Women were simply excluded from learning certain trades, carpentry being one of them, because it was thought that women either did not have the physical capacity to complete such strenuous labor or were just better suited to domestic tasks such as child-rearing, owing to their biological makeup. Therefore, the reality that Black men learned the woodworking trade (and this most assuredly meant making coffins) means that Black women's exclusions from this specialized knowledge contributed greatly to their being obscured in the undertaking trade later.

Black undertaking, especially when it left the home and became a trade in the mid-nineteenth century, was characterized by collectivity, cooperation, and self-help among Black women. The twenty-six histories captured and published in the 2010 African American Funeral Home Hall of Fame Induction speak to how Black women undertakers founded the funeral homes, expanded businesses, established burial and life insurance companies alongside the funeral home, and even migrated across states to found their own funeral homes. Gertrude Pocte Geddes, the daughter-in-law to George Geddes (founder of George D. Geddes Willis Funeral Home), expanded the business and services to ultimately reorganize the funeral home to include a life insurance company in the 1940s. After leaving the slaveholding South it was his wife, Leah McCants Miller, in 1861, who started what became the first Black funeral home in Magnolia, New Jersey. Marion Anna Smith Daniels did the same after migrating from Thomasville, Georgia, to New York City, establishing the Daniels Funeral Home on the upper west side of Manhattan. After her husband Orland passed, she raised their three children while running a successful funeral business during World War I before moving to another location.[7] Whether founders or successors, Black women undertakers were intricately part of the American Black undertaking businesses.

As "Race Women," Black Women Were Integral to Death Work

In the antebellum era Black women were central to corpse care. The first few decades of the twentieth century would find Black women as pillars of the new African American funeral home. No longer just a coffin-making, gravedigging trade, death work was now a funeral business, and the funeral home was key to its professionalization. While professionalization relied heavily on state-mandated certification and specialized school training to embalm the dead, it was the creation of the modern American funeral home, what scholars call the redomestication of the death business, that transformed the trade into a profession.[8] Redomestication, or putting death back in the home, created unique wealth-building opportunities for the Black family, from which Black women particularly benefitted. One benefit was that the role of the undertaker expanded. Instead of being narrowly defined as a coffin maker, an undertaker, sometimes now called a funeral director, was someone who cooked and spearheaded the repast, coiffed the decedent's hair, or even served as office manager and secretary—all roles traditionally held by women. Black women undertakers were fundamental to the success of their funeral home, "fashioning a domestic and religious ethos that promoted intimacy with the dead," according to Gary Laderman, a religious and cultural studies scholar who has written two pivotal books on the history and evolution of the American death care system. Another benefit was that Black women were positioned as community leaders and civic role models. Black women undertakers came to be during the country's second industrial revolution, fueled by advancements in technology and manufacturing, which produced economic opportunities for African Americans in general. This was also the "Women's Era," and women were demanding a political seat at the table, engaging in personal freedoms and individual growth. Being funeral directors in funeral homes allowed women to meld the private roles of wife and mother with the perceived public roles of professional and businesswoman. Arguably, in the Black funeral home the four roles complemented each other, giving Black women the support and authority to thrive in the modern funeral business, which relied on an intimacy, care, and concern that was the signature of this new modern funeral home, which included preneed.

Black women occupied different spaces within the undertaking trade. Nevertheless, they were undertakers and not just married to one. Booker T. Washington hinted at the partnerships and the prowess of wives but stopped short of identifying them as undertakers. When William Porter moved from Tennessee to Cincinnati, he married Ethlinda Davis around the same time Porter Undertaking was established. "[Porter] went into the undertaking business and married Miss Davis," wrote Washington, "whose efforts and judgement much of his success is due" (Washington 1907: 96).[9] As one of Cincinnati's first African American school teachers, Ethlinda Davis gained organizational and leadership skills that became part and parcel of the success of Porter Undertaking. Commenting on Jackson's "happy" marriage to Eliza (Belle) Mitchell Jackson, Washington said that the blissful union led to his wife not only inserting herself into the business but also proving herself very valuable: "Mr. Jackson was extremely happy in his marriage as his wife identified herself with his interests and has been of invaluable assistance to him" (Washington 1907: 98). Eliza (Belle) Mitchell Jackson, the first African American teacher at Camp Nelson, used, as Washington noted, "judgement" and "invaluable assistance" in the success of the undertaking businesses (98). This is a good indicator of the intellect, knowledge, and all-around decision-making power of spouses applied to the finances, administration, and the specialized tasks involved with death work.

Like Ethlinda, Eliza was trained as a "race woman," a term scholars have given to Black women of the later nineteenth and early twentieth centuries who, with higher education, found themselves as public leaders in the fight for social justice that puts their issues at the center of this fight.[10] College-educated and recognized community activists who were as committed to the uplift of their race as they were to the progression of their sex, race women were part of what the historian Evelyn Brooks Higginbotham called the "Female Talented Tenth." These women "served as a conduit of race pride and white middle-class culture," which Higginbotham interprets as "mirror[ing] whites in their behavior, values, and modes of work." (1993: 21). For Black women in death work, the latter was cancelled out. As aforementioned, death work was rooted in Black cultural norms, and because Jim Crow racially segregated not only public life but also the consumer marketplace, African Americans were able to create wealth-building opportunities (Mier 1963). Juliet E. K. Walker—founder and director of the Center for Black Business History, Entrepreneurship, and Technology and the preeminent scholar of Black business history—illustrates through her decades-long research the independent and collective ways in which Black folks from the nineteenth century onward have used thrift, community building, and self-help ideology to carve a path to economic entrepreneurial success. Walker unequivocally proves that "Blacks have participated in the American business community since Africans came here" (Walker 2009; Nicholson 2016).[11] This mix of class

and culture—the free Blacks of whom Walker speaks who are the ancestors of Higginbotham's "Female Talented Tenth"—intersects directly
with Black middle-class respectability politics.

As undertakers and funeral directors, Black women were trained, educated, valued, and respected community leaders who grounded themselves
and their funeral home businesses on middle-class respectability politics.
Hallmark scholars like Darlene Clark Hine (2007), Stephanie Shaw (1996),
and others conclude that the construction of gender within the African
American community was deliberately designed to transcend debilitating
factors of race, sex and class (see also Jeffers 1981; Simmons 2015; Hicks
2010). Shaw points out that in their communities there was no confusion
about who they were, their individual identities both public and private.
Their success was as intertwined with their personal development and
steadfastness as it was with the care and concern of the community. Black
women death workers prided themselves on providing a respectable and
proper funeral for their community members. As undertakers and funeral
directors, they abided by the same economic ethos as Washington—by
thrift and moral responsibility they would build wealth. The funeral business was lucrative, and it showed that Black-owned-and-operated businesses could thrive and be successful and respectable. Booker T. Washington was more focused on promoting the Negro Business League because it
showed this respectability, in particular the ability of Black men to adhere
to gendered norms of the breadwinner. This is why Black women undertakers were obscured in Washington's view of Black entrepreneurs.

Presumably, these women were only being "good wives" at a time when
society demanded that their identities merge and become one with their
husbands'. Although the efforts of both Ethlinda Davis Porter and Eliza
(Belle) Mitchell Jackson were downplayed and overlooked, what's clear is
that Black women were integral to death work. In her study of Black funeral
homes in the South, the historian Beverly Bunch-Lyons (2015), says that
Black women were often angel investors of Black undertaking firms, which
commonly started with only shoestring budgets. Giving even more insight
into just how Eliza and Ethlinda were central to the businesses, she writes
that "working wives contributed their earnings from teaching or other
professional jobs to the family funeral business" (61). Black women
undertakers took on the role of bookkeeper, manager, hair stylist, and
undertaker's assistant. In addition, many continued to prepare the
bodies—a task that women, regardless of race, have performed throughout

the ages. Death work performed by nineteenth-century women consisted of specialized knowledge of body preparation inclusive of decomposition and postmortem hygiene. This knowledge was passed down to apprentices.[12] In death, the decedent's home was the center, making women the lead in all tasks related to death and mourning, for example, alerting the kinship network of a death in the family and preparing the body for obsequies.

Whether involving skilled carpentry or unskilled labor, undertaking has traditionally been androcentric and independent—the idea of the lone carpenter hammering and nailing his way to entrepreneurial success during the Reconstruction era. The preoccupation with male undertakers thrust forward by the patriarchal nature of nineteenth-century labor norms minimized the presence of women undertakers. This idea is rooted in the cult of "true womanhood," the notion that a woman should be pious, pure, domestic, and submissive. These virtues helped outline and ultimately define a brand of femininity that confined women to the households and normalized men in the public sphere. Whether a part of race womanhood or "true womanhood," women, particularly Black women, had to contend with and navigate the patriarchal dynamics within their communities and the undertaking business. Therefore, it is important to recognize that, with women as co-owners and operators with their spouses, undertaking was hardly a lone male endeavor. The obituary for Robert Elliott, characterized as Baltimore's leading undertaker, mentioned that "his wife [Bettie] worked indefatigably in helping him to build up his business, and he always gave her great praise for her deep interest she took" (*Afro-American* 1916). This suggests that Bettie helped establish and develop the business, which made him known around town as the leading undertaker. Positioning Bettie's work, skill, and experience as simply "deep interest" is reminiscent of Booker T. Washington's description of Eliza (Belle) Mitchell Jackson, wife of the Lexington, Kentucky, undertaker Jordan C. Jackson.

The words in the obituary were a true testament to the growth and development of Elliott Undertaking with Bettie at the helm, especially after Robert passed away on March 31, 1916. With sporadic assistance from her brother Edward Pye and her daughter Ida Snowden, who joined a bit later around 1925, Bettie was the solo funeral directress and embalmer. Less than two months after Robert's passing, she took out an ad in the *Afro-American* headlined "Mrs. Elliott to Continue Business," where she connected the successes of Elliott Undertaking to her direct involvement, business skills, and knowledge gained from her husband as well as her expert knowledge indicated by her funeral license. In part the ad reads, "The greatness he [Robert] achieved was due greatly to the untiring energy and business tact of his wife." The ad further explains, "She spent all her time assisting her husband along all lines, thereby getting the practical experience which enables her to successfully manage the business." Case in point: Robert was working for a white undertaker, William Hickman, in 1896 when he struck out on his own, leaving Bettie to take on more than her fair share in the early days of their Elliot Undertaking business, since Robert had to split his time with Hickman. By the time Robert died, March 31, 1916, she was already licensed by the Maryland Board of Undertakers, although at the time, it was customary and easy for wives to become licensed after their husbands died. Bettie was key to Elliott Undertaking's business success: Robert was sick nearly three months before he died, and after he passed, the firm didn't miss a beat. Bettie moved, renovated, and grew the business to a higher level. Within three years of her solo ownership, she moved the business across town and "remodeled into an up-to-date establishment with funeral parlors, chapel, etc." Only seven years later, in 1926, she established four branch offices in Baltimore. This is quite an accomplishment, considering that only two horses, five hacks, hearse, and flower wagon made up all the business assets when they officially opened their business on East Street near Hillen in 1902. To put the nail in the proverbial coffin of the argument that undertakers' wives are just helpmates, Bettie accomplished all of this while simultaneously running the undertaking firm of her brother, Felix Pye Sr., a Baltimore undertaker since 1877. When he fell sick in 1923 and could no longer maintain his firm, he asked her to manage it.

Many other Black women in the death trade in Baltimore had similar experiences. Some of the nation's oldest Black male undertakers credited their success and entrusted the future of their undertaking businesses to wives, daughters, and sisters. They did this because these women were their business partners and they were great undertakers—not just their wives and kin. When funeral owner George Holland fell sick, for example, his wife Helen Holland obtained a funeral director's license, paid her nephew's way through embalming school, and took complete control of Holland Undertaking upon her husband's death in 1923. Already in its twentieth year, it prospered and grew thanks to her leadership. Helen renovated the funeral home, adding space to serve her clientele and a training center for apprenticeship undertakers to learn embalming. Similarly, Locks Funeral Home, Baltimore's (and perhaps the nation's) oldest funeral business, operational from 1860 until 2003, consistently had women at the helm. Edna Francis, the granddaughter of founder John W. Locks, was the first licensed woman undertaker in Baltimore during her two-decade-long run of the business. By 1954 her daughter-in-law, Mae Carol Locks, was not only a mortician and business manager but also a beautician to the deceased as well—beautifying the dead by styling hair and applying makeup. Likewise, in 1913 Frances Hemsley and her husband Samuel T. Hemsley were left in charge of and successfully operated Hemsley Undertaking, founded in 1876 by Samuel's father Alexander Hemsley. Samuel died in 1934, and so for thirty-plus years Frances ran the business until leaving it to her stepson Bernard Hemsley after she retired in 1968.

Nineteenth-century African American undertaking businesses undoubtedly owed their foundation and sustainment to the female members who served in the many internal roles needed for their success. Yet Black women were mislabeled as simply the wives, sisters, or daughters of undertakers. They were hardly recognized as undertakers themselves, even though they were fully involved in the business. These African American undertaking businesses thrived throughout the generations, and much if not all their success is due to the "deep interest" Washington speaks of Black women's undertaking was reinterpreted to not just fall under the expectations of the wife but to convey the earnest and sincere desire for success and longevity of a business that brings wealth and ownership and stability is the reason spouses, offspring, siblings, and in-laws worked so hard. They were just as invested in a business that would benefit the family as one that would benefit them. The harder they worked, the better the business.

Funeral Directresses, Undertakers, and Embalmers
In *The Negro in Business*, Booker T. Washington (1907: 94) writes:

The interest and even fascination with which the Negro people have always viewed the great mystery of death has given the ceremonies that are connected with this dread event a special and peculiarly important place in their social life. Out of this instinctive awe and reverence for the dead has arisen the demand for solemn and decent and often elaborate burial services. To meet this demand there has grown up a prosperous business.

At the turn of the twentieth century, African American women and men were able to take part in the cash economy via the undertaking trade. Meeting the demand for proper and culturally ascribed last rites led to wealth building, of which Washington greatly approved. African American cultural ideas regarding the importance of death have led to a demand for not only a proper burial but also one marked with intricate and extravagant detail. This extravagance, or what scholars have described as pageantry and emoting, is the core of the African American funeral, better known as a homegoing, a celebration of the decedent's life (Fletcher 2021). It was a time to honor and not be cheap. The family bought the finest casket, had the longest funeral procession, the best hearse. If Black folks had to live portrayed as one-dimensional mammies and brutes, they were determined to die as African royalty. And it was the Black funeral director who was going to see to it that they were casket sharp. The funeral director was responsible for the final public performance, and, culturally speaking, it mattered and mattered greatly. The homegoing was also a time to shout, sing, praise, and otherwise publicly emote. This emotional aspect, combined with the importance of the stylizing and care of the body, positioned Black women in death care as particularly important. Scholars have written about the "female attendant" or "lady embalmer" that was crucial element of the twentieth-century Black funeral home (Smith 2010; Plater 1996; Holloway 2002; Laderman 2005; Farrell 1980). As Michael Plater (1996) wrote, "She was the center of the consolation effort provided by African American funeral homes for the bereaved" (161–62). If the homegoing was an African transplant, then Black women funeral directors were the culture keepers and culture carriers of this death work. But as important as this role has been to funeral service, particularly as it relates to the Black experience, no scholars have talked directly about how these Black women were founding partners in the funeral home business, making it important to chronicle the ways in which they were actually involved in the funeral home from the beginning and not just discuss their overall roles. Black funeral origin stories make Black women foundational to the twentieth-century Black funeral home business.

Whereas Black men started out in the undertaking trade by driving hearses for funerals or making coffins, Black women in the early twentieth-century undertaking trade had different starting points. Historically, women took over the undertaking business either once their husbands became too infirm to service patrons or after their husbands, who were out front in operating the business, died. This was certainly the case for

Baltimore's Black women undertakers in the first decades of the twentieth century. Carrie Mason Hooper took over the George H. Hooper undertaking business when her husband George died in the decade prior. She took out an ad listing herself as the successor to her deceased husband but, more importantly, made sure to inform that the service and establishment would remain the same (fig. 2). Widowed after eight years of marriage, forty-two-year-old Ida Taylor Bailey (and second wife) announced that she would continue the business of her late husband, Charles G. Bailey, as funeral directress and embalmer. Elizabeth H. Davis became her husband's successor when James H. died in 1924.

Helen Holland in Baltimore solicited help from her brother and blood nephew when her husband was too sick to conduct business. Her husband George, who had been licensed since 1910 but was recorded as having worked in the death trade since 1898, died in 1923. Her brother and nephew served as staff to help maintain the business, and not as out-front business runners. This was a purposeful decision because she could not legally run the business under Maryland law until she received her licenses in 1923. In another instance, her brother Edward W. Pye and son-in-law Charles B. Jones were identified as employees of the widow Bettie after Robert Elliott's death. This arrangement did not work out, presumably because Edward was listed as residing in Baltimore County and was perhaps too far away, and Charles started his own undertaking business soon after his father-in-law passed away. As previously discussed, Bettie already had plans for how Elliott Undertaking would be successfully run and operated (fig. 3).

Mary A. Jones involved herself into the day-to-day operations of their Kansas-based undertaking business only after her husband, J. W., fell ill in 1917. She nursed him until he passed away four years later, and it was only then that she solely operated the business that J. W. had renamed "Mrs. J. W. Jones Memorial Chapel" in 1900 as a sign of his love and affection. She may have started her career in the death trade as a widow, but after owning, operating, and modernizing the business as the main funeral director for forty-six years, Mary was ultimately responsible for its immense growth and sustainment through Jim Crow segregation, the Great Depression, and two world wars. She studied and passed the state exam to obtain her license, and she would gain and sharpen the skills necessary to train and apprentice many up-and-coming morticians and funeral directors until her death in 1963.

She Helps in Sorrow

MRS. GEORGE HOLLAND

She is a member of Trinity AME Church and several civic groups, including the NAACP, and takes time out now and then to play cards with one of the four card clubs of which she is a member.

A berth on the AFRO's honor roll goes to Mrs. George Holland, undertaker and funeral director, who for the past seventeen years has exhibited the type of patience and rendered the kind of understanding service which has endeared her to the hearts of her fellow-citizens.

It is not an easy task to maintain calm and patience as Mrs. Holland has done during her long service to people in sorrow. Since that May day back in 1923 when George Holland died and left her the business to manage alone, Mrs. Holland has improved her parlors, chapel and morgue in order to render more efficient service, and in turn has seen more and more people turn to her for help and aid in their time of sorrow.

A quiet, modest woman, Mrs. Holland is on call at all hours of the day or night, wherever death comes, and through it all has never found the task too arduous. She attributes much of the success of the business during the past few years to her late nephew, Moncure Brown, who until his death in December, managed the business for her. He was closer to her than a son.

A native Baltimorean, Mrs. Holland has spent all her life here.

Figure 2. Top: January 6, 1922, ad announcing Mrs. George H. Hooper as successor to her husband, George Hooper. The ad identifies her as a funeral director and embalmer. Bottom: In a January 25, 1941, ad, Mrs. George Holland is featured on the Baltimore Honor Roll list. A list that honors the community's leaders and heroes. In part the ad reads: "A berth on the AFRO's honor roll goes to Mrs. George Holland, undertaker and funeral director, who for the past seventeen years has exhibited the type of patience and rendered the kind of understanding service which has rendered her to the hears of fellow-citizens. . . . Since that May day back in1923 when George Holland died and left her the business to manage alone, Mrs. Holland has improved her parlors, chapel and morgue in order to render more efficient service, and in turn has seen more and more people turn to her for help and aid in their time of sorrow."

C. & P. Phone
Wolfe 6590

Immediate Service
Day and Night

NEVER CLOSED

MRS. ROBERT A. ELLIOTT
Successor to the late ROBERT A. ELLIOTT
1725 Ashland Avenue
FUNERAL DIRECTOR AND EMBALMER
Branch Office—2109 Druid Hill Avenue, Madison 4660-J
Carriages for Funerals, Weddings and Receptions
Limousine Funerals a Specialty — Immediate Service Day and Night

Figure 3. 1928 ad announcing Mrs. Robert A. Elliott as successor to her husband, Robert A. Elliott, and identifying Mrs. Elliott as a funeral director and embalmer.

Taking a different starting point, some Black women established undertaking businesses with their husbands and brothers and so from the beginning were identified as co-owners and co-operators. In 1924 Mary Collins and her husband Malachi bought the G. F. Frazier Undertaking business, located in Jackson, Mississippi. G. F. Frazier Undertaking was priced at $14,000 and they paid $5,000 down, the equivalent of over $70,000 in contemporary times (Sanders 2014). In 1899 and at forty years old, Hattie C. Davenport founded Birmingham's Davenport and Harris Funeral Home with her brother Charles Harris. This business decision was surely a result of her and Charles moving to the big city of Birmingham. Charles had gained on-the-job experience by working for a local funeral home while he pursued higher education at Alabama A&M University. He used this crucial knowledge to branch off on his own. Married and "keeping house" by 1880 and widowed by the end of the decade, Hattie was presumably eager to move from the small rural city of Troy Pike, Alabama, to throw off restrictive gender roles. Gertrude Pocte and husband Clement, along with Arnold Moss and his wife Marie, established the Geddes and Moss Undertaking Parlor in 1909. During this time, they established a burial association that continued throughout the later redevelopment of the funeral home. During these early years, newspaper ads featured head shots of only Clement and Arnold. Later, and once Clement passed and Gertrude remarried,

1940s city directories listed a Mrs. Gertrude Geddes Willis as funeral director and business owner of Geddes Gertrude Funeral Parlor.

The women who migrated from the South to the North during the Great Migration experienced the freedom of becoming Black business owners by opening funeral homes. Those who stayed in the South worked to acquire enough capital to start funeral homes. They organized their lives to devote enough time to building the business and established themselves as community leaders. These women took risks and bet on themselves. And although their paths differed, Black women were committed to ensuring that their family funeral businesses thrived throughout the generations. Their dead husbands were depending on them to hold down the businesses in their eternal absence, and their children depended on them to sustain the family. These were race women—educated women who were realized and acknowledged as leaders in their communities. They were expected to be great.

Conclusion

Black women undertakers and funeral directors were part of a larger project of uplift and respectability that was rooted in economic advancement. As race women, they were involved leaders in numerous church-led committees, social organizations whose missions centered community improvement through economic prosperity. Their leadership, vision, and skills allowed them to grow businesses that economically benefitted not just themselves and their immediate family but also extended family and adopted kin. Many times, these women took on the role of mother to a nephew or a neighborhood youth. She trained them up in the ways of funeral service and allowed them to go off and create generational wealth. Because they were autonomous entrepreneurs, Black women funeral home owners were ignored by their contemporaries. Early to mid-twentieth-century entrepreneurs were gendered male because businesses were given family names that in a patriarchal society hid the maternal lineage. Looking at Booker T. Washington and his National Negro Business Men's League through a gendered lens allows for a more comprehensive understanding of Black life during the turn of the twentieth century and through the present.

It is imperative that Black women be given their rightful place in the twentieth-century historical narrative on death work that they helped create. This narrative is clearly traced to the corpse care enslaved Black women performed. This ritualized washing and adorning of the body hearkens back to when their ancestors, women of West Africa, particularly in Ghana among the Akan people, used the Kununum shrub for purification and ritual washing, usually done outside in a stream or large body of water. Black women used corpse care to establish and continue kinship bonds, to empower themselves, and to humanize in the face of slavery. After the institution of slavery ended, Black women continued to engage in death work as undertakers who dressed the body, coiffed the hair, and laid out the body for viewing by mourners during the wake and funeral. Working closely with husbands and fathers who made coffins and dug graves, these women acquired these new skills and then took up the trade when the patriarchs passed away. Women not only worked as undertakers in these family businesses but also invested their time, money, and energy to sustain them. They expanded the businesses and, because of their care and concern and unique position as race women, aided greatly in the modern American funeral home business.

Black women traversed through different forms of femininity, including race womanhood and "true womanhood," while resisting rigid gendered norms, sexism, and racism. As educated, skilled, and outspoken race women, they were hailed by their communities as leaders that could uplift the race. These same middle-class standards expected them to still fulfill the role of wife and mother. The funeral home, a domesticated space for the death business, was a palatable and accepted place for women to own and thrive in. Twentieth-century Black women were instrumental in developing the Black funeral home business in America, and they left a long legacy via the funeral directors and morticians of tomorrow that they trained. Black women of the later twentieth century organized and networked to tout their talents, expertise, and history. By the mid-twentieth century, Black women out-front in the funeral service. The 100 Black Women of Funeral Service understood the importance of preserving history and telling histories. Today, Black women are leading the field of funeral service. As of 2020, 67 percent of mortuary school graduates were women, and 17 percent were Black women. They are using their work as a launching pad for full inclusion. No longer catering to a Jim Crow market, Black women funeral home owners like Brandee Wilkerson, Tiffany Smith, Janet Stephens, and Barbara LaPrade see their work as breaking down racial barriers as they serve both Black and white clientele. Their success lies in their belief that they are especially equipped for their field because "women bring a special sensibility to the funeral service business" (McFarland 2022; see also Marotta 2021; Moore 2015).

....

Kami Fletcher is associate professor of American and African American history and co-coordinator of women's and gender studies at Albright College. She is the co-founder and president of the Collective for Radical Death Studies, a nonprofit committed to decolonizing death studies. Fletcher is the co-editor of both *Till Death Do Us Part: American Ethnic Cemeteries as Borders Uncrossed* and *Grave History: Death, Race, and Gender in Southern Cemeteries.*

Notes

1   These funeral homes were the 2010 Hall of Fame Inductees, awarded top honors because they were started in the nineteenth and early twentieth centuries and, in 2010, were both the nation's oldest African American funeral homes and, remarkably, still in operation. This is with the exception of Murray Henderson Undertaking, Inc. and Daniels & Sons, which closed in 1930 and around the 1990s, respectively.

2   Slave narratives talk about slaveholders gifting burial plots located at the slaveholders' feet or actually with the white family, and in both cases they presented as very generous the eternal gifts of a good death and burial. There are headstones that read "dutiful slave" and "obedient slave." The idea is to immortalize the slave and not the three-dimensional person whose freedom was kept from them in life and now death. See Library of Congress, "Born in Slavery Collection," https://www.loc.gov/collections/slave-narratives-from-the-federal-writers-project-1936-to-1938/about-this-collection/.

3   For decades, scholars of slavery have asserted how creolization, that is, the creation of the African American identity, post–American Revolution, served as resistance to the dehumanization of slavery. These scholars assert that building familial networks, fictive and real, created a culture that fought back against the commodification and exploitation of slavery. This culture extended to death and burial, allowing these familial networks to create a Black culture that humanized decedents and allowed for Black ancestors to be memorialized and to matter. For more on this, see White 1999a; Berlin 1998; Horton and Horton 2006.

4   Scholars also position second funerals as forms of Africanism, direct and indirect links to African cultural norms and practices. As a ceremony or remembrance that celebrates the next life, the spiritual life, the second funeral can be part of transmigration—the spirit is released from slavery in the Americas and heads back home to Africa. For more on the "second funeral," see Smith 2010.

5   Funeralize: to execute a funeral or prepare last rites.

6   See also the 1870 United States Census, 18th district, 7th ward city of Philadelphia, assessed May 22, 2022, through www.ancestry.com.

7   The 2010 African American Funeral Home Hall of Fame Induction Booklet, 100 Black Women of Funeral Service, National Funeral Directors and Morticians Associations, August 4, 2010.

8   Scholars agree that death work in early America was performed primarily in the home and by women. Women announced the death in the community and prepared the body for last rites. Mourning also was gendered feminine and carried forth by women in their dress and participatory roles during last rites. With the introduction of undertaking and then later embalming and the role of the funeral director, women and their central roles in death care were greatly minimized and marginalized. The introduction of the modern funeral home, which was literally located in the family home of the funeral business owners, reinstated the feminine and women into central roles in death labor. For more, see Farrell 1980 and Laderman 2005.

9   William and Ethlinda Porter are parents to Jennie D. Porter, the first African American woman principal in Cincinnati. For more, see Robinson 1998 and Ligon 2014.

10 *Race woman* is frequently used when describing the work of the National Association of Colored Women (NACW), an organization started by Mary Church Terrell and Josephine St. Ruffin in 1896. At its founding, there were already fifteen thousand members, since the NACW was an umbrella organization formed from other clubs that were part of the broader club movement. These college-educated Black women were hailed by their communities as leaders, activists, and role models. Their community work, combined with their education and burgeoning economic opportunities, allowed them to take up public space on a national stage to advocate for racial and women's equality. They also spoke out in defense of themselves, as rape and sexual assault was a national epidemic. For more on these issues, see Hine et al. 1995; Guy-Sheftall 1995; Giddings 1984; and White 1999b.

11 Juliet E. K. Walker, "African American Business, Entrepreneurship, and Capitalism, 1619–2021: Where Do We Go from Here?," webinar, March 18, 2021, Keller Center at Princeton University. https://kellercenter.princeton.edu/events /african-american-business-entrepreneurship-and-capitalism-1619-2021-where -do-we-go-here.

12 "Shrouding women," as named by the sociologist Georgeann Rundblad (1995), were women who performed "premarket death duties" that included laying the body out on the cooling board to fix and prepare for the wake and funeral, washing and dressing the body, and properly posing for coffin and burial. Before hospitals and hospice care, the sick and shut-in were cared for and ultimately died at home. If a person did not die at home, he or she was brought home for proper last rites that included funeral and family.

Works Cited

Afro American. 1908. "Negro Tells of Success: Dark Undertakers Whisper Secrets of Acquiring Wealth." August 21.

Afro-American. 1916. "Funeral of Robert Elliott." April 8.

Ball, Charles. 1837. *Slavery in the United States: A Narrative of the Life and Adventures of Charles Ball, a Black Man*. Documenting the American South. https://docsouth.unc .edu/neh/ballslavery/ball.html.

Berlin, Ira. 1998. *Many Thousands Gone: The First Two Centuries of Slavery in North America*. New York: Belknap.

Brookman-Amissah, Joseph. 1986. "Akan Proverbs about Death." *Anthropos* 81: 75–85.

Bunch-Lyons, Beverly. 2015. "'Ours Is a Business of Loyalty': African American Funeral Home Owners in Southern Cities." *Southern Quarterly* 53: 57–71.

Farrell, James J. 1980. *Inventing the American Way of Death, 1830–1920*. Philadelphia, PA: Temple University Press.

Fletcher, Kami. 2021. "Seven Elements of African American Mourning Practices and Burial Traditions." *TalkDeath*, February 8. https://www.talkdeath.com/7-elements -of-african-american-mourning-practices-burial-traditions/.

Fox-Genovese, Elizabeth. 1988. *Within the Plantation Household: Black and White Women of the Old South*. Chapel Hill: University of North Carolina Press.

Giddings, Paula. 1984. *When and Where I Enter: The Impact of Black Women on Race and Sex in America*. New York: William Morrow.

Guy-Sheftall, Beverly. 1995. *Words of Fire: An Anthology of African-American Feminist Thought*. New York: New Press.

"Henrietta S. Duterte." n.d. The Colored Conventions Project. https://colored conventions.org/Black-mobility/associated-women/henrietta-s-duterte/.

Hicks, Cheryl. 2010. *Talk with You like a Woman: African American Women, Justice, and Reform in New York, 1890–1915*. Chapel Hill: University of North Carolina Press.

Higginbotham, Evelyn Brooks. 1993. *Righteous Discontent: The Women's Movement in the Black Baptist Church, 1880–1920*. Cambridge, MA: Harvard University Press.

Hine, Darlene. 2007. "African American Women and Their Communities in the Twentieth Century: The Foundation and the Future of Black Women's Studies." *Black Women, Gender, and Families* 1, no. 1: 1–23.

Hine, Darlene, Wilma King, and Linda Reed. 1995. *We Specialize in the Wholly Impossible: A Reader in Black Women's History*. Brooklyn, NY: Carlson.

Holloway, Karla. 2002. *Passed On: African American Mourning Stories, a Memorial*. Durham, NC: Duke University Press.

Horton, James, and Lois Horton. 2006. *Slavery and the Making of America*. Oxford: Oxford University Press.

Jeffers, Trellie. 1981. "A Personal Viewpoint: The Black Black Woman and the Black Middle Class." *Black Scholar* 12, no. 6: 46–49.

Jones, Diane. 2011. "The City of the Dead: The Place of Cultural Identity and Environmental Sustainability in the African-American Cemetery." *Landscape Journal* 30, no. 2: 226–40.

Laderman, Gary. 2005. *Rest in Peace: A Cultural History of Death and the Funeral Home in Twentieth-Century America*. Oxford: Oxford University Press.

Lawrence, Bette Davis. 1988. "Henrietta Bowers Duterte: A Study in Determination." *Philadelphia Daily News*, February 8.

The Liberator. 1835. "Second Hand Clothing Establishment." August 29.

The Liberator. 1836. "Wilberforce Settlement." July 2.

Ligon, Tina. 2014. "Pioneering the Change to Be Better: Jennie Davis Porter and Cincinnati's All-Black Harriet Beecher Stowe School, 1914–1935." PhD diss., Morgan State University.

Marotta, Eric. 2021. "Focus on Black-Owned Businesses: Wilkinson 'Honored to Be Chosen' to Operate Funeral Home." *Akron Beacon Journal*, February 21. https://www.beaconjournal.com/story/news/2021/02/24/brandee-wilkinson-first-black-woman-funeral-home-operator-akron/4549577001/.

McFarland, Diana. 2022. "Black Female Funeral Owners, Directors Are History in the Making." *Star Tribune*, February 26. https://www.chathamstartribune.com/news/local/article_ba7a94ba-94d5-11ec-9df4-bb21c4bcb4da.html.

McIlwain, Charles. 2003. *Death in Black and White: Death, Ritual, and Family Ecology.* Cresskill, NJ: Hampton.

Mier, August. 1963. *Negro Thought in America, 1810–1915.* Ann Arbor: University of Michigan Press.

Moore, Doug. 2015. "African-American Woman Hopes to Break Down Racial Barrier in Funeral Home Business." *St. Louis Post-Dispatch*, February 15. https://www.stltoday.com/news/local/metro/african-american-woman-hopes-to-break-down-racial-barrier-in-funeral-home-business/article_0fdda64d-64b3-5b2e-91d4-efa3fdd051b9.html.

Nicholson, Gilbert. 2016. "Black Business History Scholar Issues Strong Words for Entrepreneurs at A. G. Gaston Conference." *Philadelphia Daily News*, February 17. Alabama News Center. https://www.alabamanewscenter.com/2016/02/17/37295/.

The Philadelphia Inquirer. 1892. "To Improve the Thirty-Third Ward." November 23.

Plater, Michael. 1996. *African American Entrepreneurship in Richmond, 1890–1940: The Story of R. C. Scott.* New York: Garland.

Ramey, Daina L. 1998. "'She Do a Heap of Work': Female Slave Labor on Glynn County Rice and Cotton Plantations." *Georgia Historical Quarterly* 82, no. 4: 707–34.

Ramey, Daina L. 2007. "'In Pressing Need of Cash': Gender, Skill, and Family Persistence in the Domestic Slave Trade." *Journal of African American History* 92, no. 1: 22–36.

Robinson, Lesley. 1998. "Jennie Davis Porter: A Leader of Black Education in Cincinnati." *Perspectives in History* 4, no. 1: 13–18.

Rundblad, Georganne. 1995. "Exhuming Women's Premarket Duties in the Care of the Dead." *Gender & Society* 9, no. 2: 173–92.

Sanders, Crystal. 2014. "Dignity in Life and Death: Undertaker Claire Collins Harvey and Black Women's Entrepreneurial Activism." *Journal of Mississippi History* 76: 111–27.

Shaw, Stephanie. 1996. *What a Woman Ought to Be and to Do: Black Professional Women Workers during the Jim Crow Era.* Chicago: University of Chicago Press.

Simmons, LaKisha Michelle. 2015. *Crescent City Girls: The Lives of Young Black Women in Segregated New Orleans.* Chapel Hill: University of North Carolina Press.

Smith, Suzanne. 2010. *To Serve the Living: Funeral Directors and the African American Way of Death*. Cambridge, MA: Harvard University Press.

Walker, Juliet E. K. 2009. *To 1865*. Vol. 1 of *The History of Black Business in America: Capitalism, Race, Entrepreneurship*. 2nd ed. Chapel Hill: University of North Carolina Press.

Warren, Jamie. 2014. "To Claim One's Own: Death and the Body in the Daily Politics of Antebellum Slavery." In *Death and the American South*, edited by Craig Thompson Friend and Lorri Glover, 110–30. New York: Cambridge University Press.

Washington, Booker T. 1907. *The Negro in Business*. Chicago, IL: Hertel, Jenkins.

White, Deborah Gray. 1999a. *Ar'n't I a Woman? Female Slaves in the Plantation South*. New York: W. W. Norton.

White, Deborah Gray. 1999b. *Too Heavy a Load: Black Women in Defense of Themselves, 1894–1994*. New York: W. W. Norton.

Lashon Daley

When Diane Tells Me a Story

Abstract: This essay examines the complex relationship that developed between ethnographer Lashon Daley and her research subject, Diane Ferlatte, over the course of Daley's master's thesis project and the years beyond. Through storytelling and narrative prose, Daley investigates the roles that grief, death, Black motherhood, and the Black southern oral tradition play within their ever-growing bond. As their relationship progresses from researcher and respondent to mother and daughter, their bond displays the connective tissue that binds one person to another through history, memory, and the common experience of loss. By exploring the performativity of Black women who are bonded by love and not blood, this essay demonstrates how Black womanhood becomes a conduit for grieving and healing.

By the evening of December 7, 2013, I had listened to all of the condolences I could handle. It was the evening of my mother's funeral, and over the past six days I had heard from friends, family members, and acquaintances whose names I had forgotten. Some graciously and some awkwardly expressed how deeply sorry they were for my loss. They wanted to know how I was doing and reminded me that if I needed anything, just ask. Like the ritual of call-and-response—their calls, my response—each conversation became scripted. Their standard apologies and my hollow thank yous were all we could muster. The pain was still too fresh, and if any of us had forgotten our lines, it was only a matter of moments before the conversation turned into a sobbing, weeping, moaning mess. As a result, we respected the script of loss and hung up our phones accordingly to cry in our respective corners. But on that sixth evening of mourning, while sitting

MERIDIANS · feminism, race, transnationalism   22:2 October 2023
DOI: 10.1215/15366936-10637663 © 2023 Smith College

in my mother's favorite chair, shell-shocked from the day, I was surprised when my cell phone rang, echoing loudly in the quiet house so much that it startled my mother's aging dog.

I was told by a family friend that the grieving process gets even more difficult after the phone stops ringing. After people who were in and out of the house on a daily basis stop coming by. After you realize that your mother isn't coming home again—ever. I didn't expect any more phone calls that evening. I had been on the phone most of the week and up until the moment I walked into the funeral home earlier in the day. I was ready for the phone calls to end—at least at that moment. I reached over and looked to see who was calling. Had it been anyone else, I would have silenced the ringer and gone back to flipping through the TV channels, but instead, I answered the call. It was Diane Ferlatte, the subject of my master's thesis project. Diane is a Grammy-nominated professional storyteller and one of the most prolific African American storytellers of our time. She wasn't calling because she knew my mother had died; she was calling because she knew that my mother was dying.

Diane and I had spoken on the phone a few times a month since August, when I had decided to withdraw from graduate school and move back home to become my mother's caregiver. Our conversations were never very long. She would ask how I was doing and ask about my mother. I would ask her how she was doing and inquire about what stories she was getting ready to perform. Sometimes we video chatted, which allowed for longer conversations and reminded me of what it was like to sit at Diane's dining-room table swapping stories. Or better yet, Diane telling me stories and me just listening in complete awe. We had done that so many times over the past year that every time I walked into her house, I headed straight for her dining-room table and took my usual seat.

The last time I sat at Diane's table before my mother's passing was on a Monday in late August. It was the day before my one-way ticket home. I walked into Diane's house, placed my things on my chair at her dining-room table, and followed her into the kitchen. I kept my head down and focused my eyes on the sunlight reflecting off the hardwood flooring. I watched as our shadows moved through the space. Diane opened her cupboard, removed two mugs, turned on her electric teapot, and waited for the water to boil. I went into her pantry, removed two tea bags, the jar of honey, and retrieved a teaspoon from the drawer. There wasn't very much to say and Diane understood that. So instead, she hugged me while tears formed in the corner of my eyes. We took our mugs back to her dining-room table, where she told me stories for the rest of the afternoon.

For Diane and me, gathering around her dining-room table, despite how haphazard it seemed, is never unintentional. As Black women, we understand that both knowledge and wisdom are shared around dining-room tables, inside kitchens where steaming pots are filled with greens, and in living rooms where mothers converse as they plait their daughters' hair.

"Hi Diane," I said, answering the phone.

I was happy to hear from her, but also heartbroken about the news I would soon convey. This time our just-checking-in conversation was going to take the same roller-coaster drop that all of my conversations had taken during the week.

"Hi Lashon," she replied, in a sing-song manner characteristic of her personality. Everything about Diane is musical: her voice, her body, her movements. The space around her is cadence in motion.

"How's everything? How's your mom?"

I twisted the top of my left ear. The constant realization that my mother was gone had me feeling as if I was continuously being thrown against a brick wall.

"Today was my mother's funeral."

Diane gasped like I knew she would because everyone did once I unveiled the news. It felt like a cosmic collision. My pain had now been transferred to someone else again. Diane's 3:00 p.m. Pacific Standard Time in Oakland and my 6:00 p.m. Standard Eastern Time in Miami had morphed and slowed down. I felt like the X-Men character Rogue, who destroys people with her touch. But like the writer I am, I was destroying people with my words.

"When did she die?" The concern in Diane's voice made me want to cry, but I didn't have any more tears. I hadn't cried all day. I had walked into the funeral parlor that morning as if I was an event planner: blazer on, smile wide, napkins and plates in hand, and my mother's eulogy on my lips. Before starting graduate school, I had been an event planner and facility supervisor; this get-it-done mentality was familiar to me. But now, hours after the funeral was over, sitting in my mother's favorite chair watching, but not watching TV, I was finally starting to take it all in.

"When did she pass?" Diane asked again. "On Monday."

"And what are you doing right now?" "I'm watching TV."

"Alone?"

My brother was visiting with some friends and my sister was at a baby shower. Believe it or not, I was happy to be home alone. It was easier to wallow in my own sorrow without someone else there to distract me with their grief.

"I don't mind," I reassured her. "I would rather be by myself."

Diane gave me her condolences like everyone else had done and I thanked her. I twisted my ear again because I was about to ask her the question I've wanted to ask her for the past year. About a month after we met, Diane told me she had cancer. She was diagnosed in 2011, but besides that we never talked about it. I was always too nervous to bring it up and Diane did not want to be confined by her illness. She had only mentioned it in passing. She'd tell me when her chemotherapy treatments were and I would try to go.

"Diane, if you don't mind me asking, what stage are you?" The words tripped out of my mouth. I couldn't bear having just lost my mother and not knowing when or if I might lose Diane too.

Diane would sometimes hint at her prognosis. I was never able to grasp the underlying urgency—I wasn't ready. I wasn't ready to acknowledge that two of the most important women in my life at the moment were battling colon cancer at the same time. I wasn't prepared to lose them both. Sometimes Diane would tell me "Who knows how much longer I have?" or "This could be my last performance at Jonesborough." She was referring to the National Storytelling Festival that occurs every October in Jonesborough, Tennessee. It's the largest storytelling festival in North America and possibly the world. Diane had only performed at the festival four times in its forty years. When she was asked to perform in 2013 during the festival's forty-first year, she believed that she might not live to see her next invitation.

"Stage IV."

Now I gasped, feeling horrible that I let my emotions show.

Her tone had been full of acceptance, but mine was of disbelief. Now I knew exactly how she felt. Our roles had been reversed. Her response sunk deep inside of me, settling into my bones like I knew cancer could do, like it had done to my mother. What made it worse is that I now knew exactly what Diane's body was going through, and I knew exactly what it could go through. I knew more about Diane's body in ways I hadn't predicted since the inception of my thesis project. Over the past eighteen months, I'd been watching Diane's body like a critic, a theorist, a student, a folklorist, a fan. Through my research, I have determined that Diane possesses a culturally educated body—a body inscribed with family histories, social constructions, age and gender delineations, and ethnic style. As a performer with more than thirty years of stage presence developed within her, her body consists of rehearsed rhythms as well as improvisation, (un)choreographed facial expressions that if mapped would fall into a system of patterns, and corporeal gestures that range from innate sign gestures to American Sign Language. Her body inhabits multiple borders of intentions, demarcating the liminal lines between improvisation and routine. Accordingly, her gestures reveal those boundaries from which her body is constructed. It is her body that took my project from being the study of folklore to folklore as it embodies both tradition and modernity. In every performance, she displays a visible demonstration of her physical pedagogy. And now with the revelation of her diagnosis, her body became even more important to me.

"Are you dying?" I asked softly.

"Not if I have anything to do with it." I could hear Diane's confidence in the bass of her voice like she was standing her ground against death. "I have too many stories to tell. Speaking of—'Bundles of Worries' have I ever told you that one?"

"No," I lied. I had heard her tell it before, but I was in the mood to hear her tell it again.

Before my mother had passed, and Diane and I had sat at her dining-room table during that last Monday in August, I had an irrational fear that she was going to shut me out of her life once I moved back home. I was nervous that maybe I would be a sad reminder to her of what cancer could do. That it could render you helpless and draw your youngest daughter back across three thousand miles to help take care of you. That it could subject you to grief you had yet to experience. That it could destroy parts of you— parts you never expected it to. I thought maybe it would be too painful for us to remain in each other's lives. Especially now, looking back and seeing that not all of my friendships made it through my grieving process. But instead, Diane has drawn me closer—accepting me not only as her biographer but also as a daughter. The more time I spend with her, the more her presence has helped ease my grief—all five ubiquitous stages of it. Hence when our anger causes us to fight from time to time, because like mother and daughter we fail to meet each other's expectations, we are quicker to forgive the verbal batting. I had learned the hard way with my mother that unforgiveness would remain living with me while it would die with her. I had to come to terms with the fact that, despite Diane's miraculous longevity, her chemotherapy treatments could stop working at any moment. Her acceptance of this eventually became my acceptance of it too. There had even come a time with my mother that accepting her mortality allowed us more freedom to express our feelings because we knew that time was of the essence.

From another perspective, accepting my mother's and Diane's mortality has also allowed me to accept my own. I even occasionally imagine how tragically poetic it would be if the three of us all succumbed to colon cancer, and this essay, years from now, becomes the prelude to my losing Diane and the prologue to whatever health scares that could befall me as a Black woman prone to hereditary cancer. I have bargained with God in hopes that my life does not become so tragically poetic and, as a result, have wallowed in my own bouts of depression more than I care to admit. But like Diane, I have more stories to tell, and this story of Diane, my mother, and me is just the beginning. It is through telling this story that I have come to realize how connected and similar the three of us are, especially Diane and me. That is the power of the Black oral tradition: not only does it change lives, creates and solidifies bonds that may not have been formed otherwise, it also strengthens the connective tissues that unite Black women. When Diane tells me a story, she's passing down generations of wisdom, morals, and histories—histories of Black women that have been pushed aside. She is also passing down stories of the oppressed, stories of rebellion, and stories of change. And rightly so, those stories give voice to other stories like the stories of my mother. This is the legacy of strength that Black women have embodied and encrypted within our DNA. Our narratives are being passed down in story, in song, in recipes, in words spoken around the kitchen table. It is these narratives that continue to give voice to my grief and fuel my desire to share my own stories of who I am as a storyteller and a scholar.

When I first heard Diane tell a story, it was at Cal Performances' *Fall Free for All* in September of 2012. It was a festival that featured free music, dance, and theater concerts. Diane was scheduled to perform that Sunday afternoon. She was one of the few storytellers participating. I had researched her work and quickly realized how her interests aligned with mine. She concentrates on African and African American folktales, weaving

American Sign Language, sung-texts, folk songs, and spirituals into her performances. So I sent her an email gushing about my interests in her work, not even noticing that I had mistakenly spelled her name wrong. I was elated when I received a reply from her husband to give her a call the next day. I wrote a reminder in my calendar to call Diane the following afternoon, and then watched videos of her on YouTube for the rest of the night.

When my last afternoon class let out, I called Diane while walking through campus toward home. She picked up after two rings.

"Hi Diane. This is Lashon. I sent you an email last night. I was hoping to do an interview with you after your performance."

"That sounds fine." Diane paused. "Lashon, where are you from?" "I'm from Miami."

"You don't sound like you're from Miami."

"Well, I just spent the last four years in New Orleans."

"No, I'm from New Orleans. You don't sound like you're from New Orleans. Are you African American?"

"Yes, but Caribbean American; my mother is from Jamaica." "Oh, that must be it," she concluded.

I knew Diane was Black because I had spent hours scrolling through photos and videos of her the night before, but I never thought about whether my being Black would be of interest to her. I have had situations like this occur before. I would have a conversation on the phone with someone, and then meet them in person to only find out years later (after becoming friends) that their first impression of my voice was that I was not Black. Since childhood, hearing my name being sputtered out by elementary school teachers, I always assumed that my name marked me as Black. However, Diane's comment caused me to wonder what kind of body she imagined when she heard my voice. For a moment, it made me reexamine the border identities of my body that I hadn't thought about for some time.

Before our phone conversation had ended, we had made plans to meet an hour before her concert to have a quick interview. I hung up the phone and called my mother. She was number two on my speed dial after my voicemail. I spoke with my mother about everything, and I spoke with her about everything quite often—four-to-five-times-a-day often, but never long conversations unless I needed them to be. They were just to check in, a habit we began when I moved to Westchester, New York, to pursue my master's in fine arts (MFA) in writing at Sarah Lawrence College. I was twenty-three years old and leaving home for the first time. I was ready for the new adventure, but I also had instilled within me my mother's fears that I could be kidnapped, raped, or mugged, even though Westchester County's violent crime statistics was rated twenty-one on a scale of one to one hundred, while Miami was a frightening eighty-four. But it was New York, after all, and my mother had watched too many episodes of *Law & Order: SVU* to believe that the statistics were true. She had seen it on TV and that's all she needed to know. So I called her in the morning on my way to school. I called her in the afternoon between classes. I called her when I was leaving school. I called her when I got home. And I called her before I went to sleep.

These series of calls lasted throughout my two years in the MFA program and into my move to New Orleans. Then they subsided slightly as I settled into southern living, but picked up again once I moved to Berkeley because I lived a block away from the infamous People's Park. When my mother helped move me in, she had seen all of the loitering for herself, so her check-in calls came in frequently, even though by that time I was twenty-nine and had lived on my own for six years.

I asked my mother what she thought about Diane's question. She told me that it was because I had a proper way of speaking and that I shouldn't be offended by such questions. I couldn't help but wonder if I had an accent, and if so, what did it sound like? My mother's Jamaican accent had never relented, but it could be watered down when she wanted it to be, which made her sound more like she was from England as opposed to the states. I wondered if that was what I sounded like: a watered watered-down version of my mother.

But I knew that it was more complicated than that. What did it mean for me to be a daughter of the African diaspora whose lineage seeped sweetened blood of sugar cane as opposed to the pure whiteness of cotton? The tension between the Afro-Caribbean and the African Americans' relationship to Blackness was not new to me. My mother's outcast status from both the white and Black communities after her immigration to the United States during the 1970s had never left her. And because it never left her, it never left me. But for Diane it seemed that I was Black enough, which meant that I had the golden ticket. The doors to the world of southern Black oral traditions were now open to me.

On the day of Diane's *Cal Free for All* performance, I walked into the Martin Luther King, Jr. Student Union, took the curved staircase up to the grand Pauley Ballroom, and asked one of the attendants for Diane. The attendant told me that my mom was here a few minutes ago, but if I waited in the room, she would be back shortly. This would be the first of many times that I would be mistaken as Diane's daughter. I corrected the attendant, letting her know that Diane was not my mother, but thanked her for the information. I walked into the room, taking in its size and the gloriousness of the light coming in from the large windows. There were a handful of people milling around: some staff and some a part of Diane's entourage. I watched and waited, spinning myself in slow circles in order not to miss her entrance. I was nervous; I wanted to make a good impression. I was already taken with Diane—her stage presence, her musical abilities, and her talent. In my mind, I was just a lowly Cal graduate student of only three weeks. Surely, she would not be impressed by me. Then Diane appeared from one of the doors toward the back of the room. She wore a bright-red head scarf that outlined her round face and accentuated her dark braids. Her red-draped knit cardigan was paired with a sunglow-yellow top and black pants. Around her neck was a long necklace with a large pendant that looked like something I wanted to shake. She walked toward the front of the room while I walked toward her. We smiled at one another. I stretched out my hand, but she didn't take it. Instead, she sang my name, elongating the L, and pulled me in for a hug.

"So nice to finally meet you," I said, even more nervous than before. "Should I ask you questions now or wait until afterwards?"

"Now because I've got work to do." Although, that's not exactly what Diane said, that's certainly what I heard. And it was true; Diane did have work to do. She had an hour-long set that was starting shortly, and I was taking up her time. We sat down in the front row. I pulled out my notebook. She turned her body toward me, but her light-brown eyes kept searching the room. I also couldn't help but watch as it began to fill up with hundreds of children and their guardians searching for seats close to the stage. Most of them had been waiting in a long line that snaked down the stairs into the student union. That's when I started to realize how famous Diane is in the storytelling world. The Pauley Ballroom can seat five hundred people, and almost every seat was taken.

The show finally started with the thumping of Diane's rhythm stick hitting the floor of the stage as she sang, "I'm so glad I'm here to share my story." She then quickly taught us a song and how to sign *yes* in American Sign Language. Our voices echoed against the walls, creating an uproar of song and laughter. Within minutes Diane had eased into her first story, a personal one about when she was a little girl, her father fought through a thunderstorm to return home to her. He knew she was scared of lightning and walked home in the pouring rain to hold her until the storm had passed. "That's the kind of daddy I had—that's love," she said, finishing the story. I could see that she was holding back tears, but in the next moment, she effortlessly moved us into another song, and we all began to sing again.

When Diane's performance had ended, I got to mill around much longer than her fans, who were obliged to exit the auditorium. Once she got her affairs in order, I went to thank her, giving her an awkward side hug. I was still nervous, but she was nice enough to ignore my awkwardness and invited me to her house anytime I wanted to come. I ended up visiting her about a month later. She was preparing for her performance at the Thirtieth Annual National Black Storytelling Festival and Conference, which was about three weeks away. She was one of three storytellers being featured at the Zora Neale Hurston Concert on the final night of the conference, a huge testament to her storytelling abilities. I watched as she sat at her dining-room table surrounded by thick books of folktales and folk songs. This is how she prepares for a tale: digging into the heart of stories until one of them speaks to her. She tried out the beginning of some of the tales on me, watching my facial expressions for clues on whether it might be a good pick.

Throughout the afternoon, Diane and I talked about the use of call-and-response in African American storytelling. She also taught me songs. We looked up videos of her storyteller friends. She showed me her catalog of work chronicled in books and awards she had received over the past thirty years. She asked me about my own history, but I didn't have the answers she was looking for. I told her that I had not grown up in a southern Black church, that my mother never sang Negro spirituals to me. Instead, I talked about my mother's Jamaican heritage, but even that I couldn't speak about in full detail. She admonished me for not knowing the particulars of my African ancestry and told me to spend more time talking with my mother and grandmother. I agreed, explaining to her that my thesis project was one of the many puzzles I was piecing together to find out more about my family's history.

"A lot of African American children are missing out on that," she started. "Songs that brought African American people through hard times, gave them hope and strength. Kids don't know them. You don't know them."

And she was right. The only Negro spirituals I knew were "Wade in the Water" and "Go Down, Moses."

Soon the afternoon turned into evening and Diane asked if I wanted to stay for dinner. "Not only do you not know any spirituals, you also don't eat meat," she joked, walking into the kitchen. I followed, making myself comfortable in her breakfast nook and watched as she flowed through the space.

"Call me the 'Quick Cornbread Queen,'" she said.

This was the second time that Diane and I had met. After being welcomed into her home and having an entire skillet of cornbread baked in my honor, I began to relax. I settled my weight into the nook, stared outside, smelling the scent of cornbread in the air, and thought to myself that Diane was someone who was going to change me for the better. That moment encompassed what years three, four, five, and beyond have continued to look like. When I ponder our cosmic connection, I consider that it stems from how similar Diane and I are—like a parallel-universe similar.

Diane and I both grew up under the rule of a strong, religious mother who understood the power of God's grace and quoted from the Bible regularly. Both of our mothers were domestic housekeepers with minimal schooling, yet a determined work ethic. Mrs. Reed, Diane's mother, told Diane about growing up in segregated Louisiana. My mother told me stories about growing up in the countryside of Jamaica. And both of our mothers were strict with us, Diane being the only girl in her family of three boys, while I'm the youngest girl with an older sister and three older brothers. Diane was very close to her mother, although she describes herself as a daddy's girl. After her father passed and Mrs. Reed was plagued by Alzheimer's disease, Diane and her husband, Tom, took Mrs. Reed in, nursing her until her death in 2006—a situation I know all too well. Besides our circumstantial similarities, Diane and I physically look alike. Our natural locks are about the same length, our brown skin just about the same shade. Even our wide smiles, high cheekbones, and smooth facial profiles match each other's. However, at five foot nine, I tower over Diane's five-foot-four stature, which for some reason makes commentators even quicker to assume that we are mother and daughter. Except for the one time in Winters, California, at an elementary school when a fourth-grade boy declared to his friend that I was Diane's sister.

Diane and I also have similar personalities. We are the chatterboxes of our families: we are more inclined to talk, to perform, and to engage with people around us, especially when given the opportunity. And when there isn't anyone around, you'll find the both of us with our nose in a book, scribbling down notes in a journal, or doing online research about a particular character or characteristic. For Diane, those characters show up in her storytelling from the likes of Brer Rabbit to Harriet Tubman to Aesop. For me, those researched characteristics show up in my writing and become unique to the characters that exist in my work.

In addition, she and I are our families' historians. We collect our families' stories and share them whenever we can. Diane shares her stories onstage, and I write them down for publishing's sake. I believe that it's the thirty-seven-year gap between us that makes Diane more orally inclined and me more literary based: she grew up listening to stories on her grandparents' porch, and I grew up checking out stories from the public library. We could have never guessed that we would both come into the world of storytelling in our early thirties—she as a storyteller, and I as an ethnographer.

Yet, despite our similarities, Diane and I also have some stark differences. When she was my age, she was married and had adopted her second child. She was a homeowner, along with her husband, and worked full-time for a union organization. As for me, I'm single, dependent-less, and recently completed my doctoral degree. Diane is a creative professional, while I'm a creative academic.

Over the course of my thesis project, these descriptors did and continued to place Diane and me on opposite sides of the creative spectrum. It is along that spectrum, that in-between space, where my constant analysis of Diane's body prevents me from simply enjoying her performances. It is also in that space where I ask Diane for an explanation about the use of her gestures, the theory behind her process, and the appropriation of her folktales. Questions she rarely answers. Instead, she tells me a story, or teaches me a song, or asks me to share one of my own. Diane is not interested in my academic rhetoric. She has admitted to me frequently that she thinks I'm wasting my time. When it comes to her performances, she doesn't see the necessity in knowing the "why" and the "how." She only sees the necessity in the now. She explains that her body just moves in the way that it moves. There is no need for me to spend time writing it all down and trying to explain it. If I watch, I will understand why. And if I do it, I will understand how.

I finally started to understand the "now" when Diane was retelling me "Bundles of Worries" on that evening of my mother's funeral. I imagined her gestures as she voiced the woman in the story who desperately wanted to swap her worries for anyone else's because she felt that her worries were too much for her to bear. I could see Diane in my mind's eye, hunched over with the imaginary heavy bundle on her left shoulder, and squinching her face in agony as she dropped the load to the floor. When she sighed, I no longer thought of Diane. Instead, I was transported into the narrative as the woman. Surely someone else's worries were lighter than mine at the moment. However, after searching for hours through all the bundles, picking them up and checking their weight on my shoulder, I inadvertently picked up my own again. It was just the right weight to match the bundle of blessings that sat on my right shoulder. While the loss of my mother felt like it was too much to bear, it unfortunately was my loss to bear. Like the woman in the story, I had inherited just the right amount of blessings to bear my loss and my grief well. Those blessings included my mother's unrelenting love and the stories she had gifted me. They also included the love resulting from my ever-growing bond with Diane and the stories she continues to tell me. Now, when Diane tells me a story, I am able to grieve my past, hope for my future, and abide in the present.

· ·

Lashon Daley is an assistant professor of English and comparative literature at San Diego State University. She earned her PhD in performance studies with a designated emphasis in new media from the University of California, Berkeley. She also holds an MFA in writing from Sarah Lawrence College and an MA in folklore from UC Berkeley. As a scholar, writer, and performer, Lashon thrives on bridging communities together through movement and storytelling.

Yalie Saweda Kamara

. . . .

American Beech
Winner of the 2023 Elizabeth Alexander Creative Writing
Award for Poetry

I don't mind when she approaches me, a stranger

on North Walnut Street, who only tells me about what she
sees while reaching two fingers in to retrieve

it from my hair. She squints a bit, fights the menace
of hot, silver, Hoosier sun, and relieves me of a problem

that, for *her*, rests too close to *me*. A deep plunge into my
curls, I wait to see how far she goes, and because I

miss the hands of the women I know, I think I'd even
let her hook her unfamiliar fingers into the lace of my wig, but

she stops short of me feeling completely like home.

It is an American Beech leaf, green as green, as opposite of red;
she pulls this weightless raft from inside the crown of me.

In small-town, downtown, there is a woman who does
not know my name, but calls herself my mirror. Haptic grace.

MERIDIANS · feminism, race, transnationalism 22:2 October 2023
DOI: 10.1215/15366936-10637555 © 2023 Smith College

She holds the leaf to my face, then releases it to flow slowly
down the vertical river of air to the pewter concrete. I don't mind

when she approaches me, a stranger on North Walnut Street,

taking a leaf, leaving her fingerprints, to sing and sing and sing
so close to our skin until I hear my own voice say: I feel you, too. How

mighty. The God portal of human touch.

....

Yalie Saweda Kamara is a Sierra Leonean–American writer, educator, and researcher from Oakland, California. Selected as the 2022–23 Cincinnati and Mercantile Library Poet Laureate (two-year term), she is the editor of the anthology *What You Need to Know about Me: Young Writers on Their Experience of Immigration* (2022) and the author of *A Brief Biography of My Name* (2018) and *When the Living Sing* (2017). Winner of the 2022–23 Jake Adam York Prize, her forthcoming full-length poetry collection, *Besaydoo*, will be published by Milkweed Editions in 2024. Kamara earned a PhD in creative writing and English literature from the University of Cincinnati, an MFA in creative writing from Indiana University, Bloomington, and an MA in French culture and civilization from Middlebury College. Kamara resides in Cincinnati where she is an assistant professor of English at Xavier University. For more, visit her website: www.yaylala.com.

Gina Athena Ulysse

....

Indigo

....

Artist Statement

For once they intuited that the human will was long intent on capture, they all conspired to rest their Truth everywhere. And in the simplest of things. Like a raindrop. And therefore, the most beautiful of things so that Truth and Beauty would not be strangers to one another.
—M Jacqui Alexander, *Of Crossings: Meditations on Feminism, Sexual Politics, Memory, and the Sacred*

....

Variations of the primary materials in this work exist all over the world.

The Kwi—made from the kalbas or calabash tree (*Crescentia Cujete*)—

are the simple, sacred, and profane holder of rasanblaj,
a gathering of ideas, things, people, and spirits,
(Though not necessarily in that order!).

The Ochre came first, a gift handed to me
by a Wiradjuri artist in Darwin
the capital of Australia's Northern Territory.

Once Kwi encountered Ochre
a new conversation began.

MERIDIANS · feminism, race, transnationalism   22:2 October 2023
DOI: 10.1215/15366936-10880014 © 2023 Smith College

There was a call
gourd became canvas
meditation on aesthetic identity
integrity before form

Then came the Ash
from burnt Pinewood
and Palo Santo.
After that,
Salt wanted to play with Indigo.

"Indigo" is part of the "Tools of the Trade or Women's Work" Kwi series.
Photo credit: © 2019 Art and digital photograph by Gina Athena Ulysse.

. . . .

Gina Athena Ulysse is a Haitian American feminist artist-scholar and professor of feminist studies at the University of California, Santa Cruz. In the last two decades, she has been concerned with the expression and representation of the dailyness of Black diasporic conditions; her rasanblaj approach to her art and writing practice entails ongoing crossings and dialogues in the arts, humanities, and the social sciences. She has been published in art catalogues as well as journals such as *Feminist Studies*, *Gastronomica*, *Frontiers*, *Journal of Haitian Studies*, *Interim Poetics*, *Kerb: Journal of Landscape Architecture*, and *Third Text*. Over the years, she has performed at a range of venues from the Bowery, the British Museum, Gorki Theatre, LaMaMa, Marcus Garvey Liberty Hall, MoMA Salon, and the MCA in Australia.

Keep up to date on new scholarship

Issue alerts are a great way to stay current on all the cutting-edge scholarship from your favorite Duke University Press journals. This free service delivers tables of contents directly to your inbox, informing you of the latest groundbreaking work as soon as it is published.

To sign up for issue alerts:

1. Visit **dukeu.press/register** and register for an account. You do not need to provide a customer number.

2. After registering, visit **dukeu.press/alerts**.

3. Go to "Latest Issue Alerts" and click on "Add Alerts."

4. Select as many publications as you would like from the pop-up window and click "Add Alerts."

Devaleena Das

What Transnational Feminism Has Not Disrupted Yet
Toward a Quilted Epistemology

Keywords: transnational feminism, epistemology, Black feminist quilting, Global South

Zeynep K. Korkman

....

(Mis)Translations of the Critiques
of Anti-Muslim Racism and the
Repercussions for Transnational Feminist
Solidarities

Keywords: anti-Muslim Racism, Black, transnational feminist solidarity, translation, Turkey

Dia Da Costa

....

Writing Castelessly
Brahminical Supremacy in Education, Feminist Knowledge, and Research

Keywords: castelessness, transnational feminism, Brahminical supremacy, Brahminical ignorance, denaturalizing merit

Sreerekha Sathi

....

When My Brown Got Colored
Living through/in the Times of White and Brahmanical
Supremacy

Keywords: woman of color, racialization, casteism, Hindutva, white supremacy

Grace L. Sanders Johnson

....

Picturing Herself in Africa

Haiti, Diaspora, and the Visual Folkloric

Keywords: Haiti, feminism, Congo, photography, visual folklore

Cherise Fung

....

In the Name of Sovereignty
Rethinking the "Tiger Bitch" and the Terrorist Bomber
in Nayomi Munaweera's *Island of a Thousand Mirrors* (2012)

Keywords: queer assemblages, female suicide bombers, national sovereignty, sexual assault, Sri Lankan literature

Rosetta Marantz Cohen and Doris H. Gray

....

A Conversation with Doris H. Gray on the Power and Limitations of Restorative Justice across History, Culture, and Gender

Keywords: restorative justice, generational trauma, Tunisian women, Arab Spring

Saher Ahmed and Amrita Hari

Young Afghan-Canadian Women's Negotiations of Gendered Cultural Scripts and Hybrid Cultural Identities

Keywords: gender identities, second generation, diaspora, Afghan-Canadian, marriage

Michaela Django Walsh

. . . .

Between Skin and Stone
A Letter to My Son, Lienzo

Keywords: thresholds, migration, motherhood, Mexico, walls

Julie Torres

"We Are Orlando"
Silences, Resistance, and the Intersections
of Mass Violence

Keywords: Latinx, mass violence, activism, gender, sexuality

Kami Fletcher

....

Black Women Undertakers of the Early Twentieth Century Were Hidden in Plain Sight

Keywords: undertaker, race women, death work, funeral home, Black women

Printed and bound by CPI Group (UK) Ltd, Croydon, CR0 4YY

13/04/2025

14656481-0001